Allotment Stories

Indigenous Americas

Robert Warrior, Series Editor

ALLOTMENT STORIES

INDIGENOUS LAND RELATIONS UNDER SETTLER SIEGE

Daniel Heath Justice and Jean M. O'Brien, Editors

Indigenous Americas

University of Minnesota Press
Minneapolis
London

Portions of "Making Mahnomen Home" by Jean M. O'Brien are adapted from "Memory and Mobility: Grandma's Mahnomen, White Earth," *Ethnohistory* 64, no. 3 (2017): 345–77. "Amikode" by Leanne Betasamosake Simpson was originally published in *A Short History of the Blockade: Giant Beavers, Diplomacy, and Regeneration in Nishnaabewin* (University of Alberta Press, 2021); reprinted with permission.

Published by the University of Minnesota Press
111 Third Avenue South, Suite 290
Minneapolis, MN 55401–2520
http://www.upress.umn.edu

ISBN 978-1-5179-0875-1 (hc)
ISBN 978-1-5179-0876-8 (pb)
A Cataloging-in-Publication record for this book is available from the Library of Congress.

Printed in the United States of America on acid-free paper

The University of Minnesota is an equal-opportunity educator and employer.

30 29 28 27 26 25 24 23 22 21   10 9 8 7 6 5 4 3 2 1

To our many Nations' warriors, diplomats, law-keepers, knowledge-holders, poets, scholars, and dreamers—past and present—and their defense of our lands, laws, and kin against the colonial logics of property lines and mapping grids.

Contents

Part IV. Resistance and Resurgence

Introduction

What's Done to the People Is Done to the Land

DANIEL HEATH JUSTICE
JEAN M. O'BRIEN

> You cannot dominate without seeking to possess the dominated.
> You cannot exclude unless you assume you already own.
> —Aileen Moreton-Robinson (Goenpul, Quandamooka First Nation),
> *The White Possessive*

This is a book about an idea—that the privatization of land is a necessary precondition for individual success and cultural modernity—and how Indigenous peoples have grappled with, responded to, and challenged the violent material and symbolic consequences of that idea. Privatization is more than policy or practice—it is a storied dispossessive process. So, too, is its restorative resistance. This book brings some of these allotment stories together in a conversation that is both timely and urgent. It foregrounds the resiliency of Indigenous community in the face of privatization, as well as how Indigenous peoples have maintained relationality with humans and other-than-human beings in spite of the disruptions wrought on the animal and plant worlds through dispossession. Such resiliency provides a firm foundation on which contemporary Indigenous resurgence dynamically imagines self-determined lives beyond the state.

The urgency of this conversation is depressingly constant. We write this introduction in the immediate aftermath of the McGirt decision (2020), in which the U.S. Supreme Court affirmed that the Muscogee (Creek) Nation's reservation boundaries in current-day Oklahoma had not been extinguished by nineteenth-century allotment legislation, while leaving open the possibility of Congress doing just that; the Amazon is aflame, in large part due to Brazil's right-wing president, Jair Bolsonaro, and his populist promise to settler industry to open up Indigenous lands to resource extraction; federal, provincial, and corporate forces use legal and extralegal processes to threaten Indigenous land and water rights activists across Canada, with the Wet'suwet'en peoples in British Columbia, the Six Nations of the Grand River in Ontario, and the Sipekne'katik First

Nation in Nova Scotia just three of many communities under settler siege. Regardless of when this introduction was written, we could have pointed to numerous immediate examples of challenge, conflict, aspiration, and even hopeful change in the relationships between Indigenous peoples and the nation-states that dominate and assert control over our homelands and our nations.

This is the context of the moment. This is the context of every moment in the structural reality of global settler colonialism. Its driving force has been the expropriation of Indigenous territories through warfare, displacement, incarceration, labor exploitation, and—especially in the twentieth and twenty-first centuries—the administrative fracturing of collective Indigenous land tenure into individually owned parcels alienable through the workings of the market. Sometimes this was done in concert with assimilationist policies meant to turn Indigenous people into laborers and consumers, but more often this was done to directly enrich settlers at Indigenous expense. Whether under the auspices of land allotment, severalty, fee simple ownership, or other individualist property schemes, the privatization (and subsequent alienation) of collectively held Indigenous territories has been—and continues to be—a fundamental mechanism of settler colonial domination and displacement across Indigenous homelands on a global scale.

It has also been, invariably, a violent process realized at every social, economic, political, ideological, imaginative, and ethical level. Along with privatization came the brutal desecration of Indigenous territories, and their restoration has been a prime focus of Indigenous resurgence detailed in many of the essays that follow. The General (Dawes) Allotment Act of 1887 in the United States is among the most notorious but by no means the only example of such land privatization schemes and their catastrophic impacts. Similar policies have been implemented in other settler states, continuing to the present day, for example, with reinvigorated focus by governments and extractive industries in Canada, Brazil, and elsewhere.[1]

We hope this volume serves as a provocation to further conversations about the structure and impact of privatization on Indigenous peoples and urges further reflection on Indigenous resilience in the face of violent property regimes. The essays that follow focus most especially on North America north of the Rio Grande, with a heavy concentration on Indigenous people in the United States. The geographic reach of the volume reflects the editors' scholarly locations and the yield our open call for contributions elicited, and we hope that their lively engagement with one another will prompt further conversations across the Indigenous world.

This volume brings Indigenous and non-Indigenous thinkers together to consider this idea and its legacies in diverse times, places, and contexts. As political policy, legal practice, analytical or artistic metaphor, and lived experience alike, allotment—and privatization more broadly—represents fragmentation, dispossession, a disruption of relations and genealogies. Its insistence on pulverizing the communal for the individual struck at the core of Indigenous identities and spirituality. It is a brutal constellation of acts, ideas, and influences, all directed toward the erasure of Indigenous communities and claims and the legitimization of settler authority and resource access. Yet the contributions to this volume also remind us that, however destructive and limited such monolithic ideologies may be, our humanity and relations are most powerfully realized in the multiplicities, the complexities, and the nuances of Indigenous peoples' agency.

Privatization schemes underscore settler colonialism as a violent, land-centered project, one that attacks Indigenous relationality attached to the land and waters. Wherever it takes place, in whatever geographic, political, or cultural contexts, as Patrick Wolfe so succinctly reminds us, "Settler colonialism destroys to replace."[2] This settler replacement logic is memorably articulated by President Theodore Roosevelt in his first annual message to Congress in 1901, where, among many other matters, he takes up the issue of allotment of Indian Territory then underway:

> In my judgment the time has arrived when we should definitely make up our minds to recognize the Indian as an individual and not as a member of a tribe. The General Allotment Act is a mighty pulverizing engine to break up the tribal mass. It acts directly upon the family and the individual. . . . The Indian should be treated as an individual—like the white man. During the change of treatment inevitable hardships will occur; every effort should be made to minimize these hardships; but we should not because of them hesitate to make the change.[3]

For Roosevelt, allotment was an explicitly ruthless process of transformation akin to social manufacturing; Indians were, to his mind, a kind of monolithic, featureless matter that only a "mighty pulverizing engine" could convert into something individualized, distinctive, and usefully human in the body politic. Not coincidentally, it is the self-congratulatory language of Gilded Age industry and its resource barons, who accumulated vast fortunes by turning trees, ore, animals, and the land itself into distributed goods, and did so through ugly systems of labor exploitation. Tellingly, these so-called natural resources were taken from lands expropriated from Indigenous peoples through betrayal, manipulation, and outright theft; privatization painted a civilized veneer of mutual consent over processes that were almost entirely violent and coercive. Roosevelt fully acknowledged that allotment would be a painful process and that people would suffer, but their pain was secondary to what he praised as the reformers' pure purpose.

Roosevelt's aggressively paternalistic position is more muted in today's privatization proposals, which tend to celebrate the idealized goals of capitalist progress, entrepreneurship, and economic opportunity over the well-documented harms of imposed assimilation, but the attitude remains: that collective Indigenous land custodianship is antiquated, primitive, antimodern, impoverishing; that collective care for lands as more than equity and resources is a retrograde and romantic pathology that holds communities back and limits individualistic ambition and achievement. When Indigenous land rights are addressed by legislation, court judgment, or negotiated framework, settler agents rarely foreground justice or restoration of Indigenous autonomy over those lands, prioritizing instead a process to fully and finally settle questions of ownership and authority, to mitigate corporate and investor uncertainty, always with the presumption that ultimate authority is and should be that of the settler state and corporations.

And as the gospel of U.S. capitalism has been spread across the world through political, military, economic, and cultural agents, the attitudes toward Indigenous peoples and landholdings that informed allotment have similarly traveled across the globe. Tellingly, however, the lessons of its myriad failures seem not to have replicated as readily. Wherever they are found, whether in Canada, Hawai'i, Aotearoa/New Zealand, Sápmi, Australia, Brazil, or any number of other regions and territories, today's privatization advocates in large part echo those of Roosevelt's time and place and are either fully ignorant of the myriad devastations and ongoing legacies of such policies, minimize their harm, or accept them as the unfortunate but inevitable cost that other people must pay for the dubious benefits of capitalist progress.

It is always Indigenous peoples who pay these costs and experience the immediate— and generational—consequences. These experiences connect through the individualism inherent in the construct of privatization, yet taking stock of the larger problem we feature in this volume demands historical and geographic specificity. This volume is not meant to be the last word on this topic but rather to suggest further interrogation of how U.S. models of privatization have been taken up and customized for Indigenous expropriation elsewhere: Latin America, Fiji, Japan, Australia, and beyond. U.S. imperialism has been central in propagating strategies of dispossession that imitate allotment schemes found throughout the Indigenous world.

Why Allotment?

Allotment Stories takes its title from the 1887 General Allotment Act—or, more colloquially, the Dawes Act—one of the most prominent, notorious, and influential examples of this worldwide phenomenon, which was advocated by white reformers and land-hungry speculators alike. For the Friends of the Indian—white social reformers, typically from upper-class East Coast urban centers—there was no greater purpose than to uphold an idea of civilization that was for them synonymous with all elements of homogeneous Protestant Americanism. Just as Black people were caught in the push and pull of uplift education and the ever more constraining limits of legalized segregation, and just as immigrants were being targeted for assimilation into the worldview of these eastern reformers, so too were Native peoples of all phenotypes—even those who, like the Cherokee Nation and other Indian Territory republics and the Kingdom of Hawaiʻi, amply demonstrated their own capacity for a different kind of civilization on their own terms and in support of their own social, political, and geographic sovereignty. For people so concerned with distinctiveness on an individual scale, cultural distinctiveness was anathema to the Friends of the Indian and other white reformers. Their charge was the ostensibly benevolent incorporation of Indians and other marginalized peoples into the social values of white Protestant America, including Christianization, assimilative education, and private landownership, for the perceived good of the targeted people, at any cost necessary.

The last of these three concerns—private landownership—was the key to the success of the others. To these largely Calvinist and evangelical activists, there could be no Christian American civilization without individual ownership of that land. Private property in the mortal sphere was linked to salvation in the afterlife, the singular authority of God reflected in miniature. It was a distinguishing mark of civilization and individual achievement. And it was not enough to embrace these principles oneself; all of society had to conform to that worldview, by force if necessary.

For the mercantile Protestant English, collective land possession was a sign of savagery and benighted primitivism. Collective landholdings were part of systems of communal decision-making and interdependence, as well as diverse cosmologies of distributed authority, and thus part of social networks that were quite resilient in withstanding reformer policies of individualism and hierarchical patriarchy. Collective social networks had to be dismantled, and one central way of doing so was by attacking the relationships that tied people to the land and strengthened their resistance. Massachusetts Senator Henry Dawes, whose name was attached to the 1887 allotment legislation, memorably described it thusly to his reformer peers at the Lake Mohonk Conference in 1885: "There was not a pauper in [the Cherokee] Nation, and the Nation does not owe a dollar. It built its own capitol . . . and built its schools and hospitals. Yet the defect of the system was apparent. They have got as far as they can go, because they hold their land in common. . . . There is no selfishness, which is at the bottom of civilization."[4]

To Dawes and his colleagues, the lands held in common by Native peoples were more than could be usefully tilled or improved upon, and were thus a foolish waste that could be more profitably exploited by others (namely, whites); if individual title created a necessary selfishness, collective title encouraged generous selflessness, which they condemned as facilitating indolence, laziness, and waste. And in the industrial period of westward expansion, driven by the rhetoric of Manifest Destiny, Indigenous landholdings had the added consequence of challenging the expansion of white populations and economic ambitions. In 1881, Carl Schurz, a prominent figure among the Friends of the Indian, offered this observation:

> When the Indians . . . have become individual property-owners, holding
> their farms by the same title under the law by which white men hold theirs,
> they will feel more readily inclined to part with such of their lands as they
> cannot themselves cultivate, and from which they can derive profit only
> if they sell them, either in lots or in bulk, for a fair equivalent in money
> or in annuities. This done, the Indians will occupy no more ground than
> so many white people; the large reservations will gradually be opened to
> general settlement and enterprise, and the Indians, with their possessions,
> will cease to stand in the way of the "development of the country."[5]

Another reformer, Hiram Price, acknowledged that "the allotment system tends to break up tribal relations. It has the effect of creating individuality, responsibility, and a desire to accumulate property."[6] Communal ties were thus quite clearly seen as intrinsically linked to land and property; individualize the latter, and the former are sure to follow.

Not surprisingly, a policy conceived of by non-Indians whose motives were a toxic mix of sincere concern for Native welfare, unreflective white supremacy, paternalism backed up with coercive violence and rigid self-righteousness, and no small amount of self-interest had none of the stated benefits for Indigenous peoples, nor did it meaningfully involve Indigenous consent. If Indian welfare was a goal, it was an abject failure of astonishing proportions—what historian Angie Debo aptly describes as "an orgy of plunder and exploitation probably unparalleled in American history."[7] If enriching settler populations at the expense of Indigenous peoples was the goal, then it was, sadly, an undoubted success. In just under fifty years, from the passage of the Dawes Act in 1887 to the formal end of U.S. allotment policy in 1934, "the General Allotment Act caused Indian land holdings to plunge from 138 million acres . . . to 48 million acres," with much of the remaining land lost in the following years through various legal, extralegal, and outright illegal means.[8] The policy imposed on Indigenous nations with the stated intention of improving their well-being had done exactly the opposite: By 1934, "two-thirds of Native Americans were either landless or without enough land to provide subsistence. The policy weakened tribal cultures and fostered the growth of a large bureaucracy in the Bureau of Indian Affairs."[9] And this is just one of many such privatization schemes imposed by settler governments around the world, policies and practices that share the paternalistic rhetoric of benevolence as well as its devastating results. In every case, Indigenous peoples' voices have been pushed to the margins, if not ignored entirely.

We start with this U.S. "landscape of dispossession" (in the words of one of the contributors, Sarah Biscarra Dilley) in large part because of its long shadow and global influence. Its function in disrupting the complex relationality that connects the human and nonhuman worlds of Indigenous people was never limited to one nation-state. While land privatization has a long history that traveled eastward with European co-lonial powers well before the American Revolution, it took on a unique quality in the United States. From there it metastasized beyond nation-state borders and boundaries and was carried with missionary zeal and foreign policy across the Pacific and Atlantic and throughout the Americas. Just as colonialism has long been a global enterprise driven by its most ardent and powerful practitioners, so too have been its diverse manifestations such as land privatization, fueled by the particular ideological and eco-nomic interests of the United States and its nation-state allies.

Diverse local contexts have resulted in diverse Indigenous experiences, but they were and remain deeply informed by the shared alienating logics of allotment. Frac-turing land, families, cultures, and more, these settler colonial projects have aimed to sever the deep reciprocity of people with place, defined through their relationality with plants and animals, the animate and inanimate world. The severing of attachment these policies mean to accomplish extends well beyond dispossessing Indigenous people of their lands and disrupting their intricate relationality: extraction of resources brings pipelines and pollution, dams and destruction, along with the carceral, religious, and educational authorities who work in tandem to manage and pathologize Indigenous resistance. And the capital that would be extracted would travel the globe, just as its originary ideology had done, and just as Indigenous resistance continues to do.

The essays in this collection bring some of those costs and consequences to the center, but not simply in reaction to privatization and allotment policies. Rather, these allotment stories consider the experience of land fragmentation and dispossession as a starting point for discussion. Just as allotment has, by and large, failed its advocates' goal of wholly destroying collective and kinship relations, so too have most such poli-cies failed to erase and replace Indigenous peoples' ties to kin, culture, and territory, though they have certainly eroded and in many cases deeply damaged those ties. While allotment policies have had very similar negative impacts on Indigenous communities around the world, those communities and their members have exercised significant agency in response, and to impressively varied ends. Indigenous peoples have consis-tently expressed creative ways of sustaining collective ties, kinship relations, and cul-tural commitments to territory, sometimes in outright defiance, but sometimes even through the very legal regimes intended to destroy them.

Genealogies of Resistance and Restoration

As noted in the title of this introduction—and to gesture to the words of Chickasaw writer Linda Hogan from Joseph Pierce's contribution to the volume—what's done to the people is done to the land. To undo these impacts, then, those material and imaginative relations must be restored. This volume is part of that ongoing scholarly and creative conversation.

The Indigenous and non-Indigenous contributors to *Allotment Stories* consider allotment and its analogous settler privatization policies in diverse contexts across the globe by centering Indigenous voices, perspectives, and experiences from multidisciplinary, multigenre perspectives. They bring scholarly analysis, family and community history, first-person testimony, and creative expression into critical conversation, illuminating the many ways that Indigenous peoples have demonstrated agency in the face of often overwhelming state and corporate pressure, and how they have navigated the relentless settler colonial demands for land privatization, while offering insights into ongoing efforts to ensure community continuity and territorial integrity.

In its own modest way, this volume offers a reversal of sorts of the individualist ethos of allotment. Whereas allotment policies have, by and large, sought to disconnect, separate, and break up collective commitments, *Allotment Stories* seeks to bring attention to the individual experiences of families, communities, and nations, and therefore bring them into meaningful collective conversation. Together and in their own specific ways, the essays gathered here illuminate the durability of Indigenous commitments to kin and culture, even in the context of world-shaking trauma. Just as the logic of elimination at the heart of settler colonialism has never completed its project of Indigenous replacement, Roosevelt's "pulverizing engine" has never fully succeeded in its purpose, although its legacies continue to affect communities across the globe. *Allotment Stories* offers creative, critical, and reflective testimonies as to why that has been—and strategic inspiration, perhaps, for those Indigenous peoples who face renewed iterations of settler privatization policies even now.

For all that settler agents have sought to disrupt Indigenous communities, it is in community that resistance has been most durable and powerfully realized. Sometimes, the community continues to struggle with its pulverizing effects long after the engine itself is a memory, with violence turned inward and lateral violence a real and present danger; at other times, the engine stops where community begins, and restoration of those ravaged ties offers hope for more sustaining ways of being and relating. These experiences, in all their complexity, contradiction, and ambiguity, are given their due in *Allotment Stories*—there is no inevitable redemptive arc, but neither is there cynical despair. The diversity of these stories, like the diversity of experience in Indigenous communities, is part of the ethos of this collection. In this way, too, it challenges settler assumptions of singularity.

An Origin Story

The impetus for this volume—its creation story—is also to be found in community; this time, a community rooted in Indigenous contexts and scholarship. It emerged during the 2017 annual meeting of the Native American and Indigenous Studies Association (NAISA) on traditional, ancestral, and unceded Musqueam territory at the University of British Columbia, in what is currently called Vancouver, British Columbia. For those unfamiliar with NAISA, it is the world's largest scholarly organization dedicated to Indigenous studies, an organization that Jeani cofounded and that Daniel had been part of from its inception. We were catching up at the opening reception and the topic of current and nascent projects came up; Daniel had mentioned interest in doing more work on Cherokee allotment matters in the former Indian Territory (currently Oklahoma), having just written extensively about it for a book project. Yet his observations about the disruptive legacies of Cherokee allotment in the former Indian Territory prompted Jeani to note that, for her own White Earth Ojibwe people, the allotment process they had encountered had brought community members to the reservation rather than having alienated them from it, something she was working through in her own project that centers the writings of her Ojibwe grandmother. Until that conversation, neither of us had stopped to consider just how different those experiences were, or that this would most certainly be the case for other Indigenous peoples throughout the United States, Canada, and beyond. Although both our tribal communities—Cherokees in northeastern Oklahoma, White Earth Ojibwes in northwestern Minnesota—grappled with the impacts of the same political movement and policy, they did so under distinctly different political, economic, geographic, and, importantly, cultural contexts and conditions, and the results were, not surprisingly, different as well. We also surmised that the experiences of land privatization in general—moving past what we imagined was an overdetermined centrality assigned to the Dawes Act in the United States—must stretch across the Indigenous world with ever-rippling contemporary manifestations. These thoughts, and our own excitement over hashing out some of our own research, seemed important points deserving of deeper consideration.

This conversation, and further reflection on the diverse ways that other Indigenous peoples experienced and responded to the forced privatization of their lands, led us to want to hear more from scholars, artists, and engaged tribal members in their circles and beyond with meaningful knowledge of these matters. As a literature scholar and a historian, we also wanted to ensure that the book did not limit its scope to scholarly analyses but also included creative, autobiographical, and mixed-format examinations of these matters, and from a range of voices both within and beyond the academy, and within and beyond familiar circles—again, to expand the circle as widely as possible and make space for voices often not included in such collections but with vital insights to share.

This volume is thus explicitly in dialogue with a global community of scholars, as much in content as in context. We have been enormously gratified to note the enthusiasm with which our call for proposals was received, as well as the impressive quality of responses; just as we had been compelled by the question of how our own Indigenous nations had experienced and responded to allotment, it was evident that others, too, from a wide range of geographic, disciplinary, and cultural positions were keen to discuss these matters with other communities and contexts. Based on that enthusiasm, we were certainly optimistic about the high caliber of contributions we would receive, but neither of us was prepared for the profound level of intellectual and emotional impact we experienced in reading through these works, or the myriad connective threads between them.

It is important to reiterate, however, that this volume does not attempt to be comprehensive, nor does it represent all geographic contexts around the world in which settler privatization schemes and practices have had an impact on Indigenous communities. Quite simply, there is no way a single volume could meet that goal. There is necessarily a tension between global coverage and making a meaningful contribution, and at the end we emphasized the latter. *Allotment Stories* is, we hope, the opening of a dialogue, one that serves as provocation for further, deeper, and more expansive work on these issues in particular.

That said, we recognize that the current volume focuses heavily on a few key areas—Indian Territory, especially Cherokee experiences; Métis concerns in the Canadian prairies; Ojibwe lands and communities of the Great Lakes region—and skews to Indigenous experiences with the U.S. and Canadian nation-states. This is in part a consequence of our own scholarly and community contexts and those of the contributors who responded to our call for proposals and were able to submit finished essays by deadline. But we were also deeply gratified to see essays that take up a broader range of experiences and contexts, especially those of the Pacific, Sápmi, Palestine, and Mexico. Clearly many other Indigenous experiences with land privatization could be embraced here from across the globe, as well as in represented regions (for example, Five Tribes Freedmen experiences of dispossession by both whites and non-Black Native people), and some of these are gestured to in various contributions. We see this already hefty volume as only one part of an ongoing conversation about the complexity and impact of privatization projects on Indigenous people; we hope it will inspire, challenge, provoke, and engage others in addressing those contexts not otherwise referenced here. We are eager to see these conversations continue long after *Allotment Stories* is in print.

Allotment Stories is certainly not the origin point of this conversation. On the larger scale of privatization and property, this interdisciplinary volume joins the work of scholars like Aileen Moreton-Robinson (whose words from *The White Possessive: Property, Power, and Indigenous Sovereignty* open this introduction), Robert Nichols, Anthony J. Hall, Susan M. Hill, and Brenna Bhandar, among others.[10] It also draws on and engages the important interventions in the specific histories of allotment by such scholars as the aforementioned Angie Debo, along with Leonard A. Carlson, Delos Sacket Otis, Francis Paul Prucha, and Wilcomb E. Washburn. Frederick E. Hoxie signaled a new, more Indigenous-focused approach to allotment with his 1984 book *A Final Promise,* and Melissa Meyer also paved the way for recent work by Lucy Maddox, Kent Carter, Kristin T. Ruppel, C. Joseph Genetin-Pilawa, Rose Stremlau, and Alaina E. Roberts, who have furthered this important new direction.[11] Indigenous artists, too, have taken up concerns relating to the impacts of these diverse policies and practices; in literature, Sarah Winnemucca, S. Alice Callahan, Lynn Riggs, Maria Campbell, Patricia Grace, Louise Erdrich, Linda Hogan, Craig Womack, Alexis Wright, and LeAnne Howe are only some of the many global Indigenous writers joining Marilyn Dumont, Rauna Kuokkanen, and Leanne Betasamosake Simpson in this volume in helping not only imagining more complex pasts but visioning more just futures.[12]

Organizing Allotment Stories

There are many ways of organizing a collection of this kind, from geography and culture to historical period, shared experience, or thematic links. We have chosen a broadly thematic approach in the hopes of placing methods, temporal considerations, geographical diversity, and theoretical framings in conversation. Before outlining that structuring of the volume, we would like to focus on a few key thematic connections between contributions to give a sense of both the diversity of topics and their meaningful links.

The first and most significant of these, not surprisingly, is family. We were explicit in our call for proposals that, just as our own family stories were central to our own understandings of the impacts and legacies of allotment (as well as to our own essays in this volume), contributors should be invited to approach the topic from their own kinship contexts, in whatever ways those seemed relevant to the discussion. And although not all of our contributors chose that direction for their works, and although not all are Indigenous themselves, a good number grounded their analyses in the intimate sphere of their own family. The impacts of allotment policy often fell hardest on Indigenous women, who have been forced to grapple with the myriad violences of heteropatriarchy in addition to settler racism, and a number of contributors grounded their allotment stories in women's experiences. Connected to this, the insidious interplay between colonial legal systems, educational practices and weaponized pedagogies, commercial interests, and politics informs a number of contributions as well.

Language and culture are important to nearly all these allotment stories—not simply the negative impact that the dispossession and dispersal of many families had on those two pillars of Indigenous life, but also the ways that communities have worked in subsequent years to restore these pillars alongside the land and relations. This in spite of the dispossessive ways that colonial political rhetoric, legal and economic theory, classroom pedagogy, and citizenship legislation have impinged upon and in many cases worked to circumscribe Indigenous agency.

Racial taxonomies of the period are also a core theme that connects many, if not most, of these contributions, and, as one of our reviewers noted, there are significant links between land, labor, and privatization throughout. Settler colonial allotment and privatization policies have always been entangled with and sometimes dependent upon or furthering other policies intended to shore up and extend white supremacy; for example, for white Protestants in the United States and throughout the British Commonwealth, the assimilative and uplift education and citizenship policies that accompanied privatization with Indigenous peoples were sites of high ambivalence, anxiety, and threat when directed toward Black people or South Asian or Eastern European immigrants. None of these issues existed in isolation, and such entanglements are both explicitly addressed and alluded to throughout these contributions.

For all that allotment was trumpeted by its advocates as an inevitability for benighted savages to aspire to an appropriate level of Christian civilization, the rhetoric of benevolent uplift was always backed up by threats of state, social, and religious violence. That violence—whether from everyday settler subjects, from church and state, legal orders, military, business interests, the tourism industry, or a combination of them all—undergirds all privatization schemes; allotment and its counterparts are mobilized by a constellation of violent settler structures. All of these allotment stories deal with either the explicit or implied violence of the process, and at all levels of settler society, with some focusing on some of these structures in particular depth. Yet they also address how Indigenous communities have confronted these structures—these are not stories of passive victimry, but of dynamic resistance, defiance, and response, even under very limited and limiting circumstances.

We have organized the essays of this volume into four parts, each punctuated by an interlude of creative writing that takes up the impact of and resistance to privatization on and within Indigenous communities. These include two contributions by Leanne Betasamosake Simpson (Michi Saagiig Nishnaabe), one of them a powerful illumination of the important stakes this volume addresses and the other a short story rooted in Nishnaabe ontologies. The other two interludes are poems by Marilyn Dumont (Cree/Métis), "Kinscapes," and by Rauna Kuokkanen (Sámi), "Long Live Deatnu and the Grand Allotment." These creative contributions are quite explicitly focused on the embraided threads of history, kinship, land, and Indigenous bodies and offer compelling and at times provocative insight into the struggle of their respective families and communities to retain their links to territory and to one another, as well as the fierce and sometimes furious love that has given fuel to that struggle.

Although many of the essays throughout are rooted in family stories (partly in response to our call), those included in part I, "Family Narrations of Privatization," use narration of family stories as a methodology or a central narrative arc. In her critical-creative contribution, Sarah Biscarra Dilley (yak tityu tityu yak tiłhini) considers the legacies of land loss and genocide in California through the experiences of her formidable foremothers, who "bent the intentions of the allotment era to respond to a disordered world, marking connection in a chain of systems meant to isolate and individuate." Daniel Heath Justice (Cherokee Nation) examines the allotment-era logics of race in Indian Territory through the account of white relatives who falsely claimed Chickasaw heritage in order to access Chickasaw lands and resources and considers the lessons in that history for those using unverified family stories to do the same today. Jean O'Brien (White Earth Ojibwe) challenges the notion of allotment as only being about movement away, not movement toward, rooting her discussion of White Earth allotment history in her grandmother's reflections on that period and the ways Ojibwes worked to bend the narrow strictures of allotment to their own needs, values, and relations. Nick Estes (Kul Wicasa, Lower Brule Sioux) considers how the bureaucratic "paper world" of twentieth-century administrative allotment worked to dispossess and alienate his family from the land and from one another, resulting in "fractions of interests in fractionated land—and, in effect, fractionated families." Sheryl Lightfoot (Anishinaabe, Lake Superior Band) chronicles how her own family grappled with the difficult and emotionally laden question of returning their individual allotments to their tribe under the Cobell Land Buy-Back Program, touched on by Estes, and what that meant for them and for the tribe itself. Joseph M. Pierce (Cherokee Nation) considers the ruptures that resulted from his father's adoption out of the tribe—an act that, in many ways, is directly rooted in the impacts of allotment on the Cherokee Nation—and what the ongoing restoration of those ties looks like for his family.

Part II, "Racial and Gender Taxonomies," includes essays that explicitly invoke the roles of racialization in privatization schemes and gender ideologies on Indigenous communities, though other essays also implicitly take up race and gender—and, we would add, class and labor—as categories of analysis. The Canadian context is elaborated by Darren O'Toole (Métis), who considers the complex function of "half-breed scrip" in dispossessing Métis people in Canada and the upper United States, a legal mechanism that recognized Métis claims while simultaneously dispossessing them. Jennifer Adese (Otipcmisiwak/Métis) examines an enormously complex family history: namely, the multigenerational impacts from "extinguishing the dead," wherein colonial authorities stripped entitlement to Métis scrip from the dead, and thus also from their descendants, to the benefit of intermarried or otherwise enfranchised whites. Jameson R. Sweet (Lakota/Dakota) attends to the nineteenth-century allotment experiences of mixed-race Dakotas in the Upper Midwest through the complexities of gender, race, patriarchy, and law, anchored by the complex consequences of a white ancestor's dispossession of his mixed children from their land rights. While homesteading is often associated with Indigenous land loss, Susan E. Gray examines how Anishinaabe women used homesteading in early nineteenth-century northern Michigan to anchor existing kinship practices and economic self-sustainability in spite of the aggressive machinations of their white male counterparts and confusion about the legal status of those lands at various legal and political levels. Placing family memory, Cherokee language, and cultural contexts alongside various documentary records involving her great-great-grandfather, Candessa Tehee (Cherokee Nation) offers a powerful account of her family's evolving understanding of their own family history, as well as the limits of the Dawes-era logics of race and tribal identity.

Though the titular theme of part III, "Privatization as State Violence," plays its role in virtually every work in this volume, the essays found here include this analytic and Indigenous resistance to state violence as a key structure. In the Pacific, and in parallel discussions that inform one another, Christine Taitano DeLisle (CHamoru) and Vicente Diaz (Pohnpeian and Filipino) consider the role of roads—in service to U.S. militarism as well as tourism—in the expropriation of Indigenous lands in Guåhan, with particular attention on how CHamoru women have worked to assert agency in a territory significantly affected by an infrastructure of settler colonial extraction and access. J. Kēhaulani Kauanui (Kanaka Maoli) analyzes the origins of the contemporary regime of land privatization in the mid-nineteenth-century Hawaiian Kingdom and how it continues to adversely affect land tenure as settler colonialism in the twenty-first century, detailing the land dispute over quieting title to a portion of land billionaire Mark Zuckerberg has amassed on the north shore of Kaua'i. Through the case study of a series of fertile land allotments coveted by a local white farmer over decades, Dione Payne (Waikato, Ngāti Tūwharetoa) provides a methodical analysis of New Zealand's long history of coercive and fraudulent land confiscation under the Māori Land Court, a practice that Pākehā used to gain title to lands Māori were actively relying on for their economic, social, and cultural well-being.

Shiri Pasternak's (Ashkenazi Jew) analysis of the Canadian legal injunction as a contemporary mechanism used to further appropriate and alienate Indigenous lands in the service of industry is a chilling reminder of just how relevant these conversations are to our own time, and how enduring the violent logics of allotment remain. William Bauer (Wailacki and Concow of the Round Valley Indian Tribes) analyzes U.S. policies of allotment, termination, and resource extraction within the rhetoric of freedom as justification for the privatization of American Indian land, labor, and resources, which has sometimes persuaded Indigenous people that privatization could work to their own advantage. Benjamin Hugh Velaise (Koyukon Athabascan) examines the enormous changes within Indigenous communities that accompanied the passage of the Alaska Native Claims Settlement Act of 1971, which introduced social and economic stratification and important questions about how Native communities manage conflicts over tradition in the new corporate existence ANCSA has brought.

Part IV, "Resistance and Resurgence," looks to a long history of Indigenous resistance to land privatization in diverse places or the resurgence of practices that look to Indigenous futurities. Pauliina Feodoroff (Sámi) and Tero Mustonen bring attention to the ways that climate change is shifting Finland's policies toward Sámi people, their reindeer culture and economy, and their land rights, and the uncertain but hopeful possibilities of both the "rewilding" of their traditional homeland through Indigenous ecological knowledge and "reterritorialization" to reverse allotment land losses and protect Sámi culture and self-determination. Kelly McDonough (Anishinaabe [White Earth] and Irish descent) illuminates the documentation of Nahuatl primordial titles within Indigenous communities across Mexico to assert their rights to their lands through transcription of oral accounts of landownership since time immemorial to confront Spanish colonialism's efforts to dispossess them. Argelia Segovia Liga demonstrates how privatization of Indigenous land in the wake of Mexican Independence (1821) dismantled *parcialidades de indios* as communal landholdings that supported Indigenous institutes beginning in the sixteenth century, imposing private property onto defiant Indigenous communities in Mexico City that paved the way for their dispossession. Munir Fakher Eldin (member of the Syrian native community in the Golan Heights) narrates the complexity of land tenure regimes under the Ottoman Empire, into the British Mandate, and then Palestinian dispossession by Zionist settlers to illustrate these struggles as nonlinear and to clear the way for subaltern Palestinian histories in Sakhina in the Jordan Valley. Local economies of Pomo labor and landownership in California are the subjects that Khal Schneider (Federated Indians of Graton Rancheria) explores in his essay, and the ways that Pomo hops harvesters asserted economic and social self-determination in spite of numerous legal and ideological barriers, culminating in a memorable encounter with the architect of U.S. allotment himself, Massachusetts senator Henry Dawes. In his study of three different Indigenous petitions from 1897 to 1929—Kanaka Maoli protesting the illegal annexation of Hawai'i, the National Council of American Indians advocating for increased rights and legal protections, and the Alaska Native Brotherhood and Sisterhood working to restore land rights—Michael P. Taylor reveals the commitment of Indigenous peoples to challenge the fragmentation of their lands and communities through their collective political voice, and to do so through the explicitly and insistently multivocal form of the petition. Megan Baker (Choctaw Nation of Oklahoma) reflects on two generations of a Choctaw family and their efforts to reverse allotment's erosion of the Choctaw language—and considers both the challenges and the possibilities of that work today. Ruby Hansen Murray (Osage Nation) meditates on what the return of the bison means to the Osage people today; although excluded from the initial provisions of the Dawes Act, the Osages were still forced to contend with privatization policies that fractionated their territories, brought murderous violence to their people, and hedged in their traditional economy.

Allotment Stories concludes with an afterword from Cherokee Nation legal scholar and former Cherokee Nation Supreme Court justice Stacy Leeds, who considers this volume and its concerns in the context of the 2020 U.S. Supreme Court decision *McGirt v.*

Oklahoma. This piece offers an important and timely perspective on not just the historical resonance of this important case but its broader significance in an uncertain time.

Wrapping up the volume is a collective composition from the contributors and editors in the form of a short glossary of key terms to help readers navigate the many legal, historical, cultural, and theoretical concepts cited throughout the essays.

Closing Thoughts

Three of the threads that weave clearly through these diverse contributions are Indigenous relationality, determination, and creativity. As previously discussed, so much of the explicit purpose and implicit function of privatization has been to destroy kinship ties—not simply those between human relatives, but those with our other-than-human relatives as well. Privatization and fragmentation make the exploitation of habitat much easier and more efficient, and a continual concern throughout many of these essays is the impacts of privatization on relations with plants, animals, and other peoples in a dynamic cosmos. Kinship, considered both broadly and in its grounded specifics, is a casualty of all privatization schemes, and the restoration of the lands brings with it a concern for restoring relations to kin beyond the human.

It is vital to remember that, for all that Indigenous communities have struggled to adapt to ever-mutating colonial pressures to surrender collective commitments and relations to land and multispecies kin, they have consistently done so, and often in surprising and unexpected ways. There is no single strategy for success, and no community has emerged from these encounters without significant losses, but while Roosevelt's pulverizing engine and its counterparts have created untold harm, they have not yet succeeded in destroying "the tribal mass."

Yet we know too well that, in Indigenous politics, the failed settler policies of one generation rise up again, sometimes in the same place with renewed vigor, sometimes in other regions where the lessons and legacies are slower to take root than the noxious ideas themselves. Just as our ancestors had to adapt their own responses to the renewed threats, so too will we, Indigenous peoples and non-Indigenous allies alike, and so will subsequent generations. We must be vigilant, and we must be agile, if our nations are to survive. Based on the stories our contributors share in these pages, in spite of continuing threats, there is abundant reason to be hopeful.

We believe that the allotment stories shared here offer insights, cautions, and inspiration to those committed to strengthening Indigenous peoples' collective rights and relations. Thank you for joining us in this conversation.

Wado and Miigwech,
Daniel and Jeani

NOTES

1. For a persuasive argument about the saliency of settler colonialism in Latin America, see Shannon Speed, "Structures of Settler Capitalism in Abya Yala," *American Quarterly* 69 (2017): 783–90.

2. Patrick Wolfe, "Settler Colonialism and the Elimination of the Native," *Journal of Genocide Research* 8, no. 4 (2006): 388.

3. Theodore Roosevelt, First Annual Message to Congress, December 3, 1901. The phrase "mighty pulverizing engine" was actually coined by eastern social reformer and "Friend of the Indian" Merrill E. Gates in an address at the Lake Mohonk Conference in 1900, and Roosevelt used it nearly word for word in his subsequent address to Congress. Francis Paul Prucha, *The Great Father: The United States Government and the American Indians* (Lincoln: University of Nebraska Press, 1984), 671.

4. Quoted in Robert J. Conley, *The Cherokee Nation: A History* (Albuquerque: University of New Mexico Press, 2005), 193.

5. Quoted in Prucha, *Great Father,* 20.

6. Hiram Price, "Allotment of Land in Severalty and a Permanent Land Title," in *Americanizing the American Indians: Writings by the "Friends of the Indian" 1880–1900,* ed. Francis Paul Prucha (Cambridge, Mass.: Harvard University Press, 1973), 89.

7. Angie Debo, *And Still the Waters Run: The Betrayal of the Five Civilized Tribes* (Princeton, N.J.: Princeton University Press, 1940), 91.

8. "Land Tenure History," Indian Land Tenure Foundation, https://iltf.org/land-issues/history.

9. William C. Lowe, "Allotment System," in *American Indian History,* vol. 1, ed. Carole A. Barrett (Pasadena, Calif.: Salem Press, 2003), 20.

10. Robert Nichols, *Theft Is Property!: Dispossession and Critical Theory* (Durham, N.C.: Duke University Press, 2019); Anthony J. Hall, *Earth into Property: Colonization, Decolonization, and Capitalism* (Montreal: McGill-Queen's University Press, 2010); Susan M. Hill, *The Clay We Are Made Of: Haudenosaunee Land Tenure on the Grand River* (Winnipeg: University of Manitoba Press, 2017); and Brenna Bhandar, *Colonial Lives of Property: Law, Land, and Racial Regimes of Ownership* (Durham, N.C.: Duke University Press, 2018).

11. Debo, *And Still the Waters Run*; Leonard A. Carlson, *Indians, Bureaucrats, and the Land: The Dawes Act and the Decline of Indian Farming* (Westport, Conn.: Greenwood Press, 1981); Delos Sacket Otis, *The Dawes Act and the Allotment of Indian Lands* (Norman: University of Oklahoma Press, 1973); Prucha, ed., *Americanizing the American Indians;* Wilcomb E. Washburn, *The Assault on Indian Tribalism: The General Allotment Law (Dawes Act) of 1887* (Philadelphia: Lippincott, 1975); Frederick E. Hoxie, *A Final Promise: The Campaign to Assimilate the Indians, 1880–1920* (Cambridge: Cambridge University Press, 1984; repr. Lincoln: University of Nebraska Press, 2001); Melissa L. Meyer, *The White Earth Tragedy: Ethnicity and Dispossession at a Minnesota Anishinaabe Reservation* (Lincoln: University of Nebraska Press, 1994); Lucy Maddox, *Citizen Indians: Native American Intellectuals, Race, and Reform* (Ithaca, N.Y.: Cornell University Press, 2018); Kent Carter, *The Dawes Commission and the Allotment of the Five Civilized Tribes* (Orem, Utah: Ancestry.com, 1999); Kristin T. Ruppel, *Unearthing Indian Land: Living with the Legacies of Allotment* (Tucson: University of Arizona Press, 2008); C. Joseph Genetin-Pilawa, *Crooked Paths to Allotment: The Fight over Federal Indian Policy after the Civil War* (Chapel Hill: University of North Carolina Press, 2014); Rose Stremlau, *Sustaining the*

Cherokee Family: Kinship and the Allotment of an Indigenous Nation (Chapel Hill: University of North Carolina Press, 2011); and Alaina E. Roberts, *I've Been Here All the While: Black Freedom on Native Land* (Philadelphia: University of Pennsylvania Press, 2021).

12. Sarah Winnemucca Hopkins, *Life among the Piutes: Their Wrongs and Claims* (1883; repr. Reno: University of Nevada Press, 1994); S. Alice Callahan, *Wynema: A Child of the Forest* (1891; repr. Lincoln: University of Nebraska Press, 1997); Lynn Riggs, *The Cherokee Night* (1936; Alexandria, Va.: Alexander Street Press, 2006); Lynn Riggs, *Green Grow the Lilacs* (1931; Alexandria, Va.: Alexander Street Press, 2008); Maria Campbell, *Halfbreed* (Lincoln: University of Nebraska Press, 1982); Patricia Grace, *Potiki* (Honolulu: University of Hawai'i Press, 1995); Louise Erdrich, *Tracks* (New York: Henry Holt, 1988); Linda Hogan, *Mean Spirit* (New York: Atheneum, 1990); Craig S. Womack, *Drowning in Fire* (Tucson: University of Arizona Press, 2001); Alexis Wright, *Carpentaria: A Novel* (New York: Atria Books, 2010); LeAnne Howe, *Shell Shaker* (San Francisco: Aunt Lute Books, 2001); and LeAnne Howe, *Miko Kings: An Indian Baseball Story* (San Francisco: Aunt Lute Books, 2007).

$85 an Acre

LEANNE BETASAMOSAKE SIMPSON

The processes of expansive dispossession, of removing Indigenous bodies, minds, and hearts from the deep relationality attaching us to and making us a part of Indigenous land, have many faces in the web of gendered colonialism and capitalist pursuit. Those faces—residential and boarding schools, the reserve and reservations systems, the Allotment Act, fraudulent treaty-making endeavors, and the Canadian Indian Act—were all designed to break our attachments to our lands and waters, our families, our cultures, languages, and spirituality, and to our political and economic systems. They set the groundwork for an influx of white settlement and infrastructure, and the extractivist economy that ensures Indigenous attachment to our homespaces is fragmented, narrow, and controlled by the state.

In the fall of 2018, "We are sorry" were the words that came out of the Canadian minister of Crown–Indigenous relations, Carolyn Bennett, to chiefs from the seven Williams Treaties First Nations in central Ontario, Canada. Bennett noted that what academics have termed the worst treaty in Canadian history "continued injustices, provided insufficient compensation and inadequate reserve lands . . . and failed to recognize and protect your treaty rights."

The apology was accompanied by a $1.1 billion settlement.

The $1.1 billion settlement seems like a lot of money, and it is, until you consider the sheer magnitude of loss. The settlement amounts to $85 an acre for the land that the Crown claims was "surrendered" by the terms of the treaty, a treaty that covered an area from the shore of Lake Ontario to Lake Nipissing in the north, from Lake Huron east to the Ottawa River. At the time of the apology, land in the Williams Treaty area sold for between $12,000 and $15,000 per acre.

$85 an acre does little for the nations of caribou, crane, eel, passenger pigeons, and salmon that are now extinct.

$85 an acre does little to compensate the deer for their destroyed homeland. It does little to reassure the beaver, turtle, pickerel, eagle, lynx, bear, wolf, and moose that their homelands will be regenerated. It does little to restore the beds of *minomiin* on our lakes, and it does nothing to remove the enclaves of private enclosure around *ninati-goog,* the maple trees.

$85 an acre does little to repair and rebalance gender relations, to refuse hetero-patriarchy, and to regenerate Nishnaabe space that values and centers queerness.

Within Nishnaabewin, a treaty that fails to protect our relations is not born out of deep reciprocity, mutual respect, or moral integrity, and it isn't a treaty relationship at all. A treaty that fails to acknowledge and affirm our preexisting treaty responsibilities to our clans isn't a treaty relationship at all.

A treaty settlement that fails to protect our relations and is not born out of deep reciprocity, mutual respect, or moral integrity is not just.

How, then, do the Michi Saagiig Nishnaabeg of the Williams Treaty area live up to our ethical responsibilities to our plant and animal relations, to our ancestors and those yet to be born, and to the anticolonial peoples with whom we share time and homespace? How, then, do the Michi Saagiig Nishnaabeg of the Williams Treaty area take care of the waterways and shorelines that run cold through our bodies? How, then, do the Michi Saagiig Nishnaabeg of the Williams Treaty area and our spiritual and ancestral relationships that constantly support us sit with, live, and act in solidarity with those to whom we are connected?

PART I

Family Narrations of Privatization

tʸiptukɨłhɨ wa tʸiptutʸɨʔnɨ, where are you from and where are you going?

patterns, parcels, and place nitspu tiłhin ktitʸutitʸu

SARAH BISCARRA DILLEY

strange weaving of wood

                      cattle

          iron

            oil

                fat

                    or

                fur

      imagined

a world

       in

    pieces

tqiłhismuʔ

fat

[ranches, missions, candles, cattle]

Where we dipped candles for forced prayer, they gave us new names. Often referred to as Obispeño Chumash, we are baptized with words again and again; an attempted transfiguration of the complex and layered relationships that make up yak titʸu titʸu, the people, into the perimeter of a mission, an *asistencia,* or a ranch.[1] Mission documents, used as legible forms of verification for recognition but also as the source of an unstable identity, decide our presence or absence in the eyes of the settler state without accounting for the complexity of our experiences or the inherent contradiction of requiring existence to be verified by the same mechanisms that dispersed, dismembered, displaced us.

Written into words and maps that remain fixed despite the life in all things, the systemic disordering of our worlds has been suspended across generations, attempting

Sarah Biscarra Dilley, *tⁱiptukiłhi wa tⁱiptutyiˀni (where are you from and where are you going?)*, video collage (still) [grayscale for print publication], 9:33, 2018.

to make such violence a new creation story. But our self-determined identities have the exponential capacity to exist beyond the codified, grounded within our own realities as Indigenous peoples and speaking from our respective centers of the world. While settlers imagine their possession, Indigenous peoples simultaneously deepen our connections—navigating narrative and physical confinement by maintaining long-standing relationships and challenging generational tensions to maintain survival. This includes relationships with other-than-human beings, place(s), and waterways, each of which contributes to a living sense of placemaking, of movement, and of alliances. Though plat maps display the world in flat, quantified dimension, it is our stories and relations that awaken the images and texts that imagine the disparate, a world in pieces. Our world is one of expansive whole, citing rivers and places with perspective in a language of family, of cultural protocol, of inspired determination. Elizabeth, Louise, Marie, Marta, Unacia, Lizzie, Mary, Maria Luisa, Leonora, Lorenza, Jacinta, Crespina; our cascade of names has always held multiple meanings, marking relation and continuum in place, a recipe, a middle name, the margin of a certificate of birth, an argument between new parents.

Like our continuance, our titled land came to be through relationship, only possible through my grandmother Louisa, the Kānaka ʻŌiwi daughter of Joaquin, son of an unbaptized *"indio"* from Veracruz, born at Mission San Diego and coming of age at San Carlos Borromeo near Monterey. Like many other displaced, dispossessed, or diasporic peoples bound up in the mission system and its subsequent enclosure of the land, Joaquin became a renown horseman, working in the 1830s and early 1840s for Kauikeaouli [Kamehameha III], herding "feral longhorns into makeshift corrals" along the slopes of holy mountains and valleys of Hawai'i or coastlines of West Maui.[2] Her father, as imbricated in colonial industry as he was, represents the bridging of Indigenous vaquero practices and then-emergent paniolo traditions, a quickening movement between California and Hawai'i, a symbol of both innovation and fracture. This moment of imperial expansion is ongoing and iterative, manifesting as shifting colonial occupations in California, land grants and land loss traced on yellowing paper, while continuing to be echoed in United States military violence across *ɬpasini,*[3] deepening further dispossession *nitspu tiɬhin ktitʸu* through use of eminent domain to build military bases, extract oil, flood valleys, or enact armed training. It reflects connections between peoples of saltwater and archipelagos existing long before colonial imposition but also the dire choices Indigenous peoples have had to make to ensure survival, including those that further distance us from who we are: our responsibilities to our own land, waters, protocols, and lifeways, as well as respect for those of other Indigenous peoples.

> what do you call a moment that never
> stopped
>   an endless stretch
>   of changing realities
>   place is (in) each of us
>   each scene is unending
>   a point of occurrence
>   implied
>   but unsuccessful
>   el camino real
>   the royal road
>   an eminent
>   domain

tspu

earth, land, mountain, world

[unratified treaties, homeland(s), and privatization]

In California, the transition between nations driving occupation disrupted many adapted lifeways and patterns of survival. Eighteen treaties were negotiated with assumed representatives from fewer than half of California's tribes after the inception of

Near the outflow of the Nacimiento River, west bank of the Salinas River, facing west, 2018 [gray-scale for print publication]. Courtesy of the author.

statehood in 1850, most of which promised large tracts of land—8.5 million acres in total—in exchange for ceding land bases that ran from the edge of the Great Basin to the sea. These negotiations were made in tandem with congressional policy that transferred newly acquired land in California to the public domain, another transfiguration through paper. While some people moved to these tracts of land allegedly set aside for them permanently, many others, like my own family, knew nothing of the treaties at all or chose not to leave the lands to which they had responsibility.

Although terms were agreed upon, the treaties were not ratified. Supported by legislation passed before California was even formally a state, the Act for the Government and Protection of Indians stated, "in no case [could] a white man be convicted of any offen[s]e upon the testimony of an Indian, or Indians," and named white settlers' ability "to obtain Indian children for indenture."[4] This law also outlawed our land management practices, like the use of cultural burning, and made being present in our homelands an act of vagrancy, formalizing dominant narratives of perceived deviance. Due to a congressional gag order, the unratified treaties remained unknown to the public until 1905. These laws, and the silences that accompany them, shape the current moment; relegating them to the realm of the historical ignores the linear pattern of policy in the United States. The profound absence of these histories when discussing recognition, as well as the restructuring of nation and state, traced through ongoing processes of displacement or gentrification, extraction, and confinement, reflects the disturbing amnesia of a settler state. Considering legislation of erasure, foundational material, and narrative histories of the United States and the State of California as governing entities, our current moment and potential futurities must account for and remain in dialogue with these ongoing realities.

My grandmother Louisa was born in 1837 to Kealalaau and Joaquin, daughter of a brief but tumultuous marriage. Documentation of her mother's life is largely absented, present only in a marriage record, divorce papers, secondhand mention, speculation, or avoidance entirely. These paths are still revealing themselves. The location of parcels awarded to her father by Kauikeaouli in Kohala, his inclusion in a list of "Ali'i and konohiki of the Kaua'ula-Lahaina Vicinity,"[5] his appointment as *konohiki* for the *ahupua'a* of Moanui, after the relocation of the Royal Seat to Hawai'i, and acreage in Waikapu thread some connection to prominent families while the swift relinquishment of most lands by the royal family and abandoned land claims awards circa 1848 speaks to a fracture. The presence of Joaquin's name on a list of passport recipients for California in 1848 coincides with the signing of the Treaty of Guadalupe Hidalgo and the transitions of conflicting colonial governance. In 1850, Joaquin passed away

Illustration adapted from detail of application filed with General Land Office, 1887, showing Louisa's mark.

of "morbid cholera," living *nitspu awaswas ktiťutiťu wa amah mutsun ktiťutiťu* at Rancho Trinidad in the Pajaro Valley and listed as a bachelor in the Mission Santa Cruz register.[6] Though her father left this world relatively penniless, it is told in our family that, as his sole heir, Louisa came into a sum of close to $100,000 in the 1850s, with $75,500 of unpaid labor still requested from Kauikeaouli, and a stone house at Lahaina listed in his last will and testament. This could also read as continued contact or relationship with her mother's family in Hawai'i.

Beginning around 1886, Louisa set out establishing documentation of her relationship to the land at Oro Fino Canyon, overlooking the San Antonio River facing north and just two hills, facing south, from the Nacimiento River. Like the now-dammed flow of each, this process was often halting and diverted. Securing ownership in the era of allotment meant meetings with the San Luis Obispo county clerk's office, a repetitive cycle of preemption claims and other forms. Misspellings made by county clerks led to many more signed affidavits and to rough buggy rides from rolling hills over the Cuesta Grade. Statements such as these arise time and time again throughout the pages of paperwork and come to stand in for the dueling literacies that enact strength and its erasure: "Officiant is unable to read or write and had to have someone else write her name." The various cash sale entries throughout this region demonstrate the dedication with which Louisa worked to make payment for the wrongs that had been done to her own people on the islands and those of the coasts and hillsides of the families she came to call her relatives. Like other Native peoples, my family bent the intentions of the allotment era to respond to a disordered world, marking connection in a chain of systems meant to isolate and individuate.

Her early childhood in two rapidly changing colonial contexts could have anchored her ideas, but she no doubt possessed the active mind and persistent knowing that has carried down our line. Like many of us, Louisa worked to repair or rewrite these histories in ways that have emanated across lifetimes, strengthening our family through intentions and marriages that are not only relational but political. This is an inherently sovereign act, especially within a landscape of dispossession.

Her navigation of the bureaucracy of the General Land Office in the 1880s as a recent widow is a testament to her strength of will, her resilience, and the long sight of her mind. Parcels were purchased for four of her eight children in later years, but the initial stages of paperwork and cash sale entries were secured for the parents-by-marriage of her son Jose Gregorio. A seamless connection to the matrifocal is present among the first parcels purchased between 1891 and 1895, secured along two distinct waterways for the parents of Mary, her daughter-in-law. Of the roughly three thousand acres scattered throughout San Luis Obispo County, purchased between 1886 and 1914, the majority of the patchwork bearing our names is sprinkled along this meandering stretch of the Nacimiento River. Since bisected by the Nacimiento Dam, some of these places rest under water while others are prevented from visit by the borders of Camp Roberts or private housing developments, seized through eminent domain.[7] These false divides continue to iterate from the first moments of contact on varied and various coasts.[8] Understanding the power of paper in settler cosmologies, she used their tools to articulate our design, weaving consistent connection in the dotted patterns of parcels that echo the intermittent use of color in coiled baskets or a string of shells.

> spanning oceans on running boards
> skirt hiked
> to shine
> > marvelous legs   back up
> to the sun
> still
> traveling
> a pretty length of shells
> > some pitch marbled lupine
> sea foam
> and sky

Sarah Biscarra Dilley, *qšimuʔ*, video collage (still) [grayscale for print publication], 3:33, 2020.

tpismuʔ

pitch, tar, *brea*

[petroleum, survey, mineral, time]

As documentation of "springs of mineral tar" within reports commissioned by the United States government pre-date or coincide with the Senate authorization and subsequent refusal to ratify the eighteen treaties negotiated with California tribes, collusion between the federal government and the state government of California is not only plausible but too timely to be coincidence.[9] John Boardman Trask, referred to as state geologist even before the founding of the Office of Geology in 1860, presided over an examination of mineral and other natural resources throughout the recently articulated boundaries of the state as requested by a California Senate and Assembly resolution on May 6, 1853. Commissioned only ten months after the denial and gag order of unratified treaties in California, this research, spanning two years, also coincides with the Pacific Railroad Survey reports conducted in 1853 by William Phipps Blake and from 1854 to 1855 by Thomas Antisell, which detail the appearance of bituminous resources from the San Francisco Bay Area and south past Los Angeles, arguing the economic value of a railway spanning "almost the entire shoreline of Southern California: Santa Cruz, Monterey, San Luis Obispo, Santa Barbara and Los Angeles."

Indians of California v. United States (1928) represents the attempted enclosure of unsettled land title created by the unratified treaties among many other iterations of displacement within the boundaries of California. Allegedly filed by the United States government on behalf of California Native peoples, this case, which describes our population(s) as "wandering" and "roving," illustrates a clear intent to undermine the legitimacy of tribal communities as people of place, ensuring a continued legislative confinement of our cultures, land, and being. Like maps of the Monterey Shale Formation, documentation of various mineral and spatial resources traces similar outline to the absence of tribal lands throughout the state, echoing the traditional land bases of many California Indigenous communities unrecognized by federal agencies as tribal nations. Combined with the dis-

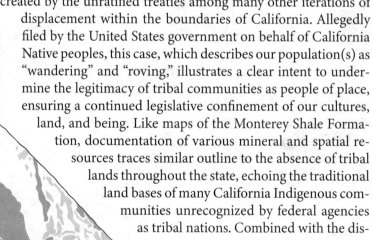

Map depicting gas and oil fields, as well as carbon sequestration, throughout California. Illustration adapted from California Geological Survey, California Department of Conservation.

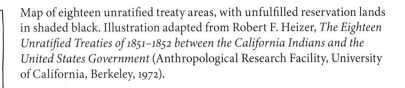

Map of eighteen unratified treaty areas, with unfulfilled reservation lands in shaded black. Illustration adapted from Robert F. Heizer, *The Eighteen Unratified Treaties of 1851–1852 between the California Indians and the United States Government* (Anthropological Research Facility, University of California, Berkeley, 1972).

possession of Indigenous lands through continued legislation, this illustrates a cartography of collusion between occupying governments.

By 1893, 24,341,000 barrels of oil were being extracted per year, making California the top producer of the era.[10] By 1981, there were over 5,500 miles of active pipelines within the state transporting petroleum.[11] By 2012, Chevron, formerly Standard Oil, was noted as being engaged in seventeen active pipeline or petroleum processing site cleanups in nitspu tiłhin ktitʸu alone,[12] due to noncompliance with policy.[13] In 2018, the Trump administration approved new drilling near tšiłkukunɨtš and shared places of prayer, within the boundary of Carrizo Plain National Monument and overlapping with the land base allegedly set aside for our people by unratified Treaty C. The San Andreas Fault, which spans the eastern boundary of this grassland, once echoed throughout a vast part of the Central Valley of California, and the abrupt mountains that arise from the meeting of earth remind us of seismic movement as a voice of dissent. In 2019, many of my family's former parcels and villages were included in the over forty thousand acres proposed for hydraulic fracturing throughout San Luis Obispo County.

Map of eighteen unratified treaty areas, with unfulfilled reservation lands in shaded black, overlaid with gas and oil fields, as well as carbon sequestration throughout the state.

the waters

we have followed

since time immemorial

seemingly drained

collecting

in   stagnant   pools

with iridescent sheen

a thin film

a lens of ages

to?

water

[transit, travel, trade]

The words of my grandmother Mary, equally cheeky and crushing, when replying to a question about where she was when the unratified Treaty C was negotiated, a direct "I don't know" while naming generations of places and relatives, the span of which she was a center. Reading the responses of relatives in the various forms of the Application for Enrollment with the Indians of the State of California under the Act of May 18, 1928 (45 Stat. L. 602), a result of the 1928 case, is an outline of an ongoing moment of enclosure but also the significant capacity of *simismuʔ* in establishing and maintaining relationship to place, despite the marginalization of matrifocal governance and patterns of movement.[14]

Of the many patents held by my relatives, secured through cash sale entry or the Homestead Act, significant parcels are held by women at the juncture of streams, mountains, or cultural confluences throughout the region and ɬpasini. California State Land Patent #18621 was processed at the San Francisco office of the Bureau of Land Manage-

13. Give the names of the Chiefs, Captains and Headmen of the Tribe or Band to which your ancestors belonged on June 1, 1852, who executed the Treaty or Treaties herein referred to, if you know them.

I do not know

Illustration adapted from excerpted page of Application for Enrollment with the Indians of the State of California under the Act of May 18, 1928 (45 Stat. L. 602), showing my grandmother Mary's hand.

ment, made out in the name of my fourth great-grandmother Leonora, listed as Leo-nor. It is through her that Cayucos is repeated from generation to generation in passing mention or a weighted vagueness—from Mary to Louise and Elvira, Lala to Cindy, to me. The parcels purchased for my grandparents, Leonora and her husband, Dionicio, reflect not only our matrifocal and gender-expansive ways of doing things but also our consistent connections between villages since time immemorial. Leonora's parcel sits between the location of tšimimuʔ, near the spring of Toro Creek, tsɨtxala, near Cayucos, and tsɨtkawayu, near Cambria, bisected by Villa Creek with Cayucos and Old Creeks nearby, and a clear view of ɫisamu, or Morro Rock. This intentional mapping of families and accompanying patterns of movement illustrate complex relationships with the land itself and with each other. Rather than completely fixed habitation, we rotate residence according to the season, use of various resources, and ceremonial calendar, making mar-riages and many other unions throughout the region an essential part of avoiding over-taxing our homeland. These networks of simismuʔ reflect the integration of material wealth, scientific understanding, and a deep knowledge of place.

Leonora was born in the 1850s of her mother's first but brief marriage, in an em-bodiment of the shifting relationships and movement within the central coastal area. According to my grandmother Lala's recollection and paperwork filed by her grand-mother Mary, Leonora was born in 1858, somewhere in Santa Barbara County, with oscillating surnames depending on location, employer, or rancho. Leonora was mar-ried at Mission San Luis Obispo de Tolosa to Dionicio, yak titʸu with connections ranging widely through Afro-Indigenous diasporas via Mexico, Huichime, Las Flores, near present-day Camp Pendleton in San Diego County, and landing *nitspu rumsen ktitʸu*.[15] Both residents of Avila at the time, their marriage reflects the long-established constellation of connections between Indigenous peoples throughout the region, both quickened and inhibited by the colonial imposition of the mission system.

These paths reflect responsibilities, often carried within families, that changed form in the era of allotment, enclosure, and labor, paid marginally to cultivate an increas-ingly wealthless world. We worked the ranches that stole our villages out from under us, claiming eminent domain or abandonment, absent humanity or extinction. Restrained through linguistic as well as physical, spatial, and economic means, we continued to assert simismuʔ, which, as living intention and action, is always growing and chang-ing. Long before such inequities, our movement followed, and follows, many patterns; tiɫhini becomes San Luis Obispo, tsɨtxala becomes Cayucos, tsɨtkawayu reimagined as Cambria, following paths of seeds into sweat and soil and colored kerchiefs. Old Creek, which follows the northern parts of Santa Rita Road, named after a ranch that employed our relatives, is halted before its outflow to the sea to provide water for a seaside town, a college, and a prison, mirroring the enclosure and incarceration that made possible its making. What they did to the land, they did to each of us in turn.

Our agency can be read into this stubborn movement, refusing to be dispossessed or abandon our responsibilities to place. Not only did intracommunity or village marriages represent a long continuum of kinship networks throughout the region, so did travel across long distances to share ceremony, materials, food, and dances. In this sense, Leonora's own lineage, past into future, has this knowledge coded into it, marking specific points of relation within broad constellations of connection as patterns taught to her daughters and granddaughters well. It is no mistake that the place marked on a patent bearing Leonora's name, the valley where she built a house and a half mile of fencing for one hundred dollars, is bisected by Villa Creek and in the shadow of Cypress Mountain. This parcel is the most divergent in location of all those purchased by Louisa. According to a letter to the commissioner of the General Land Office, proof of payment was received for the connecting parcels on July 1, 1891, though the state was delinquent in releasing the land formally until 1892. Her belonging was contested on numerous occasions, with overlapping sales and testimony from settlers claiming her absence due to illness illegitimated her ownership. Leonora, in response, challenged the state as being responsible for the true neglect and abandonment of the land, reasserting our understanding of place as interdependent with the care, maintenance, and dedication of all beings living within simismuʔ.

The purchases of each described parcel, made by Louisa, coincide with the marriage of her youngest son, Jose Gregorio, and Mary, the middle daughter of Dionicio and Leonora. Their union would eventually result in ten children, many of whom married into other prominent Indigenous families throughout the Central Coast and valleys. The fact that each of the parents' parcels is in a disparate part of the county not only recognizes the current moment of their partnership through cultural understanding, which situates "marriage" as a choice to live together, consensually dissolved through change of residence or simple relational shift, but also echoes the scope of relationships throughout our homelands and beyond. Without our stories, documentation— whether from a land office, mission record, or anthropological perspective—has little meaning. Our stories represent complex and expansive possibilities because we are speaking from a defined place, even when the language is changing.[16]

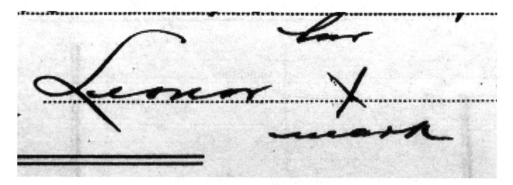

Illustration adapted from detail of California State Land Patent #18621, 1891, showing Leonora's mark.

our places
occupied by absence
    are brimming
        at the edges
           of mythologies of the settled
    are living
    in the forever
        of a dream
that made this world
        and the next
          and the next
            and the next
nitspu tʸana niłhisa šumoqini
a
      seamless
         unending
           whole

Sarah Biscarra Dilley, *tsʔiqinatʸi nitsłiłimi,* 2018. Paper, gold foil, graphite, mugwort, white sage, pine needles, polyvinyl acetate on canvas [grayscale for print publication], 48 × 36 inches.

NOTES

1. Located near *tipu* (Santa Margarita), Asistencia Santa Margarita de Cortona was an arm of Mission San Luis Obispo de Tolosa concerned with the monetization and enclosure of yak titʸu titʸu yak tiłhini homelands and a midpoint between Mission San Luis and Mission San Miguel Archangel. It remains a privately owned ranch.

2. John Ryan Fischer, *Cattle Colonialism: An Environmental History of the Conquest of California and Hawaiʻi,* Flows, Migrations, and Exchanges (Chapel Hill: University of North Carolina Press, 2015), 128.

3. Meaning "the sea" or "the one sea" in tʔinismu tiłhinktitʸu (the language of the people of tiłhini). The use of this term engages a different conceptualization of waters often described as "the Pacific," a colonial distinction of shared but distinct saltwater surrounding all continents.

4. An Act for the Government and Protection of Indians, 1850 Cal. Stat.

5. Kepā Maly and Onaona Maly, *He Wahi Moʻolelo no Kauaʻula a me Kekāhi ʻĀina o Lahaina i Maui/A Collection of Traditions and Historical Accounts of Kauaʻula and Other Lands of Lahaina, Maui,* vol. 1 (Hilo, Hawaiʻi: Kumu Pono Associates LLC, 2007), 12.

6. Meaning "in lands/worlds of the Awaswas and Amah Mutsun peoples" in tʔinismu tiłhinktitʸu (the language of the people of tiłhini).

7. At Camp Roberts, now a California National Guard post, parcels were seized as early as 1902, coinciding with violent coups and imperial expansion across łpasini, the sea. Congress did not authorize building on these lands until 1940.

8. Sāmoan scholar and collaborator Lana Lopesi reminds me that "the false divides the colonial project leaves behind change the ways in which we understand ourselves, reinforcing colonial borders. And only talking back to our individual imperial histories, rather than talking to each other across empires, can lead to an unknowing strengthening of these false divides." Lana Lopesi, introduction to *False Divides* (Wellington: BWB Texts, 2018).

9. Philip T. Tyson, George H. Derby, Edward O. C. Ord, Persifor F. Smith, Theodore Talbot, R. S. Williamson, and Bennett Riley, *Geology and Industrial Resources of California* (Baltimore: Wm. Minifie & Co., 1851).

10. Gerald T. White, "California's Other Mineral," *Pacific Historical Review* 39, no. 2 (1970): 135–54, https://doi.org/10.2307/3637433.

11. State of California, Regional Water Quality Control Board, Central Coast Region, *Staff Report for Regular Meeting of March 14–15, 2012* (2012), 26–57.

12. Meaning "in the land/world of the people of tiłhini" in tʔinismu tiłhinktitʸu (the language of the people of tiłhini).

13. State of California, *Staff Report.*

14. Often translated as "friend" or "companion" in tʔinismu tiłhinktitʸu (the language of the people of tiłhini), *simismuʔ* is derived from the verb *-sime, -simi* ("to accompany, to go with, to come with"). A translation of the noun *simismuʔ* could be "an intention to go with or accompany"— speaking to the active and ongoing principles of kinship.

15. Meaning "an Indigenous person." I do not claim specific relation where the story is still unfolding, fractured, or distant.

16. auʔ auʔ D yaptʔinismu to speak from a defined place tsʔitʸutʸu wa tsʔimonʔo

Narrated Nationhood and Imagined Belonging

Fanciful Family Stories and Kinship Legacies of Allotment

DANIEL HEATH JUSTICE

This is a story of two families—one Native, one white, both firmly rooted in the political, economic, and social struggles of the Five Tribes in Indian Territory on the cusp of Oklahoma statehood, though on opposite sides of that long siege. This is the story of the role allotment played in how they would understand and imagine themselves, their histories, and their futures. This is also a story about how the manufactured mythologies of those who worked to wrest the Territory from our nations further displace those with legitimate ties to the land and relations. The "pulverizing engine" of allotment may have largely ended as official federal Indian policy, but its dispossessive legacies continue today.

At the start of the allotment process in the late 1890s, after the Curtis Act extended key provisions of the General (Dawes) Allotment Act over the Five Tribes (the Cherokee, Chickasaw, Choctaw, Muscogee [Creek], and Seminole Nations), the Indian Territory extended over twenty million acres in what is now eastern Oklahoma. Over the course of the next decade, three-quarters of that land would be severed from collective ownership and allotted to individual citizens of the Five Tribes, with the rest expropriated for non-Native settlement and sale. Sales restrictions were lifted for many allotment holders in 1908, after which much of the allotment land swiftly passed into white possession through willing or coerced sale, fraudulent trusteeship, graft, and more insidious methods. By 1928, lands still considered restricted under Native possession (not free to be sold or taxed) had been slashed to 1,727,702 acres.[1]

Taxation and seizure of unrestricted lands was a major factor for land loss in the twentieth century, as was fractionation, where, upon the death of an original allottee, the title of the allotment would be divided equally among all heirs, while the land itself would remain intact; the fractions would diminish further with each succeeding generation, as each heir of ever-expanding family networks would possess equal shares of ever-reduced value, to the absurd point of hundreds, even thousands of co-owners of a small acreage for whom no economic sustainability for one inheritor, let alone hundreds, was possible. One researcher noted in 1942 that "most of the land allotted to citizens of the Cherokee Nation has in the short period of three decades passed into the hands of the majority white population"; the numbers have worsened in the decades since.[2] Current figures for allotment lands no longer in the possession of Five Tribes citizens are difficult to access, but Linda Donelson, the former real estate services director for the Cherokee Nation, notes that the Nation saw 4.4 million acres under its jurisdiction in 1906 reduced to 109,104 acres by 2009—a catastrophic decline in just over one hundred years and continuing.[3] (Add to this Oklahoma's notorious adverse possession legislation that explicitly facilitates land theft through squatter's rights claims, a mechanism used even today to legally alienate allotments complicated by fractionalization or geographically remote from allotment holders, especially those without the economic or physical means to monitor their property.)[4]

Yet it wasn't just land that was fragmented in the allotment of Indian Territory and the imposed dissolution of tribal governments and institutions—so too were families, communities, genealogies, political and legal orders, cultural memories, and kinship relations. While most of the published scholarly commentary on Five Tribes land allotment rightly focuses on the undeniable traumas accompanying land loss, such discussions cannot take place outside the context of the catastrophic regional influx of white settlers who hoped to gain control over Indian lands, and the existential danger they represented to the Five Tribes. That danger continues today through false family stories of vague Indigenous heritage weaponized by the descendants of the very settlers who most aggressively worked to steal those lands.

The demography of Indian Territory started shifting in the 1870s, especially with the forced introduction of railroads by the federal government as part of punitive treaty provisions after the Civil War. This included the expropriation of tribal land along the railway line as U.S. property, thus transecting the Territory with "alternate sections in a ten-mile strip on each side of the right-of-way."[5] Thousands of non-Natives came to work on the railroad and decided to stay, and as their numbers grew, they agitated for titled possession to tribal lands, pressure that only increased with the 1893 opening of the Cherokee Outlet to non-Indigenous homesteaders. The vast majority of these new claimants were white; many were European immigrants encouraged by newspaper-fueled stories of bootstrap success on the American frontier, but most were multigenerational white Americans drawn west by promises of free land and ample resources.

Land ownership was more tenuous for Black people and other racialized minorities (including a small number of Chinese and Japanese laborers); legal and extralegal violence from the white majority were constant threats to the dream of secure land tenure, class mobility, and economic stability. Black homesteaders were distinct from and sometimes in tension with Five Tribes citizen Freedmen over land access and ownership; the shared experience of anti-Black violence and discrimination—from whites and non-Black tribal citizens alike—did not always result in solidarity when it came to tribal land title, to which the Five Tribes Freedmen had hard-won and inherited rights through treaty and citizenship, family ties, history, and sometimes language and culture.

The 1890 census reveals that whites in particular outnumbered Indian citizens in the Territory by a significant margin: in the Cherokee Nation, 29,166 residents were white, 5,127 were Black, and 22,015 were citizen Indians. In the Chickasaw Nation, the disparities were even more significant, with 48,421 whites compared to only 5,223 Indians and 3,676 Black residents; this gap would grow significantly over the next decade.[6] (In both of these cases, there is no distinction between Five Tribes Freedmen and more recent Black residents, as anti-Black white and tribal authorities alike treated both as wholly non-Indian.) The 109,393 whites in Indian Territory in 1890 would number 339,560 just ten years later. In a 1907 statehood census, the demographic transformation would be even more dramatic: whites accounted for 538,512 (roughly 80 percent) of the state population; 80,649 Black residents (both Five Tribes Freedmen and non-Freedmen) numbered nearly 12 percent; while there were just 61,925 Indians not of African heritage (just over 9 percent of the total). Historian Angie Debo further elaborates on this largely white settler context with undisguised disdain:

> These newcomers had no knowledge of Indian tradition, no respect for Indian institutions. In the excitement of discovering oil fields, building cities, and placing rich land under the plow, they created a philosophy in which personal greed and public spirit were almost inextricably joined. If they could build their personal fortunes and create a great state by destroying the Indian, they would destroy him in the name of all that was selfish and all that was holy.[7]

Land-poor whites were politically empowered to push their demographic advantage in the region, aided by legions of lawyers, judges, surveyors, and other authorities who saw easy money both in helping white claimants with dubious stories get access to Native land and in manipulating or using direct violence and intimidation to separate Native people from their allotments. Accusations of bribery, perjured testimony to enrollment officials, and outright fraud were common, as were the declaration of squatter's rights (as noted, still a legal land-grab option in Oklahoma), extortion, harassment, and even murder of allotment holders and scamming of their titled descendants. Indeed, the influx of entitled and aggressive whites into Indian Territory—both intermarried and noncitizen—put enormous pressure on the social cohesion of the Five Tribes, as Eric M. Zissu points out in reference to the Chickasaws: "Whites held meetings at which they defied the tribe's attempts to limit them. They then threatened the Chickasaws, vowing to 'exterminate every member of the council from the Chief down.' By 1900, the Chickasaw Nation counted within its borders 150,000 noncitizen whites, 5,000 blacks, and only 3,100 Chickasaws."[8] In this context, options for

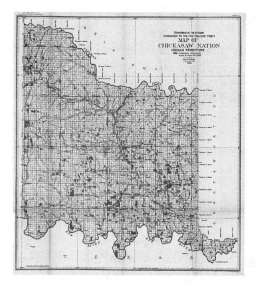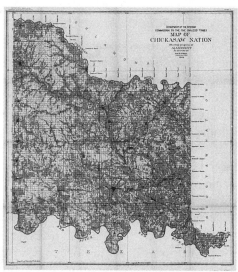

Drafted only a year apart (1903 and 1904, respectively), these two Dawes Commission maps expose the dramatic pace of allotment in the Chickasaw Nation. Pauls Valley, where J. W. Sparks tried to access Chickasaw lands, is located between the First Standard Parallel North and the Base Line, at the intersection of the Eastern Oklahoma and the Colorado and Santa Fe railway lines. Most of these allotments, like those of other Five Tribes allottees, were in non-Native hands within a couple of generations. Created by the Commission to the Five Civilized Tribes. Courtesy of the Oklahoma Historical Society.

maintaining any tribal authority over lands were increasingly limited, but the Five Tribes citizenry largely remained defiant in the face of looming privatization and the dissolution of their institutions and distinct political status.

One of the most insidious methods white settlers used to lay claim to Indigenous lands in the Territory, and one with myriad continuing impacts, was the falsification of Five Tribes heritage to be listed on rolls for land distribution. Such narratives of imagined Indianness were sometimes presented with sincerity (as with today's unsubstantiated but fervently believed stories of unnamed Cherokee great-great-grandmothers), but very often, especially during the allotment period, they were part of a widescale social and political practice of deliberate deception to secure tribal lands. These claimants were, as Debo describes them, "the most troublesome of intruders," who "had advanced some fantastic claim to citizenship, and who loudly demanded every privilege enjoyed by the Indians in spite of repeated denials of their claims by the tribal authorities."[9] Some were newcomers, but many were already firmly embedded in the Territory, protected by an incompetent federal government and manipulative white local officials with their own investments in undermining Five Tribes sovereignty. Sadly, the "fantastic claim[s]" they asserted during allotment continue to affect Indigenous nations in Oklahoma, especially Cherokees, who remain the main target for such false family histories.[10]

Through my father I am a Cherokee Nation citizen and a direct descendant of original allottees of the Dawes era and the Trail of Tears survivors and Cherokee Old Settlers who were among the first families of the reconstituted Nation in Indian Territory. Yet, through my mother's line I am also a direct descendant of Debo's white "troublesome intruders" who sought to use dubious claims about Indian identity to lay claim to tribal lands and who participated in the dispossession of Native nations and the disruption of our relations, territory, and sovereignty. These two tangled family stories together offer some insight not only into the traumas of the time but also into the ways that contemporary stories about invented Indian ancestors both reflect and perpetuate the harms of the allotment era.

My great-grandfather Amos Spears was born in 1876 in the Cherokee Nation, Indian Territory, and died ninety-nine years later in 1975, in Modesto, California, the same year I was born in Colorado. Amos was the son of Cherokee Nation citizens Charles and Mary (Crockett) Spears, an Old Settler Shields and Riley descendant through his mother and, through his father, the grandson of Elsie/Alsi Foreman and James Spears. Elsie was a member of the influential Foreman family and sister to the celebrated minister and political leader Stephen Foreman; James was a lifelong ally of Chief John Ross, served as an elected representative of the Cherokee National Council after the Trail of Tears, and signed the 1839 reunification constitution that brought the Nation back together under a single government headed by Ross. He was also implicated (along with his brothers and other relatives) in the execution of statesman and prominent Treaty Party member John Ridge, an act that would plunge the Nation into decades of internecine conflict that, even today, carries a painful legacy for descendants on both sides.

Amos and his younger brother Dennis were students in the Cherokee Male Seminary in the Nation's capital at Tahlequah at various times from 1892 to 1896, an opportunity shared by other kin, including their uncles Archibald and John Spears. The Male and Female Seminaries were among the proudest and most significant educational achievements of the Nation, with a curriculum that rivaled the New England preparatory schools from which they recruited their first teachers. Yet the seminaries would be further casualties of allotment and Oklahoma statehood: the Male Seminary burned down in 1910, and the Female Seminary was absorbed into what is now Northeastern State University.

My grandmother Pearl was born in 1906 near the now-defunct town of Vera, the second of Amos's seventeen children with his wife, Essie Bandy, likely at home on the family's primary allotment. Amos, his oldest son, Edward, and his brother Dennis had been granted allotments next door to one another just north of Tulsa; Pearl was

Pearl (Spears) Justice, later Bowers, stands beside her father, original Cherokee Nation allottee Amos Spears. Location unknown, but likely Colorado Springs or Amos's farm in eastern Colorado in the years shortly before her death of tuberculosis in 1945. Photograph from author's collection.

born too late to receive an allotment. Restrictions on Amos's allotments were removed around 1920, at which time he sold them, relocating his ever-expanding family to eastern Colorado. There, Pearl met my granddad, Jesse Jake Justice, and married young, having two children who survived infancy (Alverta and my dad, Jimmie) and one who did not (their firstborn, Alice); she would have a fourth child, a boy named Larry, after separating from Jake.

Pearl was listed as Indian on the 1910 and 1920 censuses, yet in spite of her undeniable and extensively documented Cherokee lineage and relations, both her wedding license and her later death certificate state her race as white. This is hardly surprising: to help facilitate transfer of Native lands into white ownership through marriage, and to reinforce anti-Black segregation and Jim Crow racial hierarchies, Article XXIII, section 11 of the 1907 Oklahoma state constitution explicitly categorized all people not of African heritage as legally white—the only state constitution to do so.[11] Native people without Black heritage, as well as Asian Americans and other non-Black people of color, were thus defined as legally white in Oklahoma (in law if not in social custom or personal prejudice) until 1978, when section 11 was repealed by a legislative referendum.

That legal designation carried on for my grandmother, her father, and her siblings long after they moved to Colorado, no matter how phenotypically Native they clearly were. Besides, by this time, the Cherokee Nation had been dissolved as a political entity by U.S. legislative fiat, and Amos no longer had his allotment lands in the Nation's boundaries. At the time of her wedding, Pearl was a seventeen-year-old Cherokee woman who lived on the eastern plains of Colorado, where the Ku Klux Klan was a major social and political force. In spite of being a visible woman of color married to a dark-skinned man of unspoken mixed ancestry (Jake claimed to be "Black Dutch" but was at least partly Jewish), it was safer to identify with whiteness than with Indianness in the political climate of the time and place. Even so, my father and aunt were ridiculed as "blanket-asses" by childhood bullies, and Dad in particular would deal with various iterations of anti-Indigenous bigotry throughout his long life.

Pearl and Jake separated in the late 1930s and divorced in 1940; Pearl died in the tuberculosis ward at St. Francis Hospital in Colorado Springs in 1945. Jake took custody of both my aunt Alverta and my dad until the two were old enough to leave home, while Larry, whose paternity Jake denied, was transferred to the care of the charitable Myron Stratton Home and largely disappeared from family memory. Amos came to Pearl's funeral and collected the deed to the house, which he owned, and it was the last time Dad would see him; indeed, aside from his mother's youngest brother, Gus, Dad was rarely in touch with any of his mother's kin after that point, although Alverta remained close to the extended Spears family throughout her life.

My father never ceased grieving Pearl, though for the rest of his days he never once went to visit her grave—it was just too hard, although Alverta went a few times. It wasn't until a few months after Dad died in 2019, at age ninety, that my husband, mom, and some cousins and I finally found Pearl's resting place. We were the first of my grandmother's descendants to stand in her presence since Alverta's last visit nearly fifty years before. Together we buried a handful of Dad's ashes at Pearl's grave site, finally reuniting them after a separation of nearly seventy-five years, a symbolic restoration of one more unraveled thread of kinship.

It's important to note here that this isn't at all the understanding of our history that I knew growing up. Dad was a proud "Indian" and, later in life, a reenfranchised Cherokee Nation citizen, but he wasn't raised culturally Cherokee, and therefore neither was I, nor were my siblings or cousins. We were detribalized mixed-bloods with legitimate but attenuated ties, and that reality has deeply affected how we've worked to reconnect with kin and contexts in the Nation. Until I was a young adult and began learning from near and extended relatives, Cherokee friends and teachers (and those from other Five Tribes), the archival record, and the land our family walked and lived on, everything beyond Grandma Pearl was a milky haze in history. There were no names, no relations, no controversies, scandals, documents—there were no stories *at all*. She was where our history started and ended. And it's no coincidence that this rupture substantively began the year she was born, in 1906, just as the primary push of the allotment period was wrapping up and Oklahoma statehood loomed on the horizon.

The history of my paternal Cherokee family is one of continual dispossession: first the traumas leading to and through the Trail of Tears, followed by the internecine conflict of the U.S. Civil War in Indian Territory (with kin fighting on both sides), then the fragmentations of allotment and the familial forgetting that accompanied it. When storytelling is a central way of community and family knowledge transmission, even one generation's disruption of that connecting thread—and its associated family connections—can be devastating. We can sometimes read those ruptures, but not always; we don't know why Amos sold his allotments and moved to Colorado, or why, years later, he headed to California. Certainly, the Oklahoma allotments were nowhere near big enough to support seventeen children, and many Cherokees set out to make their futures elsewhere. But other Cherokees with large families stayed put, and it's the Cherokees who kept the fires of nationhood burning who made it possible for my generation to reconnect. But allotment ravaged our extended relations, and it's only been due to a lot of hard work and a great deal of generosity from others that some of those links have been restored, even if imperfectly.

The history of my mom's family is similar—there are many things we don't know, as poverty, abuse, and constant movement seem to have unraveled much of the genealogical memory of what seems to be another motley lineage, this one largely impoverished settlers from Great Britain and western Europe. But there were certainly stories. My maternal grandfather, Jess Fay, was a lifelong miner and an inveterate grifter with more gall than charm. Yet some of Jess's stories remained consistent, such as his insistence that we were "part Blackfoot Indian" through his father's side; he was so convinced of his Indian heritage that he took up beadwork when mining in Arizona, and I still have a matching diamond-pattern belt buckle and hatband he made. Of course, the Blackfoot claim made no sense, given that the Blackfoot lands straddling the United States–Canada border were far from where that side of the family had come—namely, Oklahoma and Indiana. And my dad frankly hated Jess, for a lot of reasons, but one, I think, was Jess's breezy and uncomplicated claims to Native heritage, which Dad held with pride, but which was also the source of a great deal of pain throughout his life. (Ironically, Jess's own self-fashioning of "Indian" heritage became a grim kind of prophecy, for he would die of silicosis likely acquired from his work in the uranium mines on the Navajo Nation, thereby sharing the fate of many Diné miners.)

It would turn out to be significant that the historical period and geographic region where this Blackfoot claim was centered were those with which we're already very familiar: Indian Territory and allotment. Yet the story changed after Jess died and Mom reached out to some of his cousins. It wasn't Blackfoot, we learned, but Cherokee . . . or maybe Chickasaw. That this branch of the family had lived in Pauls Valley, Oklahoma,

CHEROKEE NATION
TOWNSHIP 23 NORTH, RANGE 13 EAST.

One of many Dawes Commission plat maps drafted to track Five Tribes allotment grants by name of allottee. The maps are a fascinating record of family relationships in a time of immense disruption. While not always possible or permitted, family members tried to ensure that their allotments were in close proximity, as seen here, where the main allotments of the author's great-grandfather Amos Spears and Amos's brother Dennis and eldest son, Edward, are together in section 27, with Riley kin nearby. Created by the Commission to the Five Civilized Tribes. Courtesy of the Oklahoma Historical Society.

firmly in the political reservation boundaries of the Chickasaw Nation, gave the latter claim some credence, and a distant cousin had some documents in her possession that, they assured us, would verify this connection. But attached to this story there was another one, which asserted that the relatives in question—by the name of Sparks—had the option of enrolling on the Cherokee or Chickasaw rolls and chose the latter given that they had lived in the Chickasaw Nation for some time. That's the story, in all its improbability: Blackfoot, then Cherokee, then Chickasaw, but maybe also Cherokee again.

As subsequent research in the Dawes records would demonstrate, these Sparks ancestors had indeed applied for citizenship in the Chickasaw Nation. And they'd been repeatedly denied.

The Chickasaws, like the other Five Tribes, had compiled extensive rolls over many decades that the Dawes Commission used to confirm legitimate tribal ties. Along with their Choctaw relatives, they also had a citizenship court that assessed claims and was particularly vigilant in ensuring that false claimants were struck from the rolls. They were understandably committed to ensuring that only legitimate tribal members were listed on the rolls, as land, resources, and relations were at stake—all of which many Chickasaw people had died to defend for future generations. And the flood of white settlers in Chickasaw territory in particular made such vigilance more than a matter of integrity or kinship—it was a matter of survival. For they had always been a relatively small community, and they had already lost so much, and many non-Indians were, as always, eager to cash in on what remained. (This was also part of the rationale for the Chickasaw Nation leadership's relentless opposition to Freedmen citizen status. It was white settlers who were the overwhelmingly real threat to the nations, not the comparatively small populations of either Five Tribes Freedmen or non-Freedmen Black homesteaders, but anti-Blackness informed Five Tribes "by blood" citizens' widespread hostility to the rightful claims of Freedmen and their descendants.)[12]

For tribal nations in the Indian Territory, who had dynamic and complex cultures, strong political and educational systems, and largely stable economies, this was a terrifying time of looming devastation. And while Five Tribes enrollment officials were busy determining eligibility for land and resource distribution and trying to keep families together as much as possible, white lawyers, judges, police, and other authorities were busy trying to undermine the process and separate them, thereby fractionating ties to kin as well as links to land. Decades of increasingly coercive allotment legislation was the tangible manifestation of that eliminationist logic.

It's vital to recall here that every illegitimate claim approved by white authorities meant that Five Tribes members, regardless of their citizenship category, once again lost land to deception and theft. There was an immediate relationship between false claims and dispossession. Many Five Tribes families tried to get their allotments close to one another in order to maintain their connections, but every false claim approved by white authorities disrupted the possibility of family proximity and broader kinship connections in tangible ways. Hostile strangers or untrusted acquaintances would suddenly be next-door neighbors who aggressively claimed rights of affiliation and increased the pressure to surrender surrounding allotments, thereby further fragmenting and distancing Indian family members from one another. Worse, still, was when Five Tribes orphans were separated from close kin and left to the machinations of court-appointed white trustees, men who scoured the region for inheriting and unprotected Native children and conspired with corrupt authorities to exploit their inheritance in shockingly cruel, even murderous ways.[13]

There were three main categories of Five Tribes citizenship: by Indian "blood," by marriage, and as Freedmen. Most enrollees were in the first category; those of the second were largely white. U.S. treaties following the Civil War stipulated that Black people enslaved by Five Tribes citizens were to be freed and granted full citizenship rights in the nations that had once enslaved them, although there were varying levels of resistance among the tribes to the enfranchisement provision, and this issue continues to be a source of ongoing pain and injustice in all the nations. (Many Freedmen were in fact affiliated with the Five Tribes "by blood," but authorities often relegated those with any known Black heritage to the Freedman rolls instead.)[14]

Reading the Sparks family allotment application brings us right to the heart of allotment tensions, economics, and politics. Page after page of testimonies, legal judgments, solicitations, and appeals. As best I can determine through this record, my maternal ancestors J. W. and Cynthia Sparks claimed rights of Chickasaw citizenship, but in a rather peculiar way. They claimed Chickasaw citizenship through marriage, but twice removed: J. W., the father, said he was entitled to Chickasaw citizenship because his ex-wife, Sarah, had previously been married to a Chickasaw citizen—Jackson Colbert (son of Chickasaw Nation governor Winchester Colbert), who had died and left her a widow. J. W. also claimed that this same ex-wife Sarah (Hughes) Colbert was a noncitizen Cherokee Indian by blood, in addition to being a Chickasaw citizen by marriage. She was demonstrably the latter, but he provided no evidence of the former, aside from yet another vague story of affiliation: he even acknowledged that "she claimed she was a Cherokee Indian by blood, but she had not been admitted to Cherokee citizenship. She was a U.S. citizen when she married [Jackson Colbert]."[15] This was as close to an admission of her non-Native status as it could be, as Cherokee kinship ties were extensively documented in over thirty-five separate censuses, rolls, and lists, not counting various treaties, judicial decrees, and other legal documents. If her relations couldn't be found in that archive and she hadn't been granted citizenship to that point, she was, in the light of all available and tribally recognized evidence, not Cherokee.

In short, J. W. Sparks—self-identified as a white man and with no Chickasaw heritage or kinship ties of his own—claimed the right of being a Chickasaw citizen solely by marriage to a white woman who was herself a Chickasaw citizen by marriage, not blood, and whom he had divorced. The Cherokee heritage claim is entirely vague and seems merely to be an added attempt to assert legitimacy, if not through his ex-wife's earlier marriage, then through her supposed Cherokee heritage (and, by extension, that of their daughter).

The citizenship-conferred-through-marriage angle was not an unusual argument in such cases. Indeed, Debo notes that it was common enough to be a particular concern to the Five Tribes in their brief to the Choctaw and Chickasaw Citizenship Court (CCCC), a tribunal that was focused specifically on applicants who were approved for citizenship by U.S. courts despite the nations' objections. She writes that the CCCC "ruled against the constitutionality of a tribal law by which intermarried citizenship was forfeited upon subsequent marriage to a non-citizen"—thus, J.W.'s wife Sarah maintained her status as a Chickasaw by marriage even after her prominent Chickasaw husband had died—but "it rejected the unconscionable claim that a white person could confer citizenship upon any white person whom he might afterwards marry and upon his white descendants."[16]

In 1898, a few years before the CCCC was established, Hosea Townsend, a judge in U.S. Federal Court for the Southern District of the Indian Territory, ordered J. W. Sparks and his daughter Cynthia to be enrolled in the Chickasaw Nation. Townsend was notorious for approving white claimants with any self-declared assertion of Indian "blood," no matter how scant or nonexistent the evidence, and the Choctaw and Chickasaw Nations were particularly opposed to his rulings, which affected them disproportionately. As Kent Carter writes in his comprehensive study of the Dawes Commission's work, "The persons admitted by . . . [Judge] Townsend were generally contemptuously referred to by tribal officials as 'court citizens,' and attorney Melvin Cornish called them a 'horde of adventurers.'"[17]

Chickasaw officials appealed Townsend's decision on J.W. and Cynthia; ultimately, the CCCC ruled in favor of the Chickasaw Nation, and Townsend's decision was vacated. Yet even then, Cynthia tried to reestablish her claim, marrying her white husband Barney a second time, this time by a Chickasaw Nation judge after their citizenship claim was dismissed, to no avail. J.W. continued to appeal the decision with multiple lawyers over the better part of a decade, pleading ill health and penury as reasons for his application to be approved, but always falling short. There were still plenty of exploitative lawyers in the Territory—and, later, the State of Oklahoma—eager to press these claims, but in the end, he was unsuccessful, and J.W. and Cynthia remained off the rolls, as did thousands of other false claimants.

But their story would not disappear. It would mutate and expand, changing through fractionated memory across the generations, down to this very day.

This brings me back to the stories of the "Blackfoot" ancestors, who become Cherokees, then Chickasaws (but maybe once again also Cherokees?), but then turn out actually to be white folks trying to steal Indian lands by claiming to be something they clearly weren't. A tangled tale, but not an unusual story for anyone with links to Oklahoma dating to this period. And, as the long controversy around Senator Elizabeth Warren's supposed Cherokee heritage demonstrates, it's still happening, now with the additional wrinkle of DNA testing being used to support dodgy and even verifiably false identity claims.

Everyone has family stories that they'd like to believe. I certainly admire the Chickasaw people I know, and I wouldn't object to being related to them. Yet there's no evidence to support the J. W. and Cynthia Sparks story, not for me, not for my mom's kin. Without a doubt, some family stories of lost connection are true. We all know people who, for reasons outside their control (adoption, residential/boarding school, family breakdown, etc.), don't know their legitimate relations or the meaningful stories that accompany them and who are doing their utmost to reweave those ties that were severed or frayed through no fault of their own. My Dad's experience of being raised largely away from his mother's kin is a case in point. Yet this legitimate work of reconnection and recovery is made infinitely harder by people who have no identifiable connection but still make claims and assert rights to resources and a platform just because they have some fuzzy, unsupportable story they want to believe.

As the Sparks story above demonstrates, just because there's a story passed down through the generations doesn't make it legitimate, nor does it make it true. It's still a story that some of my mom's cousins believe, and they've found Chickasaw people on the final roll by that last name, but these aren't the Sparkses from whom we're descended. Nothing lines up for them to be our relatives—not first names, dates, generations, or locations—but a similar name (in this case, J. B. Sparks rather than J. W.), a passed-down story, and wish fulfilment are enough for some relatives to pin certainty, and identity, on a story that just isn't true.[18]

The issue isn't simply that this story is false—it's a falsehood inextricably tied to the brutal dispossession of Chickasaw lands under allotment. Such stories aren't benign. They're profoundly embedded in white supremacy, land theft, the disruption of tribal sovereignty, and even assault and murder. It's easy to claim a vague story about an Indian ancestor when you don't know the devastating context from which that story emerged. These stories fuel continuing colonial claims of authority over Indigenous identities as well as lands, wielded without accountability to a living community. They give white voters, judges, police, lawyers, social workers, and teachers a sense of false but entitled authority, control, and domination over Native being and belonging, regardless of what Native people have to say on the matter.

It certainly doesn't escape me that my dad's family, where the roots are deep in the Cherokee Nation and its history, lost many of our own legitimate kinship stories after the disruptions and displacements of allotment from Indian Territory to Oklahoma, Colorado, and beyond, whereas my mom's paternal family firmly maintained this false narrative over that same period. My dad's people had kinship but lost our stories; my mom's people had stories but no kinship. The painful ironies pile up. Yet even on the Cherokee side there was an unsubstantiated story about vague Shawnee heritage that subsequent research has failed to support. Sometimes even Native people have these tenacious tales of mythic Indian ancestors, but we more than anyone know what they cost us and our nations.

It's easy to assume that the land swindlers were innocent in their belief in a long-lost Indian relative if you haven't read through Dawes-era documents. But these documents show just how widespread, willful, and unabashed these false claims were. White settlers weren't ashamed of their false kin claims—they actively shared them, worked with shifty lawyers to pay people who could support them, built on the narratives others used. It was shameless, public, and omnipresent. Tribal newspapers, preachers, and political leaders railed against it; white newspapers, preachers, and political leaders celebrated it. It was everywhere in public allotment discourse. People didn't often hide genuine heritage, as is frequently claimed today—rather, thousands manufactured heritage out of a disparate assortment of wishful fragments, illogical fantasies, financial ambitions, and yes, sometimes, even overtly racist lies. I'd wager that the majority of family myths about attenuated Indian ancestry date from this time. Thousands of stories that were constructed specifically to legitimize the theft of Native lands during the allotment period—and documented as such—have endured, and today they legitimize the ongoing theft of Native identities, rights, and resources, utterly divorced from kinship, familial obligations, or political acknowledgment, bolstered by slippery interpretation of sloppily applied DNA science. Our nations, and our families, have paid a heavy price for these claims.

My paternal Cherokee family's memories became fractionated after allotment, and without the collective ties to hold those memories and their associated stories together, successive generations have inherited a smaller, more fragmented, and more impoverished picture of who we are as kin and, more broadly, as a people. And just as the land was privatized, so too, now, are the manufactured stories of Indian identity from my other family line; they've now become a transmissible kind of individualized property available to anyone with the currency to claim it, but without the specificities and accountabilities of kinship, claimed at no cost and exchanged without consequence.

I don't know much about my maternal Sparks ancestors. They might have been good people genuinely convinced that their story was true. They could have been mercenary white land-grabbers trying to exploit a catastrophic policy for personal gain. Sadly, I think it was probably the latter. There were many like them, tens of thousands of land pirates that the Five Tribes had to spend precious resources, energy, time, and emotion contending with. The records are clear; the archive is substantial. What comes up again and again in the Dawes records, especially the testimonies, is how entrenched the myth of vague heritage is to the claims of white claimants, even by the late nineteenth century.

Whatever the context or the motivation, drill down far enough and over and over again we find many unnamed great-great-great-grandmother Indian princesses from vague locations lost along with the supposed records that might confirm the claim. Unsurprisingly in these narratives, those specific records always seem to be lost, in spite of the substantial relevant archive that actually exists. If as many courthouse and orphanage records burned as are claimed in some of these settler fantasies, all of Indian Territory would have been aflame for the better part of the nineteenth century.

The situation is more complicated for Black noncitizens asserting Five Tribes heritage today, for while there are similarities to the above cases, there are also important distinctions. The terrible history of Black chattel slavery among the Five Tribes is well documented; the same multigenerational sexual violence that accompanied that institution among white slavers was practiced among the Five Tribes, and there are undoubtedly numerous Black people today with Five Tribes heritage not otherwise documented in the archival record.[19] Anti-Black tribal leaders and their lawyers were generally keen to dispossess Five Tribes Freedmen from their own rights to tribal land and citizenship, attempting to sabotage Freedman allotment distribution by mobilizing anti-Blackness along with broader anxieties around land loss and false identity claims. Nevertheless, in the Dawes records some Freedmen expressed concern that unaffiliated Black homesteaders were also making false claims to their own Five Tribes citizen rights. With limited allotment land and general hostility from other tribal citizens and authorities, the risk of dispossession for Five Tribes Freedmen was materially and symbolically significant, and it came from all directions.

Each side of my family offers a kind of origin story: one to restore real but ruptured relations, the other claiming, fortifying, and refashioning the space left by such ruptures. A history of dispossessive social and interpersonal traumas deformed the processes of generational transmission in my dad's family, and the stories that could have connected us more firmly to our history and our kin were lost—some only for a while, but some perhaps forever. For my mom's paternal family, however, the fantasies of imagined Indian ancestors have a particular endurance specifically because they're disconnected from the land and kin—indeed, they depend on them. They're mobile and ever adaptable, easily commodified and exchanged and needing only minor changes to be equally applicable across nation, region, and time, untethered to the colonizing particularities of shame and wounding that made my dad's family stories so painful to hold.

J.W.'s campaign for Chickasaw citizenship solidified into a firm belief, passed through the generations, that the family has a vague and even exotic Native heritage, a quaint bit of cultural costumery like that "Indian" beaded belt buckle and hatband made by my maternal grandfather, Jess. His childhood was filled with neglect, abuse, and even incarceration as a teen, and now that I'm older I have a measure of sympathy for what this story might have meant to him, given that he felt otherwise very unloved and unwanted in the world. Being "part Indian" was a symptom of his seemingly existential need to be important. But the story is no truer for being sincerely felt, nor is it any less rooted in other people's loss and suffering. It's not the obligation of Native people today to provide meaning and identity to settler populations disillusioned with their own histories and their own impoverished relations with the land and one another.

We live in a time when Native identity is the focus of immense interest and controversy alike. Nearly every day we seem to have another commercial for DNA tests that supposedly prove Native ancestry in spite of incomplete data sets that are badly or superficially interpreted and that displace Indigenous protocols of kinmaking and affiliation.[20] These test results are increasingly mapped onto existing or emergent family stories throughout settler societies that insist on a long-dead and seemingly nameless Indigenous ancestor, and often to exploitative effect. In the United States and Canada, news items emerge with greater frequency about non-Native people gaining access to jobs, lucrative contracts, scholarship programs, and other resources in spite of having vague and stereotype-ridden identity narratives, while at the same time our own relatives and citizens are deemed not quite Indian enough or not the right kind of Indian to deserve protection as Native people under vital but besieged legislation like the Indian Child Welfare Act. With our lands now largely in non-Native hands, allotment continues to be the fragmenting, commodifying logic of dispossession on other, even more intimate levels.

It seems that in the popular American imagination, everyone is a little bit Native and can speak with authority on Native matters—all but actual Native people, that is. In too many of these vague settler stories, there's no extant, complex community, no specific lands or relations, no hard histories and ongoing struggles and continuing relations of love, courage, and commitment. Unlike in my dad's line, where there is still a strong, vibrant Nation that welcomes us into responsible relationship as verifiable kin, too many of these settler stories use Native people solely as ciphers for asserting egocentric entitlement to a romanticized identity, but without the living links or reciprocal relations that make such identities meaningful.

In settler stories of imagined belonging, there can only be the fantastical bloodlines of a placeless past, allotment identities free for the taking, not vital communities in active relationship with the world, with our ancestors, and with our descendants. As such, they become stories of erasure, not continuity; disconnection, not kinship. And that makes them dangerous.

NOTES

1. Kent Carter, *The Dawes Commission and the Allotment of the Five Civilized Tribes, 1893–1914* (Orem, Utah: Ancestry.com Inc., 1999), 226.

2. Leslie Hewes, "Indian Land in the Cherokee Country of Oklahoma," *Economic Geography* 18, no. 4 (Oct. 1942): 401.

3. Donelson quoted in Betty Ridge, "Cherokee Tribal Allotment Issues Raise Many Questions," *Tahlequah Daily Press,* March 20, 2009, https://www.tahlequahdailypress.com/news/features/cherokee-tribal-land-allotment-issues-raise-many-questions/article_6d4c6b59-c497-5283-af05-67c40d53b000.html.

4. Indian Territory was excluded from the terms of the 1906 Burke Act (and its provisions of forced competency rulings releasing trust lands from protection), which added to the hemorrhaging of land from other nations under allotment.

5. Angie Debo, *And Still the Waters Run: The Betrayal of the Five Civilized Tribes* (Princeton, N.J.: Princeton University Press, 1940), 52.

6. Debo, *And Still the Waters Run,* 13. These numbers do not distinguish between intermarried whites and noncitizens, nor between Five Tribes Freedmen and other Black Indians, and African Americans without Native heritage or citizenship, but even without these nuances the demographic disparities are stark.

7. Debo, *And Still the Waters Run,* 93.

8. Erik M. Zissu, *Blood Matters: The Five Civilized Tribes and the Search for Unity in the Twentieth Century* (New York: Routledge, 2001), 18. Of all the Five Tribes, the Chickasaws were most hostile to recognizing Freedmen rights, although admittedly none were paragons of inclusivity. Zissu does not distinguish between Chickasaw Freedmen and Black non-Freedmen in these numbers, but they most likely include both groups, given the Chickasaw Nation leadership's categorical refusal to recognize Freedmen rights and vehement assertion of any degree of Blackness with non-Chickasaw status.

9. Debo, *And Still the Waters Run,* 12.

10. Circe Sturm, *Becoming Indian: The Struggle over Cherokee Identity in the Twenty-First Century* (Santa Fe: School for Advanced Research, 2010), 15.

11. Article XXIII, Section 11 of the 1907 Oklahoma State Constitution: "Wherever in the Constitution and laws of the state, the words 'color' or 'colored race,' 'negro,' or 'negro race' are used, they shall be construed to mean or apply to all persons of African descent. The term white race shall include all other persons." See Danny M. Adkison and Lisa McNair Palmer, *The Oklahoma State Constitution* (New York: Oxford University Press, 2020), 326.

12. See Zissu, *Blood Matters,* especially chapter 4, "The Importance of Being White"; and Wendy St. Jean, *Remaining Chickasaw in Indian Territory, 1830s–1907* (Tuscaloosa: University of Alabama Press, 2011), especially chapter 3, for insightful and extensive analyses of this history.

13. Debo chronicles some of these horrors in chapter 6 of *And Still the Waters Run,* "Protection by the State."

14. Zissu, *Blood Matters,* 48–49; and Debo, *And Still the Waters Run,* 42.

15. J. W. Sparks, testimony on behalf of Barney Sparks, application for the enrollment as a citizen by intermarriage of the Chickasaw Nation, September 15, 1898, U.S., Native American Applications for Enrollment in Five Civilized Tribes (overturned), 1896, Ancestry.com online database.

16. Debo, *And Still the Waters Run,* 39.

17. Carter, *Dawes Commission,* 29.

18. The enrollment card that was photocopied and given to me by my mom's cousin as evidence of our Chickasaw heritage was for J. B. Sparks, not J. W., and it does not offer much insight aside

from confirmation of his citizenship. However, a perusal of J.B.'s second wife's rejected Dawes packet offers another troubling case of an intermarried white citizen's claim of transferrable citizenship, precisely the scenario Debo notes as a common ploy decried by Chickasaw authorities. May Sparks Dawes Packet, Chickasaw, number 1331, Applications for Enrollment of the Commission to the Five Civilized Tribes, 1898–1914, database with images Fold3 (accessed June 10, 2021), https://www.fold3.com//title/70/dawes-packets.

19. See, for example, Claudio Saunt, *Black, White, and Indian: Race and the Unmaking of an American Family* (New York: Oxford University Press, 2005); Tiya Miles, *Ties That Bind: The Story of an Afro-Cherokee Family in Slavery and Freedom* (Berkeley: University of California Press, 2006); and Darnella Davis, *Untangling a Red, White, and Black Heritage: A Personal History of the Allotment Era* (Albuquerque: University of New Mexico Press, 2018).

20. See Kim TallBear, *Native American DNA: Tribal Belonging and the False Promise of Genetic Science* (Minneapolis: University of Minnesota Press, 2013).

Making Mahnomen Home

The Dawes Act and Ojibwe Mobility in Grandma's Stories

JEAN M. O'BRIEN

When I was a kid, one of the fixtures of my life was my grandmother, Caroline Edna Wright Tonneson (called Edna by everyone), sitting in our living room. Wearing a proper dress every day, she visited with her grandkids and read the newspapers cover to cover. She also frequently scribbled away in notebooks or perused her recipes planning to cook or, more typically, bake. Usually dessert. When I was seven years old, her husband had died and Grandma, with unexplained and unexplored mobility problems, moved from her home in Mahnomen, Minnesota, on the White Earth Indian Reservation to live with us in southern Minnesota five hours south. But she never gave up her home on the reservation and she returned to her beloved Mahnomen every summer. My siblings and I hold fond memories of the small house she and our grandfather managed to build in their sixteenth year of marriage. She always had one of us in tow to help out—usually my youngest sister, Nan (unapologetically her favorite). The rest of us would go "up north" in the summer to bring them there, return later to visit and enjoy the beautiful northern Minnesota summers, then bring her back home before the onset of the bitter winter cold and in time for my siblings and me to start school.

What I didn't realize then was that she was scribbling away about her life and memories. The collective output is ten notebooks of varying sizes and lengths totaling some two hundred pages transcribed (double-spaced). These precious pages contain stories vital to our family's history and a commentary on the experiences of one family coming to a reservation long after its creation in 1867 in response to the implementation of allotment policy after 1887, which sought to divide up reservations into individually owned plots of land. Allotment instead became an engine of dispossession through much of Indian country.

As was the case with many other Ojibwe people, the implementation of reservation policy did little to stem the migratory ways of my ancestors. Ojibwe people's vast homelands involved strategic and seasonal movement among places to make a living and tend to locations of social, cultural, political, and spiritual significance—in other words, they held mobility and fixity in tension. These patterns of mobility changed over time, and those changes intensified under settler colonialism that simultaneously

Grandma with the twins,
Nan and Maggie; Julie; and
Jeani O'Brien; c. 1963.

sought to displace Indigenous people from their homelands and to fix them within reservation boundaries. As always, Ojibwe and other Indigenous people resisted these impositions even while they creatively responded to them to defend their lifeways.

My grandmother narrates how one family came to identify with the reservation assigned to them and how they incorporated it into their sense of place. This family story stretches across the nineteenth century and into the twentieth, when the incursion of non-Indians reshaped Ojibwe landscapes in complex ways that Grandma's memories reflect on. Her story surely resonates with other Ojibwe people from Minnesota, who were the targets of a reservation initiative designed to remove all Ojibwes in the state, except for those from Red Lake, onto the White Earth Reservation in the mid-nineteenth century; that initiative failed in its aim in several respects. Many Ojibwes resisted concentration, returning to places of significance to them that long antedated White Earth, and allotment policy deliberately and dramatically undermined the aim of concentrating Ojibwes on reserved land at White Earth, becoming an engine of dispossession instead.[1] Policy makers designed it that way, and in 1901 Theodore Roosevelt famously described it as "a mighty pulverizing engine to break up the tribal mass."[2] Still, White Earth remains, the recognized homeland of a nation and a place that became one of special significance for thousands of Ojibwe people. My grandmother's memories of her family's history offer a perspective on this complex place and era and, in particular, a commentary on what it meant for one family to experience allotment.

When established in the Treaty of 1867, White Earth embraced 750,000 acres, or 1,296 square miles. All but one-half of 1 percent of the land was allotted to 5,173 Ojibwes following the implementation of allotment beginning in 1889. Indian dispossession came very quickly following a series of legislative acts deliberately designed to loosen Native land and resource possession and open up the lands to non-Indian possession and exploitation: by 1933, 94 percent of Indian allotments on White Earth had passed out of their ownership through nefarious means. By that point, tribal ownership had declined to 810 acres, or one-tenth of 1 percent of the original reservation.[3] Currently, the tribe owns 10 percent of the land within the reservation boundaries, up from 6 percent in 1978; the rest is owned by the federal (15 percent), state (7 percent), and county (17 percent) governments, with 51 percent in private ownership (non-Indian and Indian individuals and the tribe—all of these lands are taxable, including tribally held land that has not yet been approved for restoration to trust status).[4]

What I am going to call Grandma's "memoirs" tell one story of her life. An enormous box of photographs in our possession, some carefully labeled on the back and others frustratingly not, provide visual and some textual details. My version of Grandma's story and her photographs are supplemented with decades of my own memories before and after she came to live with us. Grandma loved to dote on her grandchildren, she loved history, and she loved to tell stories. We grew up with them. My own mother inherited her mother's astonishing memory, and she also always told "family stories." The latter sources—my mother's memories and mine—tell a compatible but sometimes different story of Grandma's life, which is verified in the pages and pages of U.S. and Bureau of Indian Affairs (B.I.A.) census data I've mined from Ancestry.com and additional archival material housed in the Minnesota Historical Society.

Grandma's story and that of her family are inescapably stories of mobility. In Minnesota and its environs, the arrival of the railroad complicated and intensified the migratory patterns of Ojibwe peoples, providing both a means for moving and the dramatic incursion of non-Indians to the reservation (family stories and railroad stories are perfectly compatible). Mahnomen began as a railroad town, which entailed movement, adding a dimension to transience for Natives, and for the non-Indian workers, lumbermen, and land sharks it brought to the reservation in disconcerting and disruptive ways. It also brought entertainment to town that she narrates, adding texture to the social scene—itinerant bands, traveling shows, minstrels, carnivals, movies, and sports teams that enriched people's lives: "Masquerades, dances, basket socials, people came by train for these affairs from Detroit, Mn, Richwood, Ogema, Callaway, & Waubun. There were many traveling shows. Minstrel, Newman the great (a hypnotist) the Quaker Doctors . . . They would stay for weeks."[5] It conveyed children to and from boarding schools and provided a new kind of connection between towns on or near the reservation, as well as to Winnipeg, Saint Paul, Chicago, Fargo, Duluth, Jamestown, and more. And it increased the means for visiting relatives and friends on the reservation and beyond: "My Mother, Mabel, & I went on the . . . night flyer, a few times to visit Aunt Ida, & Grandma [in Detroit Lakes, just south of the reservation]. Such a thrill."[6]

The railroad brought her own father north:

> My Dad came into Moorhead as a young Beau Brummell on flat cars,
> with dozens of men, some screamed go west young man, & starve to
> death so my Dad got off, & roamed bars etc in Moorhead. My mother
> Julia E. Wright worked in a hotel as La Rues [Grandma's grandparents]
> lived along red river. My Grandpa fished off old north bridge. She met
> [him] & they married in 1887 in Fargo, ND. Roy was born in 1888.
> They moved to Duluth. My Dad worked at anything. Tended bar in
> West Duluth. Moved to Superior, Two Harbors worked on docks &
> boats. Always on move. Leo & Grace born in Duluth. Grace died at
> 6 mo. Buried at West Duluth. Then moved to Naytahwaush in 1893.
> Mahnomen in 1905. Rock Lake, N.D. in 1906.[7]

Many of the pages of Grandma's memoirs narrate the building of Mahnomen's infrastructure and are packed with names of people who came there, but this passage is loaded with her own family stories. She writes against the colonial archive by preserving her memories of her family and its far-flung connections to significant places across Ojibwe homelands and in defiance of imposed reservation boundaries. Its accounting of movement and wage labor resonates with other Ojibwe histories so ably narrated in Chantal Norrgard's book *Seasons of Change* (though her father was non-Indian who married in).[8] It is also deafening in its silences: How did her parents meet? What was life like for her grandma and the rest of her family? How did they make a living? (My mom told me he worked for a seed company in Fargo but that they lived in Moorhead.) Why did Grandma's family move to Duluth (for work it seems, but why there)? To Superior? To Two Harbors? How and why did Grace die?

Grandma repeatedly returned to the story of the family's arrival at Naytahwaush, which established the lifelong connection to a place I have no evidence they had anything to do with previously:

> Naytahwaush 1892 [Elsewhere she gives the date as 1893.]
>   One long log house, dirt floors, several families living there, with all
> of their possessions. . . . They had come in quest of Indian allotments, My
> folks from Duluth, Mn. My Grandma & Grandpa, & Aunts, & Uncles
> from Moorhead, & Fargo. They waited in long lines, at White Earth

Indian Agency for weeks to get their allotment. Some (if lucky) got land with pine (called pine claims). They always felt superior. After each one got land, they still had no home, no tools, no plows to farm the land so still stayed on the White Earth Reservation, as they said it was compulsory to retain rights.

We each received 2–80 acres of land, some good, some poor, mine poor, the Gov't came with *"pay parties,"* once a year (very officious) some full blooded Indians . . . from Dep't of Interior direct from Washington. Each received 3.00 apiece to last for 1 year. The pay party *lived high on Indians* money.[9]

My grandmother frequently talked about the injustice of allotment as implemented at White Earth; she pointed out the hardships suffered by her family and the graft that marked the entire process. She harbored resentment about the differential treatment in the division of lands, the greed of governmental officials who treated Indians condescendingly and lived parasitically off of Indian resources, and the entire process of dispossession that unfolded.

Historian Melissa Meyer, whose fine book *The White Earth Tragedy* painstakingly reconstructs the early history of White Earth and the catastrophe of allotment policy there, points out that while the Nelson Act mandated allotment in Minnesota in 1889, the greatest number of Ojibwe who came to White Earth did so in 1891, with a secondary peak around 1893–1894, and that there was an 1894 deadline for removal and allotment. Even though government officials began assigning allotments in 1891, the agent only listed three hundred families living on them in 1893, and only 61 percent of them had been recorded by 1895.[10] This is exactly the timing of Grandma's family's move to White Earth. But how did Grandma's family know about any of this? Why did they set their sights on Naytahwaush? Though I don't know how they found out or why they came to Naytahwaush, the very process of allotment drew them to White Earth: her own family, her grandparents, her aunts and uncles—a regathering of kin who clearly remained close to each other even though widely dispersed across the large traditional Ojibwe terrain.

They must have been among the last to arrive: their lands are entered as entries number 4155–4159 out of a total of 5,173 allotments made (Julia, Roy, Leo, Clarence, and Mabel).[11] My grandma was born in 1899, a few years after the family gathered in Naytahwaush, and her allotment is entered elsewhere.[12] She must have gotten one of the very last ones. These were eighty-acre plots; they gained allotments of an additional eighty acres each following the passage of the 1904 Steenerson Act.[13]

Like nearly all Ojibwes from White Earth, Grandma's family's story was one of dispossession. They lost every single acre, and the only evidence I have they ever lived on any of them comes from Grandma's memoirs:

> Charles & Julia La Rue came to White Earth Indian agency in quest of allotments. They received 2–80 acres—They lived on their land at Sandy Lake in Rosedale Township in 1890s. My grandpa was a good gardener. They only had about 2 small windows in their home—rough wooden floors—a small barn—a cow or 2. . . . Grandpa La Rue died in 1900. Buried at Beaulieu. Grandma La Rue lived with Ida Morrison [her daughter] at Detroit, Mn, & at our place in Beaulieu. She died in 1906—we were living at Rock Lake, N Dak at that time.[14]

Grandma's grandmother was Julia Aitken La Rue, daughter of fur trader William A. Aitken and Julia Hole-in-the-Day, who was the sister of the Sandy Lake then Gull Lake leader Hole-in-the-Day the elder, born around 1837. My grandmother's families are accordingly labeled as "Removal Gull Lake Ojibwe" in the B.I.A. censuses that track the families from 1894 into the 1930s on White Earth. How ironic that they lived at Sandy Lake on White Earth.

The allotments still possessed by her siblings Leo, Mabel, and Clarence in the 1910s, far removed from the one of my grandma's allotments I have located, seem to have at least been somewhere nearby the residence of their own grandparents. I'm pretty confident that they never laid eyes on at least one of my grandma's allotments, which she apparently as an entrepreneurial child trudged down to the local bank to secure a mortgage against, which then failed—this according to family lore. (An aside: of course she didn't do this. This was a common mechanism of land fraud under allotment. I am still sorting out these stories and which of Grandma's 80s became the basis for my mother's claim, settled under the White Earth Land Settlement Act of 1986 [WELSA], the year of my grandmother's death. One of her sister Mabel's 80s also came under the settlement. They are the only ones that came under the WELSA that I am aware of.) By 1909, an Indian Office investigation revealed that 80 percent of White Earth allotments had passed out of Indian hands, spurring a flurry of further investigations and lawsuits over wrongful dispossession that still have not been fully settled.[15] Grandma's allotment is located in the distant but beautiful northeast corner of White Earth that's still remote on the reservation but was located many, many miles away from those of her other family members. Here we have the genius of allotment policy in action. She was a child—what were they supposed to do with it? When I asked her about her allotment she described it as a "slough." My sisters and I tracked it down a few a years ago on a magical trip and found not a slough but a bucolic farm richly covered in grasses that maintained a herd of cattle, complete with a quaint farmhouse. We wondered who lived there and what had been the fate of that land over the long years that stretched from Grandma's ephemeral "possession" until then.

Grandma displayed a solid command of the machinery that dispossessed Ojibwes

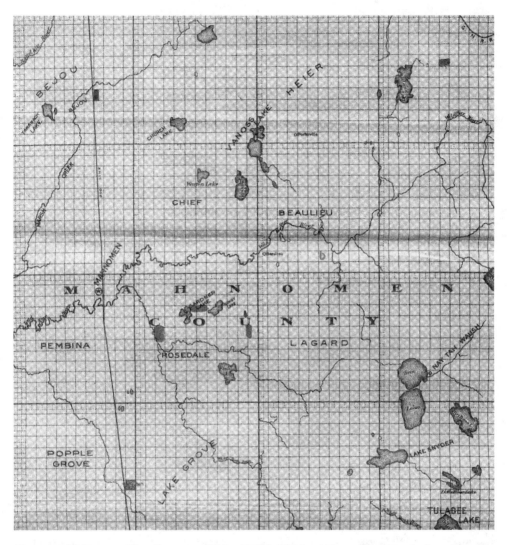

Abstract of title map of the allotment of Edna Wright in Island Township. Note the location of Rosedale Township toward the southeast of Island Township for other family allotments.

of their land under allotment: "When Clapp bill was passed, they could sell their land, they almost gave it away to land sharks that descended upon them to sell for a give away amount. Pressure was put on them to sell. . . . Each member received 2–80 acre tracts of land some good some not."[16] Elsewhere in the same tablet she notes: "The land of opportunity [for] land slickers—1906—Clapp act—sell lands not good."[17] Her memoirs provide not just a head count of those who perpetrated the land theft but a witnessing of the scandal of those who came to the reservation to trade in Indian lands. She pulls no punches in naming those she held responsible for the land theft, and the passage of years did not blunt her anger. Finding this careful accounting in her memoirs did not surprise me because I remember her narrating all of this in conversations about White Earth: "Several land offices appeared, Nels Agnes, John Carl, Houdons, McMartins, Sanders, & innumerable others. All out to capitalize. They acquired lands for little or nothing."[18] "1905—Land offices were built all over town. . . . In fact everyone was in Mahnomen to acquire Indian allotments. The Clapp Act passed in 1906 thus hundreds of eighties changed hands."[19] Note: She asserts here that the Clapp Act was passed the year after the land offices started cropping up, underscoring that the creation of a market in Ojibwe land motivated the legislation, which, if so, meant the true intent of the act to dispossess Indians rather than aid in the process of turning them into landowning farmers was obvious to those who sought to capitalize on Indian land.

But as Melissa Meyer notes, land was only part of the story of dispossession at White Earth. Subsequent legislation enabled lumber companies to strip the land of its incomparable timber resources for their enrichment. Grandma notes: "From Twin Lakes or Naytahwaush, Mn. My brother Leo Wright always told me white pine Norway pine & other gorgeous trees grew tall & stately. All the way to the [Itasca] State Park. They were logged off by Andrew Rogalski—Sprofkas [all from Perham—Chandonettes of rural Waubun, and Daigle (Frank)]. Others too."[20] Grandma loved to name names when it came to the organized theft that was allotment at White Earth: elsewhere she charged that the "pine forests all the way from Beaulieu east, [were] all logged off by greedy opportunists."[21]

In spite of these stories of rampant seizure of Ojibwe places and resources, Grandma's memoirs dwell mostly on her descriptions of early Mahnomen and what to her was a rich social and cultural life built there because of the intended and unintended consequences of allotment policy in designating White Earth *the* place for these Ojibwes. Even as she narrates a life of economic precarity, she does so to reflect on her family story with joy, humor, and nostalgia. Even while struggling against these engines of dispossession, Ojibwes made White Earth and Mahnomen their home, in their own ways.

But land privatization under allotment also reshaped Ojibwe mobility. Beginning around the 1910s, all but one of my grandma's surviving siblings (two died before the age of one, most others died in their thirties or forties) joined the early migration from White Earth that helped build the urban Indian community in Minneapolis, leaving Grandma as the only member of the nuclear family still in Mahnomen on a more or less permanent basis. As Nancy Shoemaker argues, the movement of Indians to Minneapolis beginning in the 1910s was fueled importantly by migration from White Earth in large measure because of the disastrous consequences of allotment there. She

Edna Wright Tonneson and her cousin, Laddie Lee, on Hennepin Avenue in Minneapolis.

found that the Indian population of Minneapolis stood at fewer than one thousand in the 1920s and grew to about six thousand by the end of World War II and in advance of relocation policy that greatly expanded urbanization of Indians.[22] These Indian peoples, principally Ojibwe and Dakota prior to the 1950s, provided the foundation for the vibrant activist community that sprang to national attention in the 1960s and 1970s. The Red Power movement in general and the American Indian Movement in particular emerged out of this longer history of Indian political and social organizing in the early twentieth century.[23]

Grandma stayed in Mahnomen and raised her family there, though she made frequent trips to visit relatives and friends in Minneapolis, and her children eventually moved away from Mahnomen, too. In 1922 she had married Rolfe Tonneson, who started a men's clothing store with his partner, Len Strandemo; Strandemo's is still an institution in Mahnomen—it is located across Main Street from the former Wright's Garage (once owned by my great-grandfather). My mother, Mae, was born in 1923 and

Mae Tonneson and her brother, Jack.

her brother, Jack, seven years later. Grandma's beloved sister Mabel, the first graduate of Mahnomen High School in 1913, worked as a secretary in Mahnomen and then moved to Minneapolis, where she briefly attended the University of Minnesota, before she switched to business courses and became a secretary. She seems to have been the first of the family to make the move. Her parents moved to Minneapolis in 1926 with her brother Leo and his family after her father's health failed. When her father died in 1928, her mother, Julia, moved back to Mahnomen to live with Grandma until her death in 1944. Brother Leo worked for an electric company in Minneapolis. His eight children included one son, William, who traded on his Indianness: he attained some fame as a wrestler, winning titles in venues across the United States under his given name, Bill Wright, before reinventing himself as a TV Indian wrestler, Billy Red Cloud, in the 1960s, donning Ojibwe floral motif beaded vests before trading them for the more readily discernable Plains Indian headdress (we remember watching him on Saturday evenings). His cousins included Clyde and Vernon Bellecourt, cofounders of the American Indian Movement in Minneapolis. Grandma's brother Clarence served in France in World War I, then worked in the 1930s in highway construction, where he headed the crew that unearthed and realized the significance of the "Minnesota Man" (actually determined to be the remains of an 8,000 BP woman) near Pelican Rapids south of the reservation in 1931.[24] He ended up in Seattle. This diaspora, particularly to Minneapolis, represented new nodes of Ojibwe mobility that did not negate the vital connection to White Earth. Their adaptive responses to land privatization in diaspora can be seen as a dynamic reimagining of place, now encompassing a new, vibrant pan-Indian community.

In spite of our losing Grandma's house after she passed in 1986, our last physical foothold on White Earth, the reservation remains a place of deep significance for our family. My siblings and I return when we can, less frequently than before, and we make the rounds of the places we remember from our youth and the places we've learned about from Grandma's memoirs. White Earth continues to define us in fundamental ways, even while those years of dispossession propelled us and our families away in the physical sense. Grandma's Mahnomen is very much our Mahnomen, integrated into our lives in our own ways in spite of this history of capitalist displacement.

NOTES

1. Melissa Meyer, *The White Earth Tragedy: Ethnicity and Dispossession at a Minnesota Anishinaabe Reservation, 1889–1920* (Lincoln: University of Nebraska Press, 1994).
2. Alysa Landry, "Theodore Roosevelt: 'The Only Good Indians Are the Dead Indians,'" *Indian Country Today,* June 28, 2016, https://newsmaven.io/indiancountrytoday/archive/theodore-roosevelt-the-only-good-indians-are-the-dead-indians-oN1cdfuEWo2KzOVVyrp7ig.
3. Ken Peterson, "Ransom Powell and the Tragedy of White Earth," *Minnesota History* 63 (2012): 89–101.
4. "Gaa-waabaabiganikaag/White Earth Nation," Minnesota Indian Affairs Council, http://mn.gov/indianaffairs/whiteearth-iac.html.
5. Caroline Edna Wright Tonneson, memoirs, notebook #2, 24 (pages refer to the transcribed version, all in author's possession).
6. Tonneson, memoirs, #10, 16.
7. Tonneson, #3, 1.
8. Chantal Norrgard, *Seasons of Change: Labor, Treaty Rights, and Ojibwe Nationhood* (Chapel Hill: University of North Carolina Press, 2014).
9. Tonneson, memoirs, #34, 12.
10. Meyer, *White Earth Tragedy,* 139, 60, and 65.
11. Register of Indian Allotment Entries under the Nelson Act: White Earth Reservation, Minnesota Historical Society, http://www2.mnhs.org/library/findaids/gl0009/pdf/crookston_nelson_index.pdf.

12. The large manuscript allotment ledgers in the Minnesota Historical Society show all but Grandma's allotments logged under "Supplemental" in 1893 (but they also contain jottings from 1894 and 1896—it appears to be a copy of the original ledger).

13. Meyer, *White Earth Tragedy*, 142–43 (1905 allotment) and 153 (1905 Clapp Rider).

14. Tonneson, memoirs, #8, 1–2.

15. Meyer, *White Earth Tragedy*, 160–72. The 1986 White Earth Land Settlement Act began that process but is still not complete. The settlement involved 1,900 individual allotments (nearly one-third of the total) covering more than 100,000 acres lost through "falsified affidavits, mortgages on grocery bills, sales by minor children, and illegal tax forfeitures" ("History and Issues," WELSA: White Earth Land Settlement Act, http://welsa.org). WELSA was controversial: it retroactively settled all past land transactions while providing some financial compensation for heirs of those determined to have been defrauded of their lands. The tribe also received $6 million for economic development and 10,000 acres out of government lands for the tribe. No individual lands were returned. The tribe is still trying to locate the heirs of nearly one hundred Ojibwes defrauded. Many Ojibwes wanted to hold out for land restoration.

16. Tonneson, memoirs, #4, 13.

17. Tonneson, #4, 17.

18. Tonneson, #5, 4.

19. Tonneson, #10, 40.

20. Tonneson, #4, 12.

21. Tonneson, #10, 7.

22. Nancy Shoemaker, "Urban Indians and Ethnic Choices: American Indian Organizations in Minneapolis, 1920–1950," *Western Historical Quarterly* 19, no. 4 (1988): 431–47.

23. Shoemaker, "Urban Indians and Ethnic Choices," 447.

24. Albert Ernest Jenks, "Minnesota Pleistocene Homo—An Interim Communication," *Proceedings of the National Academy of Sciences* 19, no. 1 (1933): 1–6.

The World of Paper, Restoring Relations, and the Lower Brule Sioux Tribe

NICK ESTES

My grandfather Frank was born on the Lower Brule Indian Reservation just weeks after Franklin Delano Roosevelt first took the Oval Office. It was a time of great uncertainty and possibility. Mass unemployment and poverty devastated people throughout the land—and Indian Country was no different. Everyday despair drove demands for radical change. Parts of the "Old World" descended into fascism, drawing Europe into yet another bloody civil war. In the United States, the New Deal aimed to save capitalism from its own excesses, providing federal jobs and expanding the social safety net for some. An Indian New Deal also lay on the horizon. It promised to radically overhaul Indian Affairs by halting disastrous allotment policy that ate away millions of acres of Indigenous lands and by reversing laws that criminalized Indigenous cultures and languages. By no means was the Indian New Deal a cure-all. Lakotas and Dakotas, however, "had climbed from absolute deprivation to mere poverty," the Standing Rock scholar Vine Deloria Jr. observes, "and it was the best time the reservation ever had."[1] It was, perhaps, this spirit of the times that inspired Frank's father, Ruben, to name his son Franklin Delano Estes for the progressive Democratic president most associated with New Deal reforms. Why? "Because that's what Indians do," Frank put it.[2]

He was born into a world of Indigenous kinship that had been increasingly disintegrated—like the land itself—by what he called "the paper world." A trained sociologist, Frank once used Émile Durkheim's theory of anomie in his 1963 book *Make Way for the Brules* to explain the process of Indigenous social alienation from the land itself. Frank's and Durkheim's interests aligned. They were both concerned with how societies had maintained integrity and coherence in an era when traditional social and religious ties are no longer presumed and new social institutions have come into being. Anomie, for Frank, however, described the way the rational world of the white man, which was personified in paper relations and transactions, was transposed onto the world of Indigenous relations, which were enacted through kinship and relation to the land. A world of order promising civilization and progress instead brought total disorder and social fragmentation. According to Frank, the reservation system had introduced an impersonal social environment where abstractions inked on paper attempted to insulate and mediate the interactions, sentiments, and activities among relatives, fellow tribal members, outsiders, and the land itself.[3] A prime example of the paper world exists in allotment policy and its afterlives.

This was our topic of conversation when Frank and I met for the first and last time in February 2013 in Phoenix, Arizona, where he had retired for the last decades of his life. At his kitchen table, he riffled through thick stacks of paper from the Department of the Interior on heirship and land interests. The federal courts had ruled on *Cobell v. Salazar* four years earlier in a landmark class action lawsuit spearheaded by Elouise Cobell, Blackfeet banker and tribal treasurer. The courts found that the federal government had mismanaged billions of dollars in assets for more than three hundred thousand Individual Indian Money accounts. Part of the $3.5 billion settlement awarded $1.9 billion to tribes to "buy back" individual interests in allotments to consolidate fractionated lands back into collective tribal ownership. Since by law American Indians are still wards of the government, the Department of the Interior was awarded the money that was then allocated to the Bureau of Indian Affairs to pay tribes to fix a problem these federal agencies created in the first place. It was a small fraction of what was actually lost in monetary terms (not to mention the incalculable losses of homeland and culture), and the damages dated back at least a century. Cobell and her forensic accountants had originally calculated at least $176 billion owed to individual Indian landowners.[4] Like thousands of Indigenous people, the Department of the Interior mailed Frank a packet detailing the land interests he held, which were located not only in Lower Brule but across several different Sioux reservations.

To an outsider, the papers might seem arbitrary—a mass of numbers, names, dates, and maps. To us, they held great value and mystery. "I have land up there with people I don't even know," Frank remarked, scanning the long list of names. "We are related to the same land." It seems like a paradox to be related to so many strangers, and even more confusing to be related through the land itself. At first glance, the phrase "we are related through the land" might appear like a cheap, mystical Native American daily affirmation postcard accompanied by hokey feathers, wolves, and dreamcatchers. But Frank's interpretation was quite literal: his relatives had the same legal interests in allotted lands. While allotment had ended eight decades ago, what he held in his hands was an artifact of allotment policy—a list of heirs whose claims to land, if split into individual shares, in some instances, would amount to acreage the size of a postage stamp. The land was useless, but the paper itself was not. It showed a network of familial relations. After all, each original allotment had a single common ancestor or common family. In the absence of a family tree mapping out a genealogy, we possessed inheritance papers mapping out fractions of interests in fractionated land—and, in effect, fractionated families.

That was the catastrophic consequence of allotment's two aims. The first goal, which was successful by all accounts, was a straightforward land grab. In the course of several decades, two-thirds of remaining Indigenous lands were carved up, an area about the size of what is currently the state of Montana. The second goal, which was by many accounts a failure, aimed to assimilate Native people by making them into small land-holders responsible for agricultural production and self-sufficiency. That prospect became increasingly impossible as land became fractionated and therefore unusable.

When Congress passed the General Allotment or Dawes Severalty Act in 1887, it represented a change in philosophy toward Indian administration. Instead of dealing with Native nations as political entities, it aimed to entirely bypass Indigenous leadership and to ignore tribal groupings altogether by encouraging government officials to deal directly with individuals and individual families. Allotment, or severalty (which means to separate and divide), aimed to sever Native tribes and families onto separate, individual plots of acreage without concern for traditional community life by breaking up communal land. The Board of Indian Commissioners referred to the day it became law as "Indian emancipation day." The purpose was "to abrogate the Indian tribal organization, to abolish the reservation system, and to place the Indians on an equal footing with other citizens of the country."[5]

The administration of trust land after so-called emancipation was enigmatic in practice and disastrous in outcome. The attempt to indoctrinate Native people into the European concept of private ownership by "civilizing" them through tilling the soil failed. Millions of acres became alienated and unusable because of exponential fractionation that was a result of a complex system of heirship. To ease the transition into citizenship, the titles to allotments were held in trust by the United States for a period of twenty-five years. During this time, the land could not be taxed, mortgaged, or sold without federal authorization. If an individual allottee died during this probationary period, their estate was divided among their heirs. Although the tradition of Anglo-Saxon law resolved probating an estate by physically dividing land among heirs or by selling the property and dividing the proceeds, the sale or disposal of Indian trust land was initially prohibited and then was only possible through approval by the secretary of the interior. Since Natives typically had large families and were deemed legally incompetent to manage their own affairs, government officials regarded the physical division of land as impractical. Instead of subdividing allotments into smaller plots, which would make them unsuitable for farming or ranching, land divisions happened on paper and were held in trust for the heirs. What was a highly theoretical calculation had real-world consequences. Put simply, it was an arithmetic of dispossession.

Lineage in the world of paper is usually defined according to the idealized, hetero-nuclear family. But allotment records and my family history tell a different history. One interest Frank held in an allotment north of Wanblee, on the Pine Ridge Indian Reservation, originally belonged to his mother, Cornelia Sawalla (or Narrow Strip). Her mother, Sarah Pure Woman, was the daughter of Bell Woman, one of three wives of an

Oglala man named Ptesan Wakpa (or White Cow River). The probate records show Ptesan Wakpa married all three women according to "Indian custom" and only "divorced" Cetan (or Hawk) in the same manner prior to allotment in 1889, leaving only his children with Bell Woman and Never Full as heirs. Frank recalled visiting those relatives in Wanblee with his mother: "Evidently, we had the same land because I have land up there," he said. It was a convenient way of knowing one's relatives, he thought: "That way when you go to visit some place you don't have to ask [who you're related to] because you're from the same land."

While the world of paper privileged the man as the head of the household, Frank spoke very little of his father, Ruben. He instead traced our family history mainly through his mother. Later in life, Cornelia assumed our clan name, Sawalla—which means "Shawnee" in Lakotayapi, suggesting our eastern origins—and, as far as family history and records show, she never took her husband's last name, Estes, which was the Christian custom. Ruben was the patriarch (and not in the domineering European way). It was his stories that I grew up hearing, never hers. Ruben was known as "Tongue" because he generously gave away his cattle to the hungry and poor, keeping only the tongues for himself. An *iyeska* (a translator), he also led tribal efforts to adopt the Indian Reorganization Act of 1934, which ended allotment and allowed for the creation of modern tribal councils with written constitutions. This required reading and writing—skills, Frank revealed to me that afternoon, that his father Ruben didn't possess. "He just went to third grade, and he couldn't read or write," Frank said of his father. So Cornelia read and wrote for him.

Cornelia became literate like most Indigenous children of her era. She attended a Catholic boarding school in Rosebud, where she was beaten for speaking Lakota. "They would cry, but they didn't care," Frank said, recalling his mother's stories of the Lakota girls and the beatings they received at the hands of their made-up siblings, the sisters of God, the nuns. "They'd spank their hands anyway," he said, holding out his wrinkled fingers, imitating smashing a child's hand with a rod. The scars on Cornelia's knuckles were still visible when she died. The children's tongues were scrubbed with lye and soap, to wash away the sin of their ancestors' words. That's how my grandmother Cornelia entered the world of paper, through pain and punishment—and the love of Jesus Christ.

In all the black-and-white photographs I have of Cornelia, she's smiling. She was the matriarch of the family. I imagine how she read Ruben the letters from powerful white men—congressmen, church fathers, and Indian agents—by kerosene lantern in their tar paper cabin along Mni Sose, the Missouri River. So thoroughly enmeshed in the world of paper, I find it astonishing that so little is written about her. Maybe she wanted it that way. But what she wrote captures her intellect and influence by the way she shaped the history of her family and tribe.

I had discovered Cornelia's powerful words by mistake. While conducting archival research on the Fort Randall and Big Bend Dams, I found letters written by Ruben to congressmen. The batch of correspondence has been cited in several history books (including my own) as an example of the Lower Brule Sioux Tribe's assertion of sovereignty over the Missouri River.[6] States such as South Dakota had been clamoring for river development and hydroelectric dams, to increase their power and authority over the Missouri at the expense of Indigenous people and land. While Missouri River states excluded Indigenous nations from such plans, in May 1937 the Lower Brule Sioux Tribe lodged a formal protest against river development "without the consent of the people" in a letter to South Dakota Republican congressman Francis Case.[7] The author of the letter was Ruben Estes, the first IRA chairman of the Lower Brule Sioux Tribe. But the written words belonged to Cornelia. And Case agreed with the logic of the argument, that, indeed, the jurisdiction and sovereignty of the Lower Brule Sioux Tribe, or any Sioux tribe, over the river had not been extinguished or diminished and states had to respect tribal sovereignty. I imagine Cornelia smiling as she read this news to Ruben.

Allotment attempted to paper over other aspects of Lakota history and culture that are indelibly tied to the land. For example, Pte Sa Win, White Buffalo Calf Woman, the most significant prophet in living memory, not only taught Lakotas how to live in good relations with the human and animal worlds. She also emphasized the caretaking of plant life. In one of the earliest images of Sicangu historian Battiste Good's winter count, Pte Sa Win is depicted as a white buffalo in the center of the camp circle. From her udder, corn kernels spill into water, representing the creation of life. Above her is an image of a corn stalk and a yucca plant next to a list of the animal nations—such as bears, buffalo, wolves, deer, elk, etc. In this sense, the winter count depicts the first recorded treaty among plant, animal, and human nations.[8] A woman consummated Wolakota (a peace agreement), with the aspiration to be good relatives of the earth.

Lakotas kept this first covenant in mind when they signed the 1868 Fort Laramie Treaty with the United States. While Lakota treaty-making sought harmony, balance, and inclusion among different parties, the world of paper was based on the exclusion of nonmen and nonhumans. Unlike the original covenant, which was created by a woman and included everyone and everything, treaty-making in the white world barred women's leadership. Two provisions in particular—the designation of hunting territory and farming plots—entailed the quantification of space and thus changed the Lakota relationships to land and nonhumans. Article 11 retained a vast territory set aside for the Pte Oyate, the buffalo nation: "so long as the buffalo may range thereon in such numbers as to justify the chase."[9] In turn, the military-sponsored annihilations of the buffalo herds granted white settlement to previously designated hunting territory. Often ignored, Article III allowed for the allotment of 160 tillable acres of land for every Oceti Sakowin citizen living inside the permanent reservation, an area encompassing half of the state of South Dakota west of the Missouri River. If land ran short, the treaty approved for the expansion of the reservation into adjacent or nearby territory. This was the first time individual Lakota citizenship had been so thoroughly defined on paper as fundamentally related to and measurable through the land.

Because the 1868 Fort Laramie Treaty already permitted individual allotments and farming provisions, the Dawes Act was seen as simply a land grab. Three years before the Fort Laramie Treaty, the Kul Wicasa (the Lower Brule) signed a treaty at Fort Sully establishing a "permanent reservation" at the mouth of the White River. By 1889, that reservation had been reduced in size to 446,500 acres. The opening of "surplus" reservation lands to white settlers nearly halved the reservation to 232,715 acres by 1907. By 1934, that acreage had been halved again to 122,000 acres because of the sale of individual allotments to whites. When Frank published *Make Way for the Brules,* the reservation had reached its current size of approximately 95,000 acres after the Fort Randall Dam flooded 7,997 acres in 1957 and the Big Bend Dam flooded 14,704 acres in 1963.[10]

The dams continued the project of dispossession that was set into motion by nineteenth-century extermination and allotment policy. A mixed economy of wage labor and subsistence hunting, gathering, and farming was replaced by a near dependency on work and provisions from the outside forcing many off the reservation. The dams destroyed the prime river bottomlands that once provided sustenance, shelter, firewood, drinking water, medicines, food, and game. In numbers, the Pick-Sloan Plan, as it was known, destroyed 90 percent of commercial timber and 75 percent of wildlife and wild plants on affected Sioux reservations. And nearly a third of the reservations' inhabitants were forcefully removed.[11]

The land upon which Frank and my ancestors became human was submerged, taking with it our history and culture. Years later, after Frank and I first met, my father, Ben, showed me a packet of land papers he received in the mail from the Department of the Interior. They were satellite images of my grandma Cornelia's original allotment, which is entirely underwater, forever alienated from us so long as the dams remain, but nonetheless a square 160-acre section sitting at the bottom of a riverbed. It seemed bizarre that the government kept this receipt, even mapping it across a palimpsest of multiple dispossessions.

"Opposite the *gemeinschaft* life from which the [Indian] relocatees came," Frank writes in his book, taking an academic tone, "they were suddenly set into a social environment which was basically impersonal."[12] His book's basic thesis—the more alienated Indigenous people are from the land, the more alienated they are from their own relatives—is something that has always unsettled me. The day we first met, we were two estranged relatives in Tohono O'odham territory, land we didn't belong to. But Frank's goal wasn't to prove alienation. It was to show that the Indigenous, and more specifically the Kul Wicasa, experience was one of migration, movement, and constant change. It was an observation that defied academic consensus at the time, of static and unchanging Indigenous societies. The new social institution of the paper world, however, introduced new social relations.

Frank was a scientist. In his book, the Indigenous origin story is one of movement. To his mind, American Indian migration from Asia, as purported by the Bering Strait theory, and the Siouan westward migration from the Atlantic Seaboard didn't diminish Lakota and Dakota origin stories but strengthened them because they added complexity, color, and texture to a vibrant, thriving, and ever-changing culture that couldn't be restricted in time and space. "One might even say in an over-all gesture that the underlying epitome of a great many of man's migrations was vested in freedom," he writes in the opening lines of his book, "that is, the desire to not only have the ability to move, but to practice it also. . . . And who knows, it may soon reach the height of [an] inter-planetary level."[13] The world of paper, however, brought confinement and restriction, but it couldn't halt movement, and for the Kul Wicasa, allotment, paradoxically, increased migration.

Frank found that after the creation of the Lower Brule Reservation in 1889, migration off-reservation increased. By 1963, those allottees who possessed the most land on the reservation more frequently migrated off-reservation. Those who migrated retained on average nearly twice as much land (112.41 acres) as those who stayed on-reservation (65.55 acres).[14] The reason for this paradox was that the total landholdings were of fractionated interests. Put differently, the more land one owned on the reservation, the more likely that land was unusable because of fractionation. Frank argued the Kul Wicasa lacked a terra firma "upon which to practice their patterns of life (whatever they define it to be) and for them to even feel secure with it when they desired to leave. Their venture out into the world of paper would be more dignified and less threatening if they knew that they still have, and can return to, a place to be Indian. They need not be people without refuge."[15]

Allotment made simply living with the land mercurial and near impossible. It also facilitated cultural assimilation and an attempted annihilation of our rightful relations with the land. "My parents didn't talk to me in Indian," he told me, reflecting on how the world of paper had helped shape his own relationship to his parents and siblings, who all spoke fluent Lakota.

> They didn't want me to talk in Indian. I think I know why. They thought that if I learned to talk Indian, it was going to interfere with my college or my schooling. I don't hold that against them. They thought that was the right thing to do. They would interpret for me. I didn't know that was going on until later I found out that they wanted it like that. Maybe that's why my English is so good. I can speak better English than some white people.

After Frank passed in 2015, I remembered his stories. He was never embarrassed about his upbringing or the losses he faced. His demeanor in his life and work was always forward-facing. At the end of our conversation, he told stories of his mother, Cornelia. "Indians get relatives not by blood but by kinship," he said as he described the many relatives not listed on our allotment interests. He told the stories of the sick and elderly Cornelia had adopted as brothers and sisters, the many relations that existed outside the world of paper. "Take away the item of paper," Frank writes, "and the great complex, American, social super-structure perhaps would crumble."[16]

NOTES

1. Vine Deloria Jr., "This Country Was a Lot Better Off When Indians Were Running It," *New York Times,* March 8, 1970.
2. Interview with Frank Estes, February 2, 2013. Frank's baptismal record lists him as "Franklin Delano Estes." According to him, his mother, Cornelia Swalla, changed his middle name to "Chester" when Frank enrolled in college courses, and it became his legal middle name.
3. Frank C. Estes, *Make Way for the Brules* (Lower Brule, S.D.: Lower Brule Sioux Tribe, 1963).
4. Julia Whitty, "Elouise Cobell's Accounting Coup," *Mother Jones,* September/October 2005, https://www.motherjones.com/politics/2005/09/accounting-coup-0/.
5. Quoted in S. Lyman Taylor, *A History of Indian Policy* (Washington, D.C.: United States Department of the Interior, Bureau of Indian Affairs, 1973), 95–96.
6. See, for example, Nick Estes, *Our History Is the Future: Standing Rock versus the Dakota Access Pipeline, and the Long Tradition of Indigenous Resistance* (New York: Verso, 2019); Michael L. Lawson, *Dammed Indians Revisited: The Continuing History of the Pick-Sloan Plan and the Missouri River Sioux* (Pierre: South Dakota Historical Society Press, 2009); and Robert Kelley Schneiders, *Unruly River: Two Centuries of Change along the Missouri* (Lincoln: University of Nebraska Press, 2001).
7. Ruben Estes to Francis Case, May 16, 1937, folder 157, Francis Case Papers, special collections, Dakota Wesleyan University, Mitchell, S.D.
8. Battiste Good (Brown Hat) Winter Count, Manuscript 2372, box 12, F6, National Anthropological Archives, Smithsonian Institution, Suitland, Md.
9. Treaty with the Sioux-Brule, Oglala, Miniconjou, Yanktonai, Hunkpapa, Blackfeet, Cuthead, Two Kettle, San Arcs, and Santee-and Arapaho, April 29, 1868, General Records of the United States Government, Record Group 11, National Archives.
10. F. Estes, *Make Way for the Brules,* 15–17.
11. John Ferrell, "Developing the Missouri: South Dakota and the Pick-Sloan Plan," *South Dakota History* 19 (1989): 309–15; and Lawson, *Dammed Indians,* 41–43.
12. F. Estes, *Make Way for the Brules,* 13.
13. F. Estes, 3.
14. F. Estes, 28.
15. F. Estes, 21.
16. F. Estes, 13.

"What Should We Do?"

Returning Fractionated Allotments Back to the Tribes—
One Family's Story

SHERYL LIGHTFOOT

The letters began arriving in the spring of 2014.

My uncle Don, my mother's younger half-brother, who was seventy-four years old at the time, was living in Southern California, ever since the Relocation Program had first brought him there. He had gone to work for Douglas Aircraft in Anaheim, California, during the late 1950s and had been retired for a number of years and still living in Southern California. He was the first in our family to get a letter.

When Uncle Don picked up his mail that particular spring afternoon, there was a thick letter from the Department of the Interior that included a cover letter and a number of other materials, such as instructions, a Purchasable Interests Inventory, a deed, maps, and a return envelope. The cover letter stated that Uncle Don's fractionated allotments had been identified as tracts of land that were prioritized for tribal acquisition under the Land Buy-Back Program, and he had sixty days to respond. He didn't know what to make of this letter, hadn't heard of this program, and was deeply stunned and terribly confused by this proposal. Why would the government want to buy his tiny tracts of land that were currently leased out to farmers and ranchers? What was the purpose? Who was behind this? Bewildered, he picked up the phone and made the obvious first step: he phoned me, his niece, who happened to be an Indigenous politics professor at the University of British Columbia. He hoped that I would be able to shed some light on this strange letter and explain what this program was all about. I explained that the Land Buy-Back Program was a tribal lands consolidation initiative that was part of the *Cobell* settlement. Within days, the rest of the siblings and cousins who held land rights at Sisseton-Wahpeton Oyate also received letters. Since I did not hold land rights at Sisseton-Wahpeton, I would not be receiving a letter, but I could not help but be brought into these family conversations.

"What should we do?" everyone asked. Discussion, debate, and, sometimes, emotionally charged disagreements were the immediate result. Understanding what the Land Buy-Back Program was and was intended to do was only the first step. Making a decision about what to do next was difficult, emotional, and, for some, absolutely agonizing.

Like me, Uncle Don identified as Ojibwe and was enrolled at the Keweenaw Bay community in Baraga, Michigan, which is part of the Lake Superior Band of Ojibwe. However, Don also held part of an allotment on the Lake Traverse Reservation of the Sisseton-Wahpeton Oyate (Sioux) Tribe, as well as fractionated allotments on a number of other reservations across the Upper Midwest, including our own. Like other members of his generation, he had received these various fractionated allotments after his parents passed away. He had inherited the fractionated allotment at Sisseton-Wahpeton after the death of his father many years earlier. Probate is often the means of passing down increasingly fractionated allotments with each generation. Sisseton-Wahpeton was one of the early reservations to roll out the Land Buy-Back Program, and others soon followed.

Like most American Indian families of the Upper Midwest, we come from several reservations that had been allotted at the end of the nineteenth and the early part of the twentieth centuries. Also like many American Indian families of the Upper Midwest, we have roots in multiple reservations, from both the northern and southern shores of Lake Superior as far east as what we now call Michigan, through Ontario, Wisconsin, and Minnesota, all the way west to Rosebud and Pine Ridge in what we now call South Dakota. Even in the late nineteenth and early twentieth centuries, when the U.S. government was doing everything in its power to define us and confine us to a single reservation community, our familial network remained mobile and spread out across a vast amount of land in the region, with family members marrying, divorcing, and remarrying, remaining on the move to find work, living and working across a number of reservations as well as the Canada–U.S. border. We simply refused to be confined to a single reservation. Rather, we lived as we have always done, moving and adapting as we needed to in order to survive and to thrive.

The allotments now under the Land Buy-Back Program were originally assigned to my great-grandparents' generation and, in a few cases, even one generation earlier. As my relatives often migrated for work in Minneapolis and Southern California over the decades of the mid-to-late twentieth century—and often as a revolving door with the reservation—those allotments and fractionated allotments came to be used by others, through various lease arrangements. Often, individuals hold fractionated rights to lands they have never even seen, especially if they have lived away from the reservation for many years, or as in the case of my uncle, one happened to hold land rights on a reservation other than one's own. For decades, my relatives had joked about the small checks that arrived from the Department of the Interior for lease payments on those fractionated allotments—some of them as low as a few cents each per year. My grandmother held one particular fractionated allotment in South Dakota that provided her with an annual lease payment check for twelve cents. She always chuckled when she got it. Once lease payments dropped below about ten cents, they ceased, but many in our extended family regularly received annual checks of ten dollars or less, while others received more substantial lease payments. While most of us maintained connections to relatives both on and off reservation, these ties to our original homelands, while never netting much of any financial return, often held deep emotional significance. For many of us, it was a tangible, legal tie to our homelands and to our ancestors. The idea of giving them up had never occurred to anyone.

Then, in the spring of 2014, the letters with offers to sell those land rights began arriving. The buyback offers varied substantially, depending on the fair market value of the lands based on objective appraisals, and also included a base payment of seventy-five dollars per offer. In addition, the letters noted that all land sales would also trigger contributions to the Cobell Education Scholarship Fund, without taking anything away from the amount to be paid to sellers. What had been a long-standing family joke about never getting rich off of the lease payments immediately shifted into new and much more difficult terrain. What to do about the offers to buy back our fractionated allotments and put them back into collective tribal control? How to grapple with the fact that selling meant making contributions to the scholarship fund while choosing not to sell meant the opposite? Was that a form of coercion?

Depending on the size of the fractionated allotments, the offers to buy them back were, in some cases, quite sizeable, especially considering the typically small lease payments that had trickled in over the years. However, for a handful of my relatives who had descended from allottees who had few children and grandchildren, lease payments had been more substantial over the years, and in a few cases, families still depended upon the financial returns from those leases. In these cases, there was no question about selling, especially when they considered the future return on those leases in the coming years, both for themselves and their children. They did not consider, even for a moment, the possibility of selling them back to the Tribe.

For some other relatives, especially those that lived life on the financial edge, the offer of a few hundred dollars was always enticing, and they immediately and unquestioningly accepted the offers to sell and then awaited the deposits into their Individual Indian Money accounts.

Yet, for the vast majority of the family, the answers were not so clear or so immediate. For a family that largely scattered to urban areas beginning in the 1920s and continuing through the 1970s, often far from the reservation, these land rights, while not worth very much in financial terms, did hold an emotional tie to our complex matrix of traditional and ancestral lands all over the Upper Midwest. To consider cutting those ties, voluntarily, and forever, was a jarring proposition.

What Is the Land Buy-Back Program?

The Land Buy-Back Program for Tribal Nations (or the Land Buy-Back Program, for short) formed a part of what is now often referred to as the *Cobell* settlement, which emerged out of the *Cobell v. Salazar* case, a 1996 class action lawsuit brought forward by Elouise Cobell and others against two U.S. government departments: the

Department of the Interior and the Department of the Treasury.[1] Both departments were accused of gross mismanagement of Indian trust funds, which are held by the Department of the Interior, on behalf of individual Indian owners.[2] The case settled in 2009 for $3.4 billion, of which $1.9 billion was allocated to repurchase fractionated shares of land interests that had been allotted under the Dawes Act and to bring those lands back into communal tribal ownership.[3] The Land Buy-Back Program is handled by the Department of the Interior, which also works with other departments, including the Bureau of Land Management, the Office of Policy, Management, and Budget, and the Bureau of Indian Affairs.

Under the 1887 Dawes Act, most reservation lands located within the United States were allotted to individual Indians, typically in 40-, 80-, or 160-acre parcels.[4] As these individual Indians passed away, their allotments passed to all of their heirs, in fractionated shares. Because the Dawes Act had stipulated that all "excess lands" not allotted to individual Indians could be sold off, there was no opportunity to expand the allotment landholdings of individual Indians; land could only continue to be held as fractionated allotments and then passed down. So, as each generation passed away, these same allotments then passed to their heirs, by ever smaller fractions as well. The result, over several generations, was that individual tracts of land passed to increasing numbers of heirs, sometimes hundreds or even thousands of individuals, in a deeply problematic pattern called fractionation. As the generations passed, and often intermarried, sometimes these allotments came to be held by individuals who were not eligible for tribal enrollment on any reservation but held allotments on a number of reservations.

Fractionation has been one of the largest barriers to self-determination and economic development on reservations, since divided ownership requires the consent of often a majority of landowners in order to make any changes over the use of a tract of land. As a result, fractioned land allotments rarely change use. When coupled with the checkerboard pattern of landownership on allotted reservations—where some parcels of land are held in trust, some are in fee simple, and others are allotted, all in random patterns throughout the reservation—land use planning becomes stymied as tribal governments are left unable to find larger usable tracts of land for development or other purposes. Tribes have often resorted to leases and permits in order to address this problem, with the result that individual landholders often receive tiny annual lease payments.

At the time of the *Cobell* settlement, there were approximately 92,000 fractionated tracts of land, or about 10.6 million acres, across approximately 150 reservations in the United States. Out of the 150 reservations with fractionated lands, about 90 percent were located on forty reservations, and so the program focused first on those forty. Nineteen of these forty reservations are located in the states of South Dakota, North Dakota, Minnesota, Wisconsin, and Montana.[5]

The Land Buy-Back Program was established as a part of the *Cobell* settlement in order to give individual landowners the ability to help address the fractionalization problem. Under the *Cobell* settlement, the Department of the Interior was provided with a $1.9 billion budget to purchase back fractional land interests either in trust sta-tus or as restricted fee land. Willing sellers would be offered fair market value for their fractionated shares of previously allotted lands. If landowners agreed to sell, their land interests would be consolidated and then restored to tribal trust status for the benefit of tribal members and reservations. The program's overall objective is to increase tribal ownership of reservations to greater than 50 percent of land shares in order to increase tribes' controlling interests and therefore reduce the number of land parcels standing vacant.[6]

Up to $60 million of the $1.9 billion consolidation fund is also designated for the Cobell Education Scholarship Fund, depending on the level of interests sold. Every time an individual decides to sell back their land rights, it triggers a contribution to the Cobell Scholarship. As of September 2016, the program had contributed $40 million to the scholarship fund, with $3.7 million awarded to more than one thousand under-graduate and graduate Native American students from 110 tribes.[7] So, while the deci-sion to sever land ties to a particular reservation could be very painful, it was balanced with the satisfaction of triggering a contribution to this fund for each share sold back. At the same time, another complication was that only individuals who are members of federally recognized tribes are eligible for Cobell Scholarships, so a nonenrolled individual who sold their lands back would find their own children ineligible for the Cobell Scholarship.

The program began making offers on fractioned lands in December 2013. As re-ported in the *Federal Register,* between 2013 and 2017, over 680,000 fractional inter-ests were consolidated and nearly 2.1 million acres of land were returned to tribal ownership, a full 23 percent reduction in fractionated reservation lands.[8] The 2016 annual status report shows that the program enjoyed early success, with an individual acceptance rate of more than 44 percent of offers and paying more than $900 million to landowners, restoring thirty thousand tracts of land.[9] According to the implemen-tation schedule, by mid-2021, 96 percent of all landowners with fractionated interests involving more than 98 percent of purchasable fractional interests will have been ap-proached for buyback.[10]

Under the program, fractionated lands can be restored to tribal jurisdiction and back into trust. The tribe can then use this land to benefit the community by building homes, for example, or community centers or businesses, or the tribe can elect to use it for cultural or environmental conservation. Sisseton-Wahpeton tribal chairman Rob-ert Shepherd said, "[We have] been actively acquiring fractionated lands for over three decades in an effort to reduce fractionation on the reservation. The . . . Program will further our efforts to acquire more fractionated lands, increase the tribal land base and significantly decrease further fractionation for our children and future generations. Our previous and continued efforts are made in the spirit of our inherent sovereignty and as a means of self-determination."[11] By 2016, almost three thousand holders of land rights at Sisseton-Wahpeton had received offers, and 45 percent accepted those offers, which means that in only two years, 8,861 acres moved from fractionated ownership to trust status for the Sisseton-Wahpeton Oyate.[12] While the details of how the tribe has utilized these returned lands are not available to nonmembers of the tribe, like myself, the tribe does speak of the Land Buy-Back Program as a way to express tribal sovereignty.[13] Postconsolidation, the tribe is able to exercise its self-determination in choosing how, and whether, to develop consolidated land into residential, commercial, agricultural, or other purposes on behalf of the tribe as a whole.

The Land Buy-Back Program works in several phases.[14] The first phase involves outreach, or official engagement with individual tribes and their land planning offices in order to implement the program. During this phase, agreements and memoranda of understanding are drawn up between the tribes and the program, which enable the program to support each tribe's outreach efforts to individual landholders. During the second phase, land research, the program collects data so that it can establish fair market value for the tracts of land subject to fractionated interests. This can involve mapping work and mineral assessments, which leads to the third phase, valuation, where the program determines the fair market value for each tract. Finally, in the last phase, acquisition, the Bureau of Indian Affairs Land Buy-Back Acquisition Center generates and mails purchase order packages to eligible individual landholders. After receiving these letters, individual landholders then have sixty calendar days to choose to sell back some or all of the fractional interests listed in the letter.

"What Should We Do?"

After I explained the *Cobell* settlement and the Land Buy-Back Program to Uncle Don that spring day in 2014, the first thing he said, in his usual proud but teasing tone of voice, was "Well, Professor Lightfoot, what should we do?" My response was that it was a deeply personal decision. Of course, that was only partially correct. It quickly became a collective family decision, as more letters arrived in the next several weeks to those who had inherited land rights at Sisseton-Wahpeton and more and more relatives were faced with this decision. Phones were ringing everywhere, along with Facebook messages, all faced with the deeply personal yet also collective question of what to do next.

One cousin was deeply suspicious and angry after receiving her letter of offer. "If this has the federal government behind it," she said, "I want nothing to do with it." Suspiciously, she added, "Besides, how do we even know if this is even fair market value? What did they do to determine that?" Shaking her head furiously, she continued, "I don't trust Interior to treat us fairly. They have always scammed us, always taking our land and our money, and this can only be more of the same. They fully intend to profit from our sale of the land." There was nothing anyone could say that convinced her otherwise. She didn't care to keep reliving the land theft and was having no part of this scheme. These fractionated allotments were her traditional lands, and they were going to stay that way, forever, as long as she had any say in the matter. "If the government wants my lands," she said, "they will have to come and take them from me by force. I'm not selling." Several family members agreed with her.

Another cousin, who received an offer for about $500 on an allotment he had never actually seen, was agonizing over the decision. He had spent most of his adult life in Minneapolis, far from Sisseton-Wahpeton. While he knew he had partially descended from family there, he identified primarily as Ojibwe and held land rights at scattered reservations across the Upper Midwest. Sisseton-Wahpeton was one, but not the largest or the most primary, in his mind. Yet here in his hand was an offer to sell these land rights back to benefit the Tribe. Pondering a sale was deeply emotional, as these land rights had become important icons of his identity. He felt so much cultural loss, having attended Haskell Indian Boarding School and having had his culture and language taken from him, along with his place in the reservation community. These land rights on several reservations were, for him, a tangible and deeply meaningful connection to his ancestors, to his history, and to his relatives who had remained on the reservation. While he felt a certain pull to help benefit the Tribe, the idea of severing those ties to the land—and permanently—was difficult to face. Sixty days was not long to ponder and reflect on these questions. In the end, he couldn't actually bring himself to sell and decided not to respond to the letter. Rather, he thought, he would plan to return all of his land rights to the various tribes, later, in his will.

On day fifty-nine of his sixty-day decision period, my uncle Don phoned me back. This had been an incredibly difficult decision, he told me. He had been discussing it with various siblings, cousins, children, and the few elderly aunties he still had. He had spoken to the Tribe and received some further information about their intentions for this tract of land. He had received some additional printed information from the Tribe and had visited the Department of the Interior's website in order to learn as much as he could about the program. While he respected everyone else's decisions, whatever they were, he had needed to do deep, personal reflection on his own, and in his own way. "I've decided to sell," he said. "While I can't be sure that this is, in fact, fair market value, and I can't be sure that this time the government will properly handle the land or the money, I do know that the Tribe is hoping to consolidate lands and is looking for us to help them if we can. These lands were all held by the Tribe before the government came and allotted them in the first place. I also feel good about supporting the scholarship fund." In the end, he decided that it just felt right "in his gut" to return the land to the Tribe, and he wanted to contribute to that effort. "While it is certainly a painful thing, for me as an individual, to consider severing my personal tie to these lands," he continued, "in the end, it isn't just about me, and I've decided to put the interests of the Tribe above my own. Since it's what they want and need, I'm signing the deed in front of a notary this afternoon." His return envelope went in the mail the next day, and a couple weeks later, he received an acknowledgment from the Department of the Interior, followed by a thank-you note from the tribal chairman.

Uncle Don passed away shortly after that, at the end of June, and for the first time in several generations, a fractionated allotment did not pass in additional fractions to a new generation but rather returned to the full jurisdiction and control of the Sisseton-Wahpeton Oyate. *Mitakuye Oyasin.*

NOTES

1. Cobell v. Salazar, 679 F.3d 909 (D.C. Cir. 2012).
2. Terminology use is always a decision fraught with complications and contradictions, and so an explanation of choices of terminology should always be offered. I have chosen to use the term *Indian* in this essay to refer to those who were originally allotted lands and their descendants. Following Vine Deloria Jr.'s explanation of the legal and political status of "Indians" in the United States, it is the most appropriate term for the land issues under consideration here. *Native American* tends to refer to an ethnic identity, which is not the particular subject of this essay.
3. "Frequently Asked Questions: Land Buy-Back Program for Tribal Nations," U.S. Department of the Interior, accessed August 19, 2019, https://www.doi.gov/buybackprogram/faq.
4. Dawes General Allotment Act, ch. 119, 24 Stat. 388 (1887) (codified as amended in sections of 25 U.S.C.).
5. "Maximizing the Tribal Land Buy-Back Program: How Priority Lists Can Help Tribes Influence What's Purchased," Federal Reserve Bank of Minneapolis, July 1, 2014, https://www.minneapolisfed.org/publications/community-dividend/maximizing-the-tribal-land-buyback-program-how-priority-lists-can-help-tribes-influence-whats-purchased.
6. Renae Ditmer, "A Cobell Land Buy-Back Check-Up," *Indian Country Today,* updated September 13, 2018, https://indiancountrytoday.com/archive/cobell-land-buy-back-check.
7. U.S. Department of the Interior, *2016 Status Report for Land Buy-Back Program for Tribal Nations,* November 1, 2016, https://www.doi.gov/sites/doi.gov/files/uploads/2016_buy-back_program_final_0.pdf.
8. U.S. Department of the Interior, "Land Buy-Back Program for Tribal Nations under Cobell Settlement," *Federal Register,* April 12, 2017, https://www.federalregister.gov/documents/2017/04/12/2017-07417/land-buy-back-program-for-tribal-nations-under-cobell-settlement.
9. U.S. Department of the Interior, *2016 Status Report.*
10. "Interior Announces Revised Strategy, Policies to More Effectively Reduce Fractionation of Tribal Lands," U.S. Department of the Interior, July 31, 2017, https://www.doi.gov/pressreleases/interior-announces-revised-strategy-policies-more-effectively-reduce-fractionation.
11. Native News Online Staff, "Sisseton-Wahpeton Oyate Now Part of Land Buy-Back Program," Native News Online, accessed September 2, 2019, https://nativenewsonline.net/currents/sisseton-wahpeton-oyate-now-part-land-buy-back-program/.
12. U.S. Department of the Interior, *2016 Status Report.*
13. Native News Online Staff, "Sisseton-Wahpeton Oyate."
14. "Program Phases," Land Buy-Back Program for Tribal Nations, U.S. Department of the Interior, accessed August 20, 2019, https://www.doi.gov/buybackprogram/program-phases.

Allotment Speculations

The Emergence of Land Memory

JOSEPH M. PIERCE

There are no pictures of my family on our allotment land. The memory of the land is fading, too, as those who once knew it join the ancestors. The land is not even land anymore, erased from view when the state of Oklahoma turned it into a lake. As with so many Indigenous families, loss is a common point of departure. Not just loss of land, but of human and other-than-human relations. I relate to this land through the memory of kin who were almost not my kin. Or rather, whose kinship was, like the land, severed by a technology of settler colonial erasure: adoption. My father was adopted out of the Cherokee community as a newborn. It is only through reconnecting to our Cherokee family (after fifty years apart) that we have managed to piece together a communal understanding of what endures in us, through us, as kin. Resisting these two forces of erasure—allotment and adoption—is the focus of this essay. But I am not writing to critique these forces so much as to repossess them, to speak through allotment and adoption as an act of Cherokee relation.

Shared experiences, shared stories, have provided me with guidance. When I read Chickasaw poet and novelist Linda Hogan write in *Dwellings,* "at the beginning, there was nothing and something came from it," I found myself at once inspired and conflicted.[1] In this simple juxtaposition of absence and presence, Hogan reminds us of the impermanence of the material world, its flux, and also its continuity. There is no contrast here; the conjunction is "and" not "but." She takes the unfolding of relational possibilities as linked, even coterminous. Indeed, the birth of life, the emergence of matter out of cosmic nothingness, marks an Indigenous temporality that is asynchronous and yet ongoing, emergent. Here, time is the enactment of life itself. This line reflects the possible rather than the no-longer-here. I want to propose this emergent possibility, rather than loss or erasure, as a different point of departure from which to imagine myself in relation to land and memory. I am thus primarily concerned with speculative relations with the land. By this I mean imagining what could have been and what might endure if, like in ceremony, we call our relationships with land and kin to life. I want to speculate through retelling, reengaging, with and through the memory of land-as-kin.

If life is sacred, if community is sacred, if the relationship between human and other-than-human kin is sacred—which is to say, if to be in good relations is sacred—then the only possible aim of settler colonialism is the total annihilation of the sacred. Bound to the racialized hierarchies and epistemological privileging of European knowledge, reason, and patriarchal normativity, settler colonialism depends on turning Indigenous land and bodies into capital. The transformation of relatives into things, beings into bodies, bodies into labor, and labor into capital is how the sacred is emptied of its cosmic meaning. This violent reorganization of Native life is meant to gender and heterosexualize, to remove, erase, or else assimilate. This insatiable settler colonial thirst for Native life is the basis of Western modernity. Another way of saying this is that the settler colonial order is not logical but a form of addiction. And as such, it responds not to wish fulfillment but to fear, not to nourishment but to excess. Historian Jack D. Forbes refers to this excess as *wétiko* cannibalism: white consumption of the lives of Black and Brown people through the ruthless exploitation of our bodies, lands, and resources.[2] The violence of settler colonialism is not only material—though it is material—but also psychological and spiritual. The predations of wétiko cannibalism, as Forbes points out, take place under the aegis of settler civilization, which becomes both the justification for it and the means by which it spreads.

The possibilities of resisting settler colonial capitalism do not pass through the logical articulation of history with power, power with economics, economics with the social. Rather, it is in the act of relating to (both telling the story of and associating with) the forms of life that we as Indigenous peoples know to be our kin that we find methods of resistance based in our own stories of life lived in relation. To be sure, settler colonialism depends on abrogating those stories—which are to us ongoing, experiential realities—and, thus, on the dispossession of land, kin, spirituality, and time. Settler colonialism demands that our sacred bonds of recognition and reciprocity be converted into estrangement. But by enacting the emergent lives-in-relation through which land is kin, we are not so much telling our stories as orienting ourselves in relation to history through them. Storying ourselves in relation. In this sense, living in good relations is not theory but memory, a praxis of emergence. The storying resistance that I am describing is not simply recalled but enlivened and enacted. It is this enlivening of our resistance that I am trying to feel, here, as I write these words.

Allotment

Allotment aimed to assimilate Indians into American society by isolating individual landowners, promoting patriarchal domesticity, and encouraging cash crop farming. In the case of the Cherokee Nation, of the original 7 million acres held before allotment in Indian Territory, individual Cherokee citizens retained only 146,598 acres in 1971.[3] Through coercive deals or outright fraud, Indian land was drastically reduced, families were dispersed, forced to relocate, to start over, again and again. This loss is both a point of departure and the requirement for existence within settler colonialism.

Let me provide an example. Lot 5 in Section 6, Township 11 North, Range 18 East was allotted to John Rock in 1903 after the completion of the Dawes Commission's enrollment of Cherokees in Indian Territory. In the years following the Dawes Commission, many Native families such as the Rocks found themselves unable to retain the lands they had been allotted and either sold or were forced to abandon them. In March 1952, in fact, the State of Oklahoma served notice to Rock's family that their claim to this land was to be legally quieted, forever, in court. The notice reads:

> To the unknown heirs, executors, administrators, devisees, trustees and assigns, known and unknown, immediate and remote of John Rock Cherokee roll No. 16.933, deceased, and Jeannie Rock, Dan Rock and Lee Rock, if living, and if deceased, then the unknown heirs, executors, administrators, devisees, trustees and assigns, immediate and remote of any such deceased person or persons. Defendants, Greeting.[4]

The public notice stipulates that if no heir defends the allotment in court, all rights to it will be permanently eliminated.

Here is the connection. I am one of those unknown, remote relatives—though I did not know this until somewhat recently because, as I noted earlier, my Cherokee father was adopted by a white family as a newborn. In fact, my father was born and adopted in January 1952, only two months before this notice was published.[5] Allotment and adoption are two interlocking techniques of settler colonial dispossession that converge in the body of my grandmother, my father, and me—in our shared flesh—and in the land that is our kin.

How does one claim unclaimable land?

My great-aunt Carolyn told me that the family left that land because it was about to be flooded. An infrastructure project that dammed the Canadian River would create Oklahoma's largest man-made body of water, Lake Eufaula. The Eufaula Dam turned Indian allotments into recreational facilities and profitable lakefront housing developments, as it provided hydroelectric power and irrigation for industrial cotton farming. It provided capital for white businesses at the expense of Native life. But the Rocks had left their allotment land and moved to the Oklahoma panhandle in 1951, a year before the lawsuit. Carolyn's father, my great-grandfather, told her once, "The place where I was born is under the water."

How does one claim land that is underwater?

Craig Womack tells a similar story of loss, of submergence of the land allotted to the Muskogee Creek Nation, in his novel *Drowning in Fire,* which is set in and around Lake Eufaula. Womack's central narrator, Josh Henneha, listens as his grandfather tells him: "Your daddy was borned there [under Lake Eufaula]. Now you can't get nowhere around here on the same roads you used to. All covered up."[6] The land is underwater because of a massive infrastructure project, one of the first in Oklahoma to displace Indian people in the post–World War II era, though certainly not the last. For Womack, the creation of Lake Eufaula sets off a chain reaction of cultural conflicts, as it disrupts the transmission of intergenerational memory and is exemplary of the displacement of Creeks territorially, culturally, and spiritually.

The damming of Lake Eufaula was approved in 1946, begun in 1956, and completed in 1964 by the Army Corps of Engineers. As Clint Carroll notes, in the mid-twentieth century entire communities were (once again) removed by damming projects across Oklahoma, as part of its efforts to promote recreational tourism.[7] Of course, this is not the only site where such dispossession by flooding took place. The Oceti Sakowin, for example, also struggled against numerous damming projects in the mid-twentieth century, leading up to the present-day resistance against the Dakota Access Pipeline (and the #NoDAPL movement). Nick Estes details how in 1944 the Army Corps of Engineers and the Bureau of Reclamation joined in supporting the Pick-Sloan Plan that devastated Indigenous communities along the Missouri River. This was accomplished by first seizing Indigenous land through the power of eminent domain and subsequently damming the river, flooding reservation lands, and, in the process, displacing entire communities. As Estes puts it: "The results were nothing short of genocide: by destroying the land—and with it the plants, animals, and water—the dams targeted and destroyed the very nations of people who reproduced themselves upon the soil. In this way, taking land and water also took away the possibility of a viable future."[8] I want to emphasize here, along with Estes, that flooding land is not simply an act of displacement but a genocidal maneuver meant to end Native life and relations with the land, its plants and animals, and its spirits.

The allotment period (1887–1906), Oklahoma statehood (1907), the flooding of allotment land (in the 1940s), the unilateral termination of tribal governance (in the 1950s), and the Indian Relocation Act (1956) all work in tandem and sequentially to dispossess Indigenous peoples of land, to diminish Indigenous sovereignty, and to disrupt Indigenous kinship patterns. Family displacement leads to the rupturing of kinship networks leads to assimilation leads to erasure.

Adoption

In the 1960s and 1970s, after allotment, white priests and public officials removed Indigenous children from their families at catastrophic rates. Native mothers were coerced into extinguishing their rights not to parcels of land but to children. As Margaret D. Jacobs documents, white social workers, who would often insist that they had "the best interests of the child" at heart, nonetheless could not see Indian women as fit mothers and shuttled their children away never to be seen by their families again.[9] In 1976, the Association on American Indian Affairs (AAIA) estimated that between 25 and 35 percent of Indian children had been separated from their families.[10] This crisis of Native family life eventually led to the passage of the Indian Child Welfare Act (ICWA) in 1978, which sought to stem the unidirectional flow of Native children into white households. ICWA put in place a series of protections for Native children, including the requirement that adoption agencies attempt to place Indigenous children with a member of their close or extended family, within their own tribe, or with a member of another federally recognized tribe. Testifying before the U.S. Senate in 1974, the executive director of the AAIA, William Byler, noted: "In our efforts to make Indian children white, I think it's clear that we're destroying them."[11]

Adoption is an expression of the settler colonial drive toward the impossible mandate of assimilation. Even from the very beginning of the U.S. Republic, Native children were seen as potentially assimilable into the fabric of the white nation, but only as long as they remained subservient to white interests or served to expand U.S. territorial claims.[12] But the Indian can never be made white, despite cutting his hair or teaching her to sew—can never be fully assimilated. Once more, the settler colonial repertoire of assimilation, though diverse, depends on breaking covenants, sacred bonds of kinship, in order to facilitate the expansion of technologies of control upon which modern capitalism depends.

The quieting of land titles in the first half of the twentieth century was meant to extinguish Indigenous claims to allotted parcels but also the memory of and by the land. The adoption of Native children by white families in the mid-twentieth century was carried out through coercion, was made possible by centuries of settler colonial domination, and has indelibly marked generations of Indigenous families with the pain of losing a child. In fact, the technical term for what my grandmother did when she gave my father up for adoption is *extinguish* her rights to him. The rights to a child are extinguished. The rights to land are quieted. But the child—my father, the adoptee—also lost rights through this adoption. He lost the right to his own kin, to heritage, to stories and medicine, to the land, to the ancestors. That loss is intergenerational and iterative.

Susan Devan Harness narrates a similar process in *Bitterroot: A Salish Memoir of Transracial Adoption*. As an adoptee herself, Harness's poignant reflection on the multilayered experiences of adoption and return to community speaks to how child removal is not just a technology of settler colonial erasure but also a form of psychic wounding that tears the fabric of Indigenous kinship across time and space. She gives shape to the constitutional lack, the breach, opened by her having been removed from her Indigenous community at the age of two and adopted by a white family. Decades later, Harness narrates being reunited with her mother as a form of recognition not of shared kinship but of pain: "I know we share the same pain, she and I. It's just called different names. Hers is a shame of relinquishment; mine is the hurt of abandonment.

Both are two sides of the same adoption coin."[13] What hurts most for Harness is not that her Salish family forgot her but that they remembered her as a ghost, a haunting presence of what might have been. Adoption is a method of assimilation, but as Harness points out, it creates specters rather than absences. *Relinquishment, extinguishing, quieting,* these terms mark the legal procedures through which an Indigenous child is removed from culture. Adoption, like allotment, depends on recognizing Indigenous subjectivity only in order to diminish Indigenous life. This is the mandate of settler colonial dispossession: to capture life in order to extinguish it.

Dispossession

The basis of settler colonialism is to attack Indigenous bodies in relation; it is to sever, cut, dispossess. In fact, Michi Saagiig Nishnaabeg scholar Leanne Betasamosake Simpson describes the interlocking logics of settler colonialism and heteropatriarchy as a *"foundational dispossession force."*[14] In a sense, to be an Indian is to be in a constant state of spiritual and material dispossession. To be dispossessed is to be made no longer able to hold land. But dispossession is also a form of exorcism, a casting out of evil spirits.[15] In this semiotic overlap, settler colonialism requires the expulsion from the land of both Native people and their residual, haunting presence. Dispossession is a theft of both land and souls. Expelling Native spirits, and thus severing the spiritual connection to the land—as bodies of the land—is central to the management of Native life by settler colonialism. Importantly, however, Simpson calls the opposite of dispossession not possession but "deep, reciprocal, consensual attachment."[16] The rejection of dispossession cannot be acquiescence to privatization. It must be attachment, grounded in our stories, our land, our bodies, and our ethics. This is because our land holds memories, and bodies, and spirits, and time. Our land *is* memory, and body, and spirit, and time. This is what I mean by resistance through enlivening and enacting kinship. The land is not simply named through stories of creation or relation but made whole, incorporated, embodied. Attachment is a form of kinmaking, in which we find the possibility of recognizing ourselves in relation to the land and/as ourselves.

In this vein, Jodi A. Byrd, Alyosha Goldstein, Jodi Melamed, and Chandan Reddy argue in favor of "grounded relationalities," by which they mean decolonial forms of being-with that are "situated in relation to and from the land but without precluding movement, multiplicity, multidirectionality, transversals, and other elementary or material currents of water and air."[17] The possibilities of orienting knowledges and of knowing orientations do not derive from a liberal understanding of the human as unique in its agency. Rather, to ground relations is to know the self as only ever having been in relation with others, with kin that are essentially, crucially, not only human or even material but elemental, spiritual, and kinetic. These relations are historical without being history but, rather, temporal—woven into the fabric of time and space as trace residues of the materiality of life as lived in relation. These grounded relationalities, according to Byrd, Goldstein, Melamed, and Reddy, resist the inanimacy of kin that is other-than-human. And this resistance, they argue, is aimed at undoing "economies of dispossession," "those multiple and intertwined genealogies of racialized property, subjection, and expropriation through which capitalism and colonialism take shape historically and change over time."[18] The epistemological basis of this mirrored image of colonial rule is derived from the mutability of economic and racialized subjugation of nonwhite peoples in the Americas. Dispossession and possession are not antonyms but the singular condition of possibility through which the colonial administration of bodies, land, law, and culture is authorized and made real.

Simpson proposes cultivating attachment, while Byrd, Goldstein, Melamed, and Reddy propose being with the land as a method of grounded, dynamic resistance to settler colonialism. I think this is also what Hogan means when she writes, "What happens to people and what happens to the land is the same thing."[19] This is another way of saying that the dispossession of Native land necessitates the dispossession of Native life, the draining of its epistemological significance, the wielding of proprietary logics as the basis of Western normativity. If in the first example Hogan points to the continuous relationality between absence and presence, here she points to an embeddedness, a form of imagining the land not as discrete but also in relation as kin. The claims of settler states depend on erasing Indigenous bodies from the land, Indigenous histories from the land, erasing the memory of the land itself. But in these interlocking techniques there are gaps, fissures that emerge, like air bubbling up from the depths.

Dayunisi, Water Beetle, Beaver's Grandchild

It dawned on me: I had forgotten the basics. Adrienne Keene, a fellow Cherokee Nation citizen, reminded me one afternoon as I was telling her about my ongoing struggle to claim this land that was underwater. We shared this struggle. Her family's land, like that of so many others, is also submerged. "The Water Beetle!" she exclaimed, or maybe, we exclaimed together. I had forgotten to ground myself in our stories. Dayunisi, Water Beetle, is at the heart of the Cherokee creation story. The version told to anthropologist James Mooney in the late nineteenth century begins like this:

> When all was water, the animals were above in Galunlati, beyond the arch; but it was very much crowded, and they were wanting more room. They wondered what was below the water, and at last Dayunisi, "Beaver's Grandchild," the little Water-beetle, offered to go and see if it could learn. It darted in every direction over the surface of the water, but could find no firm place to rest. Then it dived to the bottom and came up with some soft mud, which began to grow and spread on every side until it became

the island which we call the earth. It was afterward fastened to the sky
with four cords, but no one remembers who did this.[20]

Dayunisi, Water Beetle, Beaver's Grandchild, emerges from the water with the land
that will become earth, Elohi. The entire world was made from land that was once
inaccessible—land that was under the water. Here, the Under World is brought to the
Upper World (Galunlati) and there, in between, Elohi. Creation is a process of emergence. Land becomes earth as it surfaces from the water, spreading out, touching air.
Elohi is formed from a collision of elements that expands, and in that expansion, the
animals, our kin, can leave their crowded confines. The seemingly insignificant Water
Beetle has the key to the future of life. Because of Water Beetle's skill and bravery, all
of us can survive.

   As an allegory, Water Beetle brings up from the depths that which was previously
unknown, or inaccessible, but necessary for life. In this act of submerging, entering the
unknown, we journey down, but also inward, to ask questions of ourselves and meet
the mutually reinforcing responsibilities of the collective. As a cosmological beginning,
the material—that is, the land—and the philosophical are inextricably linked. Cherokee scholar Christopher B. Teuton describes this story as one of ethical reciprocity:

> The creation of Elohi is made possible by the values that arise when
> creatures recognize their shared stake in survival. Communal solidarity,
> egalitarian discussion and consensus, and individual self-sacrifice for the
> welfare of the whole are necessary conditions for finding and developing
> that new space on which the community may grow. Most important,
> these values are acted on individually, but within a social context, for all
> persons, no matter their gifts or abilities, are integral to the welfare of the
> group, and some of the most unlikely of us may become heroes.[21]

This is a journey that only Dayunisi could make, and one that positions the birth of
the world as an act of communality—a being in relation. The individual capacities of
Water Beetle are necessary to the community, which, in turn, contribute their own
capacities to the sustaining of life on Elohi.

   In some versions of this story, Dayunisi offers to travel only after the animals, our
kin, hold conference, debating how to resolve our collective problem.[22] They debate
and reach a consensus before inviting Dayunisi, who accepts the charge given to them,
to risk their life to save the others.[23] Dayunisi can exist both on land and underwater,
can see both on land and underwater, can bring up from the water the land that was
not yet land. In between these dualisms is a liminal space where perspective must shift,
a moment in which the transition occurs from water to air, from below to above, from
mud to earth. This moment of transition leads us to ask, in turn, what happens in that

particular instant when worlds collide—when the space between worlds is not really space but friction, charge, connection?

Dayunisi feels the cold of the water as they dart below. Down in these depths, the light begins to fade. They can no longer hear the ripple of the waves above, but they swim on. Dayunisi cannot know what will happen underneath the water, they cannot forecast—they can only be there in that present. Finally, they come to the soft, dark mud at the bottom of the ocean. What does Dayunisi feel now? Anxiety? Fear? They reach out—another moment of transition—and the touch of earth brings them resolve. It is one small gesture toward something that will become something else, something new. To reach down is to have faith that what they are doing is what they were meant to do, what they must do for all. And in that vast expanse of water, Dayunisi grabs hold of a small speck of mud and turns—transitions—back up toward the surface. They swim and swim. They start to see the light from the heavens above, Galunlati, where the rest of their kin are gathered, waiting. Exhausted, they emerge.

At the beginning, there was nothing and something came from it.

Dayunisi is not just a part of the past but a guide, teaching a method of engaging with time and space—and with the gaps between. Dayunisi, Water Beetle, Beaver's Grandchild, emerges from the depths of the ocean having been asked to share themselves, their life, with others, for the benefit of all, for the continuity of life as community. Dayunisi offers us a glimpse of what we must do, what we must attempt when solutions seem impossible. We dive, we grab hold, we return, we give. We must go in order to return.

I imagine myself claiming, belonging to that allotment land turned lakebed—its memories lingering under the surface of water that was once earth. I imagine belonging submerged. I imagine a something returned to nothing that waits to become again—an emergence of memory.[24] Even if I do not remember this land that is now submerged under Lake Eufaula, the land remembers me. And in that memory, that calling to memory, there is a place for me there, in the water that was once land and that can be land again. Land that returns and spreads and grows.

There are ancestors buried in that land under the water. There are memories and there are seeds from Selu, the Corn Mother, planted, waiting to emerge. There is kinship in that land, with that land; there is reciprocity as place and time. Dayunisi teaches me that I must remember, I must find in the land, and in our communities, our kin, the reciprocal relationships that endure in history as lived and enacted. Dayunisi teaches me that history is a shared experience of recognition. Community is found not in the morass of colonial bureaucracies but in storying our pasts, in remembering, attaching, grounding, reemerging.

In this essay, I have attempted to frame allotment and adoption as correlating technologies of settler colonialism that work to dispossess Indigenous families of land and kinship. Of land *as* kinship. To claim kinship as an adoptee, or as the child of an adoptee, is a process of narration of self-in-relation but also a mode of engagement with the loss that inevitably marks our bodies as liminal and spectral. While the displacement of Native children has had profound effects on the possibility of Native futures, it is also true that for us, sometimes the response to loss is already embedded within our stories of belonging, being-with, and consensual attachment. Though we may not consent to dispossession, we can consent to being good relatives. And here, finally, we see that relating is not so much a discursive maneuver as it is a mattering, an ongoing emergence of relationality. A horizon. A song.

NOTES

1. Linda Hogan, *Dwellings: A Spiritual History of the Living World* (New York: W. W. Norton, 1995), 95.
2. Jack D. Forbes, *Columbus and Other Cannibals: The Wétiko Disease of Exploitation, Imperialism, and Terrorism* (New York: Seven Stories, 2008), 24.
3. Rose Stremlau, *Sustaining the Cherokee Family: Kinship and the Allotment of an Indigenous Nation* (Chapel Hill: University of North Carolina Press, 2011), 5.
4. Milam M. King, "Notice by Publication," *McIntosh County Democrat,* March 27, 1952.
5. I have written elsewhere about my own relationship with adoption narratives. See Joseph M. Pierce, "Trace, Blood, and Native Authenticity," *Critical Ethnic Studies* 3, no. 2 (2017): 57–76.
6. Craig S. Womack, *Drowning in Fire* (Tucson: University of Arizona Press, 2001), 19.
7. Clint Carroll, *Roots of Our Renewal: Ethnobotany and Cherokee Environmental Governance* (Minneapolis: University of Minnesota Press, 2015), 88–89.
8. Nick Estes, *Our History Is the Future: Standing Rock versus the Dakota Access Pipeline, and the Long Tradition of Indigenous Resistance* (New York: Verso, 2019), 135.
9. Margaret D. Jacobs, *A Generation Removed: The Fostering and Adoption of Indigenous Children in the Postwar World* (Lincoln: University of Nebraska Press, 2014), xxv.
10. Jacobs, *Generation Removed,* xxvi.
11. *Indian Child Welfare Program: Hearings before the Subcommittee on Indian Affairs of the Senate Committee on Interior and Insular Affairs,* 93rd Cong. 6 (April 8–9, 1974).
12. Dawn Peterson, *Indians in the Family: Adoption and the Politics of Antebellum Expansion* (Cambridge, Mass.: Harvard University Press, 2017), 3–4.
13. Susan Devan Harness, *Bitterroot: A Salish Memoir of Transracial Adoption* (Lincoln: University of Nebraska Press, 2018), 157.
14. Leanne Betasamosake Simpson, *As We Have Always Done: Indigenous Freedom through Radical Resistance* (Minneapolis: University of Minnesota Press, 2017), 52.
15. *OED Online,* s.v. "dispossession (*n.*)," accessed December 31, 2018, http://www.oed.com/view/Entry/55133.
16. Simpson, *As We Have Always Done,* 43.
17. Jodi A. Byrd, Alyosha Goldstein, Jodi Melamed, and Chandan Reddy, "Predatory Value: Economies of Dispossession and Disturbed Relationalities," *Social Text* 135, no. 2 (June 2018): 11.
18. Byrd et al., "Predatory Value," 2.
19. Hogan, *Dwellings,* 89.

20. James Mooney, *Myths of the Cherokee* (Mineola, N.Y.: Dover, 1995), 239.

21. Christopher B. Teuton, *Deep Waters: The Textual Continuum in American Indian Literature* (Lincoln: University of Nebraska Press, 2010), xiii.

22. Teuton, *Deep Waters,* xi–xiii. See also Christopher B. Teuton, ed., *Cherokee Stories of the Turtle Island Liars' Club* (Chapel Hill: University of North Carolina Press, 2012), 38–40.

23. I am using the gender-neutral *they* to refer to Dayunisi.

24. For more information about submerged perspectives, see Macarena Gómez-Barris, *The Extractive Zone: Social Ecologies and Decolonial Perspectives* (Durham, N.C.: Duke University Press, 2017), 98–106.

Kinscape

MARILYN DUMONT

Land hearthless
hearthless life
land landless without
land-locked hearthless
inhabitants scatter
members disappear dissolve without land-self to hold kin
   chapan here
      kokum there
Métis line-threads extend, families fray
divide like river-lots into rebellion and road allowance
hearts fray hearth broken without home-
land without
scatter separate fragment kin kinship
kin can't kin can't ship on land-locked hearthless
land landless without land-locked without
land hearth gone

Métis people who are not on a land base have survived through
kinship ties to relatives who reconvene yearly at sites like Lac Ste. Anne
Pilgrimage, located near Edmonton, Alberta.

PART II

Racial and Gender Taxonomies

Blut und Boden

"Mixed-Bloods" and Métis in U.S. Allotment and Canadian Enfranchisement Policies

DARREN O'TOOLE

When Manitoba became a province of the Canadian federation in 1870, Section 31 of the Manitoba Act granted 1.4 million acres of land to the Métis as compensation for the purported extinction of their Indian title in the province.[1] In order to better understand the policy objectives driving the implementation of Section 31, this essay places it within the larger context of Indian policy.[2] Essentially, the Métis were conflated with "half-breeds" in both Canada and the United States. In both countries, policy singled out "mixed-bloods" or half-breeds for enfranchisement and allotment prior to the adoption of the Manitoba Act. While the enfranchisement-through-allotment policy largely failed in Canada with regard to status Indians, the use of allotment and scrip to bring about the dispersal of Métis communities parallels the implementation of allotment in the United States, first with half-breed clauses in individual treaties, then by forcing mixed-bloods onto allotments after the adoption of the Dawes Act in 1887.[3] By demonstrating that what happened to Métis lands was precisely what Canada desired in terms of its ultimate policy outcome for First Nations, this essay contradicts the claims of courts that governments did not treat the Métis the same as Indians. Prior to Canadian Confederation, it was believed that the supposed gradual civilization of Indians through allotment and enfranchisement would only take a generation or two. It was only when faced with the failure of this policy that federal Parliament turned toward more brutal disciplinary measures to ensure the assimilation of status Indians.

Allotment in the United States

In the first Canadian court decision that recognized Métis hunting rights, *R. v. Powley,* Justice Vaillancourt made a finding of fact that from 1824 to 1857, "the American government identified and included [Métis] of the Upper Great Lakes as beneficiaries of land and/or annuities in at least fifteen different treaties in what is now Michigan, Wisconsin and Minnesota."[4] While the most notorious incarnation of allotment policy is the General Allotment Act—popularly known as the Dawes Act, after Senator

Henry L. Dawes, who piloted it through Congress—the policy of allotment had a piecemeal history long before it was generalized and systematized in U.S. federal law. As early as 1877, "Secretary for the Interior Carl Schurz endorsed a general allotment bill," and such plans were "discussed in Congress in the late 1870s and early 1880s."[5] At the time, it was thought important to include "provisions restricting the sale of land after allotment" due to "the experience of tribes allotted by treaty."[6] In other words, in terms of policy learning, previous experience with allotment clauses in treaties meant the U.S. government knew well before the adoption of the Allotment Act what the probable outcome would be, were there to be no restrictions on sales.

Allotment in the United States goes back to the very beginnings of English colonization in North America. For example, in 1633, the "General Court of Massachusetts Colony declared that any of the Indians who should come to the English plantations *and live civilly* and orderly, should have 'allotments amongst the English, according to the custom of the English in like case.'"[7] Initially, at least, the goal of allotment was to integrate and assimilate Indians into the body politic of English settlers. Shortly after the United States became a sovereign nation, "Henry Knox, secretary of war under Washington, hinted at individual ownership of land in a speech sent to the Indians of the Northwest in April, 1792."[8] According to Felix Cohen, as "early as 1798 tribal lands were allotted to individuals or families," as was the case in the Treaty of June 1, 1798, with the Oneida Nation.[9] Kirke Kickingbird and Karen Ducheneaux also note that as early as the first two decades of the nineteenth century, land allotment became a process by which citizenship was granted—in other words, enfranchisement.[10]

Francis Paul Prucha reminds us that when we look at the content of treaties in the United States, it is "easy to concentrate on the land cession provisions of the treaties and see the treaties simply as a means of territorial aggrandizement, as a 'license for empire,' and thus to miss the overwhelming obsession of the United States with changing the cultures of the Indians from communally to individually based systems of property ownership and from hunting or mixed economies to yeomanry."[11] For example, after the conclusion of the 1825 treaty with the Kaw, Indian superintendent William Clark wrote that half-breed reserves "have a good effect in promoting civilization, as their attachment is created for a fixed residence and an idea of separate property is imparted without which it is vain to think of improving the minds and morals of the Indian or making any progress in the work of civilization."[12] In other words, "the mixed bloods would demonstrate, by exemplary agrarian living, the means whereby their less fortunate relatives might one day enjoy the civilizing lessons of land ownership by individuals."[13]

In November 1832, President Jackson was reelected, and he was sworn in on March 4, 1833. According to Jay P. Kinney, there "were two well-defined elements in the Indian policy of the Jackson administration."[14] The first was the segregation of Indians who were deemed unready to adopt the customs of the whites from the white population by their removal west of the Mississippi. The second was the assignment of tracts of land to individual Indians who were considered by the government "sufficiently advanced in civilization to assume the duties and responsibilities of citizenship."[15] In Kickingbird and Ducheneaux's view, it "would be fair to say that almost all of the lands east of the Mississippi allotted on an individual basis in the early treaties have long since gone out of Indian hands."[16]

If mixed-bloods were viewed as having the legal capacity to manage their individual interests, Kinney also notes that half-breeds were not always given title in fee simple, even when the government tried to separate them from full-blood Indians. Kinney finds evidence of a tendency toward the separation of half-breeds from full-bloods in Article 9 of the Treaty of July 15, 1830. In it, the Minnesota Sioux provided for a separate tract for the "half-breeds of their nation." However, half-breeds were to hold this tract "in the same manner as other Indian Titles are held" and not in fee simple. In Article 10, provision was also made for a separate tract for the use of the half-breeds of the Omaha, Iowa, Otoe, and Yankton and Santee Sioux. For Kinney, "these separate provisions for them throw light upon the instances to which reference has been made in which there was an effort to separate the mixed-bloods from the full-bloods by the assignment of lands in severalty."[17]

It was during the negotiation of the Manypenny treaties in 1854 that "a decision was made to begin a general policy of breaking down tribal societies through the deliberate use of individual allotments of tribal land."[18] Some of the Manypenny treaties provided for allotment to half-breeds. According to Kickingbird and Ducheneaux, this seems to have been racially motivated. Such allotment provisions were aimed specifically at "Christianized Indians or half-blooded traders and guides."[19] It was apparently the belief of the treaty-makers that those "who had converted to the new religion or who had sufficient white blood to understand the magic of farming" could more easily "effect a transition to civilization."[20]

If the Allotment Act evidently postdates Section 31 of the Manitoba Act, experiments with allotment in the United States preceded it by several decades. Indeed, the use of scrip to extinguish half-breed land claims also had precedents in U.S. policy. As political scientist Thomas Flanagan notes with regard to scrip being issued to fulfill the half-breed clause in the 1854 Treaty with the Chippewa, the Métis "probably never saw the scrip."[21] Similarly, subsequent to an amendment in 1864 to the Treaty with the Red Lake and Pembina Chippewa of 1863 that removed safeguards preventing the sale of half-breed grants, there was "corrupt traffic" of scrip, and "scrip and patents were issued, cancelled, and reissued in confusing succession."[22] These results were undoubtedly well known to Canadian policy makers when they decided to issue scrip to extinguish Métis title in Manitoba and the Northwest Territory.[23]

Métis as Half-Breeds

As Métis were seen as mixed-bloods—and therefore always already half-civilized simply by virtue of their white blood—it is easy to see why government officials would have targeted them for immediate enfranchisement. However, while all Métis were French Catholic half-breeds, not all French Catholic half-breeds were Métis. In 1880, Valery Havard wrote that the "true representatives" of the "race" of people he called "Métis" were "most numerous on the Red River of the North and the Winnipeg Basin."[24] The offspring of French Canadian voyageurs and Indigenous women—primarily from the Dakota (Sioux), Nakota (Assiniboine), Nēhiyawēwin (Plains Cree), and Anishinaabe (Saulteaux, Ojibwe, or Chippewa) peoples—the Métis carved out various economic niches that, while connected to the fur trade, were a step away from it. While the first generation of mixed-blood offspring in what would later become Manitoba may go as far back as the winter of 1738–1739 following the establishment of Fort Rouge and Fort La Reine, it was the Battle of Seven Oaks in 1816 that first brought to the attention of the colonial gaze their existence as a "separate and distinct tribe."[25] An official international boundary between British North America and the United States was not fixed until 1818. As borderland peoples, the Plains Métis nevertheless continued to cross the Medicine Line, whether to hunt buffalo as far west as Montana or to freight cargo between the Red River Settlement (Winnipeg) and Saint Paul, Minnesota.[26] However, the social, political, and cultural distinctions between the Métis as a collectivity and individual members of First Nations with mixed ancestry made little difference in the eyes of settler states.

What is particularly confusing in the United States is that the federal government never recognized the Métis as a distinct people, which forced many Métis to pass themselves off as half-breed relatives of, for example, their Anishinaabeg cousins in order to settle on reservations such as Red Lake and White Earth in Minnesota and Turtle Mountain in North Dakota. In the Canadian context, John Giokas and Paul Chartrand have charted out the lack of consistency on the part of the Canadian state when it has come to the legal definition of *Métis*. They identify three central sources of the confusion around Métis identity:

1. Associating English ["Scots Half-Breeds"] and French ["Métis"] mixed-ancestry groups (from Rupert's Land) as if they were the same group;
2. Including other mixed-ancestry persons whose origins may have been far removed from the Red River and Rupert's Land Métis Nation;
3. Referring loosely to persons of mixed-ancestry who may never have had Indian status, or who, having had status, may then have lost it through the status and enfranchisement rules in the *Indian Act*.[27]

With regard to the first case, section 133 of the Constitution Act of 1867 provides that all federal Parliament statutes must be adopted simultaneously in both the English and French languages.[28] For this reason, the English version of Section 31 of the Manitoba Act used the term *half-breed* while the French version used *Métis* as if they were co-terminous boundaries of identity. Furthermore, because government policy tended to reduce the Métis to individual half-breeds or mixed-bloods rather than dealing with them as a discrete polity, there was a historical tendency to simultaneously conflate all three of these sources of confusion. What interests me here with regard to allotment is the confusion between the Métis in the first group and the enfranchised Indians in the third group. Government policy initially drew a distinction between these two groups because the objective of civilizing the Indians meant focusing on criteria such as lifestyle, marriage, and residence. But the impetus of reducing the number of band members as a cost-cutting measure meant that these criteria were applied incoherently.[29] This racialization of both Métis and members of First Nations with mixed ancestry allowed for the reduction of both to a motley crew half-breed population[30]—that is, "a set of elements in which we can note constants and regularities even in accidents"[31]—a fundamental aspect of the policy of allotment. This transition from a people to a population is one of the most important knowledge-power relations underlying the policy of allotment, which targets individuals with centrifugal forces to bring about the aggregate effect of dispersal at the level of the population. Some of the first attempts are to be found in the aforementioned treaty clauses in the United States that singled out half-breeds.

Enfranchisement in Canada

The earliest statute in British North America that allowed for allotment in severalty was in Section 6 of the Act to Provide for the Instruction and Permanent Settlement of the Indians, which was adopted in Nova Scotia in 1842.[32] However, it merely provided that the commissioner of Indian affairs could "parcel out to each head of family a portion of the Reservations, with such limited powers of alienation to Indians only as the said Instructions may, from time to time, authorize."[33] Two years later, this Crown colony adopted the Act to Regulate the Management and Disposal of the Indian Reserves in This Province.[34] In effect, Section 10 of the Nova Scotia statute allowed for "allotments of not more than fifty nor less than five acres." The statute empowered the lieutenant governor to grant location tickets to "such Indians as His Excellency may deem fit objects for such exclusive appropriations." After having "resided upon and improved the same for a period of not less than ten years," an Indian could receive an absolute grant in fee simple.[35]

In 1856 in the British colony of United Canada (present-day southern Ontario and Québec), three special commissioners were appointed to investigate the failure of previous Indian policies and to report upon "the best means of securing the future progress and civilization" of Indians and the "best mode of so managing the Indian property as to secure its full benefit to the Indians, without impeding on the settlement of the country."[36] Among the recommendations of *The Report of the Pennefather Commission* (1858) was the allotment of no more than twenty-five acres to each head of family. While in severalty, this was not to be in fee simple, as it would not be possible to alienate the land to non-Indians without the approval of the government. In addition to consolidating existing laws, it was suggested that a section be added to provide for the dissolution of tribal organizations, and explicit reference was made to certain Indian treaties in the United States.[37]

Prior to its final report, the Pennefather Commission's recommendations were already being implemented in the 1857 Act to Encourage the Gradual Civilization of the Indian Tribes in this Province.[38] It was this act that not only introduced the idea of enfranchisement into Canadian law but did so through allotment in severalty. Under this act, status Indians could, under certain conditions, receive twenty hectares of reserve land in fee simple. More importantly, this statute was passed under the government of none other than John A. Macdonald and George-Étienne Cartier, who would also oversee the drafting of Section 31 thirteen years later. From the beginning, then, the Canadian policy of granting allotments to individuals in severalty with the explicit purpose of breaking up community ties can be directly linked to Macdonald and Cartier.

In 1860, the imperial Act Respecting Indians and Indian Lands transferred responsibility for Indians from the Colonial Office in London to United Canada. This allowed Canada to pass the Management of Indian Lands and Properties Act the very same year and thereby further implement recommendations of the Pennefather Commission's report. By 1860, "the basic direction for Indian policy had been set. Assimilation, with its resulting tribal destruction, stood at the center of the program."[39] In 1866, the Act to Confirm the Title to Lands Held in Trust for Certain of the Indians Resident in This Province was adopted.[40] It quieted the titles to conveyances made by married women, despite their legal incapacity to do so.[41]

In order to understand the specific effects of enfranchisement on those whom the government deemed "half-breed heads of families," one must go back to the first time Indian status was created in United Canada in 1850. Initially, any nonstatus person who married a status Indian and lived with the band was deemed Indian in the eyes of the law. The law was changed a year later from "any person" to "any woman." This essentially excluded white men who married Indian women. At this point, Indian women retained their status, as did their mixed-ancestry offspring. In 1868, these terms were extended to the entire federation under Section 13 of the Act Providing for the Organisation of the Department of the Secretary of State of Canada, and for the Management of Indian and Ordnance Lands. This was amended the following year in the Act for the Gradual Enfranchisement of Indians. Section 6 stipulated that "any Indian woman marrying any other than an Indian, shall cease to be an Indian within the meaning of this Act, nor shall the children issue of such marriage be considered as Indians within the meaning of this Act."[42] This of course generated an off-reserve nonstatus population of mixed ancestry.

Since the Métis were descendants of men who were "other than an Indian"—primarily French Canadian and Scottish—and women who would have been deemed Indian in the eyes of colonial law, it stands to reason that they would have been viewed essentially as enfranchised mixed-blood Indians after 1869. If this was not yet clear enough, just as enfranchised Indians who had received allotments were to be excluded from the Indian Act of 1876, it also explicitly excluded the Métis of Manitoba from its ambit:

> s. 3(3)(e) Provided that no half-breed in Manitoba who has shared in the distribution of half-breed lands shall be accounted an Indian; and that no half-breed head of a family (except the widow of an Indian, or half-breed who has been already admitted into a treaty), shall, unless under very special circumstances, to be determined by the Superintendent-General or his agent, be accounted an Indian, or entitled to be admitted into any Indian treaty.[43]

Despite being lumped together as a mixed-ancestry population, there was a fundamental distinction between the two groups that still clearly delineates them. While First Nations women and their children were being forced out of the Indian Act, the Métis were never allowed in. Nevertheless, the biological racialization of both groups has led to confusion with regard to Métis identity. Many of the descendants of nonstatus Indians and Métis internalized colonial categories based on race rather than polity and defined themselves in terms of Métis-as-mixed. This has been a source of confusion in terms of contemporary claims to Métis identity and was even recently perpetuated by the Supreme Court of Canada in the *Daniels v. Canada* case.[44] However, the primary political aim of nonstatus Indians in Métis and nonstatus Indian organizations was to get their status back while the Métis *stricto sensu* have never sought status under the Indian Act. The creation of the Métis National Council in 1983 was precisely due to the fact that these (cl)aims were dominating the agenda of the Native Council of Canada.[45] The recent adoption of the Gender Equity in Indian Registration Act[46] and the Act to Amend the Indian Act,[47] including the subsequent amendment removing the 1951 cutoff date, now permits descendants of First Nations women who lost their status following the coming into force of the Gradual Enfranchisement Act in 1869 to reclaim status. As they do so, the nonstatus population should gradually disappear as it is absorbed into the First Nations status population. While some may nevertheless continue to self-identify in terms of Métis-as-mixed, they will be constitutionally and legally considered Indians under the Indian Act,[48] as well as Indians rather than Métis for the purposes of Section 35(2) of the Constitution Act of 1982.[49]

Conclusion

While this essay focuses on the enfranchisement clauses in the Indian Act and the representation of Métis as immediately eligible for the franchise due to their European ancestry and their distinct lifestyle, it was the issue of scrip—along with enumerating populations, surveying, patents, and private property law—in Manitoba and the Northwest Territories after 1885 that was the primary bureaucratic mechanism for the commodification of Métis lands in Canada. Furthermore, it was a way to fast-track the enfranchisement of First Nations individuals with mixed ancestry who were singled out for half-breed scrip instead of treaty.[50] Heather Devine, James Daschuk, and Michel Hogue all note the surge in withdrawals from treaty after the North-West Rebellion in 1885.[51] Daschuk and Hogue in particular attribute this to an amendment to the Indian Act after 1885 that allowed "treaty Indians" to withdraw from treaty if they could prove they had European ancestry.[52] However, this amendment can be traced back to the consolidation of the Indian Act in 1880. In 1884, the act was again amended so as to further facilitate withdrawal from treaty. It was nevertheless the third consolidation, in 1886, that provided that "such withdrawal shall include the minor unmarried children of all such half-breed."[53]

These amendments merit several remarks. First, the fact that the amendment was not made in response to the events of 1885 only proves the point of these scholars that the sudden surge in the number of withdrawals after 1885 was not due to the pull factor of this clause but rather due to the push factor of government policies that were adopted to punish supposed rebels. Second, while the individuals who withdrew from treaty were not eligible for an allotment from reserve lands, they were almost automatically eligible for half-breed scrip under the terms of the amendment to the Dominion Lands Act in 1879. Third, the 1886 amendment brought the withdrawal clause in line with the enfranchisement clauses that declared the children of enfranchised Indians would also lose their status. Fourth, and most importantly, this clause in particular contradicts the Supreme Court of Canada's statement in *R. v. Blais* that "the record suggests that the Métis were treated as a different group from 'Indians' for purposes of delineating rights and protections."[54] What it does suggest is that all mixed-bloods—whether Métis or First Nations—were treated differently than full-bloods. It was not only the Métis people who were individually targeted for immediate enfranchisement through the use of land and money scrip—any individual Indian with European ancestry could take scrip after 1880. Moreover, the effect of scrip on First Nation communities with a high proportion of members with mixed ancestry was the same as it was for Métis communities. For example, both the Peaysis band of Lac La Biche and the Ka-qua-num band at Beaver Lake disintegrated and ceased to exist as reserves.[55] In some cases, such as that of the Sandy Bay Ojibwe, they initially took scrip but were later readmitted to treaty.[56] The long-term policy objective, however, was that the full-bloods would gradually be given the same medicine as mixed-bloods through the policy of enfranchisement. As John A. Macdonald explained in 1887, the objective of enfranchisement was "to do away with the tribal system and assimilate the Indian people in all respects with the inhabitants of the Dominion, as speedily as they are fit for change."[57] In other words, the underlying logic of allotment was nothing less than cultural genocide.[58] The policy objective for all these groups was the same as it had been in the preamble of the Gradual Civilization Act in 1857: "the gradual removal of all legal distinctions between [Indians] and Her Majesty's other Canadian subjects and to facilitate the acquisition of property and the rights accompanying it." But any such rights in land were in land as an atomized commodity and, as such, precisely what allowed the aggregate effect of the gradual dispossession of a collective land base by creating conditions favorable to the dispersal of individual members one lot in severalty at a time. As Felix Cohen wryly observes: "Allotment was then, as it has been generally ever since, an incident in the transfer of Indian lands to white ownership."[59]

NOTES

1. Manitoba Act, 1870, S.C. 1870, c. 3, *reprinted in* R.S.C. 1985, app II, no 8 (Can.).
2. For a legal interpretation of Section 31, see Paul Chartrand, *Manitoba Métis Settlement Scheme of 1870* (Saskatoon, Saskatchewan: Native Law Centre, 1991).
3. Dawes General Allotment Act, ch. 119, 24 Stat. 388 (1887) (codified as amended in 25 U.S.C.A. 331).
4. R. v. Powley, [1999] 1 C.N.L.R. 153, para. 49 (Can.). The term used in the treaties was *half-breed* and not *Métis*. In many instances, the beneficiaries of the half-breed tracts identified with their tribe and not as Métis.
5. Leonard A. Carlson, *Indians, Bureaucrats, and Land: The Dawes Act and the Decline of Indian Farming* (Westport, Conn.: Greenwood Press, 1981), 7.
6. Carlson, *Indians, Bureaucrats, and Land,* 7.
7. Jay P. Kinney, *A Continent Lost, a Civilization Won: Indian Land Tenure in America* (New York: Arno Press, 1975), 82.
8. D. S. Otis, *The Dawes Act and the Allotment of Indian Lands* (Norman: University of Oklahoma Press, 1973), 207.
9. Felix S. Cohen, *Handbook of Federal Indian Law* (New York: AMS Press, 1972), 207.
10. Kirke Kickingbird and Karen Ducheneaux, *One Hundred Million Acres* (New York: Macmillan Publishing Co., 1973), 15.
11. Francis Paul Prucha, *American Indian Treaties: The History of a Political Anomaly* (Berkeley: University of California Press, 1994), 10.
12. Quoted in William M. Unrau, *Mixed-Bloods and Tribal Dissolution: Charles Curtis and the Quest for Indian Identity* (Lawrence: University Press of Kansas, 1989), 32.
13. Unrau, *Mixed-Bloods and Tribal Dissolution,* 32.
14. Kinney, *Continent Lost,* 103.
15. Kinney, 103.
16. Kickingbird and Ducheneaux, *One Hundred Million Acres,* 16.
17. Kinney, *Continent Lost,* 97.

18. Kickingbird and Ducheneaux, *One Hundred Million Acres,* 16.

19. Kickingbird and Ducheneaux, 15.

20. Kickingbird and Ducheneaux, 15.

21. Thomas Flanagan, *Métis Lands in Manitoba* (Calgary: University of Calgary Press, 1991), 24.

22. Flanagan, *Métis Lands in Manitoba,* 25.

23. For a more in-depth analysis of the use of scrip, see Jennifer Adese's essay in this volume.

24. Valery Havard, "The French Half-Breeds of the Northwest," in *Annual Report of the Smithsonian Institution* (Washington, D.C.: Government Printing Office, 1880), 314.

25. Jennifer Brown, "Woman as Centre and Symbol in the Emergence of Métis Communities," *Canadian Journal of Native Studies* 3, no. 1 (1983): 44.

26. Michel Hogue, *Metis and the Medicine Line: Creating a Border and Dividing a People* (Chapel Hill: University of North Carolina Press, 2015).

27. John Giokas and Paul L. A. H. Chartrand, "Who Are the Métis? A Review of the Law and Policy," in *Who Are Canada's Aboriginal Peoples?,* ed. Paul Chartrand (Saskatoon, Saskatchewan: Purich Publishing Ltd., 2002), 85.

28. Constitution Act 1867, 30 & 31 Vict. c. 3, *reprinted in* R.S.C. 1985, app II, no 5 (U.K.).

29. Giokas and Chartrand, "Who Are the Métis?," 90–95.

30. Chris Andersen, *Métis: Race, Recognition, and the Struggle for Indigenous Peoplehood* (Vancouver: University of British Columbia Press, 2015).

31. Michel Foucault, *Security, Territory, Population: Lectures at the Collège de France, 1977–1978,* trans. Graham Burchell (New York: Palgrave MacMillan, 2007), 74.

32. Act to Provide for the Instruction and Permanent Settlement of the Indians, S.N.S. 1842, c 16 (Can.).

33. Act to Provide for the Instruction and Permanent Settlement of the Indians §6, S.N.S. 1842, c 16 (Can.).

34. Act to Regulate the Management and Disposal of the Indian Reserves in This Province, S.N.S. 1844, c 56 (Can.).

35. Act to Regulate the Management and Disposal of the Indian Reserves in This Province §10, S.N.S. 1844, c 56 (Can.).

36. Treaties and Historical Research Centre, P.R.E. Group, and Indian and Northern Affairs, *The Historical Development of the Indian Act* (Ottawa: 1978), 29.

37. Treaties and Historical Research Centre et al., *Historical Development of the Indian Act,* 31.

38. Roger L. Nichols, *Indians in the United States and Canada: A Comparative History* (Lincoln: University of Nebraska Press, 1998), 200. *Act to Encourage the Gradual Civilization of the Indian Tribes in the Province,* 20 Vict., 26, 10 June 1857 (Can.).

39. Nichols, *Indians in the United States and Canada,* 200.

40. Act to Confirm the Title to Lands Held in Trust for Certain of the Indians Resident in This Province, S. Prov. C. 1866, c 20 (Can.).

41. Treaties and Historical Research Centre et al., *Historical Development of the Indian Act,* 34.

42. There are evident gender implications in terms of how colonial law and policy played out with regard to the loss of status for First Nations women and their children, but the particular relevance with regard to Métis is that it effectively barred all Métis from ever claiming status under the Indian Act in the first place.

43. Act to Amend and Consolidate the Laws Respecting Indians, S.C. 1876, c 18 (Can.).

44. Daniels v. Canada (Indian Affairs and Northern Development), [2016] S.C.C. 12 (Can.).

45. See, for example, Jennifer Adese, "A Tale of Two Constitutions: Métis Nationhood and Section 35(2)'s Impact on Interpretations of Daniels," *Topia* 36 (2016): 7–19.

46. An Act to Promote Gender Equity in Indian Registration by Responding to the Court of Appeal for British Columbia Decision in McIvor v. Canada (Registrar of Indian and Northern Affairs), S.C. 2010, c 18 (Can.).

47. An Act to Amend the Indian Act in Response to the Superior Court of Quebec Decision in Descheneaux c. Canada (Procureur général), S.C. 2017, c 25 (Can.).

48. An Act Respecting Indians, R.S.C. 1985, c I-5 (Can.).

49. Constitution Act, 1982, *being* Schedule B to the Canada Act, 1982, c 11 (U.K.).

50. For an interpretation of Section 31 as a fast-track version of the enfranchisement clauses, see Paul Chartrand, "Aboriginal Rights: The Dispossession of the Métis," *Osgoode Hall Law Journal* 29, no. 3 (1991): 457–82.

51. Heather Devine, *The People That Own Themselves: Aboriginal Ethnogenesis in a Canadian Family, 1660–1900* (Calgary: University of Calgary Press, 2004), 175–79 and 193–95; James Daschuk, *Clearing the Plains: Disease, Politics of Starvation, and the Loss of Aboriginal Life* (Regina, Saskatchewan: University of Regina Press, 2013), 163–64; and Hogue, *Metis and the Medicine Line,* 190–91.

52. Daschuk, *Clearing the Plains,* 163; and Hogue, *Metis and the Medicine Line,* 190.

53. An Act for Conferring Certain Privileges on the More Advanced Bands of the Indians of Canada, with the View of Training Them for the Exercise of Municipal Powers, S.C. 1884, c 28 (Can.) (The Indian Advancement Act).

54. R. v. Blais (2003), 2 S.C.R. 236, para. 14 (Can.).

55. Devine, *People That Own Themselves,* 178.

56. Gerhard Ens and Joe Sawchuck, *From New Peoples to New Nations: Aspects of Métis History and Identity from the Eighteenth to Twenty-First Centuries* (Toronto: University of Toronto Press, 2016), 205–9.

57. Canada, Parliament, *Sessional Papers,* 50 Vict., Vol 16, No 20b (1887) at 37 (Can.).

58. "*Cultural genocide* is the destruction of those structures and practices that allow the group to continue as a group. States that engage in cultural genocide set out to destroy the political and social institutions of the targeted group. Land is seized, and populations are forcibly transferred and their movement is restricted. Languages are banned. Spiritual leaders are persecuted, spiritual practices are forbidden, and objects of spiritual value are confiscated and destroyed. And, most significantly to the issue at hand, families are disrupted to prevent the transmission of cultural values and identity from one generation to the next." Canada, *Honouring the Truth, Reconciling for the Future: Summary of the Final Report of the Truth and Reconciliation Commission of Canada* (Ottawa: Truth and Reconciliation Commission of Canada, 2015), 1.

59. Cohen, *Federal Indian Law,* 207.

Extinguishing the Dead

Colonial Anxieties and Métis Scrip at the Fringe of Focus

JENNIFER ADESE

In the winter of 2018, I sat in the consultation room at Library and Archives Canada (LAC) in the traditional and contemporary territory of the Algonquin Nation; LAC sits on unceded Algonquin land, down from Parliament Hill, the home of Canada's federal government, and on the banks of the great river—Kiji Sibi. As I untied packets of documents bound with pink and red ribbons, examining handwritten scrip documents, I kept mental note of the number of familiar names I came across, the names of my own ancestors and those of many of my Métis and First Nations friends and colleagues. As I turned to my computer to cross-reference the material in front of me with LAC's digitized scrip archive, I began to notice that a number of scrip documents were issued not in the name of the living but in the name of those who had already died by the time the scrip was applied for. A quick scan through LAC's database revealed that it was more than an anomaly. Scrip applied for or issued in the name of deceased people—children, teenagers, adults, and older people—appeared as a commonplace practice. What at first struck me as incredibly morbid upon further reflection in fact seems quite consistent with Canada's indifference to Indigenous peoples. Given that the material foundations of Canada's parliamentary buildings are made from sand taken from Algonquin burial grounds that quite likely contains mixed fragments of bone of deceased Algonquin ancestors, it is clear that Canada has long sought to extinguish and assimilate Indigenous people in life and in death.[1]

In the later decades of the 1800s, various scrip commissions were established to extinguish the Indian title to land of the people of the Métis Nation. At that time, Métis people lived in close-knit communities within the homeland of their maternal ancestors, throughout the prairies, parkland, and boreal forest of what was then referred to by Canada as the North-West. Across this wide expanse, a new nation of postcontact Indigenous people had formed in the later decades of the 1700s, with a social and economic capital, of sorts, located at the nexus of the Red and Assiniboine Rivers, presently Winnipeg, Manitoba. In the wake of petitioning and organized resistance to Canadian colonization at Red River under a provisional council led by Louis Riel, the

Canadian government entered into a treaty with the Métis Nation—one that would bring a very small part of the Métis homeland into Confederation. The 1870 Manitoba Act included a promise of recognition of Métis land rights that, although never honored, set a foundation for later conceptualizations of Métis land rights. It directly entrenched a sense of obligation on the part of the Canadian government to reckon with Métis claims to land across the homeland.

The Canadian government viewed "half-breeds" (or "mixed-bloods," though more commonly referred to in governmental documents as the former) as entitled to land by way of their ties to Indianness and their existence as what Canadian prime minister Wilfrid Laurier (1896–1911) referred to as "first occupants" of the land:

> We determined at the outset, when we acquired the territory of the Hudson Bay Company [*sic*], that we would treat the halfbreeds as we would the Indians—that is, as first occupants of the soil. It has been the policy of the British Government from time immemorial not to take possession of any lands without having in some way settled with the first occupants and giving them compensation.[2]

As Darren O'Toole discusses in the previous essay within this volume, in the later decades of the 1800s, the vast majority of Métis living at the time Canada asserted dominion over their homeland saw their rights to land extinguished via what were called scrip commissions. The scrip commissions represented a widespread, wide-reaching, and generally rushed method by which Canada worked to extinguish what it viewed as Métis people's Indian rights, which would be used within a broader assimilationist national project intent on transforming Métis into Canadian (and, by extension, British) subjects.

While some Métis tried to navigate the scrip system to entrench their rights to the land in a manner that would be recognized and protected by the Canadian colonial government, it was an irreparably damaging project for nearly all involved. Most analyses of scrip commissions focus on their impacts on and for the living; in this short intervention, I am instead interested in discussing the material and emotional impacts of Canada's extension of the scrip system to the dead and those who survive them. This essay begins by explaining the scrip system before contextualizing its existence within a wider scope of assimilatory legislation; lastly, it addresses the extinguishment of Indian title of deceased Métis people. For the government's part, scrip provided a convenient way to transform Métis land relationships from collectively held to individually held land titles, marking a sharp turn into a capitalist system of land ownership rooted in the notion that single individuals have the ability to buy and sell land. Instead of stopping here, this system also made possible the alienation of what would have been

Métis people's individually held title lands and the transfer of such title (and lands) to those who were not Métis.

One example exists in the case of my great-auntie, Annabelle Lenny. In 1876, Annabelle Lenny (Lennie) was born near the shimmering waters of White Whale Lake (presently Duffield, Alberta). She was born to my great-great-grandmother Lucille (Lucie) Gladu. Lucie was a member of the Michel Band—a mixed community of Kanien'kehà:ka (from Akwesasne and Kahnawà:ke) who moved westward in their work with the Hudson's Bay Company (HBC), prairie-based Nêhiyaw, and Métis. At the time of Annabelle's birth, the Michel Band was not yet under treaty, but on September 18, 1878, when Chief Michel Callihoo and the band's headmen—including Lucie's father, Oskinikiw (a.k.a. Joseph Gladu)—assented to treaty, the band would become a part of Treaty 6. The signing of Treaty 6 led to the establishment of their reserve, located along the trail to Manitou Sakahigan (Lac Ste. Anne) and between Lac Ste. Anne and the Métis community (and mission) of St. Albert.

Lucie's husband and Annabelle's father, John Flett Lennie, was an Orcadian apprentice blacksmith who was indentured to HBC out of Stromness, Orkney. Upon arriving to the so-called North-West or Rupert's Land, he was placed in York Factory (Manitoba), Rainy Lake (Ontario), and Island Lake (Manitoba), before moving farther west to Fort Edmonton (Alberta). After his indenture ended, he returned to Europe before rejoining HBC as a laborer, eventually falling off of HBC's payroll. Lucie and John met and established their trading post and farm life together in White Whale Lake, also living at various points in the small Métis community of Long Lake (Kinokamau/Lac én Long), about 6 miles northwest of present downtown Edmonton.

Unlike most of her siblings, who survived into old age, Annabelle did not live to see the Michel Band enter treaty and was therefore never, even briefly, a "treaty Indian." Annabelle passed away from unknown causes in May 1878, at the age of two years old, while with her parents at Long Lake. Eight years after her passing, on February 27, 1886, Annabelle's father applied to the North-West Half-Breed Scrip Commission for scrip in Annabelle's name. Through the acceptance of his claim as Annabelle's sole heir, John was entitled to receive a promissory note (a scrip certificate) from the Canadian government that could be exchanged for either $160 or $240 or 160 or 240 acres of land, determined on the basis of "age and status."[3] In the name of Annabelle, John applied for and received a scrip promissory note in the amount of $160.

To this end, and thinking about the case of Annabelle, the later stages of the essay ask: How do we make sense of the allotment of scrip to Annabelle's father, a "white man," as her sole heir? What processes were at work in this particular process of land dispossession? Lastly, what does such a practice—of extinguishing the dead—reveal to us about Canada's ultimate goals with respect to Métis and other Indigenous people? Through archival research and autoethnographic reflection on this troubling dimension of Canada's colonial land regime, I argue that Canada's extension of the extinguishment process to the dead reveals much about the country's deep fears of Indigenous peoples and the potential for disrupting Canada's attempts to seamlessly entrench itself as sovereign on Indigenous lands. Extinguishing the dead's theoretical claim to land translated to extinguishing their very existence on the land. For Métis people in particular, the extinguishment of the deceased meant that Canada, as a country that would take up two armed attacks on the Métis Nation, worked to suffocate the possibility of the Métis Nation's future, while simultaneously morbidly extricating its past.

What is commonly called "Indian title," and to a lesser extent "Aboriginal title," is a British and Canadian interpretation of Indigenous land relationships that see Indigenous people as having claim to land arising "from long and continuous use and occupancy by native peoples prior to the effective assertion of European sovereignty (although the criteria for dating this event are not well established by the courts)."[4] While Indigenous peoples generally existed as stewards and caretakers of the land with collectively held responsibilities given to them by their respective Creators, laws, and protocols, Britain and, later, Canada sought to eradicate these collective ties and transmute the relationship into a nonrelationship, structuring a system of individually held fee simple title that would enable the capitalist exchange of land. As Canada sought to engender this new way of engaging with land and, according to Frank Tough, as the federal government attempted "to deal with Métis aboriginal title,"[5] it did so through adapting a land grant method it had variously deployed as "loyalist and militia scrip (Upper Canada), military-service land scrip, indemnity scrip . . . and road labour scrip (British Columbia)."[6] Tough and Erin McGregor note that "'scrip' is a term used to denote 'a certificate, voucher, etc. establishing the bearer's right to something'" and "was issued with the intent of 'extinguishing' Indian title by granting land (or money) to individual Metis people."[7] It represented "a curious attempt to mesh two notions about property—an Indian title that had to be extinguished and a European system of varied tenures and specific rights—but which promoted fee simple title in a frontier prairie region where a system of land registry had just been laid down."[8] It is this system that would be most directly implicated in the widespread dispossession of Métis people of land.

In the fall of 1869 and into 1870, Métis politically organized and asserted their nationhood in direct opposition to Canadian imperialism. Under Louis Riel, their vociferous opposition to Canada's attempt to assume control over their homeland forced Canada to acknowledge that "the Metis and Halfbreed populations were entitled to a share of Indian title."[9] This culminated in the first of three eras of scrip for Métis, as the Canadian government sought to reckon with promises for Métis land rights arising from within the Manitoba Act of 1870 that brought the Métis Nation heartland in Red River into Confederation.[10] With respect to land, the scrip system dealing with Métis people's land rights was a five-phase process. According to Tough and McGregor, it originated with the establishment of the scrip process in Ottawa; then it moved in country during the application phase, wherein, at various scrip commission sittings, Métis claimants made application for scrip and were issued provisional scrip certificates.[11] Initially, the standard scrip amount for Métis adults was for 160 acres (or dollars), following the American-style system of land allotment.[12] Children, by contrast, were allotted 240 acres (or dollars), presumably to account for inflation at the time they reached adulthood. Later, according to Leah Dorion and Darren R. Préfontaine, scrip amounts were increased across the board to "$240 or 240 acres to accommodate the increasing price of land."[13] Criteria were minimal, and were an applicant to have been previously paid treaty monies or to have "lived as an Indian," it would be remedied by deducting treaty payment monies from the scrip amount allowable.[14] Once the application was submitted and accepted in phase two, even before any kind of assignment of land or monies had been allocated, Métis people's Indian title was considered extinguished.

The certificate was then vetted through a process of paper entitlement, issuance, and approval by the Department of the Interior in Ottawa. In the fourth phase, the Dominion Lands Office would exchange scrip coupons for a location ticket identifying an acreage of land. Finally, the applicant could apply to the Dominion Lands Office for a land patent.[15] In order to convert scrip coupons to land, during the fourth phase the individual named on the scrip coupon was required to appear at a Dominion Lands Office near where they sought to select land. These offices were "located in cities and towns across the prairies and each was responsible for administering homestead lands in a region."[16] Upon arrival to the office, the Métis scrip grantee would locate the land they wanted "by pointing to an available section on the map."[17] At this point, an application for location would be forwarded to the Lands Patent Branch in Ottawa, where it would be verified against other patents to ensure no overlapping selections had been made and to ensure there were no other issues; then, "letters patent were sent to the patentee, confirming their right to obtain title to their lands."[18]

While Métis scrip grantees were ostensibly free to choose the location of their land, until agents of the Canadian government formally surveyed lands and rendered them available as homesteading lands, many Métis had no ability to choose the lands they were already living on or nearby where they were already living: "Surveyors made attempts to ensure land that was previously occupied was in the name of the rightful occupant, but those living on unsurveyed land were technically viewed as squatters and their rights to the land they occupied were not certain."[19] It was a convoluted process intended to enable "the federal government to allot western lands to new settlers, unencumbered by prior rights of use," while at the same time upending Métis attempts to assert their rights to the land they already lived on both individually and collectively.[20]

This process thus induced Métis to a fee simple, privatized land regime with little to no guarantee that they would be able to keep their families and communities intact. It was, ultimately, a system intended to alienate Métis from their land rights and transition them to homesteading and Canadian citizenship on par with settler Canadians. Through this process, however, Métis rarely ended up as homesteaders, because at its foundation the system was designed with the best interests of Canada—and not the Métis people—at heart.

Although Métis were in effect being pulled into a system alongside prospective homesteaders, the process for the alienation of Métis land rights through the land scrip process was notably different from the process for homesteaders. According to the Rupertsland Centre for Métis Research, homesteaders "needed to complete written application and complete certain conditions to receive ownership of their land," including but not limited to living on the land "for three consecutive years and bring[ing] land under cultivation. . . . In other words, homesteaders invested their labour and capital into 'improving the land.'"[21] No such provisions existed for Métis, an element that firmly demonstrates that this process was far less about inducing Métis people to a certain way of living and ensuring that Métis would be able to viably transition to homesteading life; rather, it was a process by which the Canadian government sought to rapidly extinguish Métis land rights while simultaneously dismantling Métis communities. This process would ultimately terminate any and all (future) claims to land Métis people might have on the basis of Indian title.

This formula was replicated across all three stages of the scrip commission process: in Manitoba in the 1870s, in the North-West throughout the prairies in the 1880s, and alongside signings of Treaty 8 and Treaty 10 in the northern part of the prairies.[22] While in some instances Métis actively pushed for scrip as a method of securing land rights,[23] it was one of the only available options to them as Métis were (for the most part) denied a relationship to Canada through the treaty-making process. Prior to the 1876 passage of the Indian Act, Canada's primary oppressive legislation defining and confining the category of "status Indian" and offering a comprehensive list of restrictions on those designated as status Indians, Métis could, generally speaking, be parties to treaties as so-called half-breeds. With the passage of the act, Section 3(e) expressly outlined that no half-breed "shall, unless under very special circumstances, to be determined by the Superintendent General or his agent, be accounted an Indian, or entitled to be admitted into any Indian treaty."[24] The act was further amended in 1880 to address those Métis who had already come under treaty and with a specific mind toward reconciling the treaty and scrip systems. Those who had taken treaty would be legally "allowed to withdraw therefrom on refunding all annuity money received by him or her under the said treaty, or suffering a corresponding reduction in the quantity of any land, or scrip, which such half-breed as such may be entitled to receive from the

Government."[25] Métis were accordingly ushered toward the scrip process and, in their petitioning for recognition and affirmation of collective land rights—Métis communities at Blackfoot Crossing (1877), Cypress Hill (1878), and Edmonton and St. Albert (1880)—they were ultimately ignored.[26]

The scrip system did not exist in isolation, and in terms of legislation aimed at eliminating Indian title, it was preceded by assimilatory legislation specifically targeting First Nations. The Province of Canada passed its first piece of assimilatory legislation as the Gradual Civilization Act, which the nation-state of Canada refined with the 1869 Gradual Enfranchisement Act (and the later Indian Act of 1876, as referenced above). The 1857 Gradual Civilization Act sought to induce Indigenous peoples to enfranchise—to forfeit any Indian title claims or otherwise—by meeting a set of established criteria. According to John Tobias, the criteria were such that few European colonists might actually meet them—applicants had to demonstrate literacy, be free of debt, and be of high moral character. For Tobias, this means that a "civilized Indian" had to be more civilized than a "civilized Euro-Canadian."[27] Upon approval of their application, they were forced to select a baptismal name, given an allotment "of twenty hectares of reserve land," "placed on one-year of probation to give further proof of being civilized," and "then given the franchise (and no longer considered, at least in the eyes of Canada's law and policy, as Indians)."[28] The effects of such legislative moves ultimately led to the same—the nullifying of Indian title, the decimation of collective landholding, and inducement to capitalist property regimes for both First Nations and Métis. Enfranchisement (First Nations) and extinguishment through scrip (Métis) were thus both part of Canada's legislative effort to secure title to Indigenous lands.

Policies geared toward eliminating First Nations and Métis land rights were notably different in two ways. First, First Nations people seeking to enfranchise had to demonstrate they were more civilized than settler Canadians. Métis only had to swear that they were not living "as Indians." As previously discussed, Métis were as well not subjected to the same system as homesteaders and did not have to demonstrate an ability to cultivate farming lands. The rapidity of the system reveals that civilization was far less the goal than extinguishment. Second, policies differ in how they approach the matter of inheritance. In both instances, Indian title is treated as inheritable. Death does not nullify Indian title. But a comparative reading of two overlapping approaches to assimilatory policies reveals that inheritance appears to have operated by distinctive logics for those being enfranchised (First Nations) and those whose Indian title claims were being extinguished (Métis)—and that enfranchisement and extinguishment as they pertain to Indigenous lands and to First Nations and Métis are themselves distinct in both policy and practice. As will be laid bare, enfranchisement ultimately meant that inheritance rights for (formerly) First Nations people would see allocations of reserve land that would be returned in death—meaning that an enfranchised Indian was still an Indian and bound by some conventions of the Indian Act. By contrast, the process for Métis looked quite different and carried rather shocking implications.

In order to tease out some of the ways that inheritance has functioned—in the absence of any preexisting studies of inheritance with respect to enfranchisement (First Nations) and extinguishment (Métis)—I turn now to a brief comparative discussion of legislative approaches to inheritance. First, the Gradual Enfranchisement Act of 1869 is the first piece of enfranchisement legislation to clearly outline an approach to inheritance with respect to Indians who are enfranchised Indians under its provisions. It dictates that deceased enfranchised Indians and their heirs have some measure of inheritance right as it pertains to land. Section 14 reads:

> If any enfranchised Indian owning land by virtue of the thirteenth and sixteenth sections of this Act, dies without leaving any children, such land shall escheat to the Crown for the benefit of the tribe, band, or body of Indians to which he, or his father, or mother (as the case may be) belonged: but if he leaves a widow, she shall, instead of Dower to which she shall not be entitled, have the said land for life or until her re-marriage, and upon her death or re-marriage it shall escheat to the Crown for the benefit of the tribe, band or body of Indians to which he, or his father, or mother (as the case may be) belonged.[29]

In death, land held by an enfranchised person would be inherited first by any living children, then by any widow, and lastly, in a case where neither of those parties exist, it would revert back to Crown control—for, of course, "the benefit" of the band to which they had once belonged (and to whom the land was still presumably attached).[30] This differs somewhat from the legal practice of coverture, seeing women's entitlement to land as property as explicitly tied to their husbands. Rather, as mentioned above, were a woman to remarry, her inheritance would revert back to the Crown—it would not transfer on to her new husband.

With respect to the scrip system, as early as 1875 and in the context of Métis in Manitoba, there was recognition that "the heirs of deceased claimants" would be entitled to receive a "proportion of the inheritance" that scrip was said to represent.[31] This was later crystallized on March 2, 1900, when an order-in-council affirmed:

> it had to be further admitted that those who had died during the period of inaction were entitled to benefit through their heirs. As it was recognized by Order in Council of 6th May, 1899, that the issue of scrip in 1885 should have extended to all Halfbreeds born in the Territories before and up to that time, it follows that those thus entitled who have died should

now benefit through their heirs. The Minister, therefore, considers that deceased Halfbreeds who would if they were living be entitled to scrip, should in the proposed issue of scrip take by right.[32]

What this establishes is that it was not just land that was seen as property, and therefore inheritable, but so, too, was the very intangible right to scrip (and the potential for eventual transmuting to land) that was both property and inheritable.

It appears that members of the Privy Council worked to bridge gaps in available legislation by borrowing from other areas of inheritance law. In particular, the rationale for creating a system of heirship within the scrip system was formed through newly developed scrip legislation itself and inheritance law. In particular, the "right of representation" was put forth to rationalize the extension of inheritance rights to living heirs of deceased Métis.[33] The right of representation in the context of inheritance essentially means that an heir takes from a deceased person's estate "a share equal to that of the individual they're representing."[34] In a case where a person passes away and their child is entitled to inherit their estate, if that child has predeceased the parent, their children (the initial person's grandchildren) would inherit as representatives of their deceased parent. What we might surmise from this is that its intention is to position certain heirs as stand-ins for rightful heirs. This followed precedent set in the scrip being treated as inheritable relative to, for example, military scrip for land, where scrip was treated as land itself. What, then, does this mean in the context of scrip wherein the right of representation is being used to transfer money/land for compensation of the forfeiture of Métis people's entitlement to Indian title to white men? I will return to this question shortly.

A search of the LAC online archive populates 9,498 records when the terms *Métis, heir,* and *scrip* are input together. Some of these are, to be sure, documents related to the claims in one file. For instance, in 1875, Joseph Vivier applied as the sole heir (in spite of the fact that his wife Caroline Short was still alive) for his daughter Caroline Victoria, who died age two and a half in 1872. He "claims his daughter's share in allotment of land set apart for Métis children."[35] He also applied as the sole heir of another daughter with a different mother, Marguerite Hamelin, under the same claim.[36] In the case of William Swain, he applied as sole heir to Josephte Azure (as a Métis child), for which he received a scrip certificate for $240.[37] Baptiste Fosseneuve filed a claim (no. 1892) for five of his and Marie Desjarlais's children—Antoine (who died at one year old in 1874), Eliza (who died in January 1887 at the age of about two years old), Marguerite (who died at about eleven years old in 1886), Josue (who died in 1888 at about eleven years old), and Adelaide (who died at thirteen years old in 1890)—some of which were as money scrip and some as land scrip.[38]

In the case of Justine and Virginie Nault, who died at ages four and two in 1885 at St. Albert, their widowed mother, Philomene Nault, listed both herself and their surviving siblings—Marie Rose Nault, Adelaide Bellerose, Marcelline Nault, and John Nault—as their heirs. Each was entitled to a total of eight dollars.[39] On July 20, 1885, my great-great-grandmother Adelaide Dubé applied for scrip as a legal representative for Virginie Gariepy, Olive Desrochers, their deceased brother Narcisse (who died "without issue"—or children), and herself as heirs of their late mother, Marie Suprenant, who had passed away fifteen years earlier, on September 14, 1870, at the age of thirty years old. The sisters were issued promissory notes by the North-West Half-Breed Scrip Commission for either lands or cash totaling $160. Each of the three was entitled to one equal share amounting to $53.33 of either cash or "Dominion Lands."[40] As Tough notes, "Coupons of less than the normal value were issued to heirs who shared in the award to a deceased claimant."[41] This reflects, as well, the right of representation at work. In the aforementioned cases, however, all those making claims as heirs were themselves Métis people.

As with the Gradual Enfranchisement Act, within the scrip system inheritance rights appear to have gone first to living children. In the absence of living children, however, a deceased person's interest in scrip would be transferred first to their widow, then to their father (irrespective of whether the mother was alive), and lastly to their siblings and widowed mothers (who appear to have shared equally). As Annabelle had no living children, John Flett Lennie was able to apply for scrip as her sole heir, as a white man, and as the head of household. As scrip applications required the attestation of witnesses, witnesses would have affirmed that John was, certainly, Annabelle's father, and the details provided in the application were in fact true. Had Annabelle been alive and still a minor, her father would have had to apply on her behalf anyway.[42] But even in death, her father was seen as holding some right of representation that enabled him to apply on her behalf. Since Lucie Lennie was still alive, the implication here would be that coverture applied—that a married woman's inheritance rights were tied to her husband and that unless themselves widowed, they would never be able to access scrip of their children in such cases. Yet in the case of Adelaide Dubé and her sisters Virginie and Olive, they were allowed to apply as heirs to their deceased mother and at no point does it appear that they were compelled to turn over what they inherited through the scrip process to their husbands. If coverture did apply, then presumably any inheritance they had would become property of their husbands.

What did appear to be at work, however, was an approach that paid little attention to the symbolic and material impacts of allowing white men to extinguish the Indian title of their deceased relatives. At first glance, a purportedly equitable approach to inheritance that did not distinguish between the whiteness of John Lennie and the Indianness of Adelaide and her sisters belies the fact that the system was born from anti-Indigenous racism and Canada's desire to extinguish as many Métis claims to land as possible in whatever manner was expedient. What is most notable here, however, is that while in the case of First Nations, enfranchisement legislation makes provisions for the inheritance of property (of land itself), the scrip system makes the promise of land (or money) inheritable. It is the entitlement that is inheritable:

> When the Department decided, in retrospect, to recognize the Indian title of Métis born in the organized Territories between 15 July, 1870 and the end of the year 1885, questions were raised as to whether scrip should also be given to the heirs of deceased Métis children, who were residents of the Territories during the period of inaction, and who would have participated in a scrip claim if they had lived. The Minister of the Interior reasoned that, since the issue of scrip should have been extended to all Métis of the North-West Territories born up to 1885, "... it follows that those entitled who have died should now benefit through their heirs" (P.C. 438, 2 March, 1900, p. 2); otherwise the Aboriginal title of their heirs would not be properly extinguished. The Alberta and Saskatchewan Commission was, therefore, authorized under P.C. 438, 2 March, 1900, to accept claims from heirs of deceased Métis.
>
> However, in the Treaty 8 settlement and all subsequent settlements which would be signed in conjunction with an Indian Treaty, the heirs of deceased Métis would only be recognized in cases where a scrip recipient had died in the time period which had lapsed after filing an application with the Commission and the receipt of the actual scrip from the Department.[43]

To be clear, were land to have been conferred through the scrip system on a Métis person, no particular provisions applied beyond those that would apply to any other Canadian regarding inheritance. In fact, the government treated scrip as land/money, not just as the promise of it. But something distinctive happens wherein deceased people are cast as claimants and their prospective claim is something already immediately inheritable. If they were entitled to it in life, their heirs are therefore entitled to it in death. It is framed not as a process of aggressively extinguishing the rights of people indigenous to the land but as a benefit. Living people could make claims as the heirs of the deceased and were entitled to receive, in whole or in part, their promissory scrip notes and whatever was to become of them.[44]

Crucially, this system was not at all concerned with reserving any land for Métis people. In the case of enfranchised Indians, in the absence of legitimate heirs, land reverted back to the Crown for the benefit of the whole of the community (thus, in effect, ensuring the continuance of some form of Indian title, even for enfranchised people).

The default reversion back to the collective, even for an enfranchised Indian, marks a substantial difference from scrip processes. Land under the scrip process would forever and always be set apart from a communal or collective Métisness. It would never revert back to Indian title lands at any point. In the absence of qualified heirs making application, the entitlement to scrip simply did not exist and no entrenched mechanism was built in place to ensure that the land acquired (if ever it truly was) stayed in the hands of Métis people or communities.

This is nowhere more evident than in the fact that white men were permitted to—and often did—apply as heirs of their deceased Métis children. In the case of Annabelle (and many others, in spite of the presence of living Indigenous mothers), her white father, John, successfully applied as her sole heir. The scrip system seems to have operated in a manner that accorded inheritance to anyone who met basic relationship criteria. This omission, or its operation as intended, meant that a far greater number of scrip certificates fell into the hands of white men than scholarly research focused solely on white scrip speculators has previously accounted for.[45] Annabelle is one of thousands of Métis people whose Indian title was extinguished after their deaths, and she represents within that a disturbing practice of transferring Métis people's Indian title to white men. Someone who was able to acquire land via homesteading processes could find a much easier path to land surety by extinguishing the Indian title of their deceased Métis children; at the same time, it had the potential to sizably increase either their monetary wealth or their landholdings. While I hold space for those Métis who may have seen accessing scrip in the name of their deceased relatives as important to their survival—the promise of land or monies on the basis of their rights of inheritance to the property of their deceased relatives might provide much-needed relief in trying times, and this would have only been necessary due to the profound disruption wrought by the hyperintensive push of Canada's colonial land regime—I have found no clearly articulated rationale for granting scrip to white men beyond far too simple explanations that patriarchy (and inconsistently applied principles of coverture) meant that in some cases men and fathers held first inheritance rights.

Such an explanation feels far too convenient and far too simplistic. Canada demonstrated a clear commitment to eliminating Métis land rights, to eradicating all Indigenous ties to land. The scrip system and its approach to cases of deceased people therefore cannot be solely explained by patriarchy entrenched within the logic of British and Canadian inheritance laws. Indian title and scrip are inalienably tied to questions of land, identity, colonization, and genocide. In spite of Laurier's more positive framing, the extension of scrip to Métis arose for far more insidious reasons; we cannot excuse this fact from our minds in our analysis of the process in its entirety. While there are undoubtedly contradictions even within how scrip was administered to heirs and situations that might defy the practices I have identified here, as Canada's first prime minister and the first prime minister to oversee the creation of a scrip commission, John A. Macdonald stated in a speech to the House of Commons shortly following the Northwest Resistance in 1885: "We, at the last moment, made concessions. The Government knew . . . that we were not acting in the interests of the half-breed in granting them scrip . . . and I said 'Well, for God's sake let them have the scrip; they will either drink it or waste it or sell it; but let us have peace.'"[46] The truth lies within both Laurier's and Macdonald's descriptions of scrip. On the one hand, the British viewed so-called half-breeds as having some claim on the land and believed that the Crown (and later Canada) would be bound to honor and address this. On the other hand, scrip provided a convenient way in which to extinguish Métis entitlement to land on the basis of Indianness through a model that was not intended to be of benefit to Métis and, as Macdonald's words reflect, that was created with the full knowledge that it would, in fact, be harmful to and for Métis.

Tough and McGregor powerfully argue that while the scrip represented the potential for some measure of protection of Métis land, "in the long run, it may have, apart from a small group of scrip buyers, failed for all concerned."[47] Likewise, Maggie Siggins asserts that the scrip system process led to "the biggest land grab in the nation's history," whereby "unscrupulous white speculators" would "become fabulously wealthy by cheating Métis people out of their government-appointed scrip land."[48] Even more than this, given that Métis people derive their Indigeneity from their relationship to their homelands, the extinguishment of ties to land is tantamount to an extinguishment of Métis as an Indigenous people. The obliteration of Métis ties to land proceeded alongside other processes of Indigenous alienation and dispossession—residential schooling, the dismantling of traditional governments, the banning of ceremonial practices, and the confinement of people to reserves as holding pens during the process of civilization, to name just a few examples. Given the wholesale assault on First Nations, Métis, and Inuit, it is easy to surmise that Indigenous people were never intended to survive colonization. Even if we accept that we were to physically survive, we were never to be more than vessels emptied out of our Indigeneity and divorced from deeper relationships to land that might stand in moral and ethical opposition to Canadian nation-building and its voracious capitalist aspirations.

Métis, like other Indigenous peoples, then, remain some of the only people in the past 150 years to be forcefully made Canadian. It becomes clear that scrip's focus on extinguishing Métis land rights was as much about extinguishing whatever relationship Métis had to the land so that Canada could continue to further its conquest. By extinguishing Métis people's Indian title, the stance of the Canadian government was clearly that those who once were Indigenous must no longer be—they must instead become Canadian. By extending extinguishment to the dead, Canada tried to ensure that not only would there be no future for Métis as an Indigenous people but even those no longer living could not be left to rest as the Indigenous people they were. They, too, must be drawn up into Canada's colonizing machine, removed from Indigeneity, and forced into Canadianness. Canada wanted to ensure that it resolved the "Indian land question" in a manner so airtight as to suffocate even the no longer living. The nation must cast itself backward into the (after)life of the dead so that there will be no prospective claim left unsquashed, no possibility of future claims on the land, no Métis future or past, and no reminder that another way once was—and might yet still be possible.

NOTES

1. Randy Boswell, "Time to Acknowledge Evidence: Parliament Hill Sits on Indigenous Territory," iPolitics, November 9, 2018, https://ipolitics.ca/2018/11/09/time-to-acknowledge-evidence-parliament-hill-sits-on-indigenous-territory/.
2. Rupertsland Centre for Métis Research and the Métis Nation of Alberta, *Métis Scrip in Alberta* (Edmonton: Rupertsland Centre for Métis Research, 2018), https://cloudfront.ualberta.ca/-/media/nativestudies/rcmr/publications/rcmr-scrip-booklet-2018-final-150dpi.pdf.
3. Camie Augustus, "Métis Scrip," kā-kī-pē-isi-nakatamākawiyahk Our Legacy: Essays, http://digital.scaa.sk.ca/ourlegacy/exhibit_scrip.
4. Peter J. Usher, Frank Tough, and Robert M. Galois, "Reclaiming the Land: Aboriginal Title, Treaty Rights, and Land Claims in Canada," *Applied Geography* 12, no. 2 (1992): 113.
5. Usher, Tough, and Galois, "Reclaiming the Land," 114.
6. John C. Weaver, *Great Land Rush and the Making of the Modern World, 1650–1900* (Montreal: McGill–Queen's University Press, 2003), 280.
7. Frank Tough and Erin McGregor, "'The Rights to the Land May Be Transferred': Archival Records as Colonial Text—A Narrative of Metis Scrip," *Canadian Review of Comparative Literature/Revue Canadienne de Littérature Comparée* 34, no. 1 (2011): 36.
8. Tough and McGregor, "'Rights to the Land,'" 57.
9. Usher, Tough, and Galois, "Reclaiming the Land," 114.
10. Augustus, "Métis Scrip," 93.
11. Tough and McGregor, "'Rights to the Land.'"
12. According to Jeffrey S. Murray, parliamentarians extensively debated the size of land allotments for homesteading, with many feeling that Canada should allot lands in plots larger than the American government did because "they felt the larger-sized homesteads would make Canada a more attractive destination for immigrants." Ultimately, they settled on the same size as the American system. Jeffrey S. Murray, "Free Land!," Library and Archives Canada, March 27, 2006, https://www.collectionscanada.gc.ca/immigrants/021017-2212-e.html.
13. Leah Dorion and Darren R. Préfontaine, "Métis Land Rights and Self-Government," Gabriel Dumont Institute, May 30, 2003, http://www.metismuseum.ca/resource.php/00725.
14. See, for example, the scrip application for Lucille Gladu: Lucille Gladu, NWHB scrip claim #711, vol. 1329, series D-II-8-b, reel C-14938, RG15, LA, Library and Archives Canada, Ottawa.
15. See Figure 3, "Land Scrip—The General Model, 00.1907," in Tough and McGregor, "'Rights to the Land,'" 14.

16. Rupertsland Centre for Métis Research and the Métis Nation of Alberta, *Métis Scrip in Alberta*.

17. Rupertsland Centre for Métis Research and the Métis Nation of Alberta.

18. Rupertsland Centre for Métis Research and the Métis Nation of Alberta.

19. Rupertsland Centre for Métis Research and the Métis Nation of Alberta.

20. Murray, "Free Land!"

21. Murray.

22. To be eligible for scrip through the first two commissions, it was held that all those half-breeds who lived in the North-West prior to July 15, 1870 (the date Britain transferred its claims to Rupert's Land over to Canada and the date Manitoba entered into Confederation) would be entitled to apply for scrip.

23. Melanie Niemi-Bohun, "Colonial Categories and Familial Responses to Treaty and Metis Scrip Policy: The 'Edmonton and District Stragglers,' 1870–88," *Canadian Historical Review* 90, no. 1 (2009): 79.

24. The Indian Act, 1876, S.C. 1876, c. 18 (Can.).

25. Indian Act.

26. Indian Act.

27. John L. Tobias, "Protection, Civilization, Assimilation: An Outline History of Canada's Indian Policy," in *Sweet Promises: A Reader on Indian-White Relations in Canada,* ed. J. R. Miller (Toronto: University of Toronto Press, 1976), 130.

28. Tobias, "Protection, Civilization, Assimilation," 130. In terms of the differences in the size of land allocated to enfranchised Indians versus Métis under half-breed scrip systems, I can only surmise that this is precisely because the land allocated to enfranchised Indians came directly from the reserve—the system was intended to carve up reserves into individual allotments to gradually phase out the reserve system. Larger allotments were not possible under such circumstances. As to why enfranchisment was the focus versus extinguishment (meaning why enfranchised Indians were not subjected to a similar scrip process), I can only assume that this is because this represents an initial stage in the development of alienation and assimilation policies that become gradually refined over time. It may be that further research into enfranchisement policies will reveal additional motives on the part of Canada.

29. An Act for the Gradual Enfranchisement of Indians, the Better Management of Indian Affairs, and to Extend the Provisions of the Act 31st Victoria, Chapter 42, 1869 (Can.), https://www.aadnc-aandc.gc.ca/DAM/DAM-INTER-HQ/STAGING/texte-text/a69c6_1100100010205_eng.pdf.

30. To a separate point, I would argue that this creates a second order of enfranchisement wherein for enfranchised Indians they still do not have free and clear title—that the land can eventually become part of the reserve again, in the absence of a viable heir. This places limits on how an enfranchised person can confer their land as a part of inheritance rights. By contrast, Métis people faced no such clause—once their rights were extinguished the land was forever and always a part of Canada's capitalist land system.

31. "Métis Scrip Records," Library and Archives Canada, accessed October 18, 2018, https://www.collectionscanada.gc.ca/metis-scrip/005005-3150-e.html.

32. Privy Council Minutes 2 March 1900, R.G. 2, series 1, vol 825 (U.K.).

33. Privy Council Minutes.

34. Julie Garber, "Understanding Your Will: What Is 'Per Stirpes'?" The Balance, January 30, 2019, https://www.thebalance.com/per-stirpes-definition-in-wills-3505583.

35. Joseph Vivier, Métis and Original White Settlers affidavits scrip claim #R190–43-X-E, vol. 1324, series D-II-8-a, reel C-14934, RG15, LA, Library and Archives Canada, Ottawa.

36. Joseph Vivier, Métis and Original White Settlers affidavits scrip claim #R190–43-X-E, vol. 1324, series D-II-8-a, reel C-14934, RG15, LA, Library and Archives Canada, Ottawa.

37. Josephte Azure, NWHB scrip claim #1312, vol. 1325, series D-II-8-b, reel C-14936, RG15, LA, Library and Archives Canada, Ottawa.

38. Baptiste Fosseneuve, NWHB scrip claim #1892, vol. 1348, series D-II-8-c, reel C-14970, RG15, LA, Library and Archives Canada, Ottawa.

39. Philomene Nault, NWHB scrip claim #2926, vol. 1361, series D-II-8-c, reel C-14993, RG15, LA, Library and Archives Canada, Ottawa.

40. Marie Blandion (née Suprenant), NWHB scrip claim #614, vol. 1325, series D-II-8-b, reel C-14936, RG15, LA, Library and Archives Canada, Ottawa.

41. Tough and McGregor, "'Rights to the Land,'" 59.

42. Rupertsland Centre for Métis Research and the Métis Nation of Alberta, *Métis Scrip in Alberta*.

43. "Métis Scrip Records," Library and Archives Canada, accessed November 1, 2019, https://www.collectionscanada.gc.ca/metis-scrip/005005-3400-e.html.

44. See Tough and McGregor, "'Rights to the Land,'" 53–55.

45. At this stage, I have yet to find any indication that white women similarly engaged in a practice of applying for scrip in the name of their deceased Métis children (and, in fact, have yet to see a scrip application wherein a mother is listed as white).

46. Quoted in Niemi-Bohun, "Colonial Categories and Familial Responses to Treaty," 80.

47. Tough and McGregor, "'Rights to the Land,'" 57.

48. Siggins quoted in Warren Cariou, "Haunted Prairie: Aboriginal 'Ghosts' and the Spectres of Settlement," *University of Toronto Quarterly* 75, no. 2 (2006): 729–30.

Makhóčhe Khípi

A Dakota Family Story of Race, Land,
and Dispossession before the Dawes Act

JAMESON R. SWEET

Dakhóta wóyakapi kíŋ dé héčha (This is a Dakota story).[1] Mary Wacouta, a Dakota woman of mixed European and Dakota Indian ancestry, filed a lawsuit in 1864 with the Wabasha County District Court in Minnesota. She alleged that Artemas Sharpe, a prominent Connecticut-born farmer, had planted fields on her land and stolen hundreds of dollars' worth of crops that had been stored in her home. Through an interpreter, Wacouta testified that she had built the house and farm in 1853 on her land on the Lake Pepin reservation, a reservation explicitly for the use of mixed-ancestry Dakota Indians. "I have forbidden him in Sioux probably 10 times" from plowing her lands, she said, eventually asking her mixed-ancestry Dakota neighbor, Frank Trudell, called Hepí (Third Born Son) in Dakota, to confront Sharpe in English on her behalf. Sharpe testified that Hepí never forbid him from plowing her land. In Hepí's testimony, corroborated by his brother August Trudell, named Thatóheya (Against the Wind), however, he testified that he told Sharpe not to plow on Wacouta's land. Hepí testified that Sharpe offered him fifty dollars "if he would get Pl[ainti]ff out of possession of [her] property."[2] In this case, Sharpe attempted to dispossess Mary Wacouta out of her land and home. Indians of mixed ancestry were not exempt from land dispossession, or *makhóčhe khípi* (they steal the land), but unlike Dakota tribal lands that the American government acquired through dishonest and coercive treaties, Dakota people of mixed ancestry experienced an array of individually based dispossessive practices at the hands of non-Indian squatters, settlers, and land speculators.

The Upper Midwest was an unusual place in the mid-nineteenth-century United States as lawmakers debated the "whiteness" of Indians of mixed ancestry, and under the laws of Minnesota, Indians of mixed white and Indian ancestry held American citizenship. When the Territory of Minnesota was founded in 1849, one of the first laws of the territorial legislature was to enfranchise "persons of a mixture of white and Indian blood."[3] Those enfranchised made the best of their situation and a number of mixed-ancestry Dakota, Ojibwe, Odawa, and Métis men served in the Minnesota state and territorial legislatures between 1849 and the U.S.–Dakota War of 1862, after which the state sharply curtailed the rights of mixed-ancestry Indians.[4] On the eve of statehood, Minnesota lawmakers pondered making mixed-ancestry Indians white, best summed up by missionary Stephen Riggs in 1857: "They propose to make a new dictionary meaning of the word white so that it shall include all mixed bloods of Indian descent."[5] Indeed, whiteness and American citizenship became synonymous, while mixed-ancestry Indians of African descent were explicitly excluded from both whiteness and citizenship. This newfound whiteness also meant that the property of mixed-ancestry Indians was subject to the jurisdiction of Minnesota.

For Indians of mixed white and Indian ancestry in the Midwest, their separate status as "half-breeds" (an undefined legal term in the United States that came to mean any Indians that were "part white" and excluded those of African ancestry) under the 1830 Treaty of Prairie du Chien and their claim to fictive whiteness made them eligible to own, in addition to shared tribal lands, individual parcels of land in ways that their full-ancestry relatives could not under American law. The 1830 Treaty of Prairie du Chien created the Lake Pepin reservation on the west bank of the Mississippi and the Great Nemaha reservation in southeastern Nebraska, intended for the use of mixed-ancestry Dakota, Iowa, Omaha, and Oto Indians. This treaty was part of a series of treaties in the 1820s and 1830s that set aside land for the growing population of mixed-ancestry Indians throughout the Midwest. In addition, the treaty explicitly stated that the mixed-ancestry Dakota held their land "in the same manner, and by the same title that other Indian titles are held."[6] The muddled nature of landownership among mixed-ancestry Indians in the nineteenth century confused American lawmakers, leading an American official, E. A. Hitchcock, to proclaim, "Half-breeds are neither white men nor Indians. . . . The proper treatment of them is neither defined in the regulations, nor perhaps, established by usage."[7] White Americans sometimes considered mixed-ancestry Indians to be white, at other times Indians, and occasionally held that "half-breeds" were members of yet another racial group with a different legal status and set of legal rights. Mixed-ancestry Indians were forced to navigate these murky, ever-changing, and competing understandings of their racial status and landholding rights, which sometimes worked in their favor and sometimes not.

Cheryl Harris argues that "rights in property are contingent on, intertwined with, and conflated with race." Landownership, citizenship, and whiteness became inextricably linked; this is demonstrated in the foundation of federal Indian law, where white Americans constructed a system where they had a fundamental right to Indian land. Harris asserts that "only whites possessed whiteness, a highly valued and exclusive form of property," but in this case, Indians of mixed ancestry held a kind of "fictive" whiteness permitting them, for a time, to own property and "whiteness."[8] Dakota people of mixed ancestry acquired the Lake Pepin reservation because of their fictitious whiteness but later experienced dispossession because of their Indianness. The racial ambiguity of mixed-ancestry Dakota enabled them to own individual lands and exercise their legal rights in the American legal system through a form of white privilege, while at the same time suffering under the racist American machinery of Indian land dispossession.

Through the experiences of my ancestors, the Trudell family, I explore the ways that this racial ambiguity operated and what it meant for their landownership rights and practices. In 1855, my white great-great-great-grandfather placed his x-mark on an affidavit claiming, "I, Francis Trudell, of Dacotah County Min[nesota] Terr[itory] (near Mendota) do solemnly swear that I am a Canadian Frenchman. About twenty years ago I was married by Indian custom to a Sioux woman of the Medawahkanton [*sic*] band. . . . We live together and have seven children now living. . . . They are Half Breeds, & all live with us."[9] Francis described three different racial and ethnic categories within his own family: himself as a white French Canadian; his wife, Ičíyapiwiŋ (Woman Who Assists Them), called Mary Trudell in English, my great-great-great-grandmother, as an Indian of the Bdewákhaŋthuŋwaŋ (Dwellers at Spirit Lake) band of Dakota; and his children as "half-breeds." Francis articulated three different racial categories within his own family, but over their lifetimes the children of Ičíyapiwiŋ and Francis Trudell navigated through all three categories.

The lives of mixed-ancestry Indians have often been portrayed as on the periphery of the Indigenous experience, but I want to illuminate their lives as part of the diversity of Indigeneity and rewrite their lives and, in this case, their dispossession back into the broader narrative of the Native experience. Unfortunately for Indians of African ancestry in the Midwest, American officials typically excluded them from the categories of whiteness, Indianness, and mixedness: only one Dakota family, the two surviving children of ex-slave James Thompson and his wife, a daughter of Chief Maȟpíya Wičháŝta (Cloud Man), were deemed eligible for land at Lake Pepin; Thompson's granddaughter married a grandson of Francis Trudell and Ičíyapiwiŋ and left numerous descendants. So as not to normalize the colonial language of "blood," I use the term *mixed ancestry*. But this too is problematic in that it is a stand-in for the colonial racial and legal category of "half-breed" or "mixed-blood." Mixed-ancestry Dakota people engaged with these categories not as an identity but rather as a way to navigate within the power of the American state as a strategy of survival. Most of this population retained a Dakota identity and probably used Dakota terms that referred to their understandings of mixedness, such as *iyéska* (literally "translator") or *wašíču čhiŋčá* (children of white people).

Ičíyapiwiŋ, my great-great-great-grandmother and the matriarch of the Trudell family, was born in the spring of 1816 to Waŋbdíŝuŋ (Eagle Feather) and Thatékhoyakewiŋ (Wind Clad Woman), members of the Bdewákhaŋthuŋwaŋ band of Dakota. Francis Trudell, born Francois Perron dit Trudell about 1799 in Quebec, came to Dakota country in the summer of 1828 to work in the fur trade. He worked for the American Fur Company for several years and married Ičíyapiwiŋ in a Dakota ceremony about 1835.

They remained married until Francis's death on the Santee reservation in 1881, during which time they had fourteen children, only six of whom grew to adulthood. After the family moved from the Lake Pepin region to the Santee reservation in Nebraska in the late 1870s, Ičíyapiwiŋ spent the rest of her life there and lived to the age of ninety-five at her death in 1911.

In the thirty years from the foundation of the Lake Pepin reservation to 1860, the mixed-ancestry Dakota sent over a dozen petitions to the federal government as a strategy to protect their land. Mixed-ancestry Indians in Minnesota petitioned the government to protect their lands but also requested help as U.S. citizens, a privilege that their full-ancestry relatives did not have. Through their petitions, they successfully blocked the government from instituting a blood quantum standard for eligibility to land at Lake Pepin and requested the removal of squatters, but most often requested the government divide the land among the claimants. On October 14, 1853, the mixed-ancestry Dakota met in Wabasha to sign a petition to Minnesota Territory governor Willis Gorman. The petitioners complained that white squatters were trespassing on their reservation and that they were "destroying our best timber, and laying out a portion of our land into a town plat and offering lots for sale," and asked the governor to aid them by removing the squatters.[10] The signers of this petition perceived they were being dispossessed in two ways: by the theft of land but also through the theft of timber, which they recognized as a particularly valuable resource. Francis Trudell signed the petition on behalf of five of his mixed-ancestry children. Three weeks later, on November 5, the mixed-ancestry Dakota signed another petition, this time on the Dakota reservation in the western part of the territory. This petition bore the x-marks of the same five Trudell children and suggested "that a conveyance be made of the whole tract to the U. States, in consideration of Land Warrants, to be granted to each of the parties for as much land as they would be entitled to individually." They argued that the territorial delegate to Congress, Henry Rice, "can no doubt but accomplish what is desired."[11]

Rice did accomplish what was desired with the passage of a congressional act on July 17, 1854, offering land scrip (a legal document that entitles the bearer to a specific, guaranteed acreage) to the mixed-ancestry Dakota in exchange for their reservation, just as they had asked in their petition.[12] The act provided that each mixed-ancestry Dakota would receive land scrip for 480 acres and that it could be located on any of the unoccupied lands on the reservation or any unoccupied public lands in the United States. The act forbade the conveyance of the scrip and required the government to determine the number and names of the claimants.[13] This legislation set in motion a series of events that dissolved the Lake Pepin reservation and put the land into the hands of individuals. This turned out to be a disastrous course of action and most mixed-ancestry Dakota were cheated out of their land or scrip within a decade.

Through this 1854 law and the lengthy process that followed, the Trudell family collectively acquired 3,360 acres of so-called half-breed land. Most of that land was lost within a year of obtaining it in 1857. On May 25, 1857, on behalf of his children, Francis placed his x-mark next to their names, relinquishing their right to the Lake Pepin reservation.[14] This relinquishment was necessary under the 1854 law granting mixed-ancestry Dakota land scrip in exchange for their reservation. General James Shields, a commissioner working on behalf of the Office of Indian Affairs, signed over the scrip of the seven Trudell recipients to their father in Wabasha, as was typical in the case of minors.[15] Francis Trudell and other white fathers or husbands of mixed-ancestry Dakota women held significant power in the affairs of their Indian families in terms of trying to protect their lands and in their dispossession.

Starting just two weeks after accepting his children's scrip, Francis appeared before Judge Lemon Bates of the Goodhue County Probate Court eight times to legally complete the sale of his children's lands. Of the seven children that received scrip, Hepí was the oldest, aged about nineteen in 1857. Joseph was the next oldest at sixteen, while Thatóheya, Henry, Peter, and Levi were all under eight years old and Elizabeth was dead at the time their father sold their land. On June 11, Francis requested that the court appoint him guardian, which the court approved on July 10, with authority to sell their real estate. Francis sold most of his children's land on September 14 at auction at the Real Estate Office of Smith, Towne & Co. in Red Wing, Minnesota. The remaining lands were in Wabasha County, and Francis later received permission from the court to sell those too. Francis reported that at an auction at the Lake City Hotel in Wabasha on November 30, he sold the remaining 280 acres.[16] Francis made a small fortune of $2,600 on September 14 and acquired an additional $350 on November 30. While Francis used some of the money to buy and resell other lands, most of the money was probably squandered soon after, considering in the 1860 U.S. Census, unlike for his neighbors, the enumerator did not list a monetary value for any real estate or personal property that he might have owned.[17]

The Trudell family led an itinerant lifestyle, and the extant records suggest the family lived in poverty, which was probably the only prompt Francis needed to sell his children's land. The historical record of the Trudell family is rich with their economic activities and particularly with their indebtedness. Francis had become indebted to the American Fur Company multiple times, during and after his service with the company. Henry Sibley, a partner of the American Fur Company and resident of Minnesota, sued Francis in 1841 to recover another debt, which Francis paid out of court.[18] From the 1830s to the 1860s, to pay his debts, Francis occasionally labored for Indian traders and Indian agents. For instance, Francis labored for the Odawa Indian trader Alexis Bailly in the 1830s and 1840s, and he was paid by Indian agent Charles Flandrau for ten days of labor on the Dakota reservation in the spring of 1857.[19] Francis paid a small tax in 1848 on his personal property in Prescott, Wisconsin, on the east bank of the Mississippi, valued at fifty dollars, tied with W. C. Copley for the lowest valued property in Prescott that year.[20] At the same time, Ičíyapiwiŋ and her children occasionally received annuities as a member of Šákpe's (also known as Shakopee or "Little Six") band, and the family received $500 in 1838 for their firstborn son, Baptist Trudell, who died young, as part of a payment to mixed-ancestry Dakota in the Treaty of Washington in 1837.[21] This mix of American and Native economic practices was typical of mixed-ancestry families in the early Midwest.

The Trudell children, however, maintained a different story of their makhóčhe khípi, or dispossession, in which their father was cheated out of their land by other whites. It is unknown why the children waited so long to press their claims, but Thatóheya, also known as August Trudell, wrote to Judge S. J. Willard of the newly founded National Indian Defense Association in 1886, inquiring about the land scrip of the Trudell children. Thatóheya wrote, "Our mother is a full blood Sioux and cannot talk English, and our father was a full blood Frenchman and could not speak English. Our scrip was given him. He is dead and [we] don't know where it is. White people made him drunk and while they had him in this condition they induced him to sell some of our lands located by this scrip." Thatóheya continued, "We do not know if all the lands allowed us by the scrip was ever located. The white people there are not our friends and we cannot get its description and boundaries of these lands." Thatóheya hoped that if the Office of Indian Affairs could discover exactly where the lands were, they might be returned to the Trudell family.[22] My great-great-grandfather Levi Trudell claimed in 1886 that some of his land was now under the city of Red Wing. Levi "left there when young but was back about seven years ago, when the possessor of the 160 acres outside of town offered him $500, to sign a deed for him. Says he was then young and wild and did not sign the paper."[23] While they acquired the needed information, it did not help them regain their land in Minnesota. Indeed, as the records of the Goodhue County Probate Court reveal, their father sold their land in 1857, conflicting with their stories of how their land was lost. Because they were children at the time, and in the confusion of the U.S.–Dakota War a few years later in 1862, they may have been uncertain as to the disposition of their lands.

Forty years after their initial dispossession, in 1897, the Trudell brothers were still concerned about their land when they hired attorney D. H. Talbot to inquire to the commissioner of Indian affairs on their behalf. Talbot argued that the government had no right to issue the scrip of the children to their father and that Francis Trudell had no right to sell it, and he demanded that the Indian Office issue new scrip to the living Trudell claimants.[24] From these documents, it is unclear whether the children knew that their father had sold their land through the Goodhue County Probate Court in 1857. Regardless, the family perceived that the Office of Indian Affairs was wrong to issue "half-breed" land scrip to non-Indian fathers, and they felt that their father did not have any right to sell what was essentially Indian land. Despite their confusion over how their land had been lost, they perceived the loss of their land as illegal and a form of Indian land dispossession.

The oldest child, Hepí, called Frank Trudell in the records, was about nineteen when he located his own scrip on June 15, 1857.[25] While he held his land longer than his siblings, he too was no longer in possession of his land by 1866. After acquiring their land, mixed-ancestry Indians were subject to property taxes and to having their land confiscated and sold for failure to pay. Numerous Dakota men and women appear in Minnesota county tax books. Hepí had a tax of $2.04 assessed on his eighty-acre plot in Penn Township, McLeod County, in 1861. The notation "sold" appears in the tax book; it is unclear if Hepí or the new owner paid the tax. Hepí retained land in New Auburn Township, Sibley County, as late as 1865, when his eighty-acre parcel was assessed a delinquent property tax of $1.08 plus an additional $4.78 for the year of 1864. The year before he had been assessed $3.04 in taxes, including $0.24 in road tax and $0.86 in bridge tax.[26] He does not appear in the tax records after 1865, suggesting he sold or lost his land before the tax assessment of 1866. A number of Hepí's mixed-ancestry neighbors were also assessed property taxes; many were assessed in McLeod County in 1863, but significantly fewer than in 1861.[27] As early as September 1859, the Wabasha County treasurer sold the lands of several families for failure to pay taxes.[28] The Dakota who sold their lands had many reasons for doing so, some of them personally beneficial, but many probably felt pressure to sell in order to pay or avoid property taxes. Charles Rouleau, a white man married to a mixed-ancestry Dakota woman of the Iháŋkthuŋwaŋ (Dwellers at the End) band who received land on the Great Nemaha reservation in southeastern Nebraska, argued that "there is not 1/8 of those who have lands allotted to them here that know the nature of taxation nor can they be made to know the policy of such, as they do not find it consistent with their ideas or Indian customs."[29] The imposition of property taxes was a foreign concept in Dakota culture, nor were the recipients made aware beforehand that their land would be subject to taxes. Local governments used taxation to dispossess Native lands.

The Trudell family had means by which to acquire land that full-ancestry Indians did not. In 1856, unrelated to the mixed-ancestry lands and a year before he sold their land, Francis, the white father of the Trudell children, received a land patent for a 151-acre parcel of land he purchased from the federal government. This was a narrow strip of land between the Minnesota River and Gun Club Lake in modern-day Mendota Heights, about one mile south and on the opposite bank from Fort Snelling, and part of the lands that the Dakota had ceded in the Treaty of Mendota in 1851. The land was only a few hundred yards from the sacred site of Ohéyawahi, or Pilot Knob, where Dakota people buried their dead for generations. This land was part of the larger sacred region known as Bdóte—the confluence of the Minnesota and Mississippi Rivers—the place of creation for Dakota people. The family would have known the creation story of Bdóte, and it is likely that the family had friends and relatives buried at Ohéyawahi. A year and a half after acquiring this land, and two months after selling his children's land in Goodhue County, Francis purchased a city lot in Red Wing, Minnesota, from some of the proceeds of the sale, for $700, approximately forty-five miles southeast of his land in Mendota.[30] Here the Trudell children lived in the shadow of yet another sacred Dakota site, Ȟemníčaŋ, or Barn Bluff.

Francis Trudell bought and sold several town lots in Red Wing over the next couple of years, and sometimes those deeds only mentioned Francis, while others included Ičíyapiwiŋ, also called Mary Trudell, his wife. In October 1858, "Francis Trudell and Mary Trudell of Dakota County" sold lot ten of block seven to Edward Kiernan for $800. The deed continued, "Francis Trudell and Mary Trudell his wife the signers and sealers of the foregoing deed . . . acknowledge the same to be their own free act and deed." The document continued, "and the said Mary Trudell on an examination separate and apart from her said husband acknowledged that she executed the deed without any fear or compulsion from any one."[31] While coverture laws, in which men assumed the land and legal rights of their wives upon marriage, were beginning to be challenged by midcentury, there were no laws in Minnesota that protected the property rights of married women in Minnesota at this time. Yet the county recorder sought the consent of Ičíyapiwiŋ, a full-ancestry Dakota woman, in the sale of this land. Apparently, the county recorder only sought the consent of wives when selling land, not purchasing. A deed dated August 20, 1860, was executed by "Francis Trudell and Mary Trudell his wife" to Thomas Towne for part of their deceased daughter Elizabeth's land, but it only contained the x-mark of Francis.[32] Many white husbands, despite being non-Indians, were also able to interject themselves into the landownership matters of their Native wives and children. Francis, like many other white fathers and husbands, signed petitions concerning mixed-ancestry land, used the court system, and perfected deeds in the sale of his children's land. For mixed-ancestry women and children, American coverture and property laws collided with Indian custom, leading to uncertain property rights for the wives and children of white men.[33] County records sometimes sought the consent of Indian women in land transactions and sometimes did not. Yet, sometimes mixed-ancestry women married to white men were able to assert their property rights in court.[34]

The Trudell family also had their own legal troubles over land when they were sued for property theft. John Kennedy, a white emigrant from Canada, made a complaint in the Dakota County District Court in July of 1861 alleging that since January, members of the Trudell family had been cutting and hauling away timber from Kennedy's alleged property on Mud Hen Island in Dakota County. In the complaint, Kennedy requested an injunction from the court to direct the family to cease cutting and hauling away timber. Kennedy claimed to have made numerous requests for them to stop felling trees; the family, with their own claim to the land, simply ignored Kennedy's requests, hired men and teams of horses, and continued cutting.[35] Further legal documents of this case do not exist; the outcome of the case is unknown and the Trudell family's claim to the land is uncertain. From this evidence, it is unknown if the family was committing a criminal act or asserting its land rights. In either case, Harris's concept of "whiteness as property" is evident here; the fictitious whiteness of the Trudell family afforded them at least a semblance of legal property rights that required a lawsuit, rather than simply driving out Indians by force. What is known from this case is that the family was not intimidated by Kennedy or his threats to go to the local courts and that the family aggressively exploited land that it believed it had a right to.

Settler land associations, intended to protect against squatters and land speculators, were common in the nineteenth century. Francis Trudell was one of fifty-nine white men that revived the defunct Dakota County Association in 1855. They revived the association to combat the "trespassers and outrages [that] are almost daily committed upon the lands and property of some of the peaceful and honest citizens of Dakota County by unprincipled villains." The members elected John Kennedy, who sued the Trudell family in 1861, to be secretary of the association.[36] The intentions of this and similar associations were to protect settler lands, which resulted in a vested interest against the preservation of Indian title. As a white settler, Francis was able to take advantage of settler organizations intended to protect their land at the cost of Indian land, but he did so to protect the land of his mixed-ancestry children. Yet again, having a white father who could navigate the white American world of landownership was useful for mixed-ancestry families.

The Trudell family experienced a number of the American settler colonial dispossessive practices that confronted mixed-ancestry Dakota people, but other practices were more insidious. Speculators coerced powers of attorney from mixed-ancestry scripholders to control, sell, and locate their scrip in their name, often at rock-bottom prices. Similarly, other speculators took advantage of the poverty of mixed-ancestry Dakota to purchase their lands below market value. Outright fraud was common, especially through forged powers of attorney and unauthorized applications for duplicate scrip.[37] Unlike full-ancestry Indians, when mixed-ancestry landholders in Minnesota died, their properties were probated in the courts. This was meant to ensure that their property went to their heirs or creditors, but it also ensured that the land would not be retained by the tribe.

The family continued to live on the defunct reservation in and around the town of Wabasha during and long after the U.S.–Dakota War of 1862. This was yet another privilege of mixed-ancestry Dakota; the U.S. Army forced thousands of their full-ancestry relatives to flee the state and imprisoned and forcibly removed hundreds more. There were at least 250 mixed-ancestry Dakota Indians listed in the 1870 federal census in Minnesota, more than 75 in the town of Wabasha alone. Francis Trudell, although over sixty years of age, joined Company K of the Ninth Minnesota Infantry

Regiment as a wagoner to fight against his wife's people. Ičíyapiwiŋ's brother, Henry Waŋbdíšuŋ, fought on the Dakota side. Until 1960, the Minnesota State Constitution retained the language that mixed-ancestry Indians of European ancestry held citizenship in the state, but after the U.S.–Dakota War, white Minnesotans informally refused to recognize their rights and effectively dispossessed mixed-ancestry Indians of their land and their U.S. citizenship. It was not until the late 1870s that most of the Trudell family finally left Wabasha for the Santee reservation in Nebraska, where the federal government had forced their full-ancestry relatives to reside since 1866. Later in life, Ičíyapiwiŋ and all six of her surviving children and many of her grandchildren and great-grandchildren acquired allotments under the Dawes Act and again endured relentless dispossessive pressures from white Americans. For Indians, dispossession has never been a one-off event; they have dealt with the burden and legacies of dispossession for generations. In the early years, the Trudell family fought dispossession by signing on to petitions and exploiting lands under dispute. Decades later they appealed to the National Indian Defense Association and hired an attorney to reacquire their land or scrip. Their descendants, like other Dakota people, continue to fight dispossession, but usually at the tribal level rather than on an individual or family basis.[38] The Trudell children eventually regained their U.S. citizenship; Levi was hailed as the "first member of the Sioux nation that ever sat in a state convention" when he attended the Nebraska State Democratic Convention in 1887, having reacquired his citizenship in 1885 by taking advantage of the allotment clause in the Sixth Article of the 1868 Treaty of Fort Laramie.[39] Hepí and Thatóheya regained their citizenship in the same way, while the other three living brothers only reaffirmed their U.S. citizenship years later under the provisions of the Dawes Act.

Being a mixed-ancestry family afforded the Trudell children opportunities that full-ancestry Dakota did not have. Their white father sometimes took actions that furthered makhóčhe khípi, or Dakota land dispossession. But he also bought land in two sacred places, allowing the children to continue living there, while their full-ancestry relatives were forcibly held on a reservation far to the west. Yet these pieces of Bdóte and Ȟemníčaŋ were in the hands of their white father, and these lands were only available for purchase because their full-ancestry relatives had been forced off by the Treaty of Mendota. As with many benefits enjoyed by mixed-ancestry Indians, the Trudell family possessed this right at the expense of their kin. Like other mixed-ancestry Dakota families, the Trudell children experienced the dispossession of their land but also benefited from the dispossession of their full-ancestry relatives. Two Trudell brothers, Hepí and Thatóheya, served as go-betweens in *Wacouta v. Sharpe,* in which Mary Wacouta sought their help to keep Artemas Sharpe off her land. At the same time, Sharpe tried to bribe the Trudell brothers to help him dispossess Wacouta of her land. They were allowed to live at sacred Dakota sites, but only because of their white father. Hepí Trudell sold his land within nine years, probably to avoid paying continual taxes. At every turn, the Trudell family found themselves deeply involved in the divergent and often conflicting land interests of full-ancestry Indians, mixed-ancestry Indians, and white Americans who forced their own unfamiliar land practices on Indians in the Midwest. Cheryl Harris argues that "whiteness as property" endures, but it was a short-lived phenomenon for the Trudells and other mixed-ancestry families; they were able to engage in fictive whiteness, and therefore white property rights, only for a brief period in the nineteenth century.

NOTES

1. Throughout this essay, I use the Lakota Language Consortium orthography for Dakota words. See Lakota Language Consortium, *New Lakota Dictionary: Lakȟótiyapi-English/English-Lakȟótiyapi & Incorporating the Dakota Dialects of Yankton-Yanktonai & Santee-Sisseton,* 2nd ed. (Bloomington, Ind.: Lakota Language Consortium, 2011).

2. Wabasha County, Minnesota District Court, Civil Case Files, box 2, case #247, Mary Wacoutah v. A. T. Sharpe et al., 1866, Minnesota Historical Society (hereafter MHS).

3. An Act to Prescribe the Qualification of Voters and of Holding Office, 1849 Minn. Laws 6. The states of Wisconsin and Michigan also enacted laws at midcentury to enfranchise American Indians (in 1848 and 1850, respectively).

4. Jameson Sweet, "Native Suffrage: Race, Citizenship, and Dakota Indians in the Upper Midwest," *Journal of the Early Republic* 39, no. 1 (Spring 2019): 99–109.

5. Stephen R. Riggs to S. B. Treat, August 13, 1857, Transcripts of letters from missionaries among the Indians of Minnesota, Dakota, and Oregon, 1830–1878, Ayer MS 16, Newberry Library, Chicago.

6. Charles J. Kappler, *Indian Affairs: Laws and Treaties,* vol. 2, *Treaties* (Washington, D.C.: Government Printing Office, 1904), 307.

7. Quoted in Linda M. Waggoner, ed., *"Neither White Men nor Indians": Affidavits from the Winnebago Mixed-Blood Claim Commissions, Prairie du Chien, Wisconsin, 1838–1839* (Roseville, Minn.: Park Genealogical Books, 2002), 1–2.

8. Cheryl I. Harris, "Whiteness as Property," *Harvard Law Review* 106, no. 8 (June 1993): 1715–24.

9. Affidavit #125, Francis Trudell, record group 75, entry 529, Miscellaneous Reserve Papers, 1825–1907, box 359, National Archives, Washington, D.C. (hereafter MRP).

10. Petition of mixed-ancestry Dakota to Governor Willis A. Gorman, October 14, 1853, record group 75, entry 529, box 360, MRP.

11. Petition of mixed-ancestry Dakota to Governor Willis A. Gorman, November 5, 1853, box 360, MRP.

12. The land scrip guaranteed to the Dakota in this law and subsequent laws and treaties with other tribes in the Midwest probably influenced the issuance of Métis scrip in Canada in the following decades. At least seventy people of Dakota ancestry received Métis scrip and about a dozen acquired scrip on both sides of the border. For more on Métis scrip, see Melanie Niemi-Bohun, "Colonial Categories and Familial Responses to Treaty and Metis Scrip Policy: The 'Edmonton and District Stragglers,' 1870–88," *Canadian Historical Review* 90, no. 1 (March 2009): 71–98; Gerhard J. Ens, "Taking Treaty 8 Scrip, 1899–1900: A Quantitative Portrait of Northern Alberta

Metis Communities," *Lobstick: An Interdisciplinary Journal* 1, no. 1 (2000): 229–58; and Brad Milne, "The Historiography of Métis Land Dispersal, 1870–1890," *Manitoba History* 30 (Autumn 1995): 30–41.

13. An Act to Authorize the President of the United States to Cause to Be Surveyed the Tract of Land in the Territory of Minnesota, Belonging to the Half-Breeds or Mixed-Bloods of the Dacotah or Sioux Nation of Indians, and for Other Purposes, ch. 83, 33 Stat. 304 (1854).

14. Record group 75, entry 381, Relinquishments of Sioux Half Breeds, Lake Pepin, National Archives, Washington, D.C.

15. Record group 75, entry 379, Stubs of Land Certificates for Lake Pepin Half-Breed Sioux, 1856–1915, box 2, National Archives, Washington, D.C.; and record group 75, entry 380, Receipts for Land Certificates for Lake Pepin Half-Breed Sioux, 1857, National Archives, Washington, D.C.

16. Goodhue County Probate Court, 1854–1862, vol. 1, MHS; "Guardian's Sale," *Red Wing Sentinel* (Red Wing, Minn.), August 29, 1857.

17. 1860 U.S. Federal Census, Hastings, Dakota County, Minnesota, July 16, 1860.

18. Sioux Outfit Account, August 10, 1835, Henry H. Sibley Papers, roll 1, MHS; Balance Sheet, Sioux Outfit, 1852, Henry H. Sibley Papers, roll 9, MHS; Henry H. Sibley, Agt. Sioux Outfit v. Francois Trudell, 1841, in History Network of Washington County, *Minnesota Beginnings: Records of St. Croix County Wisconsin Territory, 1840–1849* (Stillwater, Minn.: Washington County Historical Society, 1999).

19. Account Book, 1843–1844, vol. 61, Alexis Bailly Papers, box 2, MHS; Pay Voucher to Francis Trudelle, May 20, 1857, Charles Eugene and Family Papers, box 1, MHS.

20. Dorothy Eaton Ahlgren and Mary Cotter Beeler, *A History of Prescott, Wisconsin: A River City and Farming Community on the St. Croix and Mississippi* (Hastings, Minn.: Prescott Area Historical Society, 1996), 21.

21. 1854 Mdewakanton Dakota Annuity Roll, Sioux #1 Various Bands, entry 906, Annuity Payment Rolls, 1841–1949, RG 75, National Archives, Washington, D.C.; and file 200, Claims filed under the treaty of September 29, 1837, with the Sioux of the Mississippi, 1838, Special Files of the Office of Indian Affairs, 1807–1904, microfilm, M574, roll 59, National Archives, Washington, D.C.

22. Augustus Trudell to S. J. Willard, August 28, 1886, enclosure in S. M. Hockslager to Lucius Q. C. Lamar, October 25, 1886, letter #28701, 1886, box 349, entry 91, Letters Received, 1881–1907 (hereafter LR), record group 75, National Archives, Washington, D.C.

23. Statement of Leon [Levi] Trudell, enclosure in S. M. Hockslager to Lucius Q. C. Lamar, October 25, 1886, letter #28701, 1886, box 349, LR.

24. D. H. Talbot to William Arthur Jones, Commissioner of Indian Affairs, January 25, 1898, letter #4726, 1898, box 1501, LR.

25. Red Wing Land District, Register of Sioux Half Breed Scrip Entries, 1857–1861, U.S. General Land Office Records, MHS.

26. Sibley County, Minnesota Tax Lists, 1863–1991, box 1, MHS.

27. See McLeod County Tax Lists for 1861 and 1863, MHS.

28. "Notice of Tax Sale," *Wabashaw County Herald* (Reads Landing, Minn.), August 6, 1859.

29. Charles Rouleau to William P. Dole, April 2, 1864, M234, Letters Received by the Office of Indian Affairs, Great Nemaha Agency, roll 311, National Archives, Washington, D.C.

30. Deed, William Curtis and David J. Hughes to Francis Trudell, November 4, 1857, Goodhue County, Minnesota Deeds, vol. F, roll 3, MHS.

31. Deed, Francis Trudell and Mary Trudell to Edward Kiernan, October 15, 1858, and Deed, George Wilkinson and Hannah Wilkinson to Francis Trudell, October 14, 1858, both in Goodhue County, Minnesota Deeds, vol. 1, roll 4, MHS.

32. Deed, Francis Trudell and Mary Trudell to Thomas F. Towne, August 20, 1860, Goodhue County, Minnesota Deeds, vol. K, roll 4, MHS.

33. For more on Indian women and American coverture laws, see Robert Gilmer, "Chickasaws, Tribal Laws, and the Mississippi Married Women's Property Act of 1839," *Journal of Mississippi History* 68, no. 2 (June 2006): 131–48.

34. For example, see Wabasha County, Minnesota District Court, Civil Case Files, box 1, case #65, Nancy Buisson v. City of Wabasha, 1861, and box 2, case #195, Lucy Ann Milligan v. George W. Hayes, 1864, MHS.

35. Dakota County, Minnesota District Court, Civil and Criminal Case Files, 1853–1937, box 3, John Kennedy v. Augustus Trudell, Peter Trudell, Leon Trudell, and Francois Trudell, 1861, MHS.

36. See Charter of the Dakota County Association, March 9, 1855, and list of Members of the Dakota County Association, March 10, 1855, Henry H. Sibley Papers, roll 10, MHS.

37. See numerous examples in box 360, MRP.

38. Angelique A. EagleWoman, "Re-establishing the Sisseton-Wahpeton Oyate's Reservation Boundaries: Building a Legal Rationale from Current International Law," *American Indian Law Review* 29, no. 2 (2004–2005): 239–66. A group seeking federal recognition, the Mendota Mdewakanton Dakota Tribal Community of Mendota, Minnesota, is primarily made up of descendants of scrip recipients and hopes to reacquire a land base. See their website http://mendotadakota.com/mn.

39. "A Democratic Indian Delegate," *Omaha World-Herald* (Omaha, Neb.), October 13, 1887; see also Charles J. Kappler, ed., *Indian Affairs: Laws and Treaties* (Washington, D.C.: Government Printing Office, 1904), 2: 998–1007.

Anishinaabe Women and the Struggle for Indigenous Land Rights in Northern Michigan, 1836–1887

SUSAN E. GRAY

In May 1877, E. A. Hoyt, the commissioner of Indian Affairs, and J. A. Williamson, the commissioner of the General Land Office (GLO), jointly charged E. J. Brooks, a clerk at GLO headquarters in Washington, D.C., with conducting an investigation into the conditions of Odawa and Ojibwe Indians in Michigan as a consequence of the 1855 Treaty of Detroit.[1] They instructed the clerk to pay particular attention to contested Indian homestead entries in the Traverse City Land Office District in northwestern Lower Michigan. Brooks found over forty such cases in the district, but in his December report to Williamson he chose to focus on the case of Elizabeth Na-ji-we-kwa as illustrative of "certain questions which are common to many [cases], if not all the cases, and upon the determination in which the rights of many of the parties depend."[2] Brooks's record of these cases is not attached to his report, so it is impossible to say for certain whether the homestead entries of Indigenous women like Na-ji-we-kwa were more subject to contestation by white settlers than the claims of Indigenous men were.[3] The question is, instead, why Na-ji-we-kwa's case seemed to Brooks so representative of the condition of the Anishinaabeg in northwestern Lower Michigan.

Here is Na-ji-we-kwa's story as the federal investigator told it. In 1872, Na-ji-we-kwa, a widow, made a homestead entry on a tract set aside in the 1855 treaty for bands associated with Waganakezee, the northern Odawa homeland that stretched along the eastern shore of Lake Michigan from present-day Petoskey toward the Straits of Mackinac.[4] As authorized by an 1872 act of Congress, her entry was subject to the general provisions of the 1862 Homestead Act, which allowed men and single women to file claims on 160 acres of land. They became the outright owners of their claims by "proving up"—living on the land for five years, building a permanent dwelling, and "improving" their acreage by preparing it for cultivation.[5] The 1872 act under which Na-ji-we-kwa filed her claim should not be confused with either the far broader 1875 Indian Homestead Act, which allowed Indigenous people to file under the 1862 act if they gave up their tribal affiliation, or with the homestead provisions of the General Allotment or Dawes Act of 1887. Instead, the 1872 act authorized homesteading for

Anishinaabe people in Michigan who had already been subjected to allotment and ostensible detribalization (bands continued to function as bands and federal officials to deal with them as such) under the 1855 Treaty of Detroit.[6] As Na-ji-we-kwa's case attests, however, the 1872 act proved no more successful than the 1855 treaty in securing the Anishinaabe land base.

In December 1876, four years after Na-ji-we-kwa made her entry, John S. Brubaker, a white settler, disputed the Odawa woman's claim in district court in Traverse City on the grounds that she had failed to improve it. Brubaker, according to Andrew J. Blackbird, the Odawa federal interpreter at Harbor Springs (Little Traverse), in his correspondence with George W. Lee, the Michigan Indian agent, was part of a "ring" led by John Shurtleff, the Emmet County sheriff, and L. A. Clark, the local postmaster and editor of the *Little Traverse Republican,* to harass the Anishinaabeg and seize their property in the name of the settlers' "rights" as citizens, Republican partisans, and Union Army veterans.[7] In court, Brubaker declared that "said Na-ji-we-kwa has about an acre or two chopped, not any cleared, not any house, and has never made it [the claim] her home. She lives at Cross Village [an Odawa settlement] about 3 1/2 miles from the land." Brubaker asserted not only that Na-ji-we-kwa had failed to prove up, but also that she had not bothered to show up in court, despite Brubaker's best efforts to summon her. The impending hearing had been publicized for six weeks running in the *Grand Traverse Herald,* published in Traverse City, more than sixty miles south of Cross Village. It had been impossible to notify Na-ji-we-kwa personally of her court appointment because "her residence was unknown."[8]

Having himself visited Na-ji-we-kwa's homestead, Brooks was readily able to show in his report that Brubaker's allegations against the Odawa woman were outright lies. The federal investigator used Na-ji-we-kwa's case to expose the fraud and abuse visited upon Anishinaabe people in northern Michigan as a result of the 1855 treaty, whose core purpose was to transform individual Indians into owners of private property in land alongside white settlers and thereby to absolve the federal government of further responsibility for their welfare. What implementation of the treaty instead accomplished, Brooks showed, was the destruction of the Indigenous land base, by means usually foul and never fair. Recent scholars have confirmed and added considerable detail to this story of wreckage. The focus of this essay, however, is its gendered dimension, which has received little attention. Brooks singled out Na-ji-we-kwa as Exhibit A in his depiction of the malfeasance, but beyond noting that her status as a widow made her eligible to homestead, her gender was incidental to his account. He may have been encouraged to point to the plight of an individual woman as indicative of a more general Indigenous condition by the witness of the aforementioned Odawa interpreter Andrew J. Blackbird. Blackbird's impassioned correspondence in this period with the reform-minded Indian agent George S. Lee, who was also a friend and close associate of Brooks, similarly emphasized the abuse of particular Indigenous women, such as

Margaret Boyd (Blackbird's sister) and Lucy Penaseway, at the hands of white settlers.[9] Recent scholars largely follow Brooks's and Blackbird's narratives and their examples of the abuse of Anishinaabe women.[10]

In contrast, this essay contends that thinking about Na-ji-we-kwa, Boyd, and Penaseway as women provides a fuller, more complicated understanding of the scope of the tragedy of Anishinaabe attempts to secure their land base in northern Lower Michigan. To begin, it is useful to consider Indigenous women homesteaders in comparison with their white counterparts. Case studies of homesteading in various locations in the trans-Mississippi West have shown that upward of 20 percent of nineteenth-century homesteaders were women, who proved up their claims with the same or greater degree of success as did men. Most of the female claimants, like the men, were young and single, but many older widows and some divorcées also took up land. Both men and women homesteaders tended to settle amid family and friends, and not infrequently they sought wage work to finance the development of their claims.[11]

In an age when women were only beginning to acquire legal rights to property, the question of how much economic, cultural, and psychological independence homesteading conferred upon them has been a matter of scholarly debate.[12] Homesteading certainly did give women the opportunity to manage their own financial affairs, but it was embedded, in law and practice, in a gender system predicated upon the subordination of women in families and households ruled by landowning patriarchs. Both the legislators who crafted the 1862 Homestead Act and the citizens who clamored for "free land" for several decades before its passage understood the reproduction of such families and households as foundational to nation-building. The creation and perpetuation of the American domestic empire rested on a gender system that subordinated women to men and confined women to the home, while assuring men of their independence in the form of access to land. Thus, the legislators responsible for the 1862 Homestead Act apparently never considered allowing married women to file claims, and they were dubious about permitting divorcées to do so on grounds of immorality, but they allowed single women to file with little debate. The presumption was that young women who had never married would eventually do so, and widows, who were likely responsible for dependent children, acted in a male capacity as heads of household. In light of such reasoning, it is hardly surprising that homesteading often functioned as a strategy for farming or ranching families to maximize their holdings by filing abutting entries as individuals, or that women sometimes took over homesteads upon the death of spouses or parents.[13]

The homestead entries of women like Elizabeth Na-ji-we-kwa were also embedded in a family economic system, but one very different from the structural ties that bound their white counterparts. Na-ji-we-kwa's homestead entry represented more and other than the federal government's attempt to assimilate Anishinaabe people by turning them into landowning farmers, the backbone of the republic in whose name the 1862 Homestead Law was enacted. Her entry represented the cultural strength of a gendered seasonal round that had persisted despite the forces of colonization in no small part because Odawas and Ojibwes had learned to merge landownership and some wage labor with more traditional ways of living on the land. To see how this happened, we need to backtrack from Na-ji-we-kwa's case to the 1855 treaty, which attempted to resolve the problematic status in Michigan of Anishinaabe parties to an earlier treaty compacted nearly twenty years before.

In the 1836 Treaty of Washington, Odawa and Ojibwe peoples were compelled to cede to the federal government an enormous swatch of territory: the western half of the Lower Peninsula of Michigan north of the Grand River and roughly half of the Upper Peninsula east of the Chocolay River.[14] The treaty set aside reservations for the exclusive use of different bands and conferred use rights to the rest of the domain "until the land is required for settlement." These were not provisions for the permanent residence of the Anishinaabeg in Michigan; the treaty made clear that the Indians enjoyed the "privileges of occupancy" at the pleasure of the federal government. Although not a removal treaty per se, the 1836 treaty certainly threatened removal. For a number of reasons having primarily to do with fierce Anishinaabe resistance to removal and the slowness of white settlement in northern Michigan, however, the threat was never realized. One of the more effective means that Anishinaabeg found to resist removal was to use treaty annuity monies to buy land. They were not allowed to acquire property on the reservations set aside by treaty, but they could make purchases elsewhere in the cession once it had been surveyed and brought on market. Ownership of land, on which they paid taxes, gave Anishinaabe people a claim to citizenship, a claim strengthened when Indigenous people in Michigan became state citizens in 1850.[15] Some Odawas bought land as early as the late 1830s near Protestant missions south of the cession, which had already been surveyed and brought on market.[16] The pace of purchasing quickened significantly after land in the Traverse region, as northwestern Lower Michigan is known, came on market in the early 1850s. Before 1855, for example, Anishinaabeg bought thousands of acres on the Leelanau Peninsula north and west of present-day Traverse City, amounting to more than a third of all acreage sold there in those years.[17]

This pattern of land buying was distinctive because, despite the grid system imposed by surveyors on the federal domain as a way of dividing and subdividing 640-acre sections down to parcels as small as forty acres for individual buyers, Indigenous purchases tended to circle village sites near Lake Michigan and Grand Traverse Bay, and they were not infrequently group purchases.[18] In contrast, when the missionary George N. Smith, in his capacity as federal agent, awarded allotments to eligible individual Anishinaabeg in conformity to the 1855 treaty, he tended to do so mechanically. Smith moved from northeast to southwest across the thirty-six sections of Leelanau townships designated for allotment, awarding uniform eighty- and forty-acre parcels.

Thus, although federal officials intended the 1855 treaty to absorb Anishinaabe people into the landscape of white settlement by dissolving tribal relations and allotting land in severalty, many of its Indigenous beneficiaries already had considerable experience in landownership. This experience included a deep understanding of not only the economic value of the parcels that they purchased but also the legal and political power of landownership, as represented by the warranty deed, to protect their way of life. What made these people vulnerable to settler predation, therefore, was less ignorance, as earlier scholars have claimed, than white determination to eliminate them from the Traverse region. Before the odds against them became too great, Anishinaabe landowners on the Leelanau demonstrated considerable ingenuity in adapting the American land system to Indigenous lifeways fundamentally at odds with the social and cultural values underpinning that system. Eyewitness accounts attest that these properties helped to support a seasonal round that combined subsistence-plus agriculture with fishing, some local hunting, sugaring, and gathering. All of these activities involved the participation of both sexes, but in general, farming, sugaring, and gathering were women's work, while men engaged in hunting and fishing. As the game population declined in northwestern Lower Michigan, Indigenous men increasingly spent the winters cutting and hauling cordwood to the shore, where it became fuel for lake steamers. Agriculture, traditionally female work, may have become more of a shared activity as some men acquired teams and plows. Sugaring and gathering remained under the purview of women. When men cut timber from their own properties, as opposed to jobbing for lumber companies, they selectively cut hardwood, leaving the maple trees intact for the women to organize as sugar bushes.[19] Traditionally, all of the activities associated with the seasonal round placed particular families at particular sites at particular times of the year. When federal officials and other colonial agents promoted Indigenous ownership of property in land, they envisioned the transformation of Anishinaabe men into patriarchal yeoman farmers and Anishinaabe women into wives confined to the home. But from the perspective of the seasonal round, Indigenous-owned properties supplied more of the resources under the management of women than men. Indigenous landownership thus turned the ideology of the yeoman farmer on its head.

The 1855 treaty had the potential to broaden and accelerate this trend toward Indigenous landownership. The treaty reserved land on the Leelanau Peninsula and in Waganakezee for the various bands in areas that they customarily occupied. Within these territories, each head of family was entitled to eighty acres of land, as were families of two or more orphan children under the age of twenty-one. Single individuals over the age of twenty-one were each to receive forty-acre parcels. Like the Homestead Act, allotment under the 1855 treaty allowed a good deal of leeway for female landownership, while presuming that most heads of family were male. Recipients of allotments were to be issued patents for their lands, which they could not sell for ten

Indian Woman Tapping Maple Sugar. The collection makes clear that this is an Ojibwe woman, without explicitly saying so. Photograph by Roland Reed, Native American Portraits, 1908 and 1912, Library of Congress.

years, although they were allowed to buy outright additional property within the tracts set aside for allotment. At the end of the decade, any remaining reserved land was to be brought on market.[20]

But nothing about the 1855 treaty worked as it was supposed to do. The impetus for E. J. Brooks's investigation was the smell of federal bungling, official corruption, and wholesale fraud grown so strong that it could no longer be ignored in Washington. In the Traverse region, the focus of Brooks's reports, the two major tracts set aside for allotment, were located on the Leelanau Peninsula and in the Odawa historic homeland of Waganakezee. Both areas were subjected to resurvey, delaying for several years the assignment of allotments. The greatest bureaucratic bottleneck, however, occurred in Washington. Some patents were delivered to their owners, although not until 1868, thirteen years after the treaty set the process of allotment in motion. Many Indigenous people who had chosen lands in the late 1850s, however, found themselves without legal title even as the tracts intended for allotment were thrown open to public sale. Others either had never received an allotment to begin with or had come of age since selection was carried out and were still entitled to land under the 1855 treaty.

Rather than attempt to fix the allotment process, and well aware of the clamor of white settlers for access to the remaining land in the tracts, in 1872 the federal government temporarily halted public sales and gave Anishinaabeg who had "not made selections or purchases under the 1855 treaty," and those who had "become of age since the expiration of ten years named in the treaty," six months belatedly to claim their allotment under the 1862 Homestead Act.[21] In a letter to George Betts, then the U.S. Indian agent for Michigan and soon to be exposed for conspiring illegally to remove timber from lands belonging to the Saginaw Chippewas, F. A. Walker, the commissioner of Indian Affairs, explained that since the 1855 treaty had dissolved tribal relations, the Indians were "entitled to all the rights and privileges of white citizens under the *homestead* and preemption acts." This position made single Anishinaabe women, like Elizabeth Na-ji-we-kwa, eligible for homestead entries.[22]

Awarding quarter sections of land to individual Anishinaabeg, as opposed to the maximal eighty-acre allotments under the 1855 treaty, looks like compensatory generosity on the part of Congress, but it was probably expediency. The title of the 1872 legislation signaled clearly its purpose: An Act for the Restoration to Market of Certain Lands in Michigan. Allowing some Anishinaabeg to make homestead entries would supposedly mop up the allotment mess as quickly as possible, after which the remaining reserved land would be thrown open to white homesteaders. But, to the fury of men like John S. Brubaker, Congress waited until 1875 to officially open the remaining reserved land to the "bona fide settlers" they purported to be. By "bona fide settlers," a common phrase of the period, Americans distinguished between farmers entitled to access to the public domain and speculators who reaped unearned profits from it, as well as Indigenous people who, because of their roaming ways, could not be considered settlers. Thwarted by congressional inaction, Brubaker and his associates in the Traverse region determined to seize Anishinaabe homesteads for themselves.[23]

When E. J. Brooks visited Na-ji-we-kwa's homestead in 1877, he found, contrary to John S. Brubaker's allegations, that the Anishinaabe widow had met the legal requirements for proving up her claim. Na-ji-we-kwa had over six acres in cultivation and had erected a "comfortable log house . . . about 16 × 18 feet . . . with a good bark roof, two small windows and one door." Nevertheless, the federal investigator characterized the Odawa woman's homestead as an "Indian clearing" and distinguished it from white homesteads—not in the degree but in the kind of its improvements. The Indigenous "idea of a homestead," he explained, "is a place on which to make sugar in the spring, raise a few potatoes and sufficient corn to supply their need during the year, and to have a home upon which they may at any time return" from fishing, berrying, and winter residence "in villages for comfort and social advantages and for the purpose of schooling their children." Few families owned teams, and men cleared land largely by chopping and burning brush while leaving the large trees intact. The invariable answer to Brooks's repeated question of why the Anishinaabeg did not clear land completely in the manner of whites was: "I want to save the timber so my children will have a place to make sugar."[24]

Thus, despite his outrage over the abuse that Odawa and Ojibwe people had suffered at the hands of white settlers like John S. Brubaker because the federal government could not or would not enforce its own laws, Brooks was not sympathetic to the Indigenous "idea of a homestead," regarding it as evidence that, whatever advances toward civilization Anishinaabe people in the Traverse region had made, they remained "savages," "lead[ing] a nomadic life." This understanding of Anishinaabe homesteaders as savages—one hardly knows whether to put either, both, or neither noun in quotation marks—helps to explain why Brooks singled out Na-ji-we-kwa's plight to demonstrate the crimes of settler colonialism.[25] His depiction of her at once evoked the trope of the desperate yet determined widow, the sole support of her helpless children, whom the Homestead Act was intended to succor, and a primitive woman insufficiently advanced to grasp the helping hand of a beneficent colonial state. If Brooks could grudgingly allow that the Anishinaabeg on their allotments were meeting the terms of the Homestead Act, he did not therefore approve of Indigenous people's adoption of American land law to their own purposes. No seasonal round qualified as "civilized." Very few observers of the situation in the Traverse region could declare, as did Charles L. Fraser, a local resident who corresponded with federal officials, that "it should not be required of the Indians as of the whites to stay on their Homesteads <u>all</u> the time, for it is their custom (as among the Germans and other European peoples) to live in little communities, or villages, while their farms ly [*sic*] a little way off, they being none the less residents and just as certainly improving and cultivating the land."[26] And what no one seems to have commented upon was the way that Anishinaabe women's responsibility for farming and sugaring linked Indigenous ownership of property in land—a sine qua non of "civilization"—with the perpetuation of the traditional seasonal round.

Within a few years after Brooks's investigation, this link would be broken as Anishinaabe people were forced from their lands by a white population determined to seize Indigenous property—whether acquired by allotment, homestead, or outright purchase—for themselves. One of the displaced was doubtless Na-ji-we-kwa, even though Brooks appealed her case and others to the commissioner of the General Land Office, asking that the Indigenous claimants be issued patents for their homesteads. But even patents proved no barrier to the machinations of white settlers. As Brooks detailed in an 1878 report to the commissioner of Indian Affairs, they manipulated a variety of legal instruments besides the Homestead Act to their purpose, including mortgages and tax obligations that could not possibly be met.[27] Deprived of their land base in the Traverse region, Anishinaabe men and women transformed their seasonal round yet again, incorporating more wage labor. Their work, which took them from lumber camps of the Upper Peninsula to white homes and factories in Detroit, ironically may have led them to travel farther than they had done as nomadic landowners, but that is another story.[28]

NOTES

1. Treaty with the Ottawa and Chippewa, 11 Stat. 621 (1855).
2. E. J. Brooks to J. A. Williamson, Commissioner, General Land Office, December 27, 1877, NAM, RG 75, M234, reel 413: 065–0103, National Archives, Washington, D.C.
3. There is some evidence that Indigenous women homesteaders may have been more subject than their male counterparts to harassment by white settlers. In his correspondence with Michigan Indian agents between 1866 and 1880 the Odawa federal interpreter, Andrew J. Blackbird, names twenty-one Anishinaabeg whose land claims had been threatened. Of these, eleven were women, a large number considering that only single women had access to land under the 1855 treaty and the 1872 act. Michigan Superintendency, Mackinac Agency, Letters Received, boxes 3 and 4, RG 75, National Archives, Washington, D.C.
4. In addition to the Waganakezee tract, much of the Leelanau Peninsula north and west of present-day Traverse City was reserved for Ojibwes and Odawas affiliated with Grand Traverse Bands south of Waganakezee.
5. An Act for the Restoration to Market of Certain Lands in Michigan, ch. 424, 17 Stat. 381 (1872). The classic account of the Homestead Act of 1862 is Paul W. Gates, *History of Public Land Law Development* (Washington, D.C.: U.S. Government Printing Office, 1968), 387–434.
6. Treaty with the Ottawa and Chippewa; Act of May 20, 1862 (Homestead Act), Pub. L. No. 37–64, 12 Stat. 392 (1862); and An Act to Provide for the Allotment of Lands in Severalty to Indians on the Various Reservations (General Allotment Act or Dawes Act) 24 Stat. 388–91 (1887).
7. Andrew J. Blackbird to George W. Lee, March 1, 1878; March 8, 1878; March 13, 1878; April 19, 1878; April 19, 1878; and November 5, 1878, RG 75, Michigan Superintendency, Mackinac Agency, box 3, 1876–1879, National Archives, Washington, D.C. The evidence that members of the ring were bound by partisan affiliation, Civil War service, and devotion to the local real market for land and timber at the expense of the Anishinaabeg is abundant. Ring member Charles W. Ingalls, for example, who served in Company I of the Michigan 22nd Infantry Regiment, arrived in Harbor Springs in 1874 "and was actively engaged in locating soldiers upon homesteads after the lands of the county came on market." *The Traverse Region, Historical and Descriptive, with Illustrations of Scenery and Portraits and Biographical Sketches of Some of Its Prominent Men and Pioneers* (Chicago: H. R. Page & Co, 1884), 147. See also U.S. Civil War Soldier Records and Profiles, 1861–1865, Ancestry.com, https://www.ancestry.com/search/collections/1555. Brubaker himself, a teamster turned farmer, served in Company A of the Michigan 23rd Infantry Regiment. See U.S. Civil War Soldier Records and Profiles and the 1870 and 1880 federal censuses also in the Ancestry.com database. He boasted publicly, Blackbird wrote to Lee, that he would "annul the Ind[ian] agency in . . . Michigan." Blackbird to Lee, May 18, 1878, NANA, RG 75, Michigan Superintendency, Mackinac Agency, box 3, 1876–79, National Archives, Washington, D.C.
8. Brooks to Williamson, December 27, 1877, National Archives Microforms, Washington, D.C.
9. For Blackbird's account of Boyd and Penaseway, see AJB to George W. Lee, June 4, 1878; June 27, 1878; February 10, 1879; February 27, 1879; November 10, 1879; December 10, 1879; December 22, 1879; and December 25, 1879, RG 75, Michigan Superintendency, Mackinac Agency, Letters

Received, box 3, 1876–1879, National Archives, Washington, D.C.; and AJB to George W. Lee, January 12, 1880; January 26, 1880; February 23, 1880; and December 1880, Michigan Superintendency, Mackinac Agency, Letters Received, box 4, 1880–81.

10. Charles E. Cleland, *Rites of Conquest: The History and Culture of Michigan's Native Americans* (Ann Arbor: University of Michigan Press, 1992), 248–56; Bradley J. Gills, "The Anishnabeg and the Landscape of Assimilation in Michigan, 1854–1934" (PhD diss., Arizona State University, 2008), 37–53; William James Gribb, "The Grand Traverse Bands' Land Base: A Cultural History Study of Land Transfer in Michigan" (PhD diss., Michigan State University, 1982); and Bruce Rubenstein, "Justice Denied: An Analysis of American Indian-White Relations in Michigan, 1855–1889" (PhD diss., Michigan State University, 1974), 102–38.

11. Katharine Benton-Cohen, "Common Purposes, Worlds Apart: Mexican-American, Mormon, and Midwestern Homesteaders in Cochise County, Arizona," *Western Historical Quarterly* 36 (Winter 2005): 429–52; Dee Garceau, *The Important Things of Life: Women, Work, and Family in Sweetwater County, Wyoming, 1880–1929* (Lincoln: University of Nebraska Press, 1997); Katherine Harris, "Homesteading in Northern Colorado, 1873–1920: Sex Roles and Women's Experience," in *The Women's West,* ed. Susan Armitage and Elizabeth Jameson (Norman: University of Oklahoma Press, 1987), 165–78; Elaine Lindgren, "Ethnic Women Homesteading on the Plains of North Dakota," *Great Plains Quarterly* 9 (Summer 1989): 159–73; Sheryll Patterson-Black, "Women Homesteaders on the Great Plains Frontier," *Frontiers: A Journal of Women Studies* 1 (Spring 1976): 67–88; Sherry L. Smith, "Single Women Homesteaders: The Perplexing Case of Elinore Pruitt Stewart," *Western Historical Quarterly* 22 (May 1991): 163–83; Anne Webb, "Minnesota Women Homesteaders: 1863–1889," *Journal of Social History* 23 (Fall 1989): 115–36; and Florence C. Gould and Patricia N. Pando, *Claiming Their Land: Women Homesteaders in Texas* (El Paso: Texas Western Press, 1991).

12. On women and property ownership in the nineteenth-century United States, see Norma Basch, *In the Eyes of the Law: Women, Marriage, and Property in Nineteenth-Century New York* (Ithaca, N.Y.: Cornell University Press, 1982); and Michael S. Grossberg, *Governing the Hearth: Law and the Family in Nineteenth-Century America* (Chapel Hill: University of North Carolina Press, 2004).

13. This paragraph follows the argument in chapter 3 of Tonia M. Compton's excellent dissertation, "Proper Women/Propertied Women: Federal Land Laws and Gender Order(s) in the Nineteenth-Century Imperial American West" (PhD diss., University of Nebraska, 2009), 63–97. On the family nexus and female homesteading, see Garceau, *Important Things in Life,* 112–28.

14. Treaty with the Ottawa and Chippewa at Washington, D.C., 1836, https://www.archives.gov/research/native-americans/treaties/catalog-links.

15. On state citizenship for Michigan Indians, see Deborah A. Rosen, *American Indians and State Law: Sovereignty, Race, and Citizenship, 1790–1880* (Lincoln: University of Nebraska Press, 2007), 131–36, 143–49, and 51–52. It should also be noted that Michigan Anishinaabeg were not the first to see purchases of land in fee simple as a way of preserving their autonomy and protecting their land base from the encroachment of white settlement, and they would not be the last. In the early nineteenth century, the Brotherton Nation, Christian Indians from southern New England, moved twice, to upstate New York and to Michigan Territory in what is today Wisconsin, to acquire land secure from the meddling of local, state, and federal officials. Elsewhere in

the Midwest, Wyandots bought land in Ohio after consultation with Haudenosaunee people, themselves engaged in a rear guard action to save what they could of their historic homeland. In Indiana, the Miami chief, Jean Baptiste Richardville, bought land as a way of saving at least some of his people from removal by settling them on his property. Later, in northern California, Indigenous people, whose treaties were never ratified by Congress and whose reservations were therefore not secure, saved their wages as farm workers to buy land as a way of sustaining their communities. Brad D. E. Jarvis, *The Brotherton Nation of Indians: Land Ownership and Nationalism in Early America, 1740–1840* (Lincoln: University of Nebraska Press, 2010); James J. Buss, *Winning the West with Words: Language and Conquest in the Lower Great Lakes* (Norman: University of Oklahoma Press, 2011), 73–95; James J. Buss, "Imagined Worlds and Archival Realities: The Patchwork World of Early Nineteenth-Century Indiana," in C. Joseph Genetin-Pilawa and James J. Buss, eds., *Beyond Two Worlds: Critical Conversations on Language and Power in Native North America* (Albany: SUNY Press, 2014), 97–116; C. Joseph Genetin-Pilawa, *Crooked Paths to Allotment: The Fight over Federal Indian Policy after the Civil War* (Chapel Hill: University of North Carolina Press, 2012), 29–50; Khal Schneider, "Making Indian Land in the Allotment Era: Northern California's Indian Rancherias," *Western Historical Quarterly* 41 (Winter 2010): 429–50; and Khal Schneider, "Citizen Lives: California Indian Country, 1855–1940" (PhD diss., University of California, Berkeley, 2006).

16. Susan E. Gray, "Limits and Possibilities: White-Indian Relations in Western Michigan in the Era of Removal," *Michigan Historical Review* 20 (Fall 1994): 71–92.

17. On Indian land buying on the Leelanau Peninsula before 1855, see Susan E. Gray, *Lines of Descent: Family Stories from the North Country* (Chapel Hill: University of North Carolina Press, forthcoming), chap. 5. The best account of the 1836 and 1855 treaties is Charles E. Cleland, *Faith in Paper: The Ethnohistory and Litigation of Upper Great Lakes Indian Treaties* (Ann Arbor: University of Michigan Press, 2011), 49–87.

18. This tendency is well exemplified in the founding of Waukazooville (later Northport) on Grand Traverse Bay in the early 1850s. See George Nelson Smith, Memoranda Books, entries for July 6, 1850; July 20, 1850; April 28, 1851; and May 26, 1851, Bentley Historical Library, University of Michigan, Ann Arbor, Mich.

19. On the seasonal round of the Anishinaabeg, see Cary Miller, *Ogimaag: Anishinaabeg Leadership, 1760–1845* (Lincoln: University of Nebraska Press, 2010), 21–64. On the Leelanau, the Presbyterian missionary Peter Dougherty proved a close observer of the round. See, for example, Peter Dougherty to J. C. Lowrie, Omena, February 6, 1869, box B, reel 1, vol. 1, no. 1852; Peter Dougherty, Report for 1870, February 10, 1871, box Q, reel 1, vol. 6, no. 53, Letters of Peter Dougherty, American Indian Correspondence, Presbyterian Collection of Missionaries' Letters, 1833–1893 [microfilm], Presbyterian History Society, National Archives of the PC (USA), Philadelphia.

20. The 1855 treaty was one of the first of a series of attempts to convert Indigenous peoples to "civilized" ways through landownership before the passage of the General Allotment Act of 1887. Like the later act, the Treaty of Detroit assumed that a myriad of behavioral markers of civilization, including domestic roles for subordinated women, would follow from male ownership of land in severalty. On allotment measures before the Dawes Act, see Paul W. Gates, "Indian Allotments Preceding the Dawes Act," in *The Frontier Challenge: Responses to the Trans-Mississippi Challenge,* ed. John G. Clarke (Lawrence: University of Kansas Press, 1971), 141–70.

21. An Act for the Restoration to Market of Certain Lands in Michigan, ch. 424, 17 Stat. 381 (1872).

22. F. A. Walker to George Betts, April 8, 1872, RG 75, Michigan Superintendency, Mackinac Agency, Letters Received, box 2, 1870–74, National Archives, Washington, D.C.

23. An Act to Amend the Act Entitled "An Act for the Restoration to Homestead-Entry and to Market of Certain Lands in Michigan," ch. 188, 18 Stat. 516 (1875); and An Act Extending the Time with Which Homestead Entries upon Certain Lands in Michigan May Be Made, ch. 105, 19 Stat. 55 (1876).

24. Brooks to Williamson, December 27, 1877, National Archives, Microfilms, Washington, D.C.

25. Brooks to Williamson, December 27, 1877, National Archives, Microfilms, Washington, D.C.

26. Charles L. Fraser to George S. Lee, April 12, 1878, RG 75, Michigan Superintendency, Letters Received, box 4, 1878–82, National Archives, Washington, D.C.

27. E. J. Brooks to E. A. Hoyt, Commissioner of Indian Affairs, January 12, 1878, M234, R413: 0105–0136, National Archives, Microfilms, Washington, D.C.

28. See, for example, Edmund Jefferson Danziger Jr., *Survival and Regeneration: Detroit's American Indian Community* (Detroit: Wayne State University Press, 1991); Gills, "Anishnabeg and the Landscape of Assimilation in Michigan," 142–85, 258–97; and Alice Littlefield, "Making a Living: Anishinaabe Women in Michigan's Changing Economy," in Carol Williams, ed., *Indigenous Women and Work* (Urbana: University of Illinois Press, 2012), 46–59.

ᎪᎩ ᎤᏗᏞᎩ ᏗᏮᎪᏗ ᎾᏂᏌᏭᏍᎬ ᎶᎶ

You can hear locusts in the heat of the summer

CANDESSA TEHEE

If you are out in the country, summers are loud on the land currently known as Oklahoma.[1] As the heat of day fades from intense to tolerable, the movement of air starts feeling like a breeze instead of a hair dryer on a low setting. The temperature dips slightly and insects gather in the trees to sing. The chitinous chorus of the **ᎶᎶ** / *lolo* / *locusts* can reach over one hundred decibels. Anytime I hear this sound, or even think about it, my shoulders relax as I think about sitting on a porch that exists now only in memory. The sound is synonymous with summer evenings spent outside in Cherokee Nation and I am not alone in finding it remarkable. The quote that opens this essay was included by Durbin Feeling **ᏥᎨᏒ**[2] / *tsigesv* / *their time has passed* in the groundbreaking *Cherokee-English Dictionary* authored by him and edited by William Pulte. I was one of several students he worked with over his lifetime, and during the course of our relationship as mentor and student, Durbin **ᏥᎨᏒ** would often reflect on his experiences researching the dictionary. He told me he wanted to include natural speech and recorded people speaking conversationally in many different settings. He said there was an incredible volume of language recorded through his research and the dictionary could not hold it all. He never stated the sentences chosen for inclusion were of higher importance or linguistic value. Often, however, the sentences chosen hold some cultural significance or encode an aspect of Cherokee lifeways. This sentence holds special resonance for me because hearing locusts in the heat of the summer is inextricably linked to Cherokee community, stories, family, and the land.

My family would often sit on a porch that was attached to a shell home that *ᎡᏚᏚ ᎡᎵᏏᏃ* / *edudu elisihno* / *my grandfather and grandmother* had ordered sometime after *ᎡᏚᏚ* / *edudu* / *my grandfather* finished his service in World War II. There wasn't a flat patch big enough for the house on the acreage, so concrete blocks and posts were used to level it. This tilted landscape made every corner a different height off the ground. A set of steps had been fashioned for the house from metal plates and a handrail had been welded to the metal plates. Graduated columns of concrete blocks under those metal plates made a functional, albeit steep, access point to a porch that was about four feet high. Sometimes, if all the chairs on the porch were taken, I would lie on the porch and peer through the wood slats and look for ᎦᎵᎩᎾ / *galigina* / *buck,* my grandparents' dog, who liked to laze in the cool dirt below. Years later, I learned ᎦᎵᎩᎾ was the Cherokee name of Elias Boudinot,[3] one of the signatories of the Treaty of New Echota.[4] The dog was black, of indeterminate breed, and, aside from being male, not at all like a buck. Although I never got the chance to ask either of them about his name, the lack of resemblance to an actual buck leads me to believe Boudinot may have been an inspiration.

When I think back to this porch, I can almost smell the sweet tobacco smoke that wafted up from the pipes that ᎡᏚᏚ ᎡᎵᏏᏃ / *edudu elisihno* / *my grandfather and grandmother* seemed to smoke perennially. They said the smoke kept ᏙᏌ / *dosa* / *mosquitoes* away, but occasionally pungent smoke from a Dollar General citronella candle would be added as an extra deterrent. When the ᏙᏌ / *dosa* / *mosquitoes* were really aggressive, we might even spray a little repellent from a green can. Once I asked ᎦᏙ ᎭᏗᏍᎪ Ꮎ / *gado hadisgo na* / *what is this called* as I gestured to the green aerosol can. As ᎡᎵᏏ / *elisi* / *my grandmother* dozed lightly in her chair next to him, ᎡᏚᏚ / *edudu* / *my grandfather* thought for a moment, then said, "ᏙᏌ ᏕᏖᏍᏙ / *dosa detesto.*" I was in the habit of carrying a little notebook for Cherokee words and phrases, and I immediately wrote the phrase with the translation *mosquito repellent.* I shared this phrase with Durbin ᏥᎨᏒ years later who laughed heartily then told me that the phrase's literal meaning was *mosquitoes—it scares them.*

As a lifelong student of the Cherokee language, I know that moving between Cherokee and English is not seamless. Often, translating Cherokee to English is like trying to fit ten pounds of potatoes in a five-pound sack. It just doesn't quite fit. Sometimes, trying to fit the things I learned in my youth into my contemporary life feels the same way. Telling people not to sing at the table, not to wear red in a thunderstorm, or to be careful not to slop water on your shirt while doing the dishes aren't as commonplace as they once were. I often find myself repeating stories, cautionary and otherwise, I heard from my grandparents before ᎬᎩᏲᏂᏒᎢ / *gvgiyohusvi* / *I lost them.* One of those old stories was about how, even though we are full-blood Cherokees, my great-grandpa Jess Tehee ᏥᎨᏒ / *tsigesv* / *his or her time has passed* was part Creek.

The first time I heard this story was on the front porch during a humid summer. It was a new moon and so dark outside you could hardly see your own hand in front of your face. Cherokees say this is a time of beginnings and also a good time to cut your hair if you want it to grow. We were all sitting in lawn chairs that had vinyl strips over aluminum frames. Occasionally a car would come up the narrow blacktop and pass by going toward Girty Hill or some other destination farther up Blackgum Mountain. ᎡᏚᏚ / *edud* / *my grandfather* always knew the car, even on nights when we only saw the shape of the headlights. He always quietly remarked on the passing car and its owner. I knew he was correct because, during the day, he also did this from his recliner inside the house without looking out the window. I would lean out to double-check him and he was always right. This seemed like pure magic until I realized he was identifying neighbors' cars from the distinctive sounds of their engines. Even after I figured out it was a learned skill and not omniscience, I still keenly enjoyed putting his sense of observation to the test, although I had limited time to indulge my curiosity. We were rarely inside during the day, and I needed light to identify the cars he knew from sound alone. The commercials during *The Price Is Right* game show were the only opportunity for this specific amusement. The ᎠᏛᏆᎳᎠᎣᏍᎩ / *adayvlatvsgi* / *television* would not lure us back inside until it was time for the evening news. By then, it would be too dark for me to verify any cars.

Conversations on the porch drifted between Cherokee and English but were always punctuated with laughter. The stream of stories was constant like ᎠᎺ / *ama* / *water* in the little creek that ran along part of their property line. Adults shared stories and kids listened. The cast was always changing, as ᎡᏍᏍ ᎡᏟᏏᎿ / *edud elisihno* / *my grandfather and grandmother* had eight children, seven of whom lived to adulthood and had children of their own. ᎡᏥ / *etsi* / *my mom* was the seventh in birth order and we lived with them for a while, so it seemed she, my brothers, my sister, and I were always on the porch while my aunts, uncles, and cousins came and went. The younger kids would go to the bedroom farthest from the porch and play quietly because, after dark, we were never allowed to play outside or even be too loud inside. Usually, me and my older cousins would sit and listen as the adults talked. They knew we did that and now I can only guess some of these stories were told for our benefit. They talked about neighbors when a memory was sparked by their passing car, people from ᏍᏔᏈ / *gatiyo* / *ceremonial grounds,* people from town, or something only ᎡᏍᏍ ᎡᏟᏏᎿ / *edudu elisihno* / *my grandfather and grandmother* knew. These stories about people in our community, about events from the past, and about how we came to our land were told one after another, giving me a sense of history and connection.

On one of these evenings, as lightning bugs blinked all around, I learned ᎡᏍᏍ ᎤᎥᏘ / *edud udod* / *my grandfather's father* could speak Cherokee and Creek. They started to tell stories about conversations on another porch taking place in all three languages at once. ᎡᏍᏍ / *edudu* / *my grandfather* gestured vaguely in the direction of his grandparents' house, and I realized I was the fifth generation in my family to be connected to this place in our new homeland. They continued talking about these people they remembered, gone long before I took my place on the land. Some only spoke Cherokee, some only spoke Creek, and often there was a ᎫᎴ / *gule* / *acorn* visitor who only spoke English.[5] Impromptu translation was done by bilinguals, speakers fluent in two of the three languages, and trilinguals, speakers fluent in all three languages. It amazes me to think about how quickly translation must have happened to keep the conversation going between everyone while moving between three languages. Multilingual legends were on our land back in those days, translating rapidly while summer creatures sang a chorus in evenings that were probably just like the one we were in while hearing the story retold.

One Jꮣ / *gule* / *acorn,* or ᏲᏁᎦ / *yonega* / *white person,* who came through those new Cherokee homelands was a Baptist circuit preacher who rode through the area and left a couple of Cherokee women with child. One of those women, according to ᎡᎵᏏ / *elisi* / *my grandmother,* was ᎤᎵᏏ / *ulisi* / *her grandmother.* That Baptist preacher never did return, and ᎡᎵᏏ / *elisi* / *my grandmother* said those babies were raised by the women alongside subsequent children fathered by Cherokee husbands. When a man became a husband to a Cherokee woman in those times, he became part of her family. Additionally, in Cherokee communities at that time, children belonged to their mothers. Therefore, within communities where clanship was common, Cherokee men often claimed all their wives' children as their own. By Cherokee standards, this meant as much as, if not more than, simple biology. Thereby, these Cherokee blended families erased the Baptist circuit preacher from ancestry charts and family trees, but his legacy remains enshrined in oral history. Despite the acknowledgment of paternity, he is spoken of not as an ancestor but as a passerby.

Despite the story of the ᎫᎴ / *gule* / *acorn* and an ancestor who spoke Creek, we were all considered full-blood Cherokees by our own community. This is because clan and ceremony were inextricably intertwined in what made a person Cherokee as I grew up. This was so ingrained I thought my uncle's wife wasn't Cherokee because of her lack of involvement with Cherokee ceremony. I thought this even though I knew her sister was on the Cherokee Nation Tribal Council. This may seem dissonant, but no government's measures of Cherokeeness held any meaning for us. The foundational understanding was that through ceremony and clan, we existed separate and autonomous of Cherokee government. No matter what happened in Tahlequah, the Cherokee Nation capital, or Washington, D.C., we would always be Cherokee because of ceremony and clan. There were two cousins without clans, two uncles each had daughters, but one lived in another state and visited for a few weeks each summer while the other was raised in a church patently disavowing clan and ceremonial ways. When either visited, they were rarely in situations where clanship, or lack of it, was an issue. In hindsight, this was likely not coincidence but design.

In comparison, my other cousins, my siblings, and I grew up very solidly knowing our clans and our positions within our community. We went to ᎦᏘᏲ / *gatiyo* / *ceremonial grounds* and our parents spoke Cherokee. We drank teas made from local plants and ate foods hunted, farmed, or gathered from the land. We danced together and played stickball. Once when a classmate lost money at school, they lined up the Indian kids to check pockets and backpacks. I was in that line along with all the other kids from ᎦᏘᏲ / *gatiyo* / *ceremonial grounds.* By anyone's definition, we were all full-bloods because of the way we lived. This distinction caused us to be the only ones searched when our classmate's money went missing too. The teacher took the fifty cents ᎡᏚᏚ / *edudu* / *my grandfather* had given me that morning while he waited with me for the school bus. In addition to getting robbed, I also got paddled for stealing, so it was definitely a proper mugging. If there was any advantage to that sliver of white lineage in my ancestry, it was firmly rooted in the past with the Ꭻꭺ / *gule* / *acorn* preacher where the story originated.

I have dedicated my life and my career to the Cherokee language, but I am not proficient enough to be a storyteller. I can follow the general direction of a conversation and can occasionally joke. However, I often struggle with subtlety, past tense, and the intricacies of Cherokee verb conjugation. ᎡᏟᏏ / *elisi* / *my grandmother* or ᎡᏥ / *etsi* / *my mother* would act as the interpreter for me when Cherokee was flowing swiftly on the porch. There is a deep irony that these real-time translations were to help me follow the stories and conversation rather than for the benefit of a Ꭻꭺ / *gule* / *acorn* stranger. Like many others in their generations, they thought English proficiency would equip me for success, while Cherokee fluency might hinder me in that pursuit. They didn't know the future would hold a wave of Cherokee language revitalization efforts and create new opportunities and career paths.

Since his retirement, ᎡᏚᏚ / *edudu* / *my grandfather* eschewed English, leaving ᎡᏟᏏ / *elisi* / *my grandmother* to be his intermediary. When I was with them in town, they would often prompt to speak on their behalf, as neither of them felt very confident with English. On the porch, ᎡᏚᏚ / *edudu* / *my grandfather* spoke Cherokee almost exclusively. If he used English, it was just a phrase or two because he was doing an impression of someone who only spoke English or because it was necessary to land a joke. I vividly remember him telling a lengthy story about ᎤᏥ / *utsi* / *his mom* translating for ᎤᏙᏔ / *udoda* / *his dad* to someone from the bank. She explained to the bank man that they would pay their note later because "He got no cents." The whole story was delivered in Cherokee, except for the last line, because the pun was not funny in Cherokee. The story always brought big laughs no matter how many times he told it because his delivery and comedic timing were impeccable.

However, on this evening, as the ᏄᏓ / *lolo* / *locusts* sang, he spoke in English. He said his grandfather, my great-great-grandfather, was Creek. He said he told the government he was Cherokee because he was part of the ceremonial grounds and that was what mattered. He said he thought if he claimed Creek, or even part Creek, he might be forced to leave his family in Cherokee Nation to settle among Creek people. After this short speech in English, I heard his chair creak in the darkness on the porch as he leaned back, clearly finished. Even in my youth, I knew I had heard something of great import, although I was not sure about its meaning. The stillness on the porch was only disturbed by the sputtering of the citronella candles. As ᎡᏚᏚ / *edudu* / *my grandfather* inhaled quietly on his pipe, a visible ember flared a dull orange, and the only other sound was the insects singing in the trees.

Throughout my years in elementary and middle school, I had taken part in a program called Johnson-O'Malley. It originated with a congressional act to financially assist in the education of American Indian students in the United States. Each school I attended had a different way of distributing these funds. However, one commonality was that the school's Johnson-O'Malley Program, or JOM for short, would provide limited school supplies to students. In my freshman year of high school, I became close to our JOM coordinator and she would ask me to file student forms. This is how I became aware of blood quantum and the varying degrees of Indianness in our rural school. Numbers like 1/64, 1/128, and 1/256 were common on the Certificate Degree of Indian Blood, or CDIB, cards I filed. During this time, I got my own CDIB card and stopped relying on my mother's CDIB in tandem with my own birth certificate to prove my eligibility for JOM notebooks, pencils, and pens. We sent in the requisite papers and received the CDIB card, sometimes ironically called a "white card" because it is printed on white paper under a stiff laminate. There was no hint of the complex biological heritage in my family because there in print I was listed as 4/4 Cherokee. We filed the stiff white card away at home and moved on with our lives.

From family oral history and contemporary practice, I knew my maternal side was Nighthawk Keetoowah, a Cherokee religious system marked by its apolitical stance, historic resistance to U.S. and Cherokee nationalism, and active resistance to the allotment process. As someone who dabbled in genealogy, I had ordered the interviews for some of the original enrollees in my ancestry. The Locusts and the Tehees, specifically Jess and Dora Tehee's enrollment jacket, for my maternal side and the McLemores and the Pumpkins for my paternal side. I reviewed them with interest but not with any serious scrutiny until 2013, when I was hired as executive director of the Cherokee Heritage Center (CHC) in Park Hill, Oklahoma. Through the inordinately kind and patient Gene Norris there in the Cherokee Family Research Center, a CHC department dedicated to genealogy, I was introduced to another method for genealogical research. There, I first saw my family's oral history confirmed in black and white.

Gene and Jerry Clark, a gentleman who retired from the National Archives and volunteered full-time at the center, introduced me to the Guion Miller Rolls. They explained these rolls as a list of Eastern Cherokee Indians who were applying to receive shares in a settlement. Gene and Jerry helped me to find the Guion Miller applications for Jess Tehee ᏥᎢᎡ, my great-grandfather, and Jack Tehee ᏥᎢᎡ, my great-great-grandfather. Both of the applications for the father, Jack ᏥᎢᎡ, and the son, Jess ᏥᎢᎡ, were rejected.[6] However, someone had added "Applicant a Creek" in big, bold strokes to the father's action page as well. Within both applications are statements describing Jack's mother, my great-great-great-grandmother, being taken in by the Wildcat family. It is also stated that both father and son had lived in Cherokee Nation their entire lives. None of this information was a revelation, as it was information that had long been discussed as family oral history. However, seeing it in writing did feel like validation.

Both father's and son's Miller applications took place in June 1907. This was almost five years after their enrollment interviews with the Dawes Commission.

The son's, and his wife, Dora's ᏂᎮᏡ, enrollment interview took place in June 1902, after Redbird Smith and Nighthawk Keetoowah Society leaders had been jailed and forced to comply with allotment proceedings. The son and his wife were both Nighthawks, so I theorize they refused to take part in allotment proceedings before this time. In his Dawes Commission interview, the son is asked through interpreter Wallace Thornton what degree of Cherokee blood he claims. He tells him that he is a full-blood. The next question is "What is the name of your father?"

> **A.** "Jack Tehee."
> **Q.** "Is he living?"
> **A.** "Yes, sir."
> **Q.** "He is a Cherokee by blood, is he?"
> **A.** "Yes, sir."[7]

I dearly wish there were a Cherokee transcript of this interview. Largely because I have never known a Cherokee language equivalent to the honorific *sir*. I would like to know if the use of *sir* in this exchange is a choice by the interpreter or if there is a Cherokee language equivalent that has fallen out of use. However, I would also like to know how the question of whether his father, Jack ᏂᎮᏡ, is Cherokee was posed. In any case, the Dawes Commission interview for the son further validates family oral history and provides written evidence of the story **RSS** / *edudu* / *my grandfather* told on the porch.

The information in the Guion Miller applications for the son and his father, specifically the notation of the father being rejected because he was Creek, motivated me to take a second look for a Dawes Commission interview with the father. After all, the son was on record in his Dawes interview claiming his father was a Cherokee by blood. He did so ostensibly to protect the family from any possibility of forced separation. However, five years later in his Miller application, the son is forthright about his father being Creek. Forced removal took place in 1838–1839, but the exodus to the western homelands must have been keenly remembered even in 1902 and 1907 during those official interviews. These ancestors made conscious decisions to tie our family, and themselves, to Cherokee land, thereby choosing a path for their descendants.

The father, Jack Tehee ᏂᎮᏡ, was a full-blood Creek who never lived among Creek people; he married a Cherokee woman, worshiped at Cherokee ceremonial grounds, and by family accounts spoke Cherokee and Creek equally well. Due to the similarity in father's and son's Miller applications, I expected to see a mirror of the son's Dawes application, if one existed. I expected the father had claimed to be Cherokee by blood based on the social and community markers of Cherokeeness that often outweighed biology and ancestry. However, when I found Dawes Enrollment Jacket 9292 for Jack Tehee ᏛᎭᏒ, it contained a different story. Through the same interpreter, Wallace Thornton, the father is asked, "Do you claim to be Cherokee by blood?"

> **A.** "No, sir; he is not a Cherokee. He is an Indian, he says, but he is not a Cherokee."
> **Q.** "Are you an adopted Creek?"
> **A.** "Yes, sir."
> **Q.** "Are you a full blood Creek?"
> **A.** "Yes, sir."[8]

The rhythm of the interpretation here clearly shows the interpreter's role in crafting the narrative, unlike Jess's interview that masked the role save for use of honorifics. Later notes in the jacket show the father was on an 1880 roll of Cherokee citizens as Jack Charles and on an 1896 census of Cherokee Nation citizens as Jack Charles, Creek Roll. This spurred official questions from the Dawes Commission, as a letter of inquiry to the chief clerk of the Cherokee Enrollment Division was sent from the chief clerk of the Creek Enrollment Division requesting the father's enrollment status. The inquiry states that the father is "an old soldier residing near Braggs Station" and that he submitted an application to be enrolled as a Creek citizen by blood.[9] The Cherokee Nation Enrollment Division responded with a Cherokee Nation roll card for Jack Tehee ᏛᎭᏒ and referenced Creek Enrollment Application 962 in the heading.

The Creek Enrollment Jacket for the father contains detailed information regarding his Creek ancestry. He was a member of Arbeka Deep Fork ceremonial grounds but was born and raised in Cherokee Nation. He had not returned to Creek Nation, although he is a full-blood Creek. The original Dawes application was made on his behalf by someone who knew him, and then he was called in to provide more information. During that interview, he stated, "It will be impossible for me to remove to the Creek Nation and I will relinquish my rights there rather than do so."[10] On February 28, 1907, Jack Tehee ᏛᎭᏒ was officially denied enrollment as a citizen by blood of the Creek Nation. The old soldier was born and raised in Cherokee Nation, which makes me a fifth-generation resident of this land, or sixth if you include his mother. They were two Creeks taken in by Cherokees whose descendants became full-blood Cherokees through community standard, if not ancestry. The father officially cut ties with Creek Nation, ceding his rights to Creek citizenship and ties to Creek land, to solidify his connection to his wife, to his family, to their ceremonial ground, and to Cherokee land. I now recognize the enormity of this choice for the father, an old soldier, who had not witnessed removal but had come of age in its reverberation.

The story that **RSS** / *edudu* / *my grandfather* told all those years ago was absolutely true. The son, Jess ᏍᏒᎡᏞ, had claimed his father, Jack ᏍᏒᎡᏞ, was Cherokee by blood in his Dawes interview. Possibly because he feared one, or both, of them would have been forced to relocate to Creek Nation were their Creek lineage known. In addition, the father had been living, speaking, singing, and dancing as a full-blood Cherokee among Cherokee people his whole life. Plus, he had married a Cherokee wife, and in Cherokee social organization at the time, he, and his children with her, belonged to her and to her people. It seems right this was confirmed culturally and socially. Yet, it seems profane to be confirmed legally with eight strokes from a typewriter that said, "Yes, sir." The story in our oral history was the son's and confirmed in black and white in his Dawes interview in 1902. However, it left out that his father, Jack Tehee ᏍᏒᎡᏞ, had to consciously choose to tie himself to Cherokee land and citizenship by severing his ties with Creek Nation. It also did not include the role of the Dawes Commission in recognizing his choice and denying his Creek Nation application to affirm him as a Cherokee citizen. The Dawes Commission then further affirmed him as a Cherokee by blood, although they recognized he did not have Cherokee lineage. Ultimately, the father's ties to family, community, and land propelled his Cherokee citizenship, although his available choices could not adequately, or accurately, encompass his personhood.

I take an extremely cynical view of the Dawes Commission and its decision-making process. Allotment was a land grab to make Indian lands available for white settlement. The Dawes Allotment Act broke up communal landholdings and reduced tribal land bases dramatically. It was of no consequence to Dawes commissioners whether the father received an allotment in Cherokee Nation or Creek Nation, as long as they were sure he was only counted in one place. The same interpreter and commissioners interviewed both father and son. Their applications were 9292 and 9296, respectively. They were both interviewed on June 16, 1902. Yet, although the father is noted as a full-blood Creek adopted by Cherokees, his son is noted as a full-blood Cherokee. The son referenced his father in his interview, but the questioning in the father's interview did not allow him to identify his son. Perhaps, the Dawes commissioners did not connect the two because there was no explicit statement making it clear. Perhaps, the interpreter helped the father and son in their interview answers. There is ample room for speculation on this front, but it will remain shrouded in mystery.

The story of a full-blood Creek father and his full-blood Cherokee son is only one of many intriguing cases on the Dawes Rolls. These records are rife with mistakes of all kinds. Some individuals were enrolled by neighbors or distant relatives who incorrectly guessed names and ages, as shown in the Creek Enrollment Jacket 962, where the father, Jack ᏍᏒᎡᏞ, is listed as either Jake or Jacob. As shown by my family story, each of these decisions leaves a legacy of repercussions for descendants. I heard our family story's complexities while sitting on a porch in rural Oklahoma while the locusts were singing. Now, as an adult, with children of my own, I consider the difficult choices faced by my ancestors who sought to enmesh themselves in family, ceremony, community, and land to firmly secure themselves in the wake of both Indian Removal and the American Civil War.

When I saw "Applicant a Creek" in black ink on my great-great-grandfather's Miller application, it validated all the oral history I already knew. I thought back to the moonless night on the porch when RSS / *edudu* / *my grandfather* spoke English to tell us about his Creek grandfather. That moment lives with me. The creaky aluminum lawn chairs and the tobacco smoke are unforgettable sense memories. The soft, gentle moments on the porch, enveloped by the inky night and my grandparents' patience, built a foundation of strength and resilience I would often draw on later during times of hardness and difficulty. During those moments of stillness, it felt like time moved more slowly. The folly of youth led me to believe there would always be another evening on the porch where I could ask more questions. Unfortunately, there is never enough time for all the questions you would like to ask. This is true no matter how wisely you employ each moment.

I would have loved to have brought the Miller applications and the Dawes enrollment jackets from the Cherokee and Creek applications to share on the porch. Since that time, I have also gotten more of my family's Guion Miller applications, assisted again by the deeply fabulous Gene Norris at the Cherokee Family Research Center. These documents contain a rich trove of genealogical information and go much further than the Dawes enrollment applications for the same people. Often, these two sets of applications are separated by only a handful of years. While my grandparents are not here in person to enjoy these peeks into history, I can share them with RⱧ RSⱧZ / *etsi edutsino* / *my mother and my uncle*. These are the oldest members of my family now. Once there were eight brothers and sisters, but only seven survived to adulthood. Now only four remain. A family disagreement after my grandparents passed split the remaining siblings into factions. The older two, strongly rooted in clan and ceremony, are allied, while the younger two disavowed the family, and each other, entirely. With my grandparents' passing, it seemed the staunch foundation of the family cracked like red Oklahoma clay during a drought.

The area where my grandparents lived was filled with people who had been there for generations. So much so that when someone new moved in, everyone still called the place by the old name. Even after a decade, the name of that place didn't change, and everyone still called them "the new people." In those evenings on the porch, our laughter could probably be heard up on Girty Hill, just like we could sometimes hear theirs. If we weren't laughing or listening to someone tell a story, a contented silence would fall. In that silence, the only sounds were the pipes of RⱭⱵ RSSZ / *elisi eduduno* / *my grandmother and my grandfather* as the tobacco burned and the insects singing in the trees. The quote that opens this piece was collected by Durbin Feeling ⱧⱤⱠR, renowned Cherokee linguist, in his fieldwork with Cherokee speakers. The person he recorded called those insects **ᏓᏓ** / *lolo* / locusts. This is something most people around here do. However, they are actually cicadas. Yet, regardless of what you call them, their song remains the same, and we Tehees are like that too.

NOTES

1. The chapter title is from Durbin Feeling, *Cherokee-English Dictionary* (Tahlequah, Okla.: Cherokee Nation, 1975), 146.

2. It is polite to mark a person who has passed away with this Cherokee word but not required. There will be disagreement on how it should be employed, but I use it when speaking or writing a person's proper Cherokee or English name. I do not use it for familial relationship terms.

3. As this person is a historical figure, it is common knowledge he is no longer with us. I have never heard a Cherokee speaker mark these figures with ᏥᎦᏒ / *jigesv* / *their time has passed* so I choose not to do so.

4. Treaty signed ceding Cherokee Nation lands in the east to the U.S. government and served as impetus for the Trail of Tears. Unlawful because signatories were not authorized by Cherokee Nation Council to cede land on behalf of the tribe. Led to the assassination of most signatories plus countless others; most assassinated were members of the so-called Treaty Party.

5. ᎫᏦ / *gule* / acorn is Cherokee slang for a white person. Some theorize that the caps of acorns look like hats worn by early settler colonists, while another theory holds it is inspired because an acorn is white all the way through once the hull is breached.

6. Applications Submitted for the Eastern Cherokee Roll of 1909 (Guion Miller Roll), Jack Tehee, Application 17179, and Jesse Tehee, 27748, Eastern Cherokee Applications of the U.S. Court of Claims, 1906–1909 (online database with images, Fold3, accessed June 11, 2021), https://www .fold3.com//title/73/eastern-cherokee-applications.

7. Dawes Records, Cherokee Nation, Cherokee by Blood, Jess Tehee, Enrollment Jacket 9296, Applications for Enrollment of the Commission to the Five Civilized Tribes, 1898–1914 (online database with images, Fold3, accessed June 11, 2021), https://www.fold3.com//title/70/dawes-packets.

8. Dawes Records, Cherokee Nation, Cherokee by Blood, Jack Tehee, Enrollment Jacket 9292, Applications for Enrollment of the Commission to the Five Civilized Tribes, 1898–1914 (online database with images, Fold3, accessed June 11, 2021), https://www.fold3.com//title/70/ dawes-packets.

9. Dawes Records, Creek Nation, Creek by Blood, Jack Tehee, Enrollment Jacket 962, Applications for Enrollment of the Commission to the Five Civilized Tribes, 1898–1914 (online database with images, Fold3, accessed June 11, 2021), https://www.fold3.com//title/70/dawes-packets.

10. Creek Nation, Tehee, Enrollment Jacket 962, Applications for Enrollment of the Commission to the Five Civilized Tribes, 1898–1914 (online database with images, Fold3, accessed June 11, 2021), https://www.fold3.com//title/70/dawes-packets.

Amikode

LEANNE BETASAMOSAKE SIMPSON

"OMG, Parent! What is the point of building this friggen' dam when we all know it's going to get destroyed by May and we will be right back to where we started?"

Amikoons was making even the small things in life slightly more difficult for their parents, and it was beginning to wear on Amik.[1] There was a lot of actual work left to do that did not involve selfies, picking a song and listening to it for thirty-five seconds, and incessant complaining.

"Why are we building a dam, anyway? This sucks. Let's build a selfie station."

The apocalypse could not come fast enough for Amik.

"Also, there is NO WAY I'm friggen' going swimming."

Amik hoped, prayed, and worried that Amikoons was learning something today, but they weren't sure they were. Amikwag knowledge doesn't embed itself because of one's proximity.

Amik remembered the first time they were tasked with building a dam without their parents, and it was a moment.

It was one of the sharp edges of life.

A gathering of faith and hope.

An expulsion of uncertainty.

A feeling of betrayal at being left to do something on their own that eventually, with persistence, melted into a river of humility.

"The best parts of lonely."[2]

Amik remembered wishing they had paid more attention to the details. They wished they had been more engaged and that this process was less a series of steps and lists and more learned.

Here and now, Amik wondered what Amikoons would do in a similar situation. Would they even try to build the dam on their own? Or would they just sit there and drown in their abandonment, growing it until it festered into a series of tweets that would garnish heaps of likes and retweets, reinforcing their own chosen uselessness and affirming the perceived injustice?

Amik felt like they were a hundred years old. The world had changed, without them. They felt cynical and out of touch and irrelevant, and they were.

Back in the day, before the genocide, Amikwag had a networked dam every one hundred meters, and it was perfection. Amikwag's responsibilities were a foundational part of the circuitry and the life of stream. Dams managed water levels and flooding, removed excess nutrients and chemicals, worked as caring nurseries for salmonids and frogs, and made refuges for migrating songbirds. Before the zhaagansh got here, there were between sixty and four hundred million of us, and by the early 1900s that had dropped to a hundred thousand.

Primarily because we are waterproof.

Amikoons wants to hear none of this, much less a parent lecture, so Amik lays off for now.

"Can you go cut some aspens—about fifteen centimeters in diameter?"

Amikoons leaves, headphones on, phone engaged, and Amik wonders how much longer than the required twenty minutes this will take.

Amikoons is back in one minute with no poplar.

"My teeth hurt and I couldn't find any."

Deep breaths.

"Let's go back together."

"Okay."

"Google 'How big is the biggest beaver dam.'"

"850 m."

"WTH."

"WTH."

"Google 'Nictitating membrane.'"

"It's a third eyelid. Transparent. Functions like swim goggles. Do we have these?"

It was a constant battle to get the kid to gnaw on enough wood to keep their teeth a reasonable size and functional, and all kinds of treaties were made and broken trading gnawing for screen time. Amik's gut sank with the thought that Amikoons might not be able to cut down the poplar. There was also a kind of blind faith in this with the assumption that Amik was going to be skilled enough to get Amikoons's teeth into the bark in the first place.

This is all Amik's fault. They thought they were spending a reasonable amount of time on the land, more than most. Amik took gigs building selfie stations in the parks, bars, and airports and mostly Amikoons stayed home with their screens. The stations consisted of a replicate lodge, small, but still enough for a family, some poplar branches strategically placed, a couple of blue backdrops for sky and water, human footprints, and good lighting.

Yet here they were.

Spending a week on the creek building a dam they both knew would be destroyed by the city shortly after the photos and news stories.

Yet here they were.

Yet here they were, along with resentment, cynicism, self-doubt.

Yet, here they were.

Amik wondered if their ancestors would even recognize them.

Amikoons wonders if they are going to learn anything that will improve their Minecraft beaver dam situation.

Amik selects two trees. Amikoons picks the song for chewing, asks Amik to start their tree, and Amik obliges.

Amikoons takes a mouth wide open beside the gnaw marks selfie.

Amik says, "Race you."

Amik gnaws slowly, watching Amikoons's progress out of the side of their eye. Amikoons is doing better than one might expect. It's working.

Amikoons is being an amikoons.

There is a swell of emotion in Amik, a mixture of relief, pride, and devastating sadness. A small victory that should never have been a victory in the first place.

Amik and their Amikoons carry the poplar back to the site in their mouths and place the branches on the shore.

Amikoons asks Amik for a pic of the carrying and Amik obliges because reciprocity isn't about giving back what you want, it is about giving back what is needed or what has been asked of you.

Amik eats some of the buds and branches while Amikoons finds their gummy worms.

There is a moment.

A sort of sad, crappy moment, but a moment nonetheless.

Then Amikoons takes the branch in their mouth and swims toward the dam.

NOTES

1. Translations are available at the Ojibwe People's Dictionary, https://ojibwe.lib.umn.edu/.
2. "Left and Leaving," lyrics by John K. Samson, track 7 on the Weakerthans, *Left and Leaving*, G7 Welcoming Committee Records, 2000, lyrics published in John K. Samson, *Lyrics and Poems 1997–2012* (Winnipeg: ARP Press, 2012), 40.

PART III

Privatization as State Violence

Itinerant Indigeneities

Navigating Guåhan's Treacherous Roads through CHamoru Feminist Pathways

CHRISTINE TAITANO DELISLE
VICENTE M. DIAZ

Vince and Tina: Here and There

"On this side . . . On that side . . ." This way of orchestrating not a binary but a complex and contradictory range of political, cultural, and analytic Indigenous possibilities was how our late, beloved sister, Teresia Teaiwa, once structured an experimental essay for an otherwise academic journal some twenty years ago.[1] And so, in a like-minded and similarly motivated homage to Teresia, we offer a juxtaposition in form and content, discipline and voicing—albeit laid out and ordered sequentially rather than horizontally on the page—that engages not allotment proper but a kindred example of what our editors refer generatively to as allotment's "analogous settler privatization policies."

Our example is the story of modern roadbuilding in our home, the American colony of Guam (Guåhan in the CHamoru vernacular) in the Mariana Islands, the homelands and waters of the CHamoru people.[2] The story of modern roads on Guåhan involves a tension between two (not binary) sets of forces. On the one hand, there are the insidious forces of empire that continue to lord over Guåhan's lands and waters up against Indigenous CHamoru relationalities (self-defining relations of kinship and reciprocity between humans and other living beings, including land-, water-, and airscapes). On the other hand, there are hegemonic and competing forms of Indigenous CHamoru modernities. By "Indigenous modernities" we refer to the now dominant ways that Indigenous CHamorus have adopted and consumed (and assimilated), for better or for worse, colonial ideas and practices over the past five centuries. Our goal is to call critical attention to competing Indigenous forms of modernity in search of those that do not replicate, even if unwittingly, colonial logics and relations as these, in turn, co-opt and traffic on Indigenous cultural ideas, values, and practices.

This essay begins with Vince (Pohnpeian/Filipino from Guåhan), who offers a survey of roadbuilding in Guåhan under a pre–World War II U.S. Naval regime in a voice that is not of the Indigenous CHamoru but that nonetheless seeks to model an indigenously informed critique of colonial discourse in and for his home island. Though this section appears first, as if to lay, as might be more commonly imagined and practiced, a historical and political context proper, you, the reader, might just as well begin with Tina (CHamoru, taotao Yigu, Chålan Gayineru), whose following section seeks to nudge a defiant CHamoru feminist political and cultural consciousness forward without falling into the potholes and dead ends of Guåhan's literal and figurative roads of modernity. Wishing to maintain the relatively autonomous but entangled perspectives of our critical voices, but mindful of how the sequential ordering of these perspectives within the space of a single article can also inflect readings and meanings in unintentional ways, we invite you, the reader, to choose where to proceed. We think either section works as a starting point and might even lend insight or opportunity to more expansive ways of reading and understanding in instances like these, when disciplinary and cultural points of view are offered in a single text.

Vince: Packing White *Kaskåhu*

> We are thinking seriously of calling the new road into camp "the Great White Way."
>
> —U.S. Marine Corps. Station, Guam, 1915

From the last quarter of the seventeenth century, when Jesuit missionaries operationalized its political and social hegemony over the Mariana Islands and the Indigenous CHamoru people, to its last gasp following the Spanish-American War in 1898, the seat of Spanish colonial rule in these islands moved along carabao cart paths, made of crushed coral limestone, that emanated outward, from the town of Hagåtña at the narrow and central western part of the island of Guåhan to a handful of other villages to the south, east, and north of the footprint-shaped island. Since the end of the Spanish-CHamoru wars of the seventeenth century, all but a handful of CHamorus had been forcibly relocated from the other Northern Mariana Islands and resettled in Guåhan. By the end of the nineteenth century, the majority of CHamorus resided in Hagåtña, in the port town of Sumay, or in a handful of southern villages, where they remained under watchful eyes of the resident parish priests and ruling families, even as the majority of CHamorus would try to spend as much time tending to small patches of crops and livestock at *lånchos* or tiny ranches spread out over the entire island.

Called *cascajo* in Spanish, *kaskåhu* in CHamoru, the substance of these gravel paths—and the circuits they comprised, and the relations they carried—was expanded upon and paved over dutifully by American naval officials who took over Guåhan in 1899 to transform the island into a coaling station to service America's colonial appetite across the Pacific. Packing kaskåhu into modern paved roads involved a process, still at work today, of ensuring that Guåhan remains a potent strategic military base of operations for America's interests in the Pacific and Asia, but a process that also provided much substance for the remaking of CHamoru Indigeneity. And so, somewhat like the tar that by 1918 began to hold the stuff of kaskåhu together during tropical rainstorms, roads also helped bind the terms of American hegemony to Indigenous CHamoru political aspirations, first for U.S. citizenship and then later for modern progress that, while maintaining important vestiges of pre–World War II Indigenous culture and identity, were also articulated more decidedly in terms of American exceptionalism, albeit not without ambivalence and ambiguity. "Packing kaskåhu," we might say, can stand as a useful metaphor for understanding how the navy's idea of paving roads in Guåhan solidified modern American and colonial ideas about development and the assimilation of Indigenous CHamorus through notions of cleanliness and order that were also highly racialized, gendered, and sexualized. Such were the terms for the larger stakes in roadbuilding in Guåhan. In its 1950 report, the navy would refer to America's civic project of benevolent assimilation as "the long road to rehabilitation," a colonial itinerary that, from the get-go, recognized how the interests of America in Guåhan were "intimately interwoven" with that between "the welfare of the Natives and that of the Navy."[3] Wrote Governor George Dyer in 1904:

> Conditions are such that the interests of the Naval Station and natives are intimately interwoven. The one, as an organization, cannot escape, or live far apart, from the other, and the efficiency of the first depends entirely on the welfare of the second. . . . It is therefore incumbent on us for our self-protection and efficiency to give the natives such care as they are unable to get for themselves, to see that they are kept healthy and free from contagion, are afforded practical instruction in their sole pursuit, agriculture, and to educate some of them to occupy such positions as clerks, mechanics, and intelligent laborers in the Naval Station that will eventually be established here.[4]

Roads, in this sense, were also prophylactic, kind of like colonial rubbers, used while white men—and, in time, CHamoru men—checked out and then penetrated lands now figured as wild virgins in need of a good working over as the prerequisite for achieving and protecting America's civilizational project overseas. To the extent that the record reveals a range of Indigenous CHamoru interest in road paving, the historical packing of kaskåhu into colonial roads also carried an equally complex set of Indigenous CHamoru concerns and values that were bound up in the larger project of their so-called benevolent assimilation into productive American citizens.

From 1900 to the Japanese invasion in December 1941, and in the tremendous buildup from 1944 to 1950, the U.S. Navy's Public Works division dutifully paved hundreds of miles on the island that is only thirty miles long and four to eight miles wide. Cascajo/kaskåhu roads connected, first, primary military organs, such as Apra Harbor in the upstart naval station in the villages of Sumay and Piti, with Hagåtña, the seat of the government. Later arterials would link Hagåtña and Piti to radio stations in the heights above both locales and to another strategic locale in present-day Ipao Beach in Tumon, where in 1902 the navy established a leper colony that remained until 1912, when it began forcibly deporting to the Philippine island of Culion those CHamorus afflicted with the disease.

The interest in roadbuilding—and its connection to cleaning up the island—began even before the late-1898 signing of the Treaty of Paris that ended the Spanish-American War and transferred possession of Guåhan from Spain to the United States. No sooner had Admiral George Dewey's command secured the Philippines than the Department of the Navy sent its gunboat *Bennington* and collier *Brutus* from the Philippines to Guåhan to conduct a hydrographic survey and to take possession of lands needed for a coaling station.[5] In charge was Lt. Vincendon Cottman, whose hydrographic survey linked the need to pave "a good carriage road around the island" with the need to deport the influential Spanish padres, whom he called "moral lepers," but also the need for American doctors, public pharmacies, mandatory health examinations, and teaching English.[6] Following Cottman (and his recommendations), subsequent naval governors uniformly viewed good roads as prerequisites to the benevolent task of improving the social and economic lot of the CHamorus, especially of making them a self-supporting or self-sufficient people. In a section of the aforementioned 1950 naval report, subtitled "Good Health Travels Good Roads," the navy lionized its public works and public health programs as the "team . . . which hauled the heaviest load the longest distance" (on that "long road to the rehabilitation of Guam").[7] In that jaunt, the navy identified the CHamoru population as the "heaviest load" to bear, pathologizing CHamorus as "a listless, ambitionless, unorganized mass of humanity stirred only by the hope for individual survival."[8] Thus, in the pre- and postwar years under U.S. Navy governance, all roads in Guåhan were also said to begin (and end) in America: under the navy's public works program, roads were originally classified into two types—naval and federal—according to their funding sources, although in 1917, naval governor Roy Smith felt compelled to point out that the distinction was "fictitious" in that the entire island was essentially "a naval station, and that all roads inured to the benefit of the nation's interests" anyway.[9] What follows are some highlights of the paving process and their figuration.[10]

From 1900 to 1941, the primary organs of the navy's expression—the *Guam Newsletter, The Guam Recorder,* and the naval governors' *Annual Reports* to the Department of the Navy—regularly document the progress of roadbuilding, which, by the second decade, began to extend southward, beyond Piti and Hagåtña, to the southern villages of Humåtak, Malesso', and Inalåhan, but also northward, to the villages of Dedidu and

Yigu. From Hagåtña, roads also went upward and cut inland, toward Tiyan, and yet further inland, toward the east coast, to Pågu, and then southward along the east coast to Talofo'fo' and the other aforementioned southern villages.

In 1912, roadbuilding in Guåhan would begin to receive a particularly good packing with the arrival of a road roller whose first project resulted in "fine, straight road [that] opens up a beautiful and productive part of the land."[11] Shortly, we shall see what we might call the thrust needed for romancing that beauty into something useful and productive. In 1917, the navy's public works units began to mix types of crude oils and tars, called Tarvia and bituminous macadam, with cascajo.[12] These synthetic substances served as binders, but really they were the aforementioned rubbers, in slang, inasmuch as they also protected the white cascajo (and the navy's tiny budgets) from washouts— also called "nigger heads"—that were caused by heavy rains, especially from typhoons (themselves gendered female and given women's names because both were deemed indecisive and furious in nature), that are so frequent in the tropics. By the end of the 1920s, the central and southern parts of the island were finally connected, thereby linking the most fertile farmlands with ports and markets in the central part of the island. It was, we might say, a kind of colonial circumcision of an otherwise feminized island-scape.

Public works projects like road construction involved conscripted labor. In 1901, governor Seaton Schroeder imposed a personal poll tax for men between the ages of eighteen and sixty that could be waived for those men who were willing to work on projects like roadbuilding. By the start of the second decade, the navy began to offer contracts to a new class of men who had the means and authority to manage groups of laborers, and by 1917, as a sign of ruts in the system, a Native militia known as the Insular Patrol was established to help discipline the workforce, particularly at the låncho/ranch, about which more will be said shortly.

As well, the effort to extend roads beyond connecting military installations to each other, and these installations to main towns, and eventually connect all the villages around the island, were cast in terms of penetrating natural spaces explicitly understood as virginal but improperly used. With conscripted Native labor, the navy also began to "distribute public works money over the island as far as possible" by giving contracts to individual (and sometimes to teams of) CHamorus who showed a special interest in paving roads in their localities.[13] Thus, the following examples that readers familiar with Guåhan's localities will find interesting: commencing in 1912, the Finaguayoc road in the north[14] and, in 1917, the start of an "excellent road to Pago" from Hagåtña.[15] In 1917 as well, *lancherus* from the southern villages of Talofo'fo' and Inalåhan began to negotiate with governor Roy Smith, offering to provide labor for roads if the government would build bridges over the Pågu and Ilig Rivers in their localities.[16] Indeed, throughout the prewar period, we get increasing reports of enthusiastic residents who are even willing to build roads for no pay—such as residents from Santa Rosa in the north, referred to as the "Janum [*Hånom*] Road and Gallinero [*Gayineru*] natives," who were especially interested in extending the Yigu road to the northeast coastal area of Hånom.[17] As we know, Natives are fully capable of packing themselves. And yet, CHamoru enthusiasm for roadbuilding still managed to escape, or at least was not understood by, some naval officials: admiring the completion of a road and the benefits to be had from it, governor Edward Dorn lamented, "To the average native who is of a simple and pleasure-loving disposition . . . this road represents merely an easier and more direct way of passing from town to town to his fiestas and fandangos."[18] Here, we get a glimpse of how colonial roads extended Indigenous circuits and relations.

Holding the Native Down: Agricultural Penetration of Land for Prosperity

An irony of the colonial figuration of roadbuilding for self-sufficiency is that despite three centuries of Spanish colonialism, CHamorus remained self-subsistent, not dependent on any foreign system, until *sufficiency* became translated in capitalist terms under the U.S. Navy. In 1904, governor Benjamin Stone stressed that "the prosperity of the island and its people" necessitated "good roads," which was itself a precondition for modern "agricultural production."[19] Even before the formal establishment of the navy's presence, in 1899 an American trader, Benjamin Havner, identified two major obstacles to prosperity in Guåhan: firstly, CHamorus were not a good labor force because they did not value money, and secondly, the padres, whom he described as the "only thing that will induce a Chamorro to do a decent day's work for money, or sell any of the products of his ranch," as if CHamorus were ignorant children who could only be impelled to work by their white Catholic fathers.[20] This was exactly the paternal and patronizing view that informed and upheld half a century of naval public works, like roadbuilding. In its aforementioned 1950 report, the navy boasted that in that time period, it "had guided a people from illiteracy, peonage, and apathy to where, in conservative estimate and appraisal, it had been educated to accept and intelligently to discharge the responsibilities (as well as the privileges) of citizenship."[21] In 1912, the racialized infantilization with respect to public works projects as a path to civilization as engendered in the male figure of Uncle Sam was rendered quite explicitly in a cartoon that ran in the *Guam Newsletter*.

In critically surveying the discourse of road paving on Guåhan during the naval government period (1900–1941 and 1944–1950), the site of CHamoru Indigeneity that is most at stake—the presumptive place and practice of backwardness, from whence and which CHamorus needed to be rescued and weaned—is the låncho, a particularly packed site of Indigenous life forged in relationship to foreign efforts to domesticate CHamoru Indigeneity. The låncho is typically a small plot of land, notably away from towns and villages, wherein CHamorus cultivated crops and raised livestock for

"More Like His Dad Every Day."
Illustration from the *Guam Newsletter* 4, no. 1 (July 1912): 12.

self-subsistence and barter, especially to augment hunting and fishing. It was also a space of reprieve from the always watchful eyes of the padres or colonial officials, where CHamorus could maintain vestiges of older and intimate relations with the natural and spiritual worlds. In CHamoru discourse, the låncho connotes cultural depth through antiquity as well as connectivity and continuity with *tåddong* (deep) cultural and spiritual interiority or *takhilo'* Indigeneity. It is not surprising, therefore, that the navy often lamented låncho sociality as an impediment to progress. Road-building and agricultural development amounted to first halting, then at least redirecting, CHamoru energy and mobility to and from the låncho. Roads, in this sense, were necessary solutions to ending sloth produced where Spanish despotic misrule was said to meet primitive people. That site was the låncho, and proper growth required good roads that facilitated efficient travel to such places that could also be transformed as sites of more productive labor. Of the time it took to get to the låncho, for example, a navy civil engineer, L. M. Cox, observed that "if a ranch is within an hour's walk of the town, its owner will spend two hours of his day on the road to and from his work; if at a greater distance, he will spend a day or two, or even a whole week on his farm."[22] However, Cox noticed that record time could be achieved, especially on Sundays, when the lancheru wanted to get to the cockfights held in town!

In time, the effort to get Natives to move more efficiently settled instead for getting them to remain at their lånchos longer, but more productively—that is, through modern methods and marketing. Thus did the navy launch a Back-to-the-Farm campaign—what Governor Smith referred to as "agricultural uplift" (read: colonial erection).[23] This Back-to-the-Farm (not låncho) campaign began, of course, with "improving roads" but extended to include the building of churches and schools out in the country and creating disincentives for travel and incentives for remaining in the låncho.[24] Examples included "increasing the expense of town life . . . establishing a bounty on cultivated land . . . freeing domestic animals and poultry from property taxes, and making agriculture compulsory for all persons not otherwise fully occupied, under penalty of vagrancy."[25] It was, in fact, for the enforcement of such measures that the Insular Patrol had been established. The patrol also oversaw a census of "land available for cultivation" that also counted "inhabitants by localities who are available for work" for the expressed purpose of connecting "the idle land and the idle workmen in each district."[26] In the same report, Smith observed that "traveling back and forth to the towns is being stopped. The bulls are not allowed to be tethered in the towns, and no laborers may sleep more than three miles from his work. An exception is made on Sunday."[27] To this end too, the Spanish Capuchins—scapegoated only two decades earlier—were now recruited to assist in the navy's "Back-to-the-Farm" campaign, where, to Governor Smith's satisfaction, the padres "have lent the most cordial cooperation in preaching these doctrines."[28] The new doctrine here was American modern progressivism better known as practical instruction. Taking the place of religious dogma, the new dogma involved teaching CHamorus the basic tenets of modern production beyond consumption and barter: teaching marketing and profit, and especially introducing modern, scientific methods of agricultural production. And like roads, modern agriculture was also gendered, racialized, and sexualized. A 1928 article in the *Guam Newsletter,* for example, heralded the road's potential to "open up . . . acres upon acres of virgin soil that has laid dormant since time began," particularly so if accomplished with the right "labor, capital, and improved methods of working," all of which were deemed lacking in Guam Guåhan and among CHamorus.[29] What Guåhan and Native CHamorus possessed, however, was that which, according to Patrick Wolfe, the process of settler colonialism (here through military governance) covets as it literally and symbolically eliminates Indigenous people: land.[30] And so, helping itself to CHamoru land through white Nativism's use of the first person plural *we,* the article declares, "We have the climate and the land . . . [so all that] is need[ed]" are "men from the United States induced to come here who are skilled in growing coffee, hemp. . . . Technical men to spy out the field."[31] Two months later, like some kind of pimp, the Guam Chamber of Commerce placed an advertisement titled "Wanted: American Farmers for Guam" in search of such "technical men" "in the hope that their modern methods will be of assistance and a good example to the inhabitants." The ad titillates with information about the availability of "thousands of acres of virgin government land laying waste on this island." "Here," it touts in language that is as explicitly sexual as it is racial, "is an opportunity for reputable and experienced farmers who wish to settle on this island of edenic virginity."

Itinerant Futures

I end this side part of the essay on a poem titled "Following the Flag," by one Jose C. Torres, that appeared in *The Guam Recorder* in 1925 "as a memory of my friend and *partnership* [*sic*], Antonia."

Only two and a half decades under American rule and this poem already registers interesting ambiguity and uncertainty, certainly very different from the cock-certainty of the Guam Chamber of Commerce advertisement and the racist cartoon of Guåhan as a picaninny. From one angle, the author appears to lament one of two (or both) possibilities: Americans fail to sufficiently modernize CHamorus or else CHamorus fall short of modernizing the American way. But it is also not entirely clear whether the author is lamenting failure or celebrating it, as when he ends the poem by "prais[ing] God," which can be read as sarcasm. Perhaps he is expressing gratitude that Americans weren't so successful in their efforts to modernize/Americanize the CHamorus.

122   THE GUAM RECORDER

CROSS-WORD PUZZEL NO. 4 -- SOLUTION.

FOLLOWING THE FLAG
Jose C. Torres
(I dedicate this as a memory of my friend and partnership, Antonia)

They taught the Guamanian the right way to work

And they thought the teaching was fun.

They taught them to spell and to build themselves a road

And the best way to handle a gun.

Were their salaries so big that the task was worth while

Did they save a cent of pay;

Have the average men an account with the Bank?

Never a cent, not they.

So we haven't a job and we haven't a cent;

And nobody cares a damn,

But we did our work and we have done it well

To the glory of Uncle Sam

And we've seen a lot and we've lived a lot

In this island over the sea.

Would we change with our brothers grown rich at home?

Praise be to God, not we.

"Following the Flag," by Jose C. Torres. Illustration from *The Guam Recorder* 2, no. 16 (1925): 122.

In addition to these uncertainties, there is ambiguity over how to read the title of the poem, "Following the Flag," whose meanings can fly in either direction: that is, in spite of America's teachings, CHamorus have not followed the flag properly, or, choosing "by God" not to follow the flag, CHamorus yearn for a postflag day—a day when neither the American flag nor any state flag lords over the island. While I personally like the latter but can understand and have long supported the Indigenous nationalist sentiment that would underwrite the former, my sentiment as a non-CHamoru person born and raised on Guåhan ultimately doesn't really matter when it comes to the question of CHamoru political futures. For a better sense of those possibilities, I would encourage you to do as I did: follow (or, as the case might be for you if you began with it, return to) Tina's historical analyses of CHamoru women's leadership and the older/ newer political pathways that follow this side part of the story.

Tina: Following *Famalao'an Chålan*—CHamoru Feminist Theory and Practice

> Tåya' pinekkat sin fegge. (There is no walk without footprints.)
>
> —CHamoru proverb, found in Malia Angelica Leon Guerrero Ramirez, *Los Ehemplus CHamoritus*

In CHamoru, the term *palao'an chålan* (plural, *famalao'an chålan*) literally means "woman of the road." The term is loaded with deeper meanings and greater implications for Indigenous women of Guåhan when considered in the context of women's mobilities, *kostumbren* CHamoru (traditional CHamoru custom and culture), and the U.S. Navy's "long road" of rehabilitating in public health, public education, and public works projects like hospitals, schools (and instruction in English), roads and transportation, and the introduction of modern forms of recreation, like bars, nightclubs, movies, and dances. So fraught is its meaning that even the CHamoru country singer Bobbie DeGracia-Rebanio, in her 1990 rendition of the famous 1952 Kitty Wells song "It Wasn't God Who Made Honky Tonk Angels," would capture (in her title) the CHamoru equivalent of the wild, negligent (stigmatized) woman in two words: *palao'an chålan*.

While CHamoru women entered new spaces opened up through the U.S. Navy's "long road"—nursing and teacher training schools but also bars and nightclubs—they were also at times simultaneously construed as having been drawn away from domestic and domesticated spheres of hearth and home, and of kostumbren CHamoru. CHamoru women's paths and modes of transportation themselves indexed how Guåhan's cultural and social transformation, as well as how understandings of such transformations, could likewise confine women. Take, for example, footpaths and carabao cart (*karetan karabao*) trails, which are associated with a time before the war (*åntes di i gera*) and which stood in stark contrast to the ever-increasing network of modern paved roads made of kaskåhu over which puttered U.S. military transports like jeeps and buses. The marker *åntes di i gera* evokes nostalgia for a simpler and serene way of life before it was disrupted by Japan's invasion and occupation of Guåhan (1941 to 1944) and the atrocities that occurred before American marines returned to supposedly liberate the island in 1944. Life before the war was also starkly contrasted to the hustle and bustle of postwar development. When one encounters in the archives that certain *pattera* (nurse-midwives) like Maria Taitano Aguero (Tan Marian Dogi') or Dominga Ogo Blas (Tan Inga') puttered along paved roads, one begins to understand why their Indigeneity might have been suspect or their loyalties questioned—because roads and jeeps were associated primarily with white male naval officers, but also rank-and-file soldiers and CHamoru men.[32] The word *jeep* derives from the initials *GI-Ps,* or general issue property, the same military parlance of state propriety that inspired the nickname "GI" for rank-and-file infantrymen.

"On the road" for significant periods, a pattera—particularly a younger, unmarried one—ran the risk of being called a palao'an chålan. Or, in its most negative connotation, a *puta,* as the pattera Joaquina Babauta Herrera (Tan Kina') revealed.[33] The figure of impurity and cultural abandonment, the puta was also regarded as a traitor, a collaborator. Following the work of feminist scholars who have challenged the virgin/whore dichotomy, I suggest the term *palao'an chålan* can mark a defiant and liberating moment when determined Indigenous women, in this case the pattera, transcended rigid boundaries and prescribed roles that confined them even while they continued to serve the needs and well-being of the family (*achafñak*).[34] The narrative and figure imagery of the famalao'an chålan is especially significant for thinking through colonial histories of keeping CHamoru women down—down the *via sacra,* or "sacred path," the navy's long road, and newer colonial route thoroughfares like the annual Liberation Day festivities parade route along Marine Corps Drive.[35]

If roads orchestrated Indigenous mobility (refer to Vince's side), the navy's long road of resuscitating CHamorus also entailed the emptying (and confiscating) of CHamoru lands and attempts to transform CHamoru land tenure and land-kinship relations.[36] It is in this process that we begin to discern the subjectification of CHamorus under the terms of heteropatriarchy (refer to the illustration "More Like His Dad Every Day") under the authority of naval and civilian governors and U.S. governance. This form of emptying, Aileen Moreton-Robinson argues, involves larger discursive processes by which the "possessive logics of patriarchal white sovereignty" disavow and dispossess the Indigenous subject, confining and conscripting it within modernity but in ways that leave Indigenous peoples outside the white logic of capitalism (and progress and development).[37] Anne Perez Hattori argues that the navy erased CHamoru men through forms of narrativizing a prior history of warfare during the Spanish era and the widespread epidemics that ensued, while operationalizing the power and fecundity

"Wanted: American Farmers." From *The Guam Recorder* 5, no. 4 (July 1928): 88.

88   THE GUAM RECORDER   JULY 1928

WANTED

AMERICAN FARMERS FOR GUAM

There are thousands of acres of virgin government land laying waste on this island that should be working for the needs of the world.

Governor Shapley is in favor of American farmers coming to Guam, with the hope that their modern methods will be of assistance and a good example to the inhabitants.

Here is an opportunity for reputable and experienced farmers who wish to settle on this island of edenic virginity where it is summer all winter, and the planting season is every month of the year.

Particulars concerning general information, the possibilities of securing land and growing Coffee, Sugar, Cocoa, Coconuts, Pineapples, Oranges, Lemons, Limes, Bananas, and all the tropical fruits and vegetables, including most of the garden vegetables you are familiar with, will be sent to interested parties by

THE GUAM CHAMBER OF COMMERCE
GUAM

of CHamoru women as "bearers of the race." The island, Hattori writes, was "feminized not only as a terrain from which men were literally absent" but as a "space available for the colonial penetration of a masculinized naval establishment" in which the navy saw its mission as one of rehabilitating the CHamoru race.[38]

A 1928 Chamber of Commerce advertisement (reproduced above) exemplifies well this feminized emptying and expropriation of CHamoru lands and is an example of what Patrick Wolfe calls settler colonialism's "logic of (Native) elimination."[39] These forms of emptying are also discursive modes of gendered dispossession, and, as Maile Arvin, Eve Tuck, and Angie Morrill argue, a way of "disappearing" Indigenous structures of governance and kinship, gender roles, and sexuality—all "key to making Indigenous peoples into settler state citizens."[40] The processes of feminizing, emptying, securing, and domesticating land were the colonial vehicle or, better yet, the road or path through and on which the navy subjected CHamorus not only to American agriculture but to American ideas of economic, social, and political development.

Even "More Like His Dad" Today

In 2014, the Guam Visitors Bureau (GVB) unveiled "Tourism 2020," a "road map" to rebrand the island as a family-friendly idyllic paradise "set amidst a unique 4,000-year old culture."[41] Hoping to change Guåhan's image in Asia as simply "close and cheap," the road map boasted three objectives: to make the island a "first-tier destination," to diversify its market (roughly 80 percent of tourists are Japanese), and to reach a two-million-visitor mark. Then–GVB chairperson Mark Baldyga described the road map, in military parlance, as a "hard-charging" strategic plan that would catapult Guåhan to "an entirely new level." Employing what the larger marketing industry calls a "blue ocean" strategy of "uncontested market space," GVB committed to offering visitors something it thought no other destination could: Indigenous CHamoru music, dance, art, language, cuisine, culture, and values, all within a multicultural island paradise setting.[42]

One of the island's twin engines (along with militarism) of economic development, tourism on Guåhan caters largely to Asian tourists interested in tropical exotica and access to duty-free shopping and American popular cultural entertainment. This instance of what Teresia Teaiwa has dubbed "militourism" determines much of Guåhan's social, cultural, political, and economic possibilities through the logic of order, development, and security.[43] One hundred years of American influence and two and a half years of collective memory of Japanese brutality furnish the rest of the binding (or packing, in keeping with the principal metaphor in the other side part of this essay).

Since 9/11, the U.S. military has forged a new strategic plan, which includes an overseas base realignment involving the relocation of several thousand American marines from Okinawa to Guåhan. The move has received fierce opposition from CHamorus, including the CHamoru sovereignty and independence movements, who have been rallying to halt prebuildup activities.[44] In 2009, military planners released a nine-volume, eleven-thousand-page draft environmental impact statement (DEIS) whose stated purpose was to mitigate the buildup's potential damage, going the length to acknowledge and even appearing to sympathize with local concerns over the deleterious effects on local culture and the environment. The DEIS listed the buildup's negative impacts in need of mitigation: restricted access to cultural landmarks, closure of ocean-based tourist sites, and the compromising of tourist spaces and local "sense of place." Indeed, the DEIS concluded that "the supplanting of a cultural tourism branding for one that is more militarized appears to be a strong possibility," yet also concluded that "maximum potential adverse outcome is not inevitable."[45]

Though GVB officials worried that a militourist brand could replace Guåhan's image as a culturally exotic paradise, the agency did not oppose the buildup and concluded that the positives outweighed the negatives, and that the tourism and militarism could team up, this time to mitigate the damage. GVB's concerns are understandable, given its reliance on CHamoru culture. Indeed, GVB is all about culture. When tourism was on the wane, it launched a "Guam Brand" campaign to make Native culture ubiquitous from the moment of a visitor's arrival. The campaign even rolled out a new logo featuring key symbols and values of traditional CHamoru society, like the *sinåhi* "crescent or new moon." For GVB, the curve of the moon symbolized CHamoru smiles and open arms, and the *tåsa,* or top portion of the *latte*—the stone foundation and pillars of early CHamoru society, unique to the Marianas. The crescent moon also represented the hull of the *sakman,* the CHamoru oceangoing canoe. Finally, the GVB logo evoked the crescent moon–shaped necklace made of clamshell worn by early CHamorus and revived in the late twentieth century by CHamoru grassroots activists.

The preponderance of CHamoru cultural icons in GVB marketing campaigns, in some respects, is unsurprising. GVB is an autonomous agency of the Government of Guam (GovGuam), which, although an instrumentality of the federal government, is also a stronghold of CHamoru political and cultural expression. The majority of GovGuam's employees are CHamoru, and the CHamoru language is the lingua franca in daily operations. In other words, there is something deeply Indigenous about it, and missing this point risks ignoring major expressions of CHamoru political and cultural survival. But GovGuam is also a creature of U.S. federal legislation (vis-à-vis the 1950 Guam Organic Act) through which federal oversight—congressional plenary power—is codified and institutionalized. And since Guåhan residents cannot vote in U.S. presidential elections (despite being U.S. citizens through the Organic Act) and do not have voting rights in U.S. Congress (despite having a delegate), this level of federal power over the unincorporated territory (Guåhan's official status) that the federal government does not have over any of the fifty states amounts to formal colonial rule. Despite the growing criticism of the Organic Act as a vehicle through which the United States consolidates its political power (and justifies U.S. land-takings), the mainstream and dominant Indigenous CHamoru political discourse continues to celebrate its passage as a major step along the road to political fulfillment.

It is GVB's use of nonhegemonic, subaltern CHamoru icons of political and cultural consciousness and relationalities for marketing and branding purposes, and most especially in collaboration with the military, that is especially troubling. The sinåhi is not just a quaint symbol of CHamoru cultural resurgence. First brought to light through archaeological digs of the 1970s, the sinåhi became popularized as an ornament when members of the CHamoru rights organization Nasion CHamoru (CHamoru Nation), led by the staunch activist Angel "Anghet" Santos, wore it regularly, along with shorn heads, in outward defiance of U.S. colonialism and in protest of military land confiscation and environmental degradation.[46] Its ubiquity and increased value as a commodity (sinåhi are highly desirable and can cost several thousand dollars) trouble the relations between CHamoru resurgence and resistance, political activism against U.S. militarism, and GovGuam's marketing strategies in cahoots with the military.

The Military's New Road

Like GVB, the U.S. military has been launching its own destination campaign. It comprises the old and the new—stereotypical tropical tour-of-leisure tropes with a more modernized tour of duty (as part of the Pacific Pivot and U.S.–Japan Roadmap for Realignment)—and embraces a "rich cultural and historical heritage."[47] The island is "no longer the trailer park of the Pacific," as one rear admiral had put it, but has "emerged from backwater status to the center of the radar screen" and is "rapidly becoming a focus for logistics, for strategic planning."[48]

An example of the military's new cultural branding is its $1.2 million upgrade, in response to 9/11, of the front security gate at Naval Base Guåhan Guam.[49] The gate's most distinguishing features are latte-like structures, which flank and support it. The military has also had to rebrand itself because of local opposition to the buildup. These recent conflicts continue earlier tensions with CHamoru landowners dating back to postwar land condemnations and environmental disasters. After World War II, the military owned two-thirds of the island. Today, the military controls one-third, and yet its footprint continues to encroach on *i tano i* CHamoru (the land of the CHamorus) in, for example, its off-base urban warfare training in the island's villages. It was tensions like these that led the federal government to terminate naval rule by transferring administration over the island to the Department of the Interior and to establish limited home rule in the form of GovGuam. Illustrative of such ongoing tensions for which the military has to rebrand itself as "family," "partner," and "steward" was the recently aborted plan to use the ancient CHamoru village of Pågat for live-fire training and the current plans to use the lands surrounding the CHamoru village of Litekyan.[50]

Famalao'an on the Pathways of the Ancestors

The CHamoru writer Cara Flores-Mays was having lunch at the Mermaid Tavern, a local restaurant in Hagåtña (Guåhan's capital), when she overheard known officials from the Joint Guam Program Office (JGPO) and other military personnel associated with the buildup discussing their strategy to use village mayors and wartime stories of the *manåmko'* (elderly) as a way to get local buy-in. One of them made disparaging comments about an older CHamoru man. A member of We Are Guåhan, a vocal opponent of the buildup, Flores-Mays immediately activated her social media, resulting in sharp outcry from the community. The Mermaid Tavern incident was such a setback to military-civilian-CHamoru relations that one of those officials was removed from her position and a Marine Corps leader apologized to Flores-Mays and invited her to reopen dialogue to rebuild trust. Flores-Mays refused: "You are here to sell the buildup to the community. You're here to paint it as something that is beautiful. But you can't fully understand what this community needs because you aren't connected to the land or to the bones that lie beneath it."[51]

Indeed, treasures, values, and relations considered *tåddong, ginen i mås takhilo' gi hinasso* (from the innermost recesses of the mind) also abound against settler colonialism and tourism's efforts to use an ancient CHamoru village and sacred land as an ecotourist park in Gokña in Tomhom (Tumon), the island's tourist sector. Renamed Gun Beach after the war (because of the presence of a World War II Japanese antiaircraft gun), Gokña is the site of Lina'la', the island's first cultural and ecotheme park, which features a nature trail and a zoo, at the site of a five-hundred-year-old CHamoru village. As conceived and managed under the terms of GVB-style culturalism—in fact, it is the aforementioned GVB director Mark Baldyga whose company, Baldyga Group, owns and operates Lina'la'—the village perpetuates in vintage natural history form static depictions of Natives through valorized and romanticized notions of primitivism. The park quite literally traffics in CHamoru culture, from its name, Lina'la' (which means "life, living being, existence"), to the fact that it sits atop a CHamoru burial site. A recurring justification for the desecration of ancestral burial sites at places like Lina'la' is that the U.S. military had already disturbed the site, rendering it yet another example of the insidious relations of militourism.

Together with their kin, CHamoru women leaders and queer artists and activists rallied around Gokña and stepped up to *fa'maolek* (make good or reconcile) and *fa'danche* (make right). Shortly after the park's opening, *manåmko'* and *manmaga'håga* (CHamoru women leaders) organized a sunrise ceremony, Chinachålanen i Mañaina-ta, "Creating Pathways for Our Ancestral Spirits." The ceremony consisted of a *lukao* (procession) and *inifresi* (offering). Community leader and farmer Hope Alvarez Cristobal explained that because the grave sites were disturbed, so too were the *aniti* (spirits), and thus women, as "mothers and daughters of the community," needed to offer "peace and tranquility" to the ancestors who handed down CHamoru "sovereignty and human rights." In what might be understood as an Indigenous feminist practice of maintaining genealogical cordage to land and ancestry—what I elsewhere have theorized as a CHamoru "placental politics"—Cristobal linked ideas of political self-determination and sovereignty with a long tradition of stewardship and CHamoru women caring for the well-being of community and land.[52] The inspiration and insight for an Indigenous feminist placental politics derives from the pattera's insistence on burying the newborn's placenta, or *ga'chong i patgon* (the child's companion), against U.S. navy doctors' orders to burn or discard what they regarded as toxic medical waste, and out of respect for reciprocal land-kinship relations. It is noteworthy that longtime CHamoru-language activist Bernadita Camacho-Dungca led the offering; in 1991 Camacho-Dungca composed the CHamoru "Inifresi" (pledge) to protect and defend the beliefs, culture, language, air, water, and land of the CHamorus *"ginen i más takhilo' gi hinasso-ku,"* from the innermost recesses of my (her) mind.

In this post-9/11 global antiterrorist militarization of the island, clearing and creating pathways for ancestors was (and continues to be) an enduring pathway through which Indigenous women community leaders, feminists, and queer artists and activists stepped up to do the right thing in renewing relations while furnishing counternarratives and detours to the pervasive image of Guåhan as an exotic island destination. In so doing, these CHamoru protectors of lands and waters continue to chart, steer, and advance the island down the *maolek* (good) road. In this unfinished legacy of the U.S. Asia-Pacific Pivot, there are some who continue to march, literally and figuratively, with America and America's latest political and economic road map and roadbuilding in Guåhan, while others have taken a turn, have diverted paths, and are hitting the pavement and embarking on new movements along the newer chålan of decolonization and anticolonialism. Just as earlier women like the pattera enacted alternative Indigenous modernities under the United States—insisting on old and new forms of *inafa'maolek* (a state or condition in which goodness is achieved and maintained) like the age-old embodied practice of planting the ga'chong i patgon as a way to root and thus safeguard CHamoru bodies—a new generation of famalao'an redefine and reconstruct the new terms and rules of engagement for caretaking lands, waters, and communities under a new siege of hypermilitarization, settler colonial desecration, climate change, and environmental destruction and contamination of beloved and sacred CHamoru ancestral and contemporary homelands.

NOTES

1. Teresia Teaiwa, "Lo(o)sing the Edge," *Contemporary Pacific* 13, no. 2 (Fall 2001): 343–65.
2. We follow here the official orthography for the spelling of CHamoru. We keep the spelling for the more familiar *Chamorro* when the term is cited in earlier publications.
3. United States Department of the Navy, Office of the Chief of Naval Operations, *U.S. Navy Report on Guam 1899–1950* (Washington, D.C.: Government Printing Office, 1950), 2.
4. *Annual Report of the Governor of Guam, Naval Government of Guam* (Agana, Guam: Naval Government of Guam, 1904), 2.
5. Henry Beers, *American Naval Occupation and Government of Guam, 1898–1902* (Washington, D.C.: Navy Department, 1944), 11.
6. Vincendon L. Cottman, Lt., U.S.N., "Report on Guam to the Secretary of the Navy," February 20, 1899, RG 80, 9351: 35, 3, National Archives, Washington, D.C.
7. U.S. Navy, *U.S. Navy Report on Guam,* 5.
8. U.S. Navy, 3.
9. *Annual Report of the Governor of Guam* (1917), 40.

10. This overview is culled from information from the *Guam Newsletter, The Guam Recorder,* and the Navy's *Annual Reports* that were published between 1900 and 1941. The first two were monthly serials.

11. *Guam Newsletter* 4, no. 4 (1912): 2.

12. *Guam Newsletter* 9, no. 1 (1917): 4; and *Annual Report of the Governor of Guam* (1918), 36.

13. *Guam Newsletter* 4, no. 4 (1912): 2.

14. *Guam Newsletter* 5, no. 2 (1913): 10.

15. *Guam Newsletter* 8, no. 10 (1917): 22.

16. *Guam Newsletter* 5, no. 2 (1913): 10; and *Guam Newsletter* 8, no. 9 (1917): 4.

17. *Guam Newsletter* 7, no. 3 (1915): 7.

18. Dorn quoted in Don Farrell, *The Pictorial History of Guam: The Americanization: 1898–1918* (Guam: Micronesian Publications, 1986), 137.

19. *Annual Report of the Governor of Guam* (1904), item 5.

20. Havner quoted in Anne Perez Hattori, "Colonialism, Capitalism, and Nationalism in the US Navy's Expulsion of Guam's Spanish Catholic Priests, 1898–1900," *Journal of Pacific History* 44, no. 3 (December 2009): 290.

21. U.S. Navy, *U.S. Navy Report on Guam,* 22.

22. L. M. Cox, *The Island of Guam* (Washington, D.C.: Government Printing Office, 1926), 42.

23. *Annual Report of the Governor of Guam* (1917), 40.

24. *Annual Report of the Governor of Guam* (1917), 40.

25. *Annual Report of the Governor of Guam* (1917), 40.

26. *Annual Report of the Governor of Guam* (1917), 40.

27. *Annual Report of the Governor of Guam* (1917), 40.

28. *Annual Report of the Governor of Guam* (1917), 40.

29. *Guam Newsletter* 5, no. 2 (1928): 25, 38.

30. Patrick Wolfe, "Settler Colonialism and the Elimination of the Native," *Journal of Genocide Research* 8, no. 4 (2006): 387–409.

31. *Guam Newsletter* (1928): 38.

32. *Hale'-ta I Manfåyi: Who's Who in Chamorro History, Volume I* (Agana, Guam: Political Status Education Coordinating Commission, 1995).

33. Joaquina Babauta Herrera, interview by Christine DeLisle, May 9, 1998.

34. Cherrie Moraga, "From a Long Line of Vendidas: Chicanas and Feminism," in *Feminist Studies/Critical Studies,* ed. Teresa de Lauretis (Bloomington: Indiana University Press, 1986), 173–90; and Nadine Naber, "Arab American Femininities: Beyond Arab Virgin/American(ized) Whore," *Journal of Feminist Studies* 32, no. 1 (Spring 2006): 87–111.

35. Alexandre Coello de la Rosa, *Jesuits at the Margins: Missions and Missionaries in the Marianas, 1668–1769* (New York: Routledge, 2015). For a refusal of the tourist industry's feminized and sexualized image of the CHamoru woman, refer to Desiree Taimanglo Ventura, "Starving for Saina," *Ke Kaupu Hehi Ale,* October 5, 2015, https://hehiale.com/2015/10/05/starving-for-saina.

36. Paul B. Souder, "Land Tenure in a Fortress," in *Land Tenure in the South Pacific,* 3rd ed. (Suva, Fiji: University of the South Pacific, 1987), 211–24; and Michael F. Phillips, "Land," in *Hale'-ta Kinalamten Pulitikåt: Siñenten i CHamoru: Issues in Guam's Political Development: The Chamorro Perspective* (Agana, Guam: Political Status Education Coordinating Commission, 1996).

37. Aileen Moreton-Robinson, *The White Possessive: Property, Power, and Indigenous Sovereignty* (Minneapolis: University of Minnesota Press, 2015), 191.

38. Anne Perez Hattori, *Colonial Dis-Ease: U.S. Navy Health Policies and the Chamorros of Guam, 1898–1941* (Honolulu: University of Hawai'i Press, 2004), 193, 93.

39. Wolfe, "Settler Colonialism and the Elimination of the Native."

40. Maile Arvin, Eve Tuck, and Angie Morrill, "Decolonizing Feminism: Challenging Connections between Settler Colonialism and Heteropatriarchy," *Feminist Formations* 25, no. 1 (Spring 2013): 8–34.

41. Christine Taitano DeLisle, "Destination Chamorro Culture: Notes on Realignment, Rebranding, and Post-9/11 Militourism in Guam," *American Quarterly* 68, no. 3 (September 2016): 563–72.

42. "Guam Tourism 2020 Plan," Guam Visitors Bureau, accessed August 27, 2015, 11, 7, 13, 4, 25, www.guamvisitorsbureau.com/docs/reports/guam-tourism-2020-plan/guam-tourism-2020-plan.pdf.

43. Teresia K. Teaiwa, "Reading Paul Gauguin's Noa Noa with Epeli Hau'ofa's Kisses in the Neder-ends: Militourism, Feminism, and the 'Polynesian' Body," in *Inside Out: Literature, Cultural Politics, and Identity in the New Pacific,* eds. Vilsoni Hereniko and Rob Wilson (Lanham, Md.: Rowman and Littlefield, 1999), 249–64.

44. Julian Aguon, *The Fire This Time: Essays on Life under U.S. Occupation* (Tokyo: Blue Ocean, 2006); Leevin Camacho and Daniel Broudy, "'Sweetening' the Pentagon's Deal in the Marianas," *Asia-Pacific Journal* 11, no. 1 (2013): 1–5; Tiara R. Na'puti and Michael Lujan Bevacqua, "Militarization and Resistance from Guåhan: Protecting and Defending Pågat," *American Quarterly* 67, no. 3 (2015): 837–58; and LisaLinda Natividad and Victoria-Lola Leon Guerrero, "The Explosive Growth of U.S. Military Power on Guam Confronts People Power: Experience of an Island People under Spanish, Japanese, and American Colonial Rule," *Asia-Pacific Journal* 8, no. 3 (2010): 1–15.

45. *Draft Environmental Impact Statement/Overseas Environmental Impact Statement,* Guam and CNMI Military Relocation, vol. 9: Appendices, November 2009, Appendix F: Socioeconomic Impact Assessment Study, 4–39.

46. Judy Flores, "Navigating Chamorro Art and Identity," in *Pacific Island Artists: Navigating the Global Art World,* ed. Karen Stevenson (Oakland, Calif.: Masalai, 2011), 51–68.

47. James Brook, "Looking for Friendly Overseas Base, Pentagon Finds It Already Has One," *New York Times,* April 7, 2004, www.nytimes.com/2004/04/07/us/looking-for-friendly-overseas-base-pentagonfinds-it-already-has-one.html.

48. Brook, "Looking for Friendly Overseas Base."

49. Jennifer H. Svan, "Main Gate Is Upgraded at Guam Base," *Stars and Stripes,* September 10, 2004, www.stripes.com/news/main-gate-is-upgraded-at-guam-base-1.24022; and Theresa Merto, "U.S. Navy Spends $1.2 Million on Guam Gate," *Pacific Daily News,* September 8, 2004, http://www.pireport.org/articles/2004/09/08/us-navy-spends-12-million-guam-gate.

50. Na'puti and Bevacqua, "Militarization and Resistance from Guåhan."

51. Private Facebook post, accessed October 22, 2010.

52. Christine Taitano DeLisle, "A History of Chamorro Nurse-Midwives in Guam and a 'Placental Politics' for Indigenous Feminism," *Intersections* 37 (March 2015); and Natalie Avalos, "Land-Based Ethics and Settler Solidarity in a Time of Corona and Revolution," *Arrow* (July 9, 2020): https://arrow-journal.org/land-based-ethics-and-settler-solidarity-in-a-time-of-corona-and-revolution.

Settler Colonial Purchase

Privatizing Hawaiian Land

J. KĒHAULANI KAUANUI

"Take a Tour of Mark Zuckerberg's Gigantic $100 Million Property in Hawaii" reads a headline from July 3, 2019, on Business Insider.[1] The story continues, "It's no secret that Mark Zuckerberg values his privacy. The Facebook billionaire has multiple homes . . . but one of his properties in particular is as controversial as it is beautiful." The piece features thirteen photographs of the Facebook CEO billionaire's enormous 750-acre property on the North Shore of the island of Kaua'i and explains the controversy. In 2014, Zuckerberg purchased the land, which included two separate parcels: the Kahu'āina Plantation, a 357-acre former sugarcane plantation, and Pila'a Beach, a 393-acre property with a white-sand beach. He paid a reported $100 million for both and has since spent another $45 million to purchase additional land on the island.[2] To do so, in 2016, Zuckerberg took quiet title action—legal suits to settle contested land title to multiple properties with the aim of removing competing claims or objections[3]—in an "attempt to find all the claimants to land inside his estate and buy out their shares, ensuring his privacy."[4] This is due to the fact that these are considered "kuleana lands," stemming from an 1850 law under the Hawaiian Kingdom known as the Kuleana Act, which—following the 1848 Māhele land division by the monarch of the Hawaiian Kingdom that privatized communal land—enabled the maka'āinana (common people) to acquire fee simple title to land. The act was also meant to explicitly protect their rights as Native tenants—to continue subsistence lifestyles, including rights of access, traditional gathering of food resources, and fresh water for family use.

Today, under Hawai'i state law—even in the context of the U.S. hold on the island archipelago—the Kuleana Act remains the foundation of law pertaining to Native tenant rights, protecting Native Hawaiian traditional and customary rights that trace their origins to Hawaiian Kingdom law.[5] Descendants who inherit kuleana lands from their original owner must be granted access to those properties by any future owner in order for them to exercise customary gathering rights.

In this case, contemporary and future descendants of Manuel Rapozo have a shared interest, known as "kuleana." Rapozo was a Portuguese sugarcane plantation worker who immigrated to Hawai'i in 1882 and acquired the lands in 1894 (notably after the

U.S.-backed overthrow of the Hawaiian Kingdom) and passed the property to his seven heirs. One of those descendants, Wayne Rapozo (who grew up on Kauaʻi and now lives and works in London), has served as the key spokesperson for descendants who have resisted the forced sale of the property. As reported to media, "Before Zuckerberg purchased the estate (and built his mile-long wall), it was owned by a local auto dealer and surrounded by a hog wire fence. Family members had keys to the gate and could visit the parcels or access Pilaʻa beach."[6] Rapozo explained, "Even if we lose, this has to be fought. . . . I want my nieces and descendants to know that someone thought it was wrong. . . . I want it to be known that it was resisted."[7]

At one time, Zuckerberg was pursuing eight separate lawsuits related to parcels of land that were surrounded by his Kauaʻi estate. Those being sued had a choice to either sell their partial shares or try to outbid the billionaire in a public auction (and if they lost, they could be forced to pay Zuckerberg's legal fees).[8] Many on the island—and worldwide, given the vast media coverage of the case—ask: *How did it come to this?* How could one person amass so much land in one of the places with the highest real estate prices, besides the obvious answer: because of his own wealth? This case obviously highlights the loss of land to wealthy newcomers, but here, I would like to zone in on the Indigenous piece of the story, how this property regime originated, and how it grossly affects Kanaka Maoli (Native Hawaiians) today.[9] This dispute between Zuckerberg and Rapozo—as well as Carlos Andrade, a retired history professor and partial heir to several small land parcels tied up by Zuckerberg—has its roots in Hawaiʻi's complicated history of land tenure and privatization under the Hawaiian Kingdom.

Using the Zuckerberg case as a point of departure, this essay examines the history and politics of land and property in Hawaiʻi. I offer a brief history of the privatization of Hawaiian communal land for political context and consequences. That which is commonly referred to as the 1848 Māhele land division was a process that unfolded over the course of five years with three main instruments: the creation of the Board of Commissioners to Quiet Land Titles (referred to herein as the Land Commission), enacted by statute on December 10, 1845; the 1848 Māhele division itself, which defined the separation of previously undivided land interests of King Kamehameha III and the high-ranking chiefs and lesser chiefs known as konokihi, or land stewards; and the Kuleana Act of 1850, which enabled common people to acquire fee simple title to land for the first time in Hawaiian history.

These mid-nineteenth-century developments provide a crucial genealogy for the contemporary case of Zuckerberg's holdings, which is just one among countless others.[10] Whether through the privatization of communal lands through enclosure, the U.S. government's seizure of these lands as part of its expanding territory, or the push for Hawaiian land rights, all are based on a proprietary relationship to land that undergirds its objectification and commodification.

Rapozo told media, "This case sets a horrible precedent which is un-American and un-Hawaiian. . . . They are making Hawaii look like a banana republic or colonial possession."[11] While some others have declared Zuckerberg the "face of neocolonialism,"[12] I want to examine this case as a prime example of twenty-first-century settler colonialism, given the fact that land is at the center of the controversy. Contemporary Kanaka Maoli land struggles are inextricably linked to the legacy of the U.S.-backed overthrow of the Hawaiian Kingdom in 1893, the U.S. purported annexation of 1898, and the 1959 admission of Hawai'i to the U.S. union as the fiftieth state, since all three of these historical events—constituting an occupation in the service of a broader settler colonial project of land expropriation—deeply shape and affect all land issues today. After the U.S.-backed illegal overthrow of the Hawaiian monarchy in 1893, the Government and Crown Lands of the Kingdom were joined together, and after annexation in 1898, the U.S. government managed these lands as a public trust for all of Hawai'i's residents. Once the Hawaii State Admissions Act passed the U.S. Congress in 1959, all but 373,720 acres of the Government and Crown Lands were transferred to the (new) State of Hawai'i.[13]

Even within the system of land privatization under the Kingdom, the Kuleana Act was supposed to protect land access for future generations of common Kanaka Maoli. Although these lands were first allotted under the authority of the Hawaiian Kingdom, a portion of them have been continuously reproportioned to the detriment of the Native Hawaiian people. Under the U.S. system, even while the fiftieth state has laws to protect kuleana rights, transactions such as Zuckerberg's can preempt the rights of subsequent generations.

Land Tenure and the Push for Privatization

In the mid-nineteenth century, the third and longest-reigning monarch of the Hawaiian Kingdom (founded by Kamehameha I, through war and consolidation from 1795 to 1815), Kamehameha III, facing relentless waves of Western imperialist confrontations, implemented numerous new laws to advance the government in an effort to protect Hawaiian sovereignty from European encroachment. These changes ranged from promulgating a constitution in 1840 to moving to privatize communal lands in 1848. In *Paradoxes of Hawaiian Sovereignty,* I argue that the enclosure and propertization of land established by the Mō'ī (previously the paramount chief of each island, but now the monarch) and other elites—both Hawaiian and foreign—within the model of independent statehood that met Western standards was part of a colonial biopolitical governmentality.[14] This transformation of communal landholdings is a prime example of biopower, a technology of political power that relates to the government's (in this case, the Kingdom's) concern with fostering the life of the population, and centers on the poles of discipline and regulatory controls. Individual landholdings through fee simple title became a basic dimension of social normalization by the Hawaiian Kingdom through its regulation of subjects' customary practices that were commoditized.

As the privatization measure severed ties between the makaʻāinana (common people) and the konohiki (land stewards) vis-à-vis the land itself, it also remade the relationships between and among Kanaka Maoli (of various ranks) in relation to the state (the Hawaiian Kingdom). With Westphalian sovereignty as the basis for governance that served to underwrite Western imperialism and its international political domination, the regime of private property was and remains central for the "achievement" of Hawaiian statehood. But of course, capitalism makes land into private property, which in turn is fundamental to sustaining capitalism.

Lilikalā Kameʻeleihiwa documents white settler American participation in the push for the land division process, which took place less than three decades after the missionaries arrived in 1820 to convert Kanaka Maoli to Christianity. She notes that many of those who immediately profited from the land tenure transformation were the Calvinist missionaries turned businessmen whose recommendations were crucial in promoting the change.[15] In the capitalist venture, white American and European merchants, who constituted the bulk of the foreign population in Hawaiʻi at that time, saw in the Māhele the opportunity to acquire land of their own. Foreign businessmen who were not citizens of the Kingdom also pushed for investment incentives. Though there were several rationales, the publicly stated purpose of the land division was to create a body of landed commoners who would then prosper by means of their small farms.[16] This rationale involved an inverted logic, however, because under the communal system, everyone had access to land.

The death of Kanaka Maoli was at crisis proportions since mounting epidemics caused the decline by one-half of the population from 1803 to 1831.[17] The population decline, which continued unabated through the next several decades, had many effects on society as a whole.[18] Also, as Jonathan Kay Kamakawiwoʻole Osorio explains:

> One result of the great dying off of Hawaiians was the weakening of the traditional land tenure system that had sustained the pre-Contact chiefdoms. The labor-intensive subsistence economy and extensive cultivation of mauka (upland) areas had been the basis for, and also a sign of, a healthy and prosperous civilization. The system was especially vulnerable to rapid depopulation, which inexorably led to the abandonment of thriving loʻi (taro patches) and homesteads as the labor needed to maintain them continued to diminish. Nevertheless, this weakened system might have well survived in some kind of altered form if it had not been for the Māhele.[19]

In the midst of massive depopulation due to disease, a dire part of this historical period, many believed that the privatization of land could help save Hawaiians from extinction. In this logic, the acquisition of land in fee simple (also known as freehold land) would help them in reestablishing a life of farming and bolster their survival.[20] As Osorio points out, "As far as the missionaries were concerned, the strange and, for them, uncertain land tenure was the cardinal reason for the unabated depopulation and despair within the Hawaiian community."[21] Private property was required to make the common people both industrious and prudent—"a key element of a society's recognition of individual interests."[22]

In terms of tradition, all of the land was the responsibility of the Mōʻī, who was required by ancient custom to place the chiefs in jurisdiction over the land and the people on it. Kamehameha III had to contend with the "depopulation of areas that had once been thriving agricultural communities, important to the collective food and revenue base of the entire society."[23] Hence, we can see the shift to privatization by the state as a form of colonial biopolitics—related to protecting and renewing the declining Indigenous population (and because the colonial biopolitics were why the Indigenous population was in decline to begin with). Urbanization was also a factor, as Jocelyn Linnekin notes, since "emigration came to be perceived as a problem in the 1840s, foreign residents and missionaries pressed for the establishment of individual land titles, arguing that private property would result in pride of ownership and would motivate commoners to remain on the land."[24] Yet it seems to have had the opposite effect. In any case, here was the remaking of a people, whether one understands the Māhele as a process that protected the common people's customary rights and privileged a version of the yeoman farmer model of individualization.

Osorio describes the Māhele as "the single most critical dismemberment of Hawaiian society."[25] Prior to the 1848 division, land tenure patterns were characterized by values and practices of reciprocity rather than private ownership. Hawaiian land was managed through a hierarchy of distribution rights that was contingent on chiefly politics with a succession of caretakers. The process was highly contingent and entailed a succession of caretakers, with genealogical rank being a determinative factor.[26]

Distribution itself was always in flux—not fixed, like the land itself—as exemplified by the traditional process of redistribution of lands through kalaiʻāina (land carving). Each island, or mokupuni, was ruled by a paramount chief (Mōʻī) and "divided into large sections, or moku-o-loko ('islands within,' often known simply as moku)."[27] These moku were further divided into ʻokana or kalana (districts) and each district comprised many ahupuaʻa (wedge-shaped sections of land), which varied in size. The Mōʻī allocated ahupuaʻa to lesser chiefs who entrusted the land's administration, the konohiki, who in turn administered land access for makaʻāinana who labored for the chiefs and fulfilled tributary. As Kameʻeleihiwa delineates:

> The ahupuaʻa were usually wedge-shaped sections of land that followed natural geographical boundaries, such as ridge lines and rivers, and ran from mountain to sea. A valley bounded by ridges on two or three sides,

and by the sea on the fourth, would be a natural ahupuaʻa. The word ahupuaʻa means "pig altar" and was named for the stone altars with pig head carvings that marked the boundaries of each ahupuaʻa. Ideally, an ahupuaʻa would include within its borders all the materials required for sustenance—timber, thatching, and rope, from the mountains, various crops from the uplands, kalo from the lowlands, and fish from the sea. All members of the society shared access to these life-giving necessities.[28]

Here land and ea (a Hawaiian language gloss for "sovereignty") were together linked to sustainability through reciprocity.

Jon Chinen explains that when "King Kamehameha I brought all of the islands under his control at the beginning of the nineteenth century, he simply utilized the land system in existence."[29] Chinen continues, "After setting aside the lands he desired for his personal use and enjoyment, Kamehameha I divided the rest among his principal warrior chiefs for distribution to the lesser chiefs and, down the scale, to the tenant-commoners."[30] After he died, on May 8, 1819, in accordance to his will, his son Liholiho was recognized as the new sovereign, Kamehameha II. He made only a few changes in the distribution of lands, leaving the great majority of the lands with the chief who had been rewarded by his father.[31] "These sovereign powers descended with the crown to Kauikeaouli who became King Kamehameha III upon the death of his brother in England on July 14, 1824."[32] Foreigners pressured the king and his chiefs to enact a Bill of Rights in 1839, which, he argues, was "the beginning of a complete change in the government and in the land system in Hawaii."[33] The Bill of Rights declared, "Protection is hereby secured to the persons of all the people, together with their lands, their building lots, and all their property, while they conform to the laws of the kingdom, and nothing whatever shall be taken from any individual except by express provision of the laws." It also states that a "landlord cannot causelessly dispossess his tenant."[34] These rights and laws of 1839 were published in Hawaiian as *He Kumu Kanawai, a me ke Kanawai Hooponopono Waiwai*. They "made startling changes in the authority of the chiefs and the Mōʻī by pronouncing 'God had bestowed certain rights alike on all men and all chiefs, and all people of all lands.' This declaration—codifying Christian monotheism as the state religion dictating governance—positioned everyone, chiefs and people, kanaka and haole, into one definition of people, all entitled to the rights granted by God."[35]

Kamehameha III promulgated the first constitution on October 8, 1840, which was an amended form of the Bill of Rights.[36] The constitution changed the Hawaiian government from an absolute monarchy to a constitutional monarchy, establishing a bicameral legislature consisting of a House of Nobles and a representative body chosen by the makaʻāinana who were empowered to participate in government. Another important feature was the establishment of a supreme court, consisting of the king and his advisor (and often coruler), known as the Kuhina Nui, as well as four judges appointed by the representative body.[37] Also, under the section on "exposition of the principles on which the present dynasty is founded," it is clear that there was no absolute ownership of land. As Chinen delineates, "Kamehameha I, was the founder of the kingdom, and to him belonged all the land from one end of the Islands to the other, though it was not his own private property. It belonged to the chiefs and people in common, of whom Kamehameha I was the head, and had the management of the landed property."[38] But this was the first formal acknowledgment by the king that the common people had some form of protected interest in the land, aside from "the products of the soil."[39] This protected interest arguably stands today, despite the Māhele division and its accompanying legislation.[40]

The constitution allowed for the people's vested rights to land and therefore provided a legal foundation for the Mōʻī, aliʻi (chiefs), and makaʻāinana to acquire allodial (absolute) title to land. Kamanamaikalani Beamer suggests that prior to the Western concept of rights in the Hawaiian context, vested rights could be understood as kuleana (interest, responsibility, prerogative). Beamer points out that this segment of the constitution dealt some with the ownership of land and served to codify ancient land rights held by the mōʻī, aliʻi, and makaʻāinana within the structure of the kalaʻāina. In that old system, "the mōʻī awarded lands, but they were not the mōʻī's sole property; the makaʻāinana also had rights to their ʻili, mooʻāina, pakuʻāina, kihapai, and to other resources within their ahupuaʻa."[41]

As preparation for the 1848 Māhele land division, the king created the Board of Commissioners to Quiet Land Titles, enacted by statute on December 10, 1845. Then, in 1848, King Kamehameha III first divided the lands of the Kingdom between himself and the chiefs and konohiki. Prior to the division of lands with the high chiefs and the konohiki being completed, the king had planned to subdivide his reserved lands between the government and himself—which became the Government Lands distinct from the Crown Lands.[42] These were reserved for the monarch and his descendants. As Chinen explains, the king was "deeply concerned over the hostile activities of the foreigners in the Islands and did not want his lands to be considered public domain and subject to confiscation by a foreign power in the event of a conquest."[43] The king surrendered part of his original share in the lands that became the Government Lands and reserved the smaller portion for his own use.[44]

The Kuleana Act of 1850

The Kuleana Act of 1850 enabled common Kanaka Maoli to acquire fee simple title to land for the first time in Hawaiian history. The awards made by the Land Commission to makaʻāinana were called kuleana (to have interest) awards. As several scholars note, out of 14,195 applications made for kuleana awards in 1848 among approximately 80,000 Hawaiians at the time, only 8,421 claims were awarded.[45] Most explain this small number by suggesting that few Hawaiian commoners registered their land claims, especially since they were required to pay for the survey of the lands they set out to secure, and those who did found that theirs were frequently lost to fraud, adverse possession, tax sales, and undervalued sales to speculators.[46] Others speculate that many were uninterested in small plots of rural land, especially when they required wide-ranging gathering rights to maintain a traditional subsistence lifestyle.[47] Maivân Clech Lâm offers six reasons to account for the low figure for those who participated in this institutionalized private landownership: the timeline for registering and processing the land claims was unrealistic; the maka'āinana were new to the written word and distrustful of the written law; most could not afford the survey fees; taking an award might limit their task of sustaining themselves on awarded lots only (since formerly traditional subsistence required the utilization of the whole ahupua'a); the common people preferred the old system and some tenants assumed that if they did not act to change anything, the previous land tenure arrangement would simply continue; and some probably feared that any attempt to file for kuleana lots within the ahupua'a or 'ili of the konohiki would invite reprisal. By traditional precedent, carried over into the Māhele guidelines, abandoned or uncultivated lands would revert to the konohiki of the ahupua'a.[48] Hence, kuleana lands were allowed to slip back by default into the hands of either the government or the chiefs of the surrounding land.[49]

Maka'āinana who applied for kuleana lands were referred to in general as hoa'āina (friends of the land), but the law translated the concept as "tenants" in relation to "landlords."[50] As Osorio argues, "these new designations were problematic and incommensurable with the customary definitions of Hawaiian cultural practice, in which . . . Ali'i were not landlords who owned the land and its produce. They were konohiki who had responsibilities extended above and below them. The maka'āinana were not tenants, entitled to live on and work the land as long as they paid for it in produce or labor; their entitlements were fundamentally different."[51] The roles of the maka'āinana, the konihiki, and the ali'i were all related to the ethic of malama'āina—proper care for the land.[52] This was a hierarchical system, to be sure; however, it was one based on reciprocity. Osorio suggests that, from the maka'āinana point of view, the Kuleana Act worked to try and sever all traditional ties to the chief. "If the konohiki has no right to their labor and could not deny them access that only the law guaranteed, then what was left to obligate the chiefs to the people?"[53] Here we see a new form of governmentality in relation to the rise of capitalism in the islands, through the enclosure of the ahupua'a. The relationships between the chiefs and the common people become disaffected through this process, but additionally the haole were treated with favoritism over the maka'āinana by the chiefs. Nearly a month before the maka'āinana rights to land were made explicit in the Kuleana Act, in July 1850, the legislature decided to allow haole who were not naturalized to own and sell lands.[54]

The Māhele did not in itself alter the rights of the makaʻāinana to the land because it did not convey any actual title to land.[55] Still, there is scholarly debate regarding whether the enclosure of the ahupuaʻa and the transition to royal patents ultimately had the effect of dispossession and whether the commodification of land hastened the dislocation of the common people.[56] Previous treatments of the Māhele suggest that less than 1 percent of the total land acreage passed in fee simple to the common people under the Kuleana Act.[57] David Keanu Sai was one of the first to contest the prevailing assessments and offer a radically different analysis.[58] Drawing on a report submitted as part of the minister of the interior's report to the 1882 Kingdom Legislature by W. D. Alexander (later published as *Brief History of Land Titles* in the Hawaiian Almanac in 1891), Sai argues that Kanaka Maoli tenants received title to in excess of 180,000 acres.[59] He asserts that the figure of 30,000 acres for the makaʻāinana lands is accurate only when calculated from the number of Land Commission Awards. Purchasers of portions of the Government Lands, sold as a means of obtaining revenue to increase the costs of the monarchy, were issued Royal Patent Grants, which differed from the Royal Patents issued upon Land Commission Awards, since recipients of these were not required to obtain their award from the commission. In other words, the figures would be higher with accounting of land acquisition by other means.

In addition to Sai's finding that the makaʻāinana were able to purchase more land than previously understood, there is a new wave of scholarly work by Kingdom nationalists that have reassessed the Māhele.[60] In addition to the debates about the adverse effects of the Māhele, the contemporary status of these lands and the endurance of the makaʻāinana position in relation to them is still unresolved to this day.[61] As Lâm argues, while the Kuleana Act of 1850 enabled the makaʻāinana to acquire fee simple title to land for the first time, it did not terminate their traditional rights in land, activities that were quite extensive.[62] Lâm makes the case that the act introduced a system of rights parallel to customary use practices and prerogatives, not supplanting them.[63]

The 1848 Māhele together with the Kuleana Act of 1850 formed a basic dimension of social normalization—between those marked as civilized landowners and those who were not.[64] Although a strategy by the monarch to put Hawaiians on the same playing field as the otherwise-would-be colonizers, paradoxically the plan submitted to colonial logics. This is not to disregard the agency of the Mōʻī and other chiefs but to account for the structural forces that shaped their adaptation and to assess the costs. While individual landownership was central to the making of the bourgeois subject, land rights became a venue to dispossess the common kanaka—those who fared best under the new system were Hawaiian aliʻi, missionaries, and their descendants. While the vast lands they secured are rooted in perfect title, in the contemporary period we now turn to see the relationship between settler colonialism and the amassment of great wealth by a few, the core tenet of capitalist accumulation.

Staking a Claim

The struggle over these lands Zuckerberg purchased was not simply between him and the Rapozo family; a relative of the Rapozos, Carlos Andrade, a retired professor who is also Kanaka Maoli, also had claims, which complicated matters.[65] The title to the four parcels Zuckerberg moved to buy was divided between hundreds of descendants, including Andrade, who claims to be the only family member to have ever lived on or cared for the lands. Zuckerberg partnered with Andrade "to file a quiet title lawsuit in 2016 to have a judge force Rapozo family members to sell their fractional interests in their land because it would not be possible to subdivide the property into equitable pieces for so many people."[66] The lawsuit claimed that there could be as many as three hundred partial owners of these four parcels. Andrade, who reportedly cared for and lived on the property in recent decades while also paying taxes for the land, wanted to acquire the parcels for his immediate family and his own descendants. Andrade's attorney, Harvey L. Cohen, explained that he is the rightful heir to the parcels and that the lawsuit is simply a legal process allowing them to compensate partial owners for fractional shares that are otherwise useless to them. As Cohen put it, "It is not reasonable or practical for 138 parties to own and control 2.35 acres. . . . The quiet title process exists to address such matters, so that there is a clear owner based on an individual's ownership interests and history with the land."[67] Andrade, who is the great-grandson of Manuel Rapozo, first learned of the parcels in the 1970s. At the time, he was a new father and he and his wife were struggling to find affordable housing. In turn, his aunt suggested they move to "Grandpa's land." Andrade and his wife then "had the land surveyed, cleared it, planted gardens and restored its irrigation system and taro pond-fields" and made other improvements.[68] In response to controversy over the lawsuits, Andrade noted:

> I am unaware of any other descendant of Manuel Rapozo who has at-tempted to make use of the lands or who has offered to assist in paying the property taxes or to contribute to clearing the lands and having them surveyed. . . . I have spent more than half my life tending to these lands. Hopefully, my family and I will be able to do so well into the future. I pursue these actions of my own volition in order to make that dream a reality.[69]

In 2016, Zuckerberg addressed Andrade's claim to the lands: "He is 72 years old, retired, and wants to clear up the titles of these kuleana so he can pass the land on to his children. . . . He will continue his quiet title action and upon completion his family will have ownership of those kuleana. He has been a steward of his family lands and we support him in this effort."[70] Because Andrade could not afford the cost of quiet title litigation, he partnered with Zuckerberg. The media magnate tried to justify the quiet title action by insinuating he was doing the other claimants a favor: "For most of these folks, they will now receive money for something they never even knew they had. No one will be forced off the land."[71] Due to the controversial nature of the case, Zuckerberg withdrew as a plaintiff.

Andrade pursued things, despite speculation that the CEO helped Andrade by financially supporting both the litigation and bidding. It was reported that Northshore Kalo LLC was willing to pay the legal fees of Andrade's case to clear up the title issues relating to the property, which would enable him to take full ownership and compensate his relatives (fellow descendants) for their shares. Then the *Honolulu Star-Advertiser* investigated and found that the LLC was a shell corporation controlled by Zuckerberg.[72] Northshore Kalo withdrew from the lawsuit as a plaintiff in 2017 but continued to buy up partial shares from other defendants.[73] And because the entity "had already acquired an ownership stake in the kuleana by paying individual Rapozo descendants for their tiny fractional stakes in the land, the LLC was automatically listed among the defendants in the case."[74]

By March 2019, Andrade won three out of the four parcels at public auction, submitting a $1,060,000 bid for approximately two acres.[75] Meanwhile, the Rapozo family succeeded in outbidding him for the fourth parcel (5,227 square feet) in a $700,000 bid, or so it seemed. In early June 2019, at a court hearing to finalize the outcome of the March auction, "Andrade was able to reopen the bidding and win the title to all four of the parcels for a total of $2,145,000."[76] As reported, the final amount more than doubles the figure that he appeared to be able to pay earlier.[77]

In response, the Rapozo family and several other related holdouts then filed a separate claim suggesting that Andrade's alleged cooperation with Zuckerberg was improper.[78] Attorneys for the descendants who were holdouts argued in court documents that Andrade and Northshore Kalo used misrepresentations to acquire some of those shares. They claimed that Andrade falsely told relatives that the land would "stay in the family" and that Northshore Kalo took advantage of people's mistaken belief that it was a taro farm, given that *kalo* in Hawaiian is the word for taro. They sued Andrade, stating: "We have not been afforded an opportunity to conduct discovery and find the truth concerning who has truly funded the quiet title case and who is truly funding the bidding of $2.145 million as part of forced sale of the Rapozo family kuleana."[79] But the judge rejected these arguments and ordered the auction.[80] At the time the land sold, "North Shore Kalo owned a greater portion of the kuleana than Andrade or any of his relatives, with 44% of the kuleana shares."[81]

After the sale, the Rapozos filed another lawsuit, again highlighting what they saw as misrepresentation and malfeasance. But state circuit judge Randal Valenciano dismissed their lawsuit, ruling that the issues raised in the case were redundant to those in the earlier quiet title case and should have been handled in that process.[82] Meanwhile, many noted the disturbing irony that Andrade would be willing to sell to a foreigner

(Zuckerberg as a white person who also is not from Hawai'i in any sense) in this way, done through auction in this case, rather than keeping Hawaiian lands "in Hawaiian hands." Additionally, Rapozo noted that Zuckerberg and Andrade have created a model for how a "tag team tango of billionaire and dissident cousin" can dispossess "ordinary middle-class families that don't have $40bn to play games with other people's lives."[83]

One of the other descendants who refused to sell is twenty-four-year-old Alika Guerrero, who teaches Native Hawaiian culture and language at a resort on the island of Maui. As reported in the media, he had never set foot on the property but still wanted to maintain connection to the land.[84] He spoke to media in the lobby of another Maui hotel where his mother, fifty-seven-year-old Jennie Guerrero, works in the housekeeping department.[85] She owns a 0.45 percent share of the property, which she wanted to pass on to her three sons. Her son reported that the day they learned of the lawsuits, "both of us had the same response. Our family name is not going to be attached to anything to do with a billionaire buying up land in Hawaii and having us sell out our ancestral land."[86] He went on to say, "For people like myself, our connection to land and ancestral property is more than just about money. . . . We've been dispossessed for the last 150 years at least, so every little bit to us matters."[87]

On July 23, 2019, a Fifth Circuit judge—Kathleen Watanabe, who had presided over the dispute since 2016—ruled that Andrade did not have to turn over accounting documents to the relatives who wanted his financial statements disclosed to the court. They had hoped the judge would order the discovery to determine whether he violated court procedure by colluding with Zuckerberg in the legal case. In denying the motion asking for the financial disclosure, the judge ruled that "if the former-kuleana shareholders want to appeal her decision to finalize the sale of the land to Andrade, they would have to put up over half a million dollars to compensate the remaining shareholders for delays caused by the appeal, in the event that the higher court upholds Watanabe's ruling."[88] To date, none of Andrade's relatives have further appealed.

Conclusion

On July 2, 2020, a petition launched by Mia Brier went live on Change.org, "Stop Mark Zuckerberg from Colonizing Kauai."[89] Addressed to the Department of Hawaiian Home Lands and Hawai'i governor David Ige, it states:

> Mark Zuckerberg is the sixth richest man in the world . . . and he is suing
> Native Hawaiians in Kauai for their land so he can build a mansion.
> They have built lives there. They have built families there. Hawaiians
> are already mistreated enough as is. We need to let them have this. Their
> land is important to them. He's building a mansion to what? Live in

Kauai for two months out of the year? This is inhuman. It is sick. He needs to be stopped. He could literally build a house anywhere else. There are plenty of open spaces no one has claimed. Yet he has to pick a place where people are trying to make a living and support their families? It's disgusting. Don't let the privileged steal things that don't belong to them any longer. If you sign this petition, you could potentially save lives and families. Don't stay silent about this just because he's rich. The rich have enough already. They're greedy. This is greedy. He has ten homes already. INCLUDING surrounding properties to insure his privacy. He has enough. Like this is ridiculous.[90]

It is unclear what prompted the petition in terms of the timing in summer 2020, given all that transpired earlier in what appears to be a closed case. But here it seems a (presumably) non-Kanaka ally put forth a callout, since although the petition asserts that Zuckerberg "needs to be stopped," the petition does not specify what should or could be done to that effect.

In response to the petition, a spokesperson for the Zuckerberg family office stated that "the premise of this petition is false." The statement reads:

Mark is not suing native Hawaiians and no one has been forced off of the land. At the beginning of 2017, Mark withdrew as a plaintiff from the process to clear title on the land he purchased in Kauai. Before Mark acquired the land, it was set to be subdivided by a commercial developer and built into 80 homes. Instead, the property is being used as a working ranch and family retreat, designed in partnership with local families and experts to help create and maintain sustainable agriculture activities while preserving its natural beauty and protecting native wildlife.[91]

Note how this defense positions Zuckerberg as a savior on at least three counts: protector of the land, saving it from being developed, while also sustaining it through environmental preservation. The assertion continues:

Portions of the land are leased to local farmers and other portions are set aside as protective areas for endangered native species. The buildings on the land will cover about 1 percent of the land or less. Beyond the ranch, Mark and Priscilla have made commitments to Kauai charitable organizations that help to improve the island's education and health care systems, promote conservation and help to promote efforts to recover from flooding and COVID-19.[92]

Indeed, in April 2020, along with Priscilla Chan, his wife, Mark Zuckerberg followed up by offering a $1 million donation from the Chan Zuckerberg Initiative to support social services and health care needs on the island.[93] These include the Wilcox Medical Center, the Hawaii Community Foundation (for the Hawaii Resilience Fund), and the Āina Hoʻokupu O Kīlauea in support of local farmers.[94] They had given funds before to the American Red Cross and Mālama Kauaʻi to support flood relief efforts on the North Shore.[95] However much these funds are needed, charity in the form of donations is no stand-in for land.

As my own auntie Puanani Rogers—an elder and well-known sovereignty leader in the Hawaiian nationalist movement—told the media in response to the Zuckerberg case: "You malama (care for) the ʻāina. It's for your children and great-grandchildren. How dare they make decisions for my great-grandchildren."[96] She is not a claimant, but her point cuts to the core of what constitutes kuleana in Hawaiian cultural terms, if not the law: to protect the land for future generations. Among Kanaka Maoli today, there is an enduring belief that land is a birthright, not property. The concept of kuleana predates the property definition it is now used for in the law—and it is a deep Hawaiian principle, a robust combination of privilege *and* responsibility.

In response to the Zuckerberg case, some politicians and officials have called for a reform of the state law that created the quiet title and partition process, which may serve as a stopgap. However, this sort of fix-it remedy does not get to the root issues of the U.S. settler colonial legal frame regulating the sale of lands, nor the problems with privatization in the first place.

At the time of this writing, it is unclear whether Andrade has sold the parcels or if any of his relatives been paid for their interests in the property.

NOTES

1. Rebecca Aydin, "Take a Tour of Mark Zuckerberg's Gigantic $100 Million Property in Hawaii," *Business Insider*, July 3, 2019, https://www.businessinsider.com/mark-zuckerberg-hawaiian -property-photos-2014-10. Coverage of this case has been detailed in venues as diverse as *Forbes*, the *Guardian, Vice*, the *Wall Street Journal, USA Today*, and the *Garden Island*. Andrew Gomes, "4 Parcels within Mark Zuckerberg's 700-Acre Kauai Estate Sold at Auction," *Star Advertiser*, March 22, 2019, https://www.staradvertiser.com/2019/03/22/breaking-news/kuleana-parcels -within-mark-zuckerbergs-kauai-estate-being-auctioned-today; "Family Considers Appeal over Kuleana Land Purchase on Kauai," Hawaii News Now, June 8, 2019, https://www.hawaii newsnow.com/2019/07/08/family-considers-appeal-over-kuleana-land-purchase-kauai; and Julia Carrie Wong, "Zuckerberg's Hawaii Estate: Battle's Latest Turn 'Devastates' Local Family," *Guardian*, June 6, 2019, https://www.theguardian.com/us-news/2019/jun/06/zuckerbergs -hawaii-estate-battles-latest-turn-devastates-local-family.

2. Aydin, "Take a Tour."

3. Wex, Legal Information Institute, s.v. "Quiet title action," https://www.law.cornell.edu/wex/quiet_title_action.

4. "Family Considers Appeal over Kuleana Land Purchase on Kauai"; and Wong, "Zuckerberg's Hawaii Estate."

5. D. Kapuaʻala Sproat, "Avoiding Trouble in Paradise: Understanding Hawaiʻi's Law and Indigenous Culture," *Business Law Today* 18, no. 2 (November/December 2008): https://apps.americanbar.org/buslaw/blt/2008-11-12/sproat.shtml.

6. Julia Carrie Wong, "'A Blemish in His Sanctuary': The Battle Behind Mark Zuckerberg's Hawaii Estate," *Guardian,* January 17, 2019, https://www.theguardian.com/us-news/2019/jan/17/mark-zuckerberg-hawaii-estate-kauai-land-rights-dispute.

7. Wong, "'A Blemish in His Sanctuary.'"

8. Wong, "'A Blemish in His Sanctuary.'"

9. Wong, "'A Blemish in His Sanctuary.'"

10. There are cases of haole (foreign or white) elites in Hawaiʻi who have amassed vast tracts of Hawaiian land that show how even when ostensibly legal, massive land acquisition within private property regimes—literally part and parcel to contemporary settler colonialism—were made possible only through the Māhele land division in the first place. In earlier work, I examine two cases of haole (foreign, in this case white) elites in Hawaiʻi who have amassed vast tracts of Hawaiian land—in one case nearly an entire island—and assert perfect title to them. The first case is that of Harold F. Rice, who holds an immense segment of the island of Maui, and the second is Larry Ellison, who recently purchased 98 percent of the island of Lānaʻi. See J. Kēhaulani Kauanui, *Paradoxes of Hawaiian Sovereignty: Land, Sex, and the Colonial Politics of State Nationalism* (Durham, N.C.: Duke University Press, 2018).

11. Wong, "'A Blemish in His Sanctuary.'"

12. Wong, "'A Blemish in His Sanctuary.'"

13. Jon M. Van Dyke, *Who Owns the Crown Lands of Hawaiʻi?* (Honolulu: University of Hawaii Press, 2008).

14. Kauanui, *Paradoxes of Hawaiian Sovereignty.* For another look at allotment in Hawaiʻi, see J. Kēhaulani Kauanui, *Hawaiian Blood: Colonialism and the Politics of Sovereignty and Indigeneity* (Durham, N.C.: Duke University Press, 2008). In it, I uncover the history of the Hawaiian Homes Commission Act of 1920 (HHCA). The HHCA was passed by U.S. Congress to provide for the "rehabilitation" of the native Hawaiian people—defined as individuals having at least 50 percent Hawaiian blood—through a government-sponsored homesteading program. Pursuant to provisions of the HHCA, the Department of Hawaiian Home Lands provides direct benefits to native Hawaiians in the form of ninety-nine-year homestead leases for residential, agricultural, or pastoral purposes. *Hawaiian Blood* looks at how the arbitrary correlation of ancestry and race imposed by the U.S. government on the Indigenous people of Hawaiʻi has had far-reaching legal and cultural effects. With the HHCA, the federal government explicitly limited the number of Hawaiians included in land provisions, and it recast Hawaiians' land claims in terms of colonial welfare rather than collective entitlement. Moreover, the exclusionary logic of blood quantum has profoundly affected cultural definitions of indigeneity by undermining more inclusive Kanaka Maoli notions of kinship and belonging.

15. Lilikalā Kameʻeleihiwa, *Native Land and Foreign Desires: Pehea Lā E Pono Ai? How Shall We Live in Harmony?* (Honolulu: Bishop Museum Press, 1992), 15.

16. Kameʻeleihiwa, *Native Land and Foreign Desires,* 297.

17. Jonathan Kay Kamakawiwoʻole Osorio, *Dismembering Lāhui: A History of the Hawaiian Nation to 1887* (Honolulu: University of Hawaii Press, 2002), 11.

18. As Osorio notes, figures range from 93 percent to 95 percent depopulation by the end of the nineteenth century. Osorio, *Dismembering Lāhui,* 9–10. See David Stannard, *Before the Horror: The Population of Hawaii on the Eve of Western Contact* (Honolulu: University of Hawaii Press, 1989).

19. Osorio, *Dismembering Lāhui,* 47.

20. Douglas Shigeharu Yamamura, *A Study of Some of the Factors Contributing to the Status of Contemporary Hawaiians* (PhD diss., University of Washington, 1949), 233–34; Jocelyn Linnekin, *Sacred Queens and Women of Consequence: Rank, Gender, and Colonialism in the Hawaiian Islands* (Ann Arbor: University of Michigan Press, 1990); and Kameʻeleihiwa, *Native Land and Foreign Desires,* 297.

21. Osorio, *Dismembering Lāhui,* 32.

22. Osorio, 32.

23. Osorio, 32.

24. Linnekin, *Sacred Queens and Women of Consequence,* 198.

25. Osorio, *Dismembering Lāhui,* 44.

26. Linnekin, *Sacred Queens and Women of Consequence,* 85.

27. Kameʻeleihiwa, *Native Land and Foreign Desires,* 27.

28. Kameʻeleihiwa, 27.

29. Jon J. Chinen, *The Great Mahele* (Honolulu: University of Hawaii Press, 1958), 5.

30. Chinen, *Great Mahele,* 5.

31. Chinen, 5.

32. Chinen, 5.

33. Chinen, 7.

34. Cited in Chinen, 7.

35. Osorio, *Dismembering Lāhui,* 25.

36. Osorio, 25.

37. Osorio, 25.

38. Chinen, *Great Mahele.*

39. Chinen, 7–8. Here he uses the term *form of ownership,* but it is unclear whether by 1840 the concept of ownership was apt to describe the king's recognition that the makaʻāinana had a place within this communal land that went deeper than their labor upon it for him.

40. Maivân C. Lâm, "The Kuleana Act Revisited: The Survival of Traditional Hawaiian Commoner Rights in Land," *Washington Law Review* 64, no. 2 (1989): 233–88.

41. Kamanamaikalani Beamer, *No Mākou Ka Mana: Liberating the Nation* (Honolulu: Kamehameha Publishing, 2014), 129.

42. The Hawaiian Kingdom Crown and Government Lands are the national lands of the Hawaiian nation that remain at the center of contemporary sovereignty struggle. Together they constitute approximately 29 percent of the total land area of what is now known as the State of Hawaiʻi and almost all the land claimed by the state as public lands. According to Section 5(f) of the 1959 Hawaii State Admissions Act (Pub. L. No. 86-3, 73 Stat. 4), they are to be used for specific purposes—whether retained or sold, with proceeds from the sale or income therefrom—including "support of the public schools and other public educational institutions, for the betterment of the conditions of native Hawaiians, as defined in the Hawaiian Homes Commission Act, 1920, as amended,

for the development of farm and home ownership on as widespread a basis as possible for the making of public improvements, and for the provision of lands for public use." These lands were claimed by the U.S. federal government when it unilaterally annexed the Hawaiian Islands through a joint resolution by the U.S. Congress in 1898, after they had been ceded by the Republic of Hawai'i, which had established itself a year after the armed and unlawful overthrow of the Hawaiian monarchy in 1893. Newlands Resolution, To Provide for Annexing the Hawaiian Islands to the United States, 30 Stat. 750 (1898).

43. Chinen, *Great Mahele,* 25.

44. Until a later law prevented their alienation by the Crown, Kamehameha III administered these lands through his agents as any citizen under the system of private property ownership might; the monarch could sell, mortgage, or lease at will, and the revenues resulting were diverted to his personal use. See Jean Hobbs, *Hawaii: A Pageant of the Soil* (Stanford, Calif.: Stanford University Press, 1935), 46.

45. Kame'eleihiwa, *Native Land and Foreign Desires,* 295.

46. Kame'eleihiwa, 295; Lâm, "Kuleana Act Revisited," 262; and Chinen, *Great Mahele,* 31. Linnekin points to four statutes enacted in 1850 that, in combination, "made it impossible for commoners to subsist on the land without participating in the market economy, either through produce sales, cash cropping, or wage labor" (Linnekin, *Sacred Queens and Women of Consequence,* 195). One was the Kuleana Act that allowed commoners the right to be awarded their land in fee simple; the second was a law giving foreigners the right to own land in the Kingdom; the third opened three more ports to foreign commerce on Hawai'i Island, which had up until that point only been allowed in Lahaina on Maui Island and Honolulu on O'ahu Island; and the fourth abolished payment of taxes in kind, requiring Hawaiians to pay land, labor, and poll taxes to the Kingdom in cash. By the mid-1840s, government taxes had to be paid in cash, which forced people in areas remote from foreign commercial activities to shift to port towns to earn the necessary money. These changes also made for the development of a different process of class formation. Carolyn Ralston also explores the shift in common Kanaka Maoli lives, noting that between 1778 and 1854, life patterns for the maka'āinana changed from those of affluent subsistence farmers who were self-sufficient in terms of nearly all the essentials of life to those of a class of unskilled and predominantly landless peasants who were dependent on their own labor to supply the food and increasing number of foreign goods required to sustain life. Carolyn Ralston, "Hawaii, 1778–1855: Some Aspects of Maka'āinana Response to Rapid Cultural Change," *Journal of Pacific History* 19, no. 1 (1984): 21–40.

47. Mari J. Matsuda, "Native Custom and Official Law in Hawaii," *Internationales Jahrbuch für Rechtsanthropologie* (1988): 137.

48. Lâm, "Kuleana Act Revisited."

49. Linnekin, *Sacred Queens and Women of Consequence,* 201.

50. Osorio, *Dismembering Lāhui,* 53.

51. Osorio, 48.

52. Kame'eleihiwa, *Native Land and Foreign Desires,* 30–31.

53. Osorio, *Dismembering Lāhui,* 55.

54. Osorio offers a sustained treatment of these changes in Hawaiian governance and how the haole were empowered in serious ways. But, as he notes, when the nobles in the legislative council introduced their Act to Abolish the Disabilities of Aliens to Acquire and Convey Lands in Fee Simple Title on July 9, 1850, they met opposition from the representatives. Osorio, 55.

55. Lâm, "Kuleana Act Revisited," 259; and Chinen, *Great Mahele*, 20.

56. Matsuda, "Native Custom and Official Law in Hawaii," 137. Also, Linnekin maintains that the land division accelerated migration to nascent urban centers in the islands. She notes, "It is ironic that emigration was thus used as a justification for the individualization of title, for the land division was perhaps the single event most responsible for land abandonment." Linnekin, *Sacred Queens and Women of Consequence,* 198–99.

57. Until recently, the assertion of broad dispossession and the figure of 1 percent prevailed in the literature. See Chinen, *Great Mahele*; Lâm, "Kuleana Act Revisited"; Matsuda, "Native Custom and Official Law in Hawaii"; Osorio, *Dismembering Lāhui*; Kameʻeleihiwa, *Native Land and Foreign Desires*; and Noenoe K. Silva, *Aloha Betrayed: Native Hawaiian Resistance to U.S. Colonialism* (Durham, N.C.: Duke University Press, 2004).

58. Sai argues that the real dispossession for the makaʻāinana originated from the Bayonet Constitution—forced on King Kalākaua in 1887—that institutionalized property qualifications for the enfranchisement of citizens. David Keanu Sai, email message to author, March 28, 2006.

59. David Keanu Sai, email message to author, March 28, 2006; and Sai, review of *Kahana: How the Land Was Lost* by Robert Stauffer, *Contemporary Pacific: A Journal of Island Affairs* 15, no. 1 (2005): 237–40.

60. As I detail in *Paradoxes of Hawaiian Sovereignty,* some Hawaiian scholars suggest that the process protected more rights for the makaʻāinana by securing them in perpetuity, while others argue that the Māhele was a condition for but not a sole determinative factor in land dispossession of the common people. A key factor in these different interpretations of the Māhele starts with different understandings and interpretations as to the main purpose of the division itself.

61. Sai, email message to author, March 28, 2006.

62. Lâm, "Kuleana Act Revisited," 244.

63. Lâm, 259; and Chinen, *Great Mahele,* 20, 27–28.

64. Kauanui, *Paradoxes of Hawaiian Sovereignty.*

65. "Family Considers Appeal over Kuleana Land Purchase on Kauai."

66. Wong, "'A Blemish in His Sanctuary.'"

67. Wong, "'A Blemish in His Sanctuary.'"

68. Wong, "'A Blemish in His Sanctuary.'"

69. Wong, "'A Blemish in His Sanctuary.'"

70. Wong, "'A Blemish in His Sanctuary.'"

71. Audrey McAvoy, "Facebook CEO Trying to Buy Out Land Near His Hawaii Estate," AP News, January 19, 2017, https://apnews.com/article/aa791dc7ceed42dd87a912edf9bbdfb2.

72. Wong, "'A Blemish in His Sanctuary.'"

73. When the quiet title suit was filed in December 2016, Andrade owned about 14 percent of the parcels, and Northshore Kalo owned about 24.1 percent. By the time the judge ordered the auction in November 2018, Andrade's share had increased to 27.1 percent and Northshore Kalo's to 43.9 percent. According to real estate records reviewed by the *Guardian,* Northshore Kalo paid out more than $450,000 in seventy-one different transactions in the course of increasing its stake. See Wong, "'A Blemish in His Sanctuary.'"

74. Carl Loehrer, "Judge Sides with Andrade," *Garden Island,* July 24, 2019.

75. Gomes, "4 Parcels within Mark Zuckerberg's 700-Acre Kauai Estate Sold at Auction."

76. Wong, "Zuckerberg's Hawaii Estate."

77. Wong, "Zuckerberg's Hawaii Estate."

78. Wong, "Zuckerberg's Hawaii Estate."

79. Wong, "Zuckerberg's Hawaii Estate."

80. Wong, "Zuckerberg's Hawaii Estate."

81. Loehrer, "Judge Sides with Andrade."

82. "Kauai Land Sale Lawsuit Linked to Facebook's Zuckerberg Is Dismissed," Hawaii News Now, June 15, 2019, https://www.hawaiinewsnow.com/2019/06/14/kuleana-land-sale-lawsuit-dismissed-over-redundant-issues.

83. Wong, "'A Blemish in His Sanctuary.'"

84. Wong, "'A Blemish in His Sanctuary.'"

85. Wong, "'A Blemish in His Sanctuary.'"

86. Wong, "'A Blemish in His Sanctuary.'"

87. Wong, "'A Blemish in His Sanctuary.'"

88. Loehrer, "Judge Sides with Andrade."

89. Matthew Impelli, "Petition to Stop Mark Zuckerberg from 'Colonizing' Hawaii Island with His New Mansion Goes Viral," *Newsweek*, July 2, 2020, https://www.newsweek.com/petition-stop-mark-zuckerberg-colonizing-hawaii-island-his-new-mansion-goes-viral-1515020; and Jason Murdock, "Petition for Zuckerberg to Stop 'Colonizing' Hawaii Island Doubles in a Day," *Newsweek*, July 3, 2020, https://www.newsweek.com/facebook-mark-zuckerberg-hawaii-island-kauai-change-petition-signatures-land-deal-1515228.

90. Mia Brier, "Stop Mark Zuckerberg from Colonizing Kauai," Change.org petition, https://www.change.org/p/stop-mark-zuckerberg-from-colonizing-kauai.

91. Impelli, "Petition to Stop Mark Zuckerberg."

92. Impelli, "Petition to Stop Mark Zuckerberg."

93. "Mark Zuckerberg's Rare $1 Million Kauai Relief Donation," *Beat of Hawaii*, April 12, 2020, https://beatofhawaii.com/mark-zuckerbergs-rare-1-million-kauai-relief-donation.

94. "Mark Zuckerberg's Rare $1 Million Kauai Relief Donation."

95. "Mark Zuckerberg's Rare $1 Million Kauai Relief Donation."

96. Gomes, "4 Parcels within Mark Zuckerberg's 700-Acre Kauai Estate Sold at Auction."

The Enduring Confiscation of Indigenous Allotments in the National Interest

Pōkaewhenua 1961–1969

DIONE PAYNE

Indigenous land utilization in Aotearoa New Zealand prior to settler colonization focused on *whānau* (extended family units) and *hapū* (groups of whānau, subtribe) under a system of *take whenua* (the basis of land or birth), a term used to describe cultural philosophies and practices associated with customary Māori land tenure. Generally speaking, four main take associated with take whenua include *take taunaha* (naming rights), *take tūpuna* (by ancestry), *take raupatu* (by conquest), and *take noho* (by occupation).[1]

Following initial European contact from the 1700s, Waikato, a tribe in the North Island of Aotearoa New Zealand, took advantage of trade opportunities, including the incorporation of European fruits, vegetables, and animals. Waikato became proficient in polycultural agriculture and horticulture that fed the whānau and hapū and supplied a growing immigrant settlement in Auckland in the early nineteenth century and international markets around the world. Their produce included flour, wheat, pigs, wood, potatoes, onions, carrots, turnips, marrows, beans, apples, quinces, cherries, grapes, watermelons, oats, barley, tobacco, cabbages, peaches, maize, kumara, fish, bundles of grass, goats, and kauri gum.[2]

From 1852 to 1856, Māori sent 285,937 bushels of wheat, 90,798 bushels of maize, and 3,975 tons of potatoes into Auckland by coastal transport or canoe for trade.[3] One estimate of the value of this produce is considered to be in the vicinity of £16,000 annually—or in today's currency, £936,480 or USD$1,372,967 over that four-year period.[4] This is a considerable contribution by Māori to the local economy, given that Māori used relatively labor-intensive tools. Their communal social systems also allowed Waikato Māori to maximize their productive output and thereby feed the starving settlers that had newly arrived in Auckland.[5]

Māori contribution to the colony also included a significant settlement at Rangiaowhia, a town in Waikato that was considered the "showplace of Māori agriculture, granary of the North Island as well as a major cattle breeding area without peer in the colony."[6] Māori showed they were able to adapt and adopt tools, crops, and animals while implementing improvements in conjunction with their own horticultural and animal husbandry techniques.[7]

In addition to supplying food to Auckland, the then capital of the colony (1841–1865), the Waikato *iwi* (groups of hapū, tribe) also provided for the security of the capital from a perceived attack by the Ngāpuhi tribe in Northland. This dual role helped to secure peace and security in the Auckland and Waikato regions during that time.

For Māori, their rights to their land and their undisturbed use of it had been secured under Article 2 of the Treaty of Waitangi, which had been signed in 1840. Article 2, like the rest of the Treaty of Waitangi, had a Māori and an English version. The Māori version promised that the Crown would uphold the *rangatitratanga* (absolute authority) that Māori had over their own affairs, lands, and *taonga* (all their possessions). In the English version, this was translated as Māori having an "undisturbed possession of their properties, including their lands, forests, fisheries, for as long as they wished to retain them."[8] The English version also guaranteed to the Crown the right of preemption in Māori land sales, whereby Māori could only dispose of their land to the Crown. In the meantime, Māori continued to develop their economic expansion and to capitalize on their trade with the colony, while maintaining autonomy over their lands.[9] For the settlers, however, the major impediments to their ongoing interests and colonization were Māori customary title and a reticence by Māori to part with their land, particularly those lands settlers considered wasteland. For the settler government, wasteland was any Māori land not directly occupied or utilized for cultivation.

Settlers had brought with them a system of productivity that was based on John Locke's seventeenth-century theory of property rights, which considered that land was owned and improved by individuals and any land that was perceived as unutilized was wasteful and should be surrendered to those better able to utilize it.[10] Access to wasteland in Aotearoa became an important issue for settlers, and in 1846 Governor Hobson was given clear instructions that any "Māori customary rights to land beyond their habitations and cultivations" were considered unutilized and therefore wasteland.[11] By 1854, the settler government passed the Waste Lands Act allowing the Crown to thenceforth purchase, or confiscate, those lands it considered wasteland.

Māori, however, had no such concept of wasteland, given that they utilized regional practices and networks of seasonal *kainga nohoanga* for *mahinga kai* (food-gathering settlements) that saw large territories utilized to fish, hunt, bird, and cultivate. As an example, bushland used for hunting kererū, tui, weka, kaka, or kiwi or for gathering kōuka, aruhe, berries, fungi, and palms was often considered scrubland that settlers believed needed to be broken in, farmed, or mined.[12] Danny Keenan argues, "As the subsequent deadlock between sales and settler aspirations grew, settlers became increasingly intolerant of Māori refusals to sell land, which threatened the expansion of settlement and economic prospects. Demands increased that Māori be forced to part with their land, with all rights removed."[13] Immediately following the signing of the Treaty of Waitangi, and despite all the assurances of Māori autonomy, settler and colonial interests focused on the acquisition, by any means possible, of Māori land and the development and expansion of their own economies.[14] In doing so, and by virtue of the concept of Lockean productivity, settler and colonial interests became immediately at odds with Māori.[15]

Māori needed an intermediary or advocate to halt the continued harassment of settlement demands for their land, and in 1858 Pōtatau Te Wherowhero, a Waikato *rangatira* (chief), was elected by a number of iwi and hapū representatives at Pūkawa to become the first Māori king under the *Kīngitanga* (King Movement).[16] His son, Tāwhiao, succeeded him in 1860, when Waikato's economic success spurred a pervasive resentment by settlers and an unrelenting desire to access Māori land for their own independent development.[17]

The creation of the Kīngitanga removed settler ability to access land and was considered a "land league" that impeded settler development and rejected British sovereignty. For some, the Kīngitanga was an act of treason and a divisive threat to the colony.[18] In reality, the Kīngitanga was established not to oppose the government but to advocate for Māori interests and retain Māori land. In 1857, Governor Gore Browne considered that the Kīngitanga maintained their loyalty to the Queen and "desired to have a chief of their own election, who should protect them from every possible encroachment on their rights, and uphold such of their customs as they were disinclined to relinquish."[19] However, settlers perceived that Waikato had supported other iwi who had fought against the Crown to maintain their lands and thereby supporting rebellion against the Crown. In 1861, the Crown addressed a manifesto to Waikato demanding that they "should make at once an unreserved surrender of all they had done for themselves and be content to receive in exchange vague reassurances of some good to be done for them hereafter by a power which had, up to that time, done next to nothing, and in whose promises they had ceased to trust."[20]

The forced eviction of Waikato settlements in Auckland (such as Ihumatao) and the subsequent invasion of Waikato on July 12, 1863, by Crown forces were focused on bringing the Kīngitanga under the dominion of the English Monarch, to decisively defeat the Kīngitanga through armed conflict, and to facilitate the wholesale confiscation of their land.[21] By fabricating hysteria that Waikato was about to invade Auckland, an area they had provided protection against other tribes for the settler colony, the settlers were able to convince London that war was required and the funds to suppress rebellion were necessary.[22]

The invasion was facilitated by three key pieces of legislation: the New Zealand Settlements Act 1863 (which allowed for the confiscation of land from those considered to be in rebellion against the Crown), the Suppression of Rebellion Act 1863 (which gave the military authority to repel or crush a rebellion), and the New Zealand Loan

Act 1863 (which sought to raise a loan from England that was secured against sales of future confiscated lands). At its conclusion, the invasion resulted in the confiscation of 1.2 million acres in Waikato "causing displacement, economic deterioration and those of Ngāti Hine descent in Waikato to be placed in native reservations or land allotments with little immediate means of survival."[23]

Once confiscated, those lands were surveyed, subdivided, and administered into town and rural allotments for ex-militia and newly arrived settlers under the Department of Lands and Survey, which was established in 1858. The department was also responsible for farm development, including identifying underutilized and unproductive Crown and Māori land for sale to settlers. This dichotomy between the Crown and settler Lockean attitudes to land and the Māori concept of take whenua has become an enduring legacy for Māori land use and development.

Ngāti Hine ki Waikato

Ngāti Hine are a hapū of Waikato located in the Waikare area and within the Crown's survey boundaries of the Parish of Whangamarino. One of the kainga nohoanga and *pā* (fortified village) of Ngāti Hine included Pōkaewhenua, which is situated at the northeasternmost point of the parish. Pōkaewhenua was inhabited by both Ngāti Hine and Ngāti Marae but is also associated with other hapū, such as Ngāti Mahuta. Ngāti Hine has had unbroken take tūpuna and take noho in Pōkaewhenua and Waikare, with documented accounts as early as 1807 when Ngāti Hine went into battle with Te Rauangaanga (father of Pōtatau Te Wherowhero) against Pikauterangi and his allies at Hingakākā.[24]

Parish of Whangamarino

The Parish of Whangamarino encompasses 95,775 acres, all of which were confiscated following the invasion of Waikato during the 1860s. In 1863, the Compensation Court was established to determine the claims for compensation for those Māori who could prove they were loyal to the government but whose land had been confiscated as a result of proclamations by the Crown for the Waikato region. The court heard claims initially by loyal Māori and then later by rebel Māori following the invasion. By 1900, the Compensation Court had set aside approximately 6,663 acres within the Parish for Waikato Māori, and in 1910, 4,073 of those acres were set aside in nineteen allotments and advertised in the *New Zealand Gazette* for title investigation.[25] Those entitled to the nineteen allotments were Māori considered to have been made landless as a result of the invasion of Waikato and labeled rebels against the Crown. Lot 512 was one of those allotments set aside as a Native reservation for Ngāti Hine in 1883 and was situated on Pōkaewhenua.[26]

During the invasion of Waikato in 1863, those residing in Pōkaewhenua fought with Tāwhiao against the Crown forces and, in doing so, were labeled rebels and had their lands confiscated under the New Zealand Settlement Act. When lands were finally returned to identified Waikato rebels, there were additional stipulations applied under the Waikato Confiscated Lands Act of 1880 that insisted that rebels must continuously occupy their lands for two years or they were forfeited again to the Crown. Once claims were established in the Compensation Court, those claims were referred to the Native (and later renamed Māori) Land Court for official title to be granted.

Pōkaewhenua Confiscation

Lot 512 was granted through the Māori Land Court to members of Ngāti Hine in 1927, following forty years of investigation by the Native and Māori Land Courts. In 1930, Lot 512 was partitioned by the Māori Land Court into six allotments—Lot 512 blocks A to F—and included the granting of title to 198 Waikato Māori, Te Ao Mārama Tamehana being one of the grantees. Although the partition lines were submitted to the court, none of the partitions were surveyed or Māori landowners consulted or advised of those allotment boundaries. Te Ao Mārama and her whānau therefore maintained their *whare* (houses), plantations, and *iho whenua* (places where placenta are buried) across the wider block. By 1960, however, a Pākehā (European) farmer named Reginald John Ellmers utilized the Māori Affairs Act 1953 to apply to the Māori Land Court to lease two of the allotments, Lots 512E and F, to develop a sheep or beef farm.[27] Ellmers's application came on the back of two pieces of legislation and an international trade agreement with Britain.

Food for Britain

One of the key policies that supported the confiscation of Māori land in the 1950s and 1960s was an ongoing focus on supporting the Food for Britain campaign. In 1940, New Zealand entered into a bulk purchase agreement with Britain that saw every available acre of land brought into production to support Europe's recovery after World War II. This saw all of New Zealand's meat, wool, and dairy products exported to Britain. As an example, in the five-year period to 1947, New Zealand sent 80 percent of its butter exports, 93 percent of its cheese, and 74 percent of its meat to Britain.[28] To ensure all available land was bent to this purpose, Parliament focused on perceived unproductive Māori land as its primary target by ensuring Māori land was removed from its owners and then put into production by an individual farmer utilizing scientific methods of farming.[29] Scientific farming was the agricultural practice of using exotic grasses, plant management, fertilizers, and alternative farming techniques to promote greater production levels.[30]

Rather than focusing on sustaining the livelihood of Māori owners who were occupying and utilizing the remaining allotments left to them following a devastating colonial period, government legislation and policies instead focused on ensuring that Māori land was productively utilized for the nation's benefit. Ordinarily, the property rights of landowners ensured undisturbed control and ownership by non-Māori landowners. For Māori, however, their land was controlled by government agencies that insisted on productive utilization that deliberately excluded its owners' interests.

In 1950, the Māori Purposes Act was passed and stipulated that the Māori Land Court, if and whenever it deemed satisfied, could dispose of Māori land that was considered unoccupied, not kept properly cleared of weeds (which included native species of edible or usable flora), or that "the owners of the land have neglected to farm or manage . . . diligently."[31] This included land that was perceived as not being used to its best advantage in the interests of the owners and in the public interest.[32] The second piece of legislation was the Māori Affairs Act, which went further by including two additional clauses. They key section reads as follows:

> 387. The Court may appoint the Māori Trustee as agent to dispose of unproductive land—(1) Where with respect to any Māori freehold land or European land owned by Maoris [*sic*], the Court is satisfied—
>
> (a) that the land is unoccupied; or
> (b) that the land is not being kept properly cleared of weeds . . .
> (c) that any rates payable in respect of the land . . . have not been paid and that the amount of the said rates or moneys has been charged upon the land; or
> (d) that the owners of the land have neglected to farm or otherwise manage the land with due diligence and that in consequence of their neglect the land is not being used to proper advantage,—
>
> it may on application by the local authority of the district or by any person interested make an order in respect of that land or a defined portion thereof appointing the Māori Trustee to be the agent of the owners for the purpose of this Act.[33]
>
> 397. The Māori Trustee may, for any reason that he thinks sufficient, refuse to accept the application of any owner for a lease of land under this Part of this Act.[34]

The inclusion of "rates" and the ability by a "local authority of the district" or any interested person allowed for an application by Ellmers to the Māori Land Court to alienate land, while the Māori Purposes Act provided the national interest focus by ensuring the bulk purchase agreement with Britain was honored. However, it was the Māori Trustee that became a key collaborator with the Māori Land Court.

The Māori Trustee

The Māori Trustee had extraordinary powers to acquire, lease, or sell Māori allotments or convert uneconomic shares into its own name for redistribution. The key powers and functions of the Māori Trustee were, inter alia: the administration of the estate and property of deceased Māori, those with a disability, or minors; the control and alienation of allotments that were in Māori reservations, in trusts, or under Court orders; the execution of instruments of alienation as agents for Māori landowners; and the collection and distribution of rents and other money from the alienation of Māori allotments.[35] One of its more relevant functions, however, was as an agency for alienation whereby:

> 39. In a special way, the Māori Trustee is appointed agent of the owners under Court orders to arrange alienations of Māori lands which are lying idle and unproductive or are covered with noxious weeds or in respect of which rates are not paid.[36]

These two agencies (the Māori Land Court and Māori Trustee), the accompanying legislation (Māori Purposes and Māori Affairs Acts), and a national interest focus to fulfill a commitment to Britain nullified the treaty rights guaranteed to Māori and instead helped to facilitate a sixfold administrative process to determine the merits of Ellmers's application. This was undertaken while the owners of Lots 512E and 512F were still occupying and utilizing their own land.

Contemporary Confiscation

To lease or buy Māori land in the 1960s required a valuation (from the Department of Valuation), a district officer assessment (Department of Māori Affairs), a noxious weed inspector (Local Council), a confirmation of survey (Department of Lands and Survey), an assessment of current utilization and possible future utilization (Department of Lands and Survey and Department of Māori Affairs), and meetings of owners to discuss and vote on resolutions to lease or sell their land (Māori Land Court).[37] In Lot 512, all of these processes were utilized from 1961 to 1969 to determine the most effective and productive use of the land, starting with Lots 512E and F in 1960.

Lots 512E and F were occupied and utilized by their Māori owners and included a dairy farm, orchards, and gardens. As noted above, in 1960 a Pākehā farmer applied to the Māori Land Court under the Māori Affairs Act 1953 under Part XXV to lease these two allotments.[38] Under Part XXV, Māori-owned land considered unproductive could be disposed of by the Māori Trustee in the national interest. The Māori Land Court's administrative role to consider whether the two allotments could be disposed of was initiated by ordering a valuation of the allotments. During this time, the farmer had indicated his proposed lease fee, which fell short of the recommended valuation. To ensure the allotments were brought into production, the judge ordered that the resolution be changed from lease to sale and that all or any restrictions for a sale be removed, including declaring the allotments to be wasteland.[39] The acquisition of wasteland by the Crown, from Māori either forcibly or for £1 or less per acre, was considered lands taken under confiscation in the nineteenth century.[40] The term *wasteland* fell out of use in the courts post-1900, so its reutilization in the 1960s was out of step with the time, given its connotations as a tool for confiscation. Its use as a means to sell Lots 512E and F strongly indicated the court's coercive practice in the Waikato during that time. As each of the processes were completed, the Māori owners failed to stop the sale of their land, which was irretrievably alienated in 1961 in the national interest.

To further develop the remainder of Lot 512, the court consolidated the remaining allotments still in Māori ownership (Lots 512B, C, and D) on October 3, 1963. (Lot 512A had already been leased by the Maori Trustee shortly after Lots 512E and F were sold.) The court argued that none of the allotments could by themselves be utilized as an economic unit. In the judge's opinion, all three remaining allotments needed to be used together and should the owners decide against leasing or selling their allotment, the judge could pass the land over to the Māori Trustee to act as an agent to negotiate a lease for twenty-one years.[41]

The owners of Lot 512B rejected proposals from Pākehā farmers to have their land sold or leased. To avoid the Local Council taking their land for £14 due to unpaid rates, one of the Māori landowners was able to facilitate a purchase of the allotment and, within a year, the land was leased to a local farmer and has been in lease since 1968. In Lot 512C, the Local Council applied to the court in 1964 under the Māori Affairs Act and Rating Act to be the receiver for Māori owners failing to pay £11 in rates, and subsequently the allotment was put into a twenty-one-year lease.[42] Like Lot 512B, Lot 512C has been in a lease arrangement since then.

For Lot 512D, the alienation application was submitted for the purchase of their allotment in 1964 and was similarly rejected by their owners. Assessment of the allotment showed that owners had been planting crops on twenty-five acres of their land, with additional horticultural and agricultural activities.[43] So despite occupation and productive use by the owners, the court still appointed the Māori Trustee on June 13, 1968, to lease the block to non-Māori for twenty-one years from September 19, 1968.

By 1969, all six allotments were reconfiscated by the Māori Land Court in the national interest. The rationale applied by the Māori Land Court was a perceived failure by Māori landowners to productively utilize their land.[44] Although the declaration of these blocks as wasteland in the 1960s was historically redundant in the twentieth century, Lots 512E and F were sold by the Māori Land Court, with the remainder of Lot 512 subsequently alienated by lease. The majority of Lot 512 and its partitions have been in lease since the original eviction of its owners in the 1960s.

Conclusion

The Treaty of Waitangi assurances under Article 2 were nullified for Waikato by government invasion and confiscation. Pōkaewhenua demonstrates that confiscation endured well into the twentieth century. The utilization of the Māori Land Court and Māori Trustee and relevant clauses of legislation concerning Māori allotments clearly illustrates that Māori interests were superfluous to settler and non-Māori interests and their Lockean philosophy of land productivity. The minimal land provided for Ngāti Hine in the 1880s at Pōkaewhenua, although legally confirmed in 1930, became the focus of ongoing harassment from local farmers and systemic racism within a Māori Land Court that employed coercive practices to confiscate and devalue Māori land utilization by its owners.

The word *sale* conjures examples of scenarios where two willing parties agree to an exchange of commodities, in this case land allotments. The coercive sales practices by the Māori Land Court of Ngāti Hine allotments at Pōkaewhenua demonstrate that despite active and vocal opposition by owners to sell their land, national interests imperatives emboldened confiscatory practices disguised as sales. Pōkaewhenua is only one area of Aotearoa New Zealand where this type of confiscation occurred. It is so recent that memories survive in living whānau members of its enduring impact on them, and to date no contemporary Waitangi Tribunal claim has focused on this type of confiscation, despite the 2,501 registered claims submitted.

NOTES

1. George Asher and David Naulls, *Maori Land,* no. 29 (New Zealand Planning Council, 1987).
2. John Williamson, "Return of Native Produce Imported into the Ports of Auckland and Onehunga" [1865] I *AJHR* E12 at 4–14 (N.Z.).
3. R. P. Hargreaves, "The Maori Agriculture of the Auckland Province in the Mid-nineteenth-Century," *Journal of the Polynesian Society* 68, no. 2 (1959): 74.
4. Hargreaves, "Maori Agriculture of the Auckland Province," and the U.K. National Archives website and MoneyConverter.com for today's currency values. Please also note that pounds, shillings, and pence have been converted to decimal currency.
5. Robert Mahuta, "Tainui, Kīngitanga, and Raupatu," in *Justice and Identity: Antipodean Practices,* ed. M. Wilson and A. Yeatman (Wellington: Bridget Williams Books Ltd., 1995), 20.
6. Mahuta, "Tainui, Kīngitanga, and Raupatu," 20. See also, D. Payne, "Mai Rangiriri ki Pokaewhenua: The Confiscation of Pokaewhenua in the National Interest—1961–1969" (PhD diss., Victoria University, Wellington, N.Z., 2014), 71.

7. Graham Harris and Percy Tipene, "Māori Land Development," in *State of the Māori Nation: Twenty-First Century Issues in Aotearoa,* ed. Malcolm Mulholland et al. (Auckland, N.Z.: Reed Publishing Ltd., 2006), 69.

8. "The Treaty of Waitangi/Te Tiriti o Waitangi: Meaning of the Treaty," Waitangi Tribunal, accessed October 7, 2019, www.waitangitribunal.govt.nz/treaty-of-waitangi/meaning-of-the-treaty.

9. J. B. McKinney, "The Evolution of a Legal Title to Land Formerly Held under Maori Custom and Usage, or The Effect of Native Land Laws on Maori Custom" (master's thesis, Victoria University College, 1939), 27.

10. Payne, "Mai Rangiriri ki Pokaewhenua," 52.

11. Payne, 54.

12. Keith Sinclair, *The Origins of the Maori Wars* (Wellington: New Zealand University Press, 1957), 5.

13. Danny Keenan, *Wars without End: The Land Wars in Nineteenth-Century New Zealand* (Auckland, N.Z.: Penguin Books, 2009), 51.

14. Keenan, *Wars without End,* 51.

15. Payne, "Mai Rangiriri ki Pōkaewhenua," 73.

16. Turongo House, *Tawhiao: King or Prophet* (Hamilton, N.Z.: Waikato Raupatu Lands Trust, 2000), 25.

17. House, *Tawhiao,* 25.

18. C. Orange, *The Treaty of Waitangi* (Wellington: Allen & Unwin, 1987), 143.

19. William Martin to William Fox, "Observations on the Proposal to Take Native Lands under an Act of the Assembly, 16 November 1863, in Papers Relative to Confiscation of Native Lands" [1864] I *AJHR* E2b at 11 (N.Z.).

20. Martin to Fox, "Observations on the Proposal" at 12.

21. Keenan, *War without End,* 207.

22. D. McCan, *Whatiwhatihoe: The Waikato Raupatu Claim* (Wellington: Huia Publishers, 2001), 46; and Keenan, *War without End,* 215.

23. Payne, "Mai Rangiriri ki Pōkaewhenua," 90.

24. Pei Te Hurinui Jones, *King Pōtatau* (Wellington: Journal of the Polynesian Society, 1959), 46. See also Leslie G. Kelly, *Tainui* (Wellington: Polynesian Society Inc., 1949), 237, for the date of Hingakākā.

25. Payne, "Mai Rangiriri ki Pōkaewhenua," 224.

26. Payne, 113.

27. M. A. Brook — *Lot 512F Parish of Whangamarino* (1960) 1 Auckland Thames Alienations MB 249.

28. Department of Agriculture, *Farming in New Zealand* (Wellington: Hutcheson, Bowman, and Stewart Ltd., 1950), 287–88.

29. Department of Agriculture, *Farming in New Zealand,* 96.

30. Department of Agriculture, 85.

31. Māori Purposes Act 1950, s 34 (N.Z.).

32. Māori Purposes Act 1950, s 34 (N.Z.).

33. Māori Affairs Act 1953, s 387 pt 2 (N.Z.).

34. Māori Affairs Act 1953, s 397 (N.Z.).

35. Department of Maori Affairs, "The Minister of Maori Affairs,'" 16 December 1957, Maori Affairs (AAMK), series 869, W3074/3, Archives New Zealand, Wellington.

36. Department of Maori Affairs, "The Minister of Maori Affairs."

37. Payne, "Mai Rangiriri ki Pōkaewhenua," 127.

38. Brook, *Lot 512F Parish of Whangamarino.*

39. M. A. Brook — *Lot 512E and 512F Parish of Whangamarino* (1961) 4 Waikato Maniapoto MB 284–86.

40. See M. McGillivary, "Return of the Crown Lands in Each Province Showing the Extent Acquired by Confiscation" [1871] I *AJHR* C4a (N.Z.).

41. D. Payne, *Riro Whenua Atu: The 1960s Confiscation of Waikato Land at Pōkaewhenua* (Auckland, N.Z.: Hakari Rau Limited, 2018), 129.

42. Payne, *Riro Whenua Atu,* 132.

43. Darby Finlayson in M. A. Brook — *Lot 512D2 Parish of Whangamarino Section 438* (1968) 46 Waikato MB at 141.

44. Payne, *Riro Whenua Atu,* 36.

"Why Does a Hat Need So Much Land?"

SHIRI PASTERNAK

What Is Crown Land?

If we look at a political map of Canada, it is striking how much of the land is claimed by the Crown. Eighty-nine percent of the country has been roughly divided between the federal and provincial governments.[1] In the westernmost province of British Columbia, 94 percent of the province is claimed as B.C. Crown land.[2] Other regions, particularly the northern territories, fall almost entirely under federal jurisdiction, save for some modern treaty settlement lands and municipalities. Indian reserves also fall under federal jurisdiction, in the sense that "Indians and the lands reserved for Indians" are federally governed, but also because reserves are lands held "in trust" by the federal government. They occupy 0.02 percent of the total national land base that spans 10 million square kilometers (or over 6 million square miles) of mostly Crown lands.[3] It is hard to think of a better illustration of the colonial geography of Canada than this spatial distribution. Besides, as Stó:lō writer Lee Maracle once quipped: "Why does a *hat* need so much land?"[4]

Crown lands find their source in a number of colonial legalities, including British royal charters and the confederation acts of this successor state. Since the eleventh century, British law established in the doctrine of tenure that only the Crown could properly own land. This doctrine became Canadian law through the regulatory concept of the doctrine of reception—premised on a void of law in the new territory into which British subjects filled the vacuum with their common law.[5] To this day, the Crown—an entity that has changed radically since first contact (both in Britain and Canada)—presumes to hold underlying title to all lands in the country.

So, that's the story of Crown land. But enforcing ancient British property law in the face of Indigenous territorial authority requires considerable real violence. Therefore, the answer to Lee Maracle's rhetorical question about why a hat needs so much land cuts to the heart of colonization. The Crown, after all, is neither intact nor integral and bears little continuity with the political entity that established the doctrine of tenure or made the first treaties or confederated as a new dominion. But though *the Crown* is an ambivalent representation of power, *Crown land* is very directly connected with the regulatory powers of governments to sell and reap rewards for the use of these lands. As laid out in the Constitution Act, 1867, the federal government has jurisdiction, for example, over interprovincial and international energy projects, navigable waters, and military forces. Provinces have jurisdiction over the extraction of local natural resources, including oil, gas, and energy projects, as well as forestry and mining. These powers confer the legal authority under settler law to issue permits, licenses, leases, and grants to third parties to extract resources and develop these lands.

For First Nations in Canada, however, the founding of this country had little to formally offer in the jurisdiction basket. All of their lands were divided between the hats. Then, nearly a decade after dominion was granted by Britain, the early Indian Acts were consolidated into *the* Indian Act, 1876, and restrictions on First Nations' authority to govern were laid out in painstaking and exhaustive detail that limited band council jurisdiction to reserves.[6] Though formal acknowledgment of Indigenous governance was not extended, the new colony was in practice a "paper empire" that was not immediately successful at the widespread dispossession it claimed to have achieved.[7] As the provinces were gradually carved out of Indigenous national territories, the authority of the new state was constantly tested, and legal strategies to define and defend Crown lands were devised. In the late nineteenth century, for example, lands treated between Canada and First Nations were suddenly subsumed under provincial jurisdiction. This development partially unfolded through the court's interpretations of treaties that domesticated U.S. doctrines of discovery.[8]

Treaties did not gain constitutional protection until 1982, when Indigenous peoples' rights to defend their hunting, fishing, trapping, and other traditional practices were acknowledged and affirmed. Further court cases to define Section 35 rights—"the existing aboriginal and treaty rights"—to the land itself placed Indigenous peoples in direct competition with Crowns that may seek to maximize revenues through their sale.[9] In British Columbia, for example, the energy, utilities, and residential sectors account for 58 percent of tenures on Crown land, amounting to around 13 percent of total annual provincial government revenue.[10] So, while the vast area of Crown land on political maps depicts an empty and unoccupied space—save for some Indian reserves, small settlements, and an urban population strung out along the southern U.S.–Canada border—mapping extractive practices offers a much more revealing depiction of the scale of contemporary land alienation. It is not simply a matter, in other words, of lands being stolen, but rather that the nature of alienation may render them impossible to ever be returned. For example, mining claims alone darken Crown lands with activity and investment.[11]

Here in this allotment story, I want to illustrate through a contemporary land struggle a key legal and military mechanism for maintaining the proprietary interest of Crown land, as well as foregrounding contestations against it. One of the most dramatic conflicts over Crown land is unfolding on the territory of the Wet'suwet'en people in British Columbia. It involves a form of forced removal to access, claim, and exercise control over Crown lands: the injunction.

In December 2018, Coastal GasLink Pipeline Limited, a subsidiary of TransCanada PipeLines Limited, served an injunction to the Unist'ot'en clan associated with the Yikh Tsawwilhggis (Dark House) of the C'ilhts'ëkhyu (Big Frog Clan) of the Wet'suwet'en Nation (one of thirteen hereditary *Yihks,* or clans). The company sought to clear the path for a liquified natural gas (LNG) pipeline to transport diluted bitumen (or "dilbit") from northern British Columbia to the Kitimat port. Two members of the Unist'ot'en are named in the suit—spokesperson Freda Huson and Chief Smogelgem. They filed a response to the injunction stating that, under Wet'suwet'en law, they were under no obligation to offer access to their territory: as they write, "One of the firmest Wet'suwet'en laws holds that one cannot enter another's territory without asking for and receiving the head chief's permission. Trespassing on house territories is considered a serious offence."[12] Yet the province had authorized the use of their lands for a pipeline project that all the Wet'suwet'en hereditary chiefs unanimously opposed. So, how does the injunction resolve this impasse for the state?

This is a site within a structure of colonization where we can observe how Crown land works through a form of simultaneous socialization and privatization of Indigenous lands—the former through the sovereignty claims of the state that render these lands titled to the Crown and the latter through the exercise of jurisdiction to sell those claimed lands to a private corporation. The forced removal of Unist'ot'en people from the path of the pipeline was not so much a failure of the legal system but a realization of its insistence that the proprietary interests of Indigenous peoples are subordinate to the Crown and its regulatory powers. In this case, we also see how Anuk Nu'at'en (Wet'suwet'en law) and the responsibilities it upholds foreground the emptiness of a tenure system that claims to fill a void already governed by Indigenous political and legal orders.

What Is an Injunction?

First Nations are granted little control to authorize economic activity on their lands. Most of the time, companies have already cleared the gate of provincial authorization when First Nations are engaged and consulted.[13] When Indigenous peoples express dissent against these regulatory decisions, a common strategy of containment exercised with increasing frequency is the injunction.[14] In plain terms, an injunction is a legal tool that restrains someone from doing something. Indigenous peoples and industry alike use injunctions to intervene in urgent matters. In fact, some of the most important Aboriginal rights cases in Canada have been launched through the exercise of this legal action, for example, in *Haida Nation v. British Columbia.*[15]

Secwepemc leader Art Manuel called injunctions a "legal billy club" because they are designed to move rightful title holders off their land through force.[16] In terms of the Unist'ot'en injunction, it was the *Delgamuukw v. British Columbia* Supreme Court of Canada decision that affirmed Aboriginal title as an Indigenous interest in the land that is sui generis, distinct from other forms of land title, proprietary, and held communally by the nation.[17] The appellants were Wet'suwet'en and Gitxsan hereditary chiefs, who brought the case to court on behalf of their houses, claiming ownership and jurisdiction over thirty-six thousand miles of their territory governed by seventy-one houses. The very nation that first succeeded in defining Aboriginal title as an underlying proprietary interest was now being removed from these same lands through a low-level lever—the equivalent of an emergency stop cord on a train.

Delgamuukw found Aboriginal title to be "held by Aboriginal nations or polities that are the descendants or successors of the Aboriginal people that were in exclusive occupation of their traditional territories at the time of Crown assertion of sovereignty."[18] The *Delgamuukw* case also raised the bar of Indigenous jurisdiction from a requirement of consultation to consent, as the court stated: "Some cases may even require *the full consent of an aboriginal nation,* particularly when provinces enact hunting and fishing regulations in relation to aboriginal lands."[19] Though the burden of proof for Aboriginal title and the cost of bringing a case to court remain substantial barriers, Indigenous peoples' governing authority over their lands opened the door for participation in the resource economy in new ways.[20]

Meanwhile, to get an injunction in Canada, an applicant must simply pass three tests set out in *RJR-MacDonald Inc. v. Canada.*[21] First, the issue must be deemed "serious"; second, the applicant must prove "irreparable harm" is being caused that cannot be remedied with money; and third, the applicant must show that in the "balance of convenience," those requesting injunctive relief are the most disadvantaged. Of course, this third criterion is highly subjective. Time and time again, with few exceptions, the courts appear to have decided that the short-term economic losses of resource companies outweigh the long-term commitment of Indigenous governments to caretake their lands—for example, at Aamjiwnaang, Barriere Lake, and Elsipogtog.[22] Not only has this stopgap mechanism been exercised to remove people from their lands and alienate their jurisdiction, these judgments create precedents defining proper title holders in the process of adjudicating internal First Nation disputes.[23] That is a lot of power for a court action that need not weigh Aboriginal rights, which when treated as a criminal offense can result in jail time and serious fines, even on unceded Indigenous lands.

Who Can Authorize Consent?

From the start of media coverage of the Unist'ot'en blockade against Coastal GasLink, the definition of Wet'suwet'en land as Crown land was everywhere. CBC reported,

"Companies trying to use the area say they're trying to use public roads *to access Crown land,* and some have ferried their crews to nearby worksites by helicopter" (*emphasis added*).[24] But as Tlingit scholar Anne Spice writes, "At Unist'ot'en Camp, the hosts remind visitors, 'this is not Canada, this is not British Columbia: this is unceded Wet'suwet'en territory.'"[25] Here is where injunctions and the concept of Crown land come to a head.

The Wet'suwet'en land defenders named in the Coastal GasLink injunction have made a permanent home on their ancestral lands, constructing traditional pit houses, gardens, and a healing lodge. The camp itself lies on the GPS coordinates of multiple proposed pipelines. Spokesperson for the Unist'ot'en Freda Huson draws attention often to the integral role of the people to protect the life-giving territory from endangerment—this is what she and many others were raised to understand about their role on the land. As the Wet'suwet'en Nation's original affidavit to the B.C. Environmental Assessment Office regarding the pipeline states, "Each House group is an autonomous collective that has jurisdiction over one or more defined geographical areas known as the House territory."[26] Their jurisdiction is not a human-centered form of political authority but rather forms part of a broader governance system with their relations. As the hereditary chiefs state:

> Within the context of Wet'suwet'en society, this ownership is considered to be a responsibility rather than a right. Hereditary Chiefs are entrusted with the stewardship of territories by virtue of the hereditary name they hold, and they are the caretakers of these territories for as long as they hold the name. It is the task of a head Chief to ensure the House territory is managed in a responsible manner, so that the territory will always produce enough game, fish, berries and medicines to support the subsistence, trade, and customary needs of house members. The House is a partnership between the people and the territory, which forms the primary unit of production supporting the subsistence, trade, and cultural needs of the Wet'suwet'en.[27]

Despite this clear notice regarding governance of the region, Crown land designation helped authorize a series of institutional responses to remove the hereditary stewards of the land. Because this was considered public property, police enforcement was triggered by the legal action to move in and supposedly protect the contract British Columbia had made with Coastal GasLink. Therefore, in December 2018, this Wet'suwet'en governing order was set into physical motion to defend the territory from the injunction enforcement. A neighboring clan, the Gidumt'en, also erected a checkpoint to stop the injunction enforcement against their kin. Gidumt'en Clan spokesperson

Molly Wickham was arrested on her land along with fourteen others by the Royal Canadian Mounted Police (RCMP). The RCMP soon arrived at the Unist'ot'en checkpoint, where the people opened the gate to avoid the violence but made clear their opposition. "I will slide this 2 × 4 over under duress for fear of RCMP action," said a Wet'suwet'en man who slid open the gate.[28]

The Unist'ot'en Camp may act to blockade against industrial infrastructure and development, but as the group describes, the camp is not "a blockade"—rather, "it is a permanent, non-violent occupation of Unist'ot'en territory, established to protect our homelands from illegal industrial encroachments and to preserve a space for our community to heal from the violence of colonization."[29] "This is our house group's work. It's a shared vision and purpose," Unist'ot'en house group member Dr. Karla Tait stated.[30] It is so much deeper than the claim of a hat.

While the injunctions temporarily removed people from the pipeline construction, the work of upholding Anuk Nu'at'en continues. The socialization of Crown lands invests Canadians in a promise of growing prosperity and secure employment that relies on the alienation of Indigenous lands through privatization. The alienation of land, though, also socializes the risk of Indigenous rights to the resource economy. It deepens racial antagonisms between Indigenous peoples and those precariously employed or with ownership stakes in its boom and bust cycles. But the most insecure of all is the political mindset that refuses to consider the horizon ahead—the conditions for life to thrive on the territory—and the protectors with the knowledge to care for it. What the Unist'ot'en struggle can teach us all about the twinned problem of injunction-alienation is that, for Canadians, if Crown land is ours, it is also ours to give back.

NOTES

1. By contrast, public lands in the United States account for only 40 percent of the country. U.S. Census Bureau, *Statistical Abstract of the United States, 1991,* 11th ed. (Washington, D.C.: 1991), 201. But the distribution of these lands is heavily skewed toward twelve western states where 92 percent of federally owned acres can be found. "Federal Land Ownership by State," Ballotpedia, accessed February 28, 2019, https://ballotpedia.org/Federal_land_ownership_by_state.

2. Province of British Columbia, Ministry of Forests, Lands, and Natural Resource Operations, *Crown Land: Indicators and Statistics Report* (Victoria, B.C.: 2011).

3. DIAND, *Resolving Aboriginal Claims: A Practical Guide to Canadian Experiences* (Ottawa: Department of Indian Affairs and Northern Development, 2003).

4. Lee Maracle, "Prequel—Colonialism 101: Dear Harper, A Primer on Canadian Colonialism" (panel at Indigenous Sovereignty Week, Toronto, Ontario, October 25, 2009).

5. John Borrows, *Canada's Indigenous Constitution* (Toronto: University of Toronto Press, 2000); Kent McNeil, "Exclusive Occupation and Joint Aboriginal Title," *U.B.C. Law Review* 48 (2015): 821; and Ian Johnson, *Pre-Confederation Crown Responsibilities: A Preliminary Historical Overview,* Treaties and Historical Research Centre (Ottawa: Indian and Northern Affairs Canada, 1984).

6. J. S. Milloy, "The Early Indian Acts: Development Strategies and Constitutional Change," in *Sweet Promises: A Reader on Indian-White Relations in Canada,* ed. J. R. Miller (Toronto: University of Toronto Press, 1991).

7. Brian Slattery, "Paper Empires: The Legal Dimensions of French and English Ventures in North America," in *Despotic Dominion: Property Rights in British Settler Societies,* ed. John Maclaren, Andrew Buck, and Nancy Wright (Vancouver: UBC Press, 2005); and John L. Tobias, "Canada's Subjugation of the Plains Cree, 1879–1885," *Canadian Historical Review* 64 (1983): 519–48.

8. Kent McNeil, "Social Darwinism and Judicial Conceptions of Indian Title in Canada in the 1880s," *Journal of the West* 38 (1999): 68.

9. Constitution Act, 1867, 30 & 31 Vict. c 3 (U.K.).

10. Province of British Columbia et al., *Crown Land: Indicators and Statistics Report.*

11. Yellowhead Institute, *Land Back: A Yellowhead Institute Red Paper,* https://redpaper.yellow headinstitute.org.

12. Chantelle Bellrichard, "Defendants Accuse Coastal GasLink of Trying to 'Subvert Authority' of Wet'suwet'en Hereditary Chiefs," CBC News, February 21, 2019, https://www.cbc.ca/news/indigenous/wet-suwet-en-coastal-gaslink-injunction-court-filings-1.5028237.

13. Arthur Manuel, *Unsettling Canada: A National Wake-Up Call* (Toronto: Between the Lines, 2014).

14. There are two kinds of injunctions: a permanent injunction that is awarded after a trial and an interlocutory injunction that is more immediate and used when people think a trial will take too long. This second type of injunction is the one most often used by companies to restrain Indigenous peoples from blockading or by Indigenous peoples to stop development on their lands.

15. Haida Nation v. British Columbia (Minister of Forests), [2004] 3 S.C.R. 511 (Can.).

16. Arthur Manuel, *Reconciliation Manifesto: Recovering the Land, Rebuilding the Economy* (Toronto: Lorimer, 2018).

17. Respectively, Delgamuukw v. British Columbia, [1997] 3 S.C.R. 1010, para. 190, 115, and 140 (Can.). While in the latter case, the court distinguishes Aboriginal title from fee simple property, the chief justice states that it is "a right to the land itself" and clearly a proprietary interest.

18. Kent McNeil, "Aboriginal Title and Indigenous Governance: Identifying the Holders of Rights and Authority" (All Papers Working Papers Collection, https://digitalcommons.osgoode.yorku.ca/all_papers/264/), 17.

19. Delgamuukw v. British Columbia, para. 168 (emphasis added).

20. Tsilhqot'in Nation v. British Columbia, [2014] 2 S.C.R. 257 (Can.). The court also put limits on this right. In *Delgamuukw,* the Supreme Court found that Aboriginal title is not an absolute right but a legal burden on the Crown's title (para. 145). Therefore, the Crown and Indigenous peoples must take one another's interests in the land into account. Aboriginal title is also constrained by the requirement that the land remain intact to preserve Indigenous use ("inherent limit") (para. 125). It is also constrained by potential infringement by the state, although the state must pass a justification test established in the case law on Aboriginal rights (para. 165). See also *Tsilhqot'in,* where the Supreme Court wrote that the state must show that its infringement of section 35(1) rights is justified by demonstrating that "(1) it complied with its procedural duty to consult with the right holders and accommodate the right to an appropriate extent at the stage when infringement was contemplated; (2) the infringement is backed by a compelling and substantial legislative objective in the public interest; and (3) the benefit to the public is proportionate to any adverse effect on the Aboriginal interest" (para. 125). See also Kent McNeil, "How Can Infringements of the Constitutional Rights of Aboriginal Peoples Be Justified?" *Constitutional*

Forum 8, no. 2 (1997): 33–39; and Kent McNeil, "The Post-Delgamuukw Nature and Content of Aboriginal Title," *Centre for First Nations Governance* (May 2000).

21. RJR-MacDonald Inc. v. Canada (Attorney General), [1995] 3 S.C.R. 199 (Can.).

22. Canadian National Railway Co. v. Plain, [2012] ONSC 7356 (Can.); Wawatie c. PF Résolu Canada Inc., [2014] QCCA 1840 (Can.); and SWN Resources Canada, Inc. and Louis Jerome et al, Nov. 22, 2013, Madame Justice J. L. Clendening, F-C-279-13 (Can.).

23. For example, Campbell v. British Columbia (Minister of Forests and Range), [2011] BCSC 448 (Can.); and Moulton Contracting Ltd. v. British Columbia, Appeal Decision, [2015] BCCA 8 (Can.).

24. Betsy Trumpener, "RCMP Planning Mass Arrests at Pipeline Protest Camp, Northern B.C. Chiefs Fear," *CBC News,* August 28, 2015.

25. Anne Spice, "Fighting Invasive Infrastructures: Indigenous Relations against Pipelines," *Environment and Society: Advances in Research* 9 (2018): 52.

26. *Wetsuweten Title and Rights and Coastal GasLink* (Office of the Wet'suwet'en, 2014), 2.

27. *Wetsuweten Title and Rights and Coastal GasLink,* 2.

28. Linda Solomon Wood, "Force Is Not Consent," *National Observer,* January 14, 2020.

29. Unist'ot'en, "TransCanada Litigation Threatens Unist'ot'en Territory," November 13, 2018, https://unistoten.camp/press-release-transcanada-litigation-threatens-unistoten-territory.

30. Unist'ot'en, "TransCanada Litigation Threatens Unist'ot'en Territory."

Stories of American Indian Freedom

The Privatization of American Indian Resources
from Allotment to the Present

WILLIAM BAUER

In November 2016, news wires reported that the Native American Affairs Coalition (NAAC), a group that advised then-President-Elect Donald Trump, recommended privatizing American Indian reservation lands. The proposal caused quite a stir throughout Indian Country. Cherokee Markwayne Mullin, representative from Oklahoma and member of the NAAC, responded to the criticisms by stating that the coalition actually wanted to reduce Environmental Protection Agency (EPA) restrictions on Indian lands in order to make it easier for tribal governments to drill for oil and develop other natural resources. The NAAC believed that the EPA prevented natural resource extraction on trust lands and that private lands would free tribes from dealing with what they consider a bloated federal bureaucracy.[1] American Indians have heard similar stories before. Since the nation's founding, Americans have attempted to privatize American Indian labor, land, and resources, and they have done so by invoking a language of "freedom." Americans promised that privatized resources would free or emancipate American Indians from something that held them back.

This essay explores American and Indigenous stories about allotment, termination, and natural resource extraction. So-called Friends of the Indian have used the language of freedom to support policies aimed at privatizing American Indian labor, land, and resources. American Indians, for various reasons, supported these policies because they believed these policies offered opportunities to exercise sovereignty and self-determination. American Indians possessed their own understandings of these policies, but they could not have anticipated their consequences.

The language of freedom functions in transit, moving from historical moment to historical moment, to undergird United States settler colonialism.[2] Under settler colonialism, colonizing nations seek to extract land from Indigenous people, to remove Indigenous people from the land and replace them with settler families, and to eliminate Indigenous people. Settler colonial processes are not one-off events, rather they are a structure that continues into the present day.[3] By exploring the concepts of freedom and sovereignty, one can see how these ideas are entangled with capitalism.[4] The capitalist marketplace's promises of freedom, protection, and sovereignty have been both full of potential and full of danger.

In the 1880s, Friends of the Indian, a collection of farmers, railroad interests, and politicians, recommended allotting reservations—dividing communal reservation lands into individual parcels, distributing them to heads of Indian households, and transferring surplus lands to the public domain for sale to non-Indians. Reformers hoped that American Indians would become self-sufficient farmers on their private landholdings. Allotment was one of several policies, including the creation of the off-reservation boarding school system, that intended to assimilate American Indians. When the United States passed the General Allotment Act in 1887, supporters called it the Indian Emancipation Act, echoing Abraham Lincoln's Emancipation Proclamation.[5]

What did allotment emancipate American Indians from? Supporters argued that allotment freed American Indians "from the shackles of the reservation system."[6] Friends contended that reservations prevented American Indians from integrating into the body politic as citizens. Merrill Gates, of the reform organization the Board of Indian Commissioners, said, "For American Indians there is no way into the privileges of American citizenship except by allotment—by land in severalty."[7] Once freed from communal ownership, private lands would allow American Indians to integrate into the United States as citizens and they would "obey the laws" of the United States.[8] Here we have a conventional understanding of American freedom: freedom means that American Indians become citizens of the United States, absorbed into the liberal democracy, subject to the same rights and privileges of other American citizens, such as the ability to vote or pay taxes.

Reservations also kept American Indians beholden to tribal governments, which reformers called "arbitrary," "incompetent," and "corrupt."[9] Orville H. Platt, a senator from Connecticut, argued that "mixed-blood" and white men who married Indigenous women monopolized communal landholdings in Indian Territory. He claimed that in the Creek Nation, 61 people held 1,237,000 acres. "They are not Indian republics," Platt said of the government of the Five Tribes (Cherokees, Creeks, Choctaws, Chickasaws, and Seminoles), "they are white oligarchies." Allotment, then, would free full-blood Indians from the "rapacious . . . white Indian" and their pawn governments.[10]

In addition to liberating American Indians from a nebulous legal status and allegedly corrupt tribal governments, reformers argued that communal lands impeded the development of American Indians and their economies. Under a system of communal landholding, American Indians could advance no further. Merrill Gates said, "To hold land in common cuts the nerve of all industry and individual effort."[11] Massachusetts Senator Henry Dawes, after whom the General Allotment Act of 1887 was named, famously stated that without private property, American Indians lacked "selfishness, which is at the bottom of civilization."[12] Allotment intended to free American Indians from communal reservations, which, they argued, prevented American Indians from participating in capitalist marketplaces. J. S. Murchison, an American lawyer for full-blooded Cherokees, said, "I believe firmly that on the whole, if the restrictions were removed so that they could go out freely into the market and offer their lands to the best buyer and get the best price for it that the market affords, [private property] would be a decided advantage to them."[13] Private property would inculcate American values—such as industry, effort, and selfishness—and permit American Indians to fully engage in U.S. economic systems.

Given that allotment was fundamentally an attack on American Indians' lands and that many American Indians opposed the policy, it may be surprising that some American Indians supported allotment. On northern California's Round Valley Reservation, American Indians believed that allotment would allow them greater control over their lands. The Round Valley Reservation is located approximately 180 miles north of San Francisco and is home to seven different tribes. Between 1855 and 1880, the federal government failed to prevent American squatters from grazing cattle on reservation lands. Round Valley Indians believed that allotment offered an opportunity to retake control over reservation lands from a corrupt and inefficient Bureau of Indian Affairs. Concow leader Dan Wright insisted to government officials, "I need land from six mile wide from river to river, I ought to have it, I need more land, mountain land." Yuki leader John Brown agreed with Wright, "We want to have this valley land, right in this valley." Round Valley Indians revealed what they would do with the land once they gained control over it. Daniel Webster, a Concow leader, said, "In ten or twenty years from now our children must have stock. . . . We need lots of land to pasture hogs and a few head of cattle." Webster, then, saw an Indigenous future in allotment, one in which his descendants had access to land and livestock. A Yuki leader named Abraham Lincoln added, "We like to have our hunting ground out through this mountain across out here for hunting ground, as soon as I get through my work I go hunting out in the hills." Round Valley Indians supported allotment to retain control over their lands (something the federal government failed to do) and engage in multisource economies, not just farming. They did not, though, demand that the government transform their lands into private holdings.[14]

American Indian politicians also supported allotment. Perhaps the most well known was Charles Curtis, an enrolled member of the Kaw Nation and Republican representative from Kansas (later senator and vice president of the United States). Curtis wore his Kaw identity proudly throughout his early political career. He ended stump speeches with "I am one-eighth Kaw Indian and a one-hundred per cent Republican."[15] Curtis styled himself as a paragon of allotment policy; he claimed he was a "self-reliant, hard-working, loyal, honest and 'self-made' man in the highest sense."[16] Curtis boasted that he had done more than anyone else to protect Indian sovereignty.[17] He did this by proposing bills and laws that transformed communal and trust resources into individual and private ones. Curtis's most famous piece of legislation was the Curtis Act, which forced allotment and dissolved tribal governments in Indian Territory.[18] In 1902, he also authored the bill that allotted the Kaw Reservation.[19] Reservation Indians and national politicians, then, did not support allotment because it promised freedom; they supported allotment because it promised more control over lands and resources and allowed American Indians to develop positive traits for the capitalist marketplace.

Although supporters of allotment claimed that they were giving freedom to American Indians, reformers and American Indian politicians' support for allotment dispossessed American Indians of their lands. Curtis dabbled in the language of freedom for American Indians, and he was closely aligned with railroad, oil, and coal corporations, which salivated over Indian Territory's resources.[20] Similarly, Senator Platt expressed a desire to protect full-bloods, and he described the untapped resources in Indian Territory that needed to be moved into capitalist markets. He said of Indian Territory, "This country is about as large as the State of Indiana, equals that State in fertility of soil, salubrity of climate, and surpasses it probably in coal, minerals, and valuable timber."[21] Merrill Gates made similar remarks about Seneca lands in New York. Gates lamented what historian Frederick Jackson Turner calls the "closing of the frontier": "We no longer have a superabundance of good public land. Men who have seen millions of acres given to great railroads[,] have felt 'we have land enough for all,' [but] now that we begin to approach the limit of the nation's landed largess, [they] grow impatient of the possession of any land by the Indian." For Gates, the solution was opening up American Indians' lands: "We all feel that in time there must be an end to the holding of millions of acres of land for small bands of Indians to roam over. With due regard to the equities of treaties made under widely different conditions, and always in the spirit of seeking to do what is best for the Indians, we feel that the Government of the United States must secure to Indians as individuals the land which they are to hold."[22] Although reformers and others might use the language of freedom to promote allotment, access to land and natural resources motivated allotment policy.

In the 1940s and 1950s, the United States launched another effort to provide freedom to American Indians. In the aftermath of World War II and at the beginning of the Cold War, federal officials wished to "get out of the Indian business" by settling claims against the United States and then terminating the trust relationship. Many politicians were bent on reducing the size of the federal government, after President Franklin D. Roosevelt increased the size of the government to fight the Depression and World War II. Additionally, politicians offered democracy and capitalism as antidotes to authoritarianism and communism in Russia. Critics argued the Indian Reorganization Act of 1934, for instance, increased the size and scope of the federal government and kept American Indians dependent on the federal government. In 1944, the Indian Claims Commission Act created the Indian Claims Commission (ICC), a special court that enabled American Indians to bring land claims against the United States. In 1953, President Dwight Eisenhower signed into law House Resolution 153, also called the Indian Freedom Act, which enabled the United States to terminate the trust relationship with American Indian tribal governments. Once the United States settled any lingering claims by American Indians, it could wipe its hands clean of its responsibilities to American Indians.[23]

Reformers resuscitated language and ideas from the allotment era to advance termination-era policies. The ICC and termination, another batch of Friends of the Indian argued, would make American Indians equal citizens of the United States. They claimed that reservations and the trust relationship prevented American Indians from freely participating in the United States. HCR 153 declared that American Indians would be "subject to the same laws and entitled to the same privileges and responsibilities of other Americans."[24] In addition, termination-era policies would privatize communally owned resources. Nevada Senator George Malone argued that communal reservations represented "natural Socialist environments."[25] Malone and others reasoned that if the United States was waging an ideological battle against the U.S.S.R. abroad, it should also contest that battle at home. As with the allotment era, federal officials believed that termination policies would make American Indians equal citizens in the United States and permit them to equally participate in the capitalist markets.

Some American Indians believed that termination policies could advance sovereignty and self-determination projects. American Indians in Southern California relied on a long history of advocating for home rule in their support of termination. Southern California Indians believed that termination would allow them to escape an overbearing and neglectful Bureau of Indian Affairs.[26] In Washington State, historian Laurie Arnold writes, American Indians on the multitribal Colville Reservation supported termination in order to regain the north half of their reservation, lost during the allotment era.[27] In Wisconsin, some Menominees voted for termination because congressional officials purposefully connected a vote in support of termination with a vote in favor of distributing an ICC settlement.[28] From the outset, the ideas of termination—reduced BIA oversight, regaining land, and proper dispensation of claims money—garnered support from American Indians who sought more control over their lives and resources.

Termination-era policies transformed communal resources into private assets. After a claim was successfully won against the United States, Congress distributed the money to people as per capita payments. In California, Native people won a $12 million claim against the United States for failing to ratify treaties and compensate Native people for taking their lands. Each individual California Indian received a check for $150.[29] Under termination, the United States also divided American Indians' resources equally among the people. Termination transformed Menominees from citizens of a nation into individual shareholders, which gave them a right to vote on board members.[30] The effort to privatize American Indians' communal resources continued for the next two decades. In 1971, the Alaska Native Claims Settlement Act transformed Alaska Natives into individual corporate shareholders.[31]

Some of the tribes first tapped for termination were those with abundant natural resources, such as the Menominee and Klamath, who had vast timber resources that also would be freed for exploitation. Termination policies devastated the Menominee and Klamath. By 1989, poverty and health problems persisted among the terminated Klamath people. Menominees, meanwhile, lost access to health care and education facilities and saw unemployment rates double.[32] Termination policies pruned other Indigenous nations' resources. On the Quinault Reservation in Washington, the Bureau of Indian Affairs moved so many allotments out of the federal trust that non-Indians owned one-third of the reservation land.[33] As with the allotment era, promises of freedom obscured an American desire to extract resources—timber and land—from American Indian nations and people.

In 2016, another group of so-called friends suggested the privatization of American Indians' resources. In the twentieth and twenty-first centuries, the United States has continued to extract natural resources—such as oil and natural gas—from American Indian lands. For example, the United States eagerly drilled for oil from the Osage Nation's "underground reservation." During and after World War II, the United States mined for uranium on the Navajo Nation. In the aftermath of the 9/11 terrorist attacks, Republican President George W. Bush promoted domestic energy production to avoid an overreliance on importing oil from the Middle East or South America. In combination with technological developments that made it easier to extract oil from shale through fracking and hydraulic mining, the federal government and oil and gas corporations sought to exploit coal and natural gas reserves on the northern Plains and in Oklahoma to slake the nation's thirst for fossil fuels. These more recent efforts coincided with continued efforts to shrink the size of the federal government. As with the allotment and termination eras, American Indian communal lands figure prominently in these national and global developments.[34]

After the United States elected Donald Trump in 2016, the Native American Affairs Coalition recommended moving communal and trust lands into the private market to reduce what Republicans see as excessive restrictions on the extraction of natural resources. The NAAC believes that the Environmental Protection Agency puts too many restrictions on trust lands; private lands would then free tribes from dealing with another federal bureaucracy. Representative Markwayne Mullin, Cherokee of Oklahoma and head of the coalition, stated: "We should take tribal land away from public treatment. As long as we can do it without unintended consequences, I think we will have broad support around Indian country."[35] The policy seemingly had wide support with federal officials. Then Secretary of the Interior Ryan Zinke suggested that many American Indians would take an "off-ramp" to escape the Indian Reorganization Act, leave trust status, and become corporations.[36]

Some American Indian politicians supported these policy suggestions. Mullin asserted that any policies advocated by the NAAC would support "tribal sovereignty and self-determination."[37] Ross Swimmer, former Principal Chief of the Cherokee Nation and coalition member, added, "It has to be done with an eye toward protecting sovereignty."[38] Representative Sharon Clahchischilliage, Navajo from New Mexico, added, "I am outraged that Indian Country is prevented from harnessing our own energy resources by ever-increasing regulations." She continued, "[With the Trump administration] we will block the bureaucrats holding Native American businesses back and bring new jobs into our communities."[39] For Mullin, Swimmer, and Clahchischilliage, privatized lands would empower American Indians in entering the natural resource extraction industry. Further, privatized lands would enable American Indians to chart their own paths forward and reduce federal oversights.

As with allotment and termination, some tribal nations on the Plains would appreciate cutting red tape as they seek to utilize oil, natural gas, and other natural resources to generate revenue and economic self-determination. Mark Fox, chairman of the Three Affiliated Tribes in North Dakota, explained: "The time it takes to go from lease to production is three times longer on trust lands than on private land. If privatizing has some kind of meaning that rights are given to private entities over tribal land, then that is worrying. But if it has to do with undoing federal burdens that can occur, there might be some justification."[40] Indigenous leaders supported the NAAC policies in order to avoid what they consider to be an overbearing federal government.

As with allotment and termination, though, supporters of privatization policy consistently mentioned the large amount of natural resources under Indigenous control at the same time they spouted ideas of freedom. News wires noted that Indigenous nations possess one-fifth of the nation's oil and gas, along with untapped coal reserves.[41] Further, politicians, such as Mullin and Clahchischilliage, have much in common with Charles Curtis, their allotment-era contemporary. Energy companies donate considerable funds to both representatives' campaign budgets. In addition, Swimmer was a partner in Energy Transfer Partners, who owned the Dakota Access Pipeline.[42] Supporters of privatization remain economically invested in the corporations and companies that seek to extract American Indian resources. Further, American Indian studies scholars have linked an increase in the number of murdered and missing Indigenous women to "man camps" that have sprouted up on or near reservations.[43] The United States' drive to develop a domestic energy policy, then, has relied on Indigenous land and political support while endangering Indigenous women.

Since the 1880s, the United States has supported policies that intended to privatize

American Indian land, resources, and labor. In the 1880s and 1890s, allotment divided communal lands, distributed them to heads of household, and transferred so-called surplus lands to the public domain. In the 1950s, the United States attempted to compensate American Indians for treaty claims and terminate the trust relationship with American Indian nations. In 2016, the Trump administration floated the idea of transferring communal trust lands into private lands in order to expedite the extraction of oil, natural gas, and other natural resources.

In all three instances, politicians argued that communal resources hindered American Indian freedom. Allotment, termination, and the coalition promised to free American Indian people, lands, and resources from communal restrictions so that they could enter American society and capitalist marketplaces. Throughout the nineteenth, twentieth, and twenty-first centuries, American Indians have supported all three policies. California Indians, Charles Curtis, and Markwayne Mullin support policies in the name of sovereignty and self-determination. Yet, American Indians on reservations have engaged with sovereignty differently than national American Indian politicians.

The history of allotment, termination, and natural resource extraction is part of a long history of the structure of settler colonialism. That is, the United States has attempted to privatize American Indian land, labor, and natural resources and it has used the language of freedom to do so. Allotment was called the Indian Emancipation Act. In the 1950s, termination, also called the Indian Freedom Act, promised citizenship and free access to capitalist marketplaces. In 2016, the Native American Affairs Coalition, with which I began this essay, supported privatization of land to free American Indians from excessive government regulation that prevents them from entering the capitalist marketplace. As scholars, Indigenous politicians in Washington, D.C., and on reservations, and others debate these potential policy changes, I hope they remember that the previous policies aimed at privatizing American Indians' resources have produced Indigenous poverty, not freedom. Under allotment, American Indians lost 70 percent of their land base. Under termination, Menominees and Klamaths lost natural resources, land, and social services. Natural resource exploitation on the Plains has already caused environmental damage and social problems. Then as now, the story of freedom is not the same as the story of self-determination.

NOTES

1. Valerie Volcovici, "Trump Advisors Aim to Privatize Oil-Rich Indian Reservations," Reuters, December 5, 2016.
2. I borrow the idea of "transit" from Jodi Byrd, *The Transit of Empire: Indigenous Critiques of Colonialism* (Minneapolis: University of Minnesota Press, 2011). As Joanne Barker notes, sovereignty is both culturally and historically contingent; the meaning of sovereignty changes according to the time and people involved. Joanne Barker, "For Whom Sovereignty Matters," in

Sovereignty Matters: Locations of Contestation and Possibility in Indigenous Struggles for Self-Determination (Lincoln: University of Nebraska Press, 2006), 1–32. For debates on the meaning of sovereignty in American Indian studies, see Taiaiake Alfred, "Sovereignty," in *A Companion to American Indian History,* ed. Philip Deloria and Neal Salisbury (Oxford: John Wiley & Sons, 2004), 460–74; Wallace Coffey and Rebecca Tsosie, "Rethinking the Tribal Sovereignty Doctrine: Cultural Sovereignty and the Collective Future of Indian Nations," *Stanford Law & Policy Review* 12 (Spring 2001): 191–222; and Scott Richard Lyons, "Nationalism," in *Native Studies Keywords,* ed. Stephanie Nohelani Teves, Andrea Smith, and Michelle Raheja (Tucson: University of Arizona Press, 2015), 168–79.

3. For a helpful introduction to settler colonialism, see the work of Patrick Wolfe, especially *Settler Colonialism and the Transformation of Anthropology: The Politics and Poetics of an Ethnographic Event* (New York: Cassell Press, 1999) and "Settler Colonialism and the Elimination of the Native," *Journal of Genocide Research* 8, no. 4 (2006): 387–409; see also J. Kēhaulani Kauanui (Kanaka Maoli) and Patrick Wolfe, "Settler Colonialism: Then and Now," *Politica & Societa* 1, no. 2 (2012): 235–58; and Dean Itsuji Saranillio, "Settler Colonialism," in *Native Studies Keywords,* ed. Stephanie Nohelani Teves, Andrea Smith, and Michelle Raheja (Tucson: University of Arizona Press, 2015), 284–300.

4. For entanglement, see Jean Dennison, *Colonial Entanglement: Constituting a Twenty-First Century Osage Nation* (Chapel Hill: University of North Carolina Press, 2012); and Maeve Kane, "'Covered with Such a Cappe': The Archaeology of Seneca Clothing, 1615–1820," *Ethnohistory* 61 (Winter 2014): 1–25.

5. D. S. Otis, *The Dawes Act and the Allotment of Indian Lands* (Norman: University of Oklahoma Press, 1973), x. Helpful studies of allotment include Janet McDonnell, *The Dispossession of the American Indian, 1887–1934* (Bloomington: Indiana University Press, 1991); Emily Greenwald, *Reconfiguring the Reservation: The Nez Perces, Jicarilla Apaches, and the Dawes Act* (Albuquerque: University of New Mexico Press, 2002); Rose Stremlau, *Sustaining the Cherokee Family: Kinship and the Allotment of an Indigenous Nation* (Chapel Hill: University of North Carolina Press, 2011); and Nicole Tonkovich, *The Allotment Plot: Alice C. Fletcher, E. Jane Gray, and Nez Perce Survivance* (Lincoln: University of Nebraska Press, 2012).

6. *25th Annual Report of the Board of Indian Commissioners for 1893* (Washington, D.C.: Government Printing Office, 1889), 6.

7. *Hearings before Committee on Indian Affairs of the House of Representatives in Favor of the Bill (H.R. 12270) for the Allotment of Lands in Severalty among Seneca Nation of New York Indians and for Other Purposes* (Washington, D.C.: Government Printing Office, 1902), 33.

8. Wilcomb E. Washburn, *The Assault on Indian Tribalism: The General Allotment Law (Dawes Act) of 1887* (Philadelphia: J. P. Lippincott Company, 1975), 47; and *Hearings before Committee on Indian Affairs,* 32.

9. *Hearings before Committee on Indian Affairs,* 33.

10. Orville H. Platt, "Problems in the Indian Territory," *North American Review* 160 (February 1895): 200 and 199; and Alexandra Harmon, *Rich Indians: Native People and the Problem of Wealth in American History* (Chapel Hill: University of North Carolina Press, 2010), 156.

11. *Hearings before Committee on Indian Affairs,* 34.

12. *Proceedings of the Third Annual Meeting of the Lake Mohonk Conference of the Friends of the Indian Held October 7 to 9, 1885* (Philadelphia: Sherman & Co. Printers, 1886), 43.

13. *Report of the Select Committee to Investigate Matters Connected with Affairs in the Indian Terri-*

tory with Hearings November 11, 1906–January 9, 1907, 2 vols. (Washington, D.C.: Government Printing Office, 1907), 1: 200.

14. Speeches Made by Indians at Round Valley Indian Agency, February 21st, 1891, relative to the quantity of land which they desire for grazing and timber growing purposes, RG 75, Special Case Files, 1821–1907, Special Case #43, box 48: 11360–1891, National Archives, Washington, D.C. For a history of squatters in Round Valley, see Kevin Adams and Khal Schneider, "'Washington Is a Long Way Off': The 'Round Valley War' and the Limits of Federal Power on a California Indian Reservation," *Pacific Historical Review* 80 (November 2011): 557–96.

15. William E. Unrau, *Mixed-Bloods and Tribal Dissolution: Charles Curtis and the Quest for Indian Identity* (Lawrence: University of Kansas Press, 1989), 112.

16. Unrau, *Mixed-Bloods and Tribal Dissolution,* 116.

17. Unrau, *Mixed-Bloods and Tribal Dissolution,* 118, 121.

18. Julie Reed, *Serving the Nation: Cherokee Sovereignty and Social Welfare, 1800–1907* (Norman: University of Oklahoma Press, 2016), 257; and Unrau, *Mixed-Bloods and Tribal Dissolution,* 122.

19. Unrau, *Mixed-Bloods and Tribal Dissolution,* 113–14, 118–19.

20. Unrau, *Mixed-Bloods and Tribal Dissolution,* 113.

21. Orville H. Platt, "Problems in the Indian Territory," *North American Review* 160 (February 1895): 196.

22. *Hearings before Committee on Indian Affairs,* 33.

23. For an overview of termination policy, see Donald Fixico, *Termination and Relocation: Federal Indian Policy, 1945–1960* (Albuquerque: University of New Mexico Press, 1986); and Kenneth R. Philp, *Termination Revisited: American Indians on the Trail to Self-Determination, 1933–1953* (Lincoln: University of Nebraska Press, 1999). Important works that address termination and specific American Indian nations include Nicholas Peroff, *Menominee Drums: Tribal Termination and Restoration, 1954–1974* (Norman: University of Oklahoma Press, 1993); R. Warren Metcalf, *Termination's Legacy: The Discarded Indians of Utah* (Lincoln: University of Nebraska Press, 2002); David R. M. Beck, *Seeking Recognition: The Termination and Restoration of the Coos, Lower Umpqua, and Siuslaw Indians, 1855–1984* (Lincoln: University of Nebraska Press, 2009); and Edward Charles Valandra, *Not without Our Consent: Lakota Resistance to Termination, 1950–1959* (Urbana: University of Illinois Press, 2010).

24. *Kappler's Indian Affairs: Laws and Treaties,* 7 vols. (Washington, D.C.: Government Printing Office, 1971), 6: 614–15.

25. Quoted in Paul C. Rosier, "'They Are Ancestral Homelands': Race, Place, and Politics in Cold War Native America, 1945–1961," *Journal of American History* 92 (March 2006): 1309.

26. Heather Ponchetti Daly, "Fractured Relations at Home: The 1953 Termination Act's Effect on Tribal Relations throughout Southern California Indian Country," *American Indian Quarterly* 33 (Fall 2009): 427–39.

27. Laurie Arnold, *Bartering with the Bones of Their Dead: The Colville Confederated Tribes and Termination* (Seattle: University of Washington Press, 2012).

28. Charles Wilkinson, *Blood Struggle: The Rise of Modern Indian Nations* (New York: W. W. Norton, 2006), 182–84.

29. Kenneth M. Johnson, *K-344: Or, the Indians of California vs. the United States* (Los Angeles: Dawson's Book Shop, 1966); and Kat Whitely, "Exploring California Indian Testimony during the 1966 California Indian Judgment Fund Hearings" (paper presented at the Tenth Annual Native American and Indigenous Studies Association Meeting, Los Angeles, May 17–19, 2018).

30. Wilkinson, *Blood Struggle,* 72.

31. See, for instance, Benjamin W. Thompson, "The De Facto Termination of Alaska Native Sovereignty: An Anomaly in an Era of Self-Determination," *American Indian Law Review* 24, no. 2 (1999/2000): 421–54.

32. Wilkinson, *Blood Struggle,* 83–84, 184.

33. Alexandra Harmon, *Reclaiming the Reservation: Histories of Indian Sovereignty Suppressed and Renewed* (Seattle: University of Washington Press, 2019), 96–97.

34. For representative studies of twentieth-century natural resource extraction, see Terry P. Wilson, *The Underground Reservation: Osage Oil* (Norman: University of Oklahoma Press, 1985); Doug Brugge, Timothy Benally, and Esther Yazzie-Lewis, eds., *The Navajo People and Uranium Mining* (Albuquerque: University of New Mexico Press, 2007); Traci Brynne Voyles, *Wastelanding: Legacies of Uranium Mining in Navajo Country* (Minneapolis: University of Minnesota Press, 2015); and Manu Karuka, *Empire's Tracks: Indigenous Nations, Chinese Workers, and the Transcontinental Railroad* (Berkeley: University of California Press, 2019), 185–200.

35. Volcovici, "Trump Advisors Aim to Privatize Oil-Rich Indian Reservations."

36. "Secretary Zinke Advocates 'Off-Ramp' Taking Lands Out of Trust," Indianz.com, May 3, 2017, https://www.indianz.com/News/2017/05/03/secretary-zinke-advocates-offramp-for-ta.asp.

37. Volcovici, "Trump Advisors Aim to Privatize Oil-Rich Indian Reservations."

38. Volcovici, "Trump Advisors Aim to Privatize Oil-Rich Indian Reservations."

39. Lorraine Chow, "Trump Advisors Plan to Privatize Native Lands to Tap into Oil Rich Reservations," *Ecowatch,* December 5, 2016, https://www.ecowatch.com/trump-privatize-native-lands-2129506421.html.

40. Volcovici, "Trump Advisors Aim to Privatize Oil-Rich Indian Reservations."

41. Volcovici, "Trump Advisors Aim to Privatize Oil-Rich Indian Reservations."

42. Chow, "Trump Advisors Plan to Privatize Native Lands."

43. See, for instance, Joanne Barker, "Confluence: Water as an Analytic of Indigenous Feminisms," *American Indian Culture and Research Journal* 43, no. 3 (2019): 26–28.

The Incorporation of Life and Land

The Alaska Native Claims Settlement Act

BENJAMIN HUGH VELAISE

The 1971 Alaska Native Claims Settlement Act (ANCSA) was an unusual and untried case in the extinguishment of Aboriginal title to land.[1] In the early 1960s, a generation of Alaska Native leaders took a step outside the historic federal–Indian law playbook. Whereas the federal government had traditionally acted as a trustee of Native American land, Alaska Native leaders recognized the holes in this reservation system and negotiated their own land claim settlement along entirely different praxes.

While Secretary of State William H. Seward purchased the Territory of Alaska from Russia in 1867, it was not until nearly a century later that land claims became salient due to a convergence of structural forces. The first half of the twentieth century set in place the need for a land claim settlement—the discovery of gold, the migration of settlers, and rising tensions between the United States and the Soviet Union. But it was not until the 1957 discovery of oil in Prudhoe Bay, driven by massive oil interests that sought to build a pipeline extending throughout the state, that a land claim became urgently necessary.[2] Leveraging the demand for oil, Alaska Natives rejected traditional trusteeship, insisting on private, fee simple landownership instead.

On Saturday, December 18, 1971, President Richard Nixon signed ANCSA into law. Alaska Natives, all at once, had achieved what they had been working toward for over a decade, the largest land settlement in United States history. Alaska Natives received fee simple absolute title of up to forty-five million acres of land and a total sum of $962.5 million as compensation for the extinguishment of land claims. ANCSA mandated the establishment of twelve for-profit Alaska Native regional corporations tasked to manage the land and payments. In addition to the twelve regional corporations, ANCSA established over two hundred village corporations.[3] The logic followed that through economic self-sufficiency, predicated on developing land and resources, Alaska Natives would realize a better future. The social well-being of communities would improve, while also allowing communities to become participants in the state's economy and achieve economic and political power through for-profit Native corporations. Faced with an entirely experimental and improbable task, ANCSA marked the incorporation of Indigenous life and land.

In December 1971, the resource economy that ANCSA introduced produced a society that was forced to take up a new form of self-worth, effecting a new kind of social stratification. Once defined along kinship ties and cultural sources of power and privilege, ANCSA effected a devaluation of this social and cultural power along Western axes that put economic, Western skill-bearers in control of operations. In turn, economically defined conceptions of power and privilege transformed traditional village rank order into capitalist class-based stratifications.[4] As an act that catered to the American oil industry and the state of Alaska itself, ANCSA also created a small ruling elite class—a class of Native trailblazers that emerged to lead the charge in sustaining corporations, villages, and business relations.[5]

Through the 1960s, those that maintained social influence during the land claim movement became those that soon occupied the corporate governing positions. In the Kodiak region, for instance, Alutiiq Natives born in the early 1900s who grew up to occupy corporate managerial positions were almost entirely those of mixed blood. Outsiders termed this generation of leaders in southeastern, coastal Alaska as the "Kodiak Creole." The Kodiak Creole were those believed to be the "middle class" of the community, as many of their "fathers . . . were Scandinavians and Americans who arrived in Alaska at the turn of the century and intermarried with [then] local Russian-Alutiiq Native women." Alutiiq Natives, those part white, are noted to be the first generation to no longer speak the Alutiiq language fluently. Once these Natives were placed in Wrangell and Mount Edgecumbe boarding schools—as part of the federal Indian boarding school program—assimilation into American culture was reportedly easier for these Natives to manage.[6] The result was a generation of Natives educated by Western instructors and more readily accepted into white society, a generation that could negotiate and collaborate with non-Native professionals, capable of transforming the assimilation into purposeful action.

In "The Rise of an Alaskan Native Bourgeoisie," Arthur Mason traces the development of this Alaska Native elite class. Members of this elite class became "subjects (e.g., Native capitalists) in the dual manner of being subjected to the conditions of the world they live in and, simultaneously, being the agent of knowing and doing in the world."[7] Put differently, Native managers of the corporations balanced, and continue to balance, the ethical problematics within corporate operations that have gone to "displace traditional routines in modern life."[8] Balancing disposition, tradition, spirituality, and collective memory with their institutional positions and corporate responsibilities, ANCSA created a framework whereby leaders were ultimately obligated to choose between profit and tradition in their operations.

In December 1986, the Alaska Native Review Commission—a federal commission established to assess the benefits and shortcomings of ANCSA a decade after its passage—gathered to hear the thoughts and experiences of over a thousand Alaska Natives from across the regions. At the heart of nearly all testimonies published was this conflict between profit and tradition that ANCSA manufactured: "I hope that the claims act will not force our people to relate our human values to the paper and plastic world that seem inherent in corporation stocks. . . . We have too many proud values to lose such valueless non-human, much less non-Native means of survival," Tim Towaralz (Unalakleet) announced. "Survival means identifying our values and living with them as is our custom, passing them on to our children," he continued.[9] While ANCSA had been operating in full swing for over a decade, it is clear that knowledge of the land in practice and the many strong cultural ties embedded therein continued to resist the corporate responsibilities and integration of Western markets.

The testimonies equally laid claim to the inaccessibility felt inherent in the corporations' formations, raising questions as to how the Native corporations would remain profitable and avoid bankruptcy. John Borbridge (Tlingit), former vice president of the Alaska Federation of Natives, presented his account of what the settlement's imposition ultimately amounted to: "They set us down and said, 'You're a corporation, now act like one.' It would be like setting a bunch of Wall Street people down in the Arctic and saying, 'Now go catch a whale.'"[10] In short, the apparent lack of experience Natives had in the business realm troubled Alaska Natives and raised questions surrounding the corporations' viability.

In 1973, Judith Kleinfeld, professor of psychology at the University of Alaska Fairbanks, compiled a report for the Alaska Native Foundation on the "professional, technical, and clerical manpower needs of regional and village corporations established under ANCSA." Kleinfeld's study held that between 1969 and 1973, an average of only twenty-one Natives had received a bachelor's degree in Alaska per year. She estimated that between four hundred and six hundred "professionally educated" Natives were required for the total sum of corporations, where the discrepancy between what was had and what was needed produced systems of education that carelessly rushed to fix the lack of personnel. While at the time Natives had organized "crash training programs" to submerge villages in best practices for the management of their corporations, Kleinfeld argues that this approach was "inferior," where efforts would have been better spent in devising long-term strategies to educate Natives on corporate management.[11] The blatant lack of infrastructure in place to submerge villages into their now fully operating Native corporations ultimately rendered village corporations powerless and entirely dependent on the regional corporations for the management of resources, land, and profit.

Moreover, few Natives were interested in becoming involved in their corporations to begin with. Individuals had no choice but to fill corporate positions, or else villages would forfeit land and cash granted under the act. The process of incorporation was far from organic and was embedded in the corporations' constructions. While corporations are usually established to exploit an economic opportunity previously discovered, ANCSA reversed this convention. ANCSA required Natives to form corporations first and then try to find and create economic opportunities to sustain themselves.[12] Because Native corporations were established by government fiat, Native corporations were constructed with no incentive other than an understanding that Alaska Natives now maintained a billion-dollar fund and ownership over their land. In turn, the lack of engagement supplemented by an astounding lack of experience directly led to reliance upon non-Native professionals.[13]

The only option was to accept help from those outside Alaska Native communities. White professionals who helped build the village and regional corporations played a hand in manufacturing their corporate identities and establishing procedures along Western conventions rather than Native ones. This is not to imply, however, that Natives stood idle; rather, it was the opposite. Natives strategically hired white managers to aid their initiatives, specifically identifying investment opportunities to generate revenue. Despite the impossibility of success, Native corporations continued to manage their assets, generate revenue, and pay out dividends to shareholders. Thus, perhaps the issue was not so much that white professionals were depended on but rather that corporations depended on white institutions and investments to sustain growth and economic success into the future. Because there was no long-term plan to equip Natives with the necessary skills and education, the economic self-sufficiency that the corporations were established on in the first place was undermined within the first three years of the act's passage.

By the second decade of the act's passage, Native corporations were operating in full swing—"economically secure" but "much less profitable."[14] The corporate structures' viability—the very fact they continued to exist, hold shareholder conventions, maintain essential leaders in the state—empowered Natives to believe in the promise and potential of ANCSA. In turn, while corporations within the first decade of the act's passage ignored tradition in light of their struggle to stay afloat, many nearing the brink of bankruptcy, in the second decade, at the heart of the tradition–profit conflict seemed to be the remaking of values along Western axes. In his testimony to the Alaska Native Review Commission, Weaver Ivanoff (Unalakleet) held ANCSA's failures were primarily embedded in its structural reworking of society:

> We've had a feeling of unity under our traditional council, under our
> Native way of life; we've shared it. That sharing made us a unified body.
> But now we have the stocks and the shareholders, and we have individual
> pieces of land, and we have money. And that has made villages split up.
> It's made people in villages who lived together all these years sharing and
> getting along split up.[15]

The term *tribal shareholder* introduced a new membership category within Native Alaska. This designation stands apart from tribal membership—where tribal membership remains within the village's or tribe's purview—but is an earmark of one's Native identity nonetheless. Alaska Natives born before December 18, 1971, were granted one hundred shares of their Native corporations. Those born after this date (known as the "afterborns") were excluded. This created two classes of Natives—some that earned hundreds, if not thousands, of dollars a year, and others that did not. Importantly, Native corporations have control over how to direct their stock, and these directives have further widened the disparities. While opening tribal shareholder registries would include afterborns—securing participation of younger generations—it would also "dilute" the value of the initial stocks distributed.[16] Simply put, ANCSA's provisions were unclear and shortsighted.

By 1991, shareholder dividends across the twelve regional corporations ranged from zero to seventeen thousand dollars.[17] Because certain Native corporations sat on resource-rich land, those corporations were put at an economic advantage to others. ANCSA Section 7(i) required corporations to share 70 percent of the "net revenue" from subsurface development and timber, though the definition of *net revenue* did not include the gains from special tax preferences. The money generated from tax windfalls far surpassed income from development, leading to years of costly litigation between the village and regional corporations as to ANCSA's intended definition of *net revenue*.[18] As the disparities grew wider and increasingly apparent, so did each corporation's social mandate. The Arctic Slope Regional Corporation (ASRC), for instance, maintains the property-taxing power over the Prudhoe Bay oil field. The ASRC's funds and influence surpass others, where, as a consequence, the ASRC can fulfill its mission to "actively manage our businesses, our lands, and resources, our investments," but also "our relationships to enhance Iñupiaq cultural and economic freedom."[19] According to Doyon, Limited CEO and president Aaron Schutt (Athabascan), ASRC's commitment to cultural revival is due to exactly this:

> They're big enough—2.5 billion dollars a year—Doyon is 300 million. You have to be that big to be able to make that economic choice—we owe our primary obligations to the shareholders. We need to be economically successful for our shareholders to support us and for us to maintain our [people's] jobs.[20]

ANCSA requires Alaska Native corporations to prioritize profit; the successful development of land and business means continued ownership over land, an increase in shareholder dividends, and the success of the company. While the resource-rich corporations can balance their profit directives with programs that work to sustain tradition, others cannot, at least to the same extent. Doyon, Limited, for instance, takes on a different approach to shareholders' social well-being. Doyon provides college scholarships for shareholders, as well as vocational training for the jobs Doyon offers—some of it through educating shareholders on oil drilling. Through these channels, Doyon is able to employ shareholders in its business operations and sustain new sorts of collective ties. But while resource-rich corporations have enjoyed unparalleled financial success—almost entirely because of their know-how and resource operations—it is important to note that their success is often used as a smoke screen in championing ANCSA as a whole.

Aaron Schutt believes in cultural revitalization in the Doyon region, but he equally understands that Alaska Native prosperity needs to "keep up with modern times." Schutt supposes that "ultimately, culture is the people themselves." He continues, "[Doyon is] a corporation, we're not going to be cultural champions as an organization. Even if we had all the money in the world, that wouldn't be our mandate." Schutt's perspective exemplifies one side of this discourse—the idea, per Schutt, that "the work of culture has to be done by the people."[21] It is true—Native corporations were not established to protect the maintenance of traditions and culture so much as to manage the land, create economic opportunities, and generate profit through resources for their Native shareholders. It is merely an ethical obligation, as Alaska Native people, that Native corporations choose to invest money in cultural revival. But while this may be so, it stands that regional corporations continue to direct themselves with leadership principles and mission statements that hold the financial well-being as the means through which the health of their communities can be sustained—in health, but culture too.

Native corporations have scaled to become so much more than they were in 1971. They are responsible not just for their shareholders but for their Native and non-Native employees, their investments, and their subsidiaries. It is undeniably remarkable— Alaska's economy is inextricably bound to the twelve regional corporations and the many Alaska Native groups they represent. In 2017, *Alaska Business* magazine reported that nine of the top ten largest Alaska-owned businesses (in terms of gross revenue) were Native corporations.[22] It is hard to say how much of this financial wealth reaches each individual shareholder, but it does increase political capital. In his 1985 *New York Times* article, Andrew Yarrow writes: "Once virtually without influence in political affairs, natives now play a major role. Passage of the native-claims act . . . bolstered the feeling that 'being a native is a good thing.'"[23] Following this, it stands that because Native corporations are responsible for the economic health of the villages and shareholders, then, by extension, they should be responsible for the cultural integrity of the community too. As Walter Carlo—an early member of the Fairbanks Native Association and longtime Doyon, Limited board member—told me in our interview, "We're not practicing a lot of our traditions—we say we are, but we're really not. You look at all of the suicides, the drinking, the drugs—that's not part of our culture." The practice of subsistence hunting and fishing, the essence of Alaska Native spirituality, and the relationship Natives maintain with their land and resources are what make up the cultural fabric of a community—a cultural fabric that defines the health of the people. Carlo continued: "I know that with spirituality, power comes with that. Lots of power. In good health."[24] It would be irresponsible to outright separate the financial health and social well-being of a village from the maintenance of this cultural fabric.

The question as to how responsible ANCSA corporations must be remains ambiguous. What is known, however, is that when corporations are forced to prioritize revenue over the social health of their communities, the result is the loss of culture and tradition. Yet, as Jessica Cattelino asks in a different context pertaining to the Seminole, "Does money . . . erode those values and practices that people call 'culture' and 'tradition'? Does culture have a currency, and how can its value be represented? Such questions are not neutral for indigenous people who aim to pursue economic gain with money while also remaining distinctively indigenous."[25] Thus, how do ANCSA CEOs reconcile this truth—the decaying of culture and knowledge that has existed since time immemorial—with the predominantly one-sided, for-profit machines—which claim a Native identity—that they operate? In our interview, Schutt duly argued that the settlement gave Alaska Natives agency like none other: "The settlement has enabled Native people here to have dramatically better economic success than just about any other aboriginal peoples in the world," where it is through this economic success that Doyon, Limited has effectively been able to endow cultural preservation programs and Athabascan linguistic courses for the betterment of shareholders. Sealaska Corporation also has sponsored computerized linguistic programs, where oral histories and traditional tribal music are now available to shareholders online. Both Doyon, Limited and NANA Corporation have opened cultural heritage museums in their headquarters, where a large majority of corporations have equally financed cultural revival camps that aim to teach subsistence practices—including smoking salmon and picking berries. Cultural revival has become a profession in and of itself. Many Native corporations have incorporated their ethnographic symbols. Licensing Native motifs, for instance, is another key example of how cultural integrity meets corporate responsibility at a crossroads. While this cultural production may be symbolic, its importance is grounded in a shared perspective that culture is not static. While some disagree with this perspective, the licensing of Native culture is nonetheless a development that seeks to connect past and future, Alaska Native knowledge and corporate responsibility.

But is it enough? Alaska Natives have progressed—for certain families in specific regions, Alaska Natives have reached the middle class. Poverty rates are half what they were at the time of ANCSA's passage.[26] Alaska Native regional corporations, tribal governments, and federal, municipal programs continue to bring relief to many of the issues that U.S. colonial domination imposed through the centuries. 1959 statehood, ANCSA, and federal recognition of certain villages throughout the state have worked to benefit Native peoples too. Native villages operate schools, have more efficient trapping and fishing equipment, and have motorized transport—and some have internet access, TVs, and satellite dishes. Native corporations have massive, visible headquarters in Fairbanks and Anchorage, graduates from the country's top institutions, substantial scholarship funds, and an enormous stake in the state's economy and politics for an Indigenous group—a voice that is heard, though not always listened to. But the fact remains that an overwhelming number of the peoples that make up the category of Alaska Natives continue to exist on the economic margins of society, well below the poverty line, dropping out of high school at rates three times the national average.[27] Generations of oscillating policies, ambiguity, and requirements on the part of the state and federal governments have produced a system whereby Alaska Natives walk among two distinct worlds, caught between two vastly different ways of being.

While there are no answers at the moment, as the settlement is far too young to account for this future and threatening challenge, leaders such as Carlo, Schutt, and Ivanoff are not forgetting, and will not forget, where they come from and what their predecessors achieved. Alaska Natives are a population of empowered people who understand, firsthand, that advancement and solutions to the problems we face come from within. With each new challenge that presents itself, it is critical for leaders to "walk in the corporate as well as the village world"—to remember "we have always been tribal people."[28] Ultimately, ANCSA corporations should do what they can to sustain traditional values and subsistence traditions. Yet, an inevitable reality penetrates the possibility of profit and tradition coexisting together; that is, time stops for no one, and the corporations—by virtue of what they are—have no choice but to secure profits, stay afloat, and keep up.

NOTES

1. The Alaska Native Claims Settlement Act, 85 Stat. 688 (1971); and Gary Anders, "The Role of Alaska Native Corporations in the Development of Alaska," *Development and Change* 14, no. 4 (1983): 555–75.
2. Eve Tuck, "ANCSA as X-Mark: Surface and Subsurface Claims of the Alaska Native Claims Settlement Act," in *Transforming the University: Alaska Native Studies in the 21st Century* (Minneapolis: Two Harbors Press, 2014), 240–72.
3. Alaska Native Claims Settlement Act, 690–716.
4. Arthur Mason, "The Rise of an Alaskan Native Bourgeoisie," *Études/Inuit/Studies* 26, no. 2 (2004): 5–22, https://doi.org/10.7202/007643ar.
5. Mason, "Rise of an Alaskan Native Bourgeoisie," 5.
6. Mason, 7.
7. Mason, 7.
8. Mason, 6.
9. "Thousands Testify across Alaska on ANCSA," Alaska Native Review Commission, excerpts from transcripts of proceedings, *Alaska Native News Magazine,* December 1986.
10. Andrew L. Yarrow, "Alaska's Natives Try a Taste of Capitalism," *New York Times,* March 17, 1985.

11. Judith Kleinfeld et al., *Land Claims and Native Manpower: Staffing Regional and Village Corporations under Alaska Native Claims Settlement Act of 1971* (Bureau of Indian Affairs, National Science Foundation, and the University of Alaska, Fairbanks, 1973), iii–vi.

12. Ernest Burch, "Native Claims in Alaska: An Overview," *Études/Inuit/Studies* 3, no. 1 (1979): 7–30.

13. Gary C. Anders and Kathleen K. Anders, *Limited Means and Rising Expectations: The Politics of Alaska Native Corporations* (Juneau: University of Alaska, Juneau, School of Business and Public Administration, 1985), 7.

14. Martha Hirschfield, "The Alaska Native Claims Settlement Act: Tribal Sovereignty and the Corporate Form," *Yale Law Journal* 101, no. 6 (1992): 1331–55.

15. "Thousands Testify across Alaska on ANCSA."

16. Tuck, "ANCSA as X-Mark," 255.

17. Steve Colt, *Two Views of the New Harpoon: Economic Perspectives on Alaska's Native Regional Corporations* (Anchorage: Institute of Social and Economic Research, University of Alaska Anchorage, 1998), 3.

18. Colt, *Two Views of the New Harpoon,* 68.

19. "About," Arctic Slope Regional Corporation, May 9, 2019, https://www.asrc.com/about.

20. Aaron Schutt (Athabascan), interview with author, Anchorage, Alaska, August 16, 2017.

21. Schutt, interview.

22. "2017 'Elements of Enterprise' Top 49ers Winners Announced by Alaska Business," *Alaska Business,* October 25, 2018.

23. Yarrow, "Alaska's Natives Try a Taste of Capitalism."

24. Walter Carlo (Athabascan), interview with author, Fairbanks, Alaska, August 11, 2017.

25. Jessica R. Cattelino, *High Stakes: Florida Seminole Gaming and Sovereignty* (Durham, N.C.: Duke University Press, 2008), 12.

26. Stephanie Martin and Alexandra Hill, "The Changing Economic Status of Alaska Natives, 1970–2007," *Institute of Social and Economic Research Webnote* 5 (July 2009): 5.

27. Martin and Hill, "Changing Economic Status of Alaska Natives," 1.

28. Byron Mallott (Tlingit), interview with author, Middletown, Conn., September 3, 2017.

Interlude

Long Live Deatnu and the Grand Allotment

RAUNA KUOKKANEN

What did I learn at school
About us
About the river?

Grand Allotment[1]
Happened elsewhere to other people
I didn't learn how it privatized lands
Was left unfinished up here
The "excess" land appropriated by the state

Which, as it happens, was most of it

Parcels of which now sold to holiday makers
Piece by piece
While "Sámi land rights" remain
Unrecognized
"Complicated"
"Creating conflicts"

The rest owned individually
By small-scale Sámi farmers
Who besides their small plots of fields and forests
"received" some fishing rights
Attached to those parcels of land

Which since the road was built in 1958
Have also been sliced up and sold

To buy boat engines
Snowmobiles
Cars
To modernize

Sliced up and sold
To southern tourists
Who come to catch the biggest salmon
In "the best salmon river in Europe"

I catch nothing
I don't even have the right to
Golgadit, buođđut[2]

But I fish anyway
I did and will not
Purchase a license
I have it

I am from here
My relations are here
Both sides of the river

Like a line in the sand
You draw a boundary in water
We are still relatives
We still speak the same language

Although they tried taking away
that too

I am from here
I am "Non-local Sámi"

Our family's hereditary right to fish
Does not apply to me
Have fallen out of use
"Local Sámi" in my family
Not able to

What did I learn at school?
I didn't learn to
Golgadit, buođđut

Who will teach my children?
What will they learn?

*"The biggest threat to Deatnu and the culture is
that we don't have descendants who know
how to buođđut or golgadit—people who understand Deatnu."*[3]

I sit by the banks of the River Deatnu
In the landscape
In the place
Where I have spent
All my summers

Long Live Deatnu

Min johtolat, min čanastat

Our artery
Our bond that binds us together

Slowly moving past the untold sand dunes
In which the boat gets stuck
unless you know the channel *exactly*
that changes every year

Our lives, our knowledge, our livelihoods, our connection
with the river and its salmon
Is strong
Counts for nothing
in management and decision-making

Is taken away piece by piece
By each piece of land on the river being sold

Traditional knowledge
Becomes a belief system[4]

Only *data* counts
In protecting
the salmon stocks?
Somebody else's interests?

2017 Deatnu Agreement
Signed by Norway and Finland
While Sámi representatives sit in the hall
Outside the negotiation room

"Consultation" is a user-friendly term
It shape-shifts
According to the needs
Of the powerful

2017 Deatnu Agreement
Mentions no Sámi fishing rights
Creates a new category of rights holders

Cabin owners on the Finnish side of the river[5]
In Norway, even the Ministers in the Government
Not quite sure
How it happened
They are "looking into it"

Declared a moratorium
On the new Deatnu Agreement

A resurgence movement
For Sámi self-determination

Protest against ongoing acts of settler colonialism

Against fishing regulations
Disapproved by Sámi rights holders
Advanced by stakeholders
Who have cabins up here
And powerful positions down south

Ellos Deatnu

Defies the fishing regulations
Demands answers from the states
How and when
Did you receive the control
Right to govern
Make decisions
Over the river?

Legal fiction
Is magic
Everywhere

But we're on it.

NOTES

1. A land reform in Sweden, which began in the mid-eighteenth century (when Finland was part of the kingdom of Sweden) and continued up until 1960s in northernmost Finland. The purpose of the Grand Allotment (*isojako* in Finnish, *storskiftet* in Swedish) was to eliminate the problems caused by the traditional division of the farmland for the purposes of increasing agricultural production and its efficiency. In the process, the previous narrow, scattered strips of farmland were consolidated into fewer and bigger blocks. In addition to the consolidation of fields, the previously common forest and pasture lands of the village were privatized by dividing them up among the farms. It was further stipulated that the "leftover commons" after the farms had been allotted were declared as the Crown (state) land. This was the start of state forest ownership, which is significant especially in northern Finland where the state still considers owning 90 percent of all land. See, e.g., Jouko Sillanpää, "Ylä-Lapin Isojaot Ja Saamelaisten Maaoikeudet," *Maanmittaus* 81, no. 1–2 (2006).
2. Two forms of traditional net fishing in Deatnu. Golgadit is practiced with a drift net and buođđut with a weir.
3. A traditional Sámi fisher at a community meeting held in Fanasgieddi in 2018, cited in Aslak Holmberg, "Bivdit Luosa—To Ask for Salmon: Saami Traditional Knowledge on Salmon and the River Deatnu in Research and Decision-Making" (master's thesis, UiT the Arctic University of Norway, 2018), 79.
4. See Morten Falkegard et al., *Status of the River Rana Salmon Populations 2016* (Working Group on Salmon Monitoring and Research in the Tana River System, 2016).
5. See Holmberg, "Bivdit Luosa," 72–73.

PART IV

Resistance and Resurgence

Indigenous and Traditional Rewilding in Finland and Sápmi

Enacting the Rights and Governance of North Karelian ICCAs and Skolt Sámi

TERO MUSTONEN
PAULIINA FEODOROFF

Finland, situated between the boreal taiga that starts in Russian Siberia and the Baltic, as well as the European Arctic, is in many ways an exception to questions of Indigenous and traditional wilderness communities, biodiversity and species, and climate change. This essay focuses on new models of Indigenous and community land rights, rewilding, and equity through an exciting model that returns land governance to traditional owners using purchases from the private markets.

The majority of the remaining global biodiversity is located in Indigenous and traditional community lands. However, the status and ownership of these lands vary greatly, whether they are used for conservation, recreation, industrial land uses, or otherwise. These lands can be private, public, a mix of the two, or Indigenous owned.

In this short research essay, we, writing from a twin Finnish-Sámi research point of view, discuss the questions of the transition of community-controlled lands for both the Finnish (Suomi) and Sámi traditional customary viewpoints. We wish to highlight this as a radical, progressive, cutting-edge Suomi–Sámi dialogue of a new kind, leaving old models of thought behind and exploring progressive actions that deliver both for the land and for the people.

While some of these actions may be critically reflected on, we do believe they are representing a set of new solutions in a context (in Finland) where no communal rights have been recognized. Additionally, our approach restores and heals the past damages on lands and rivers through community-led processes of applying Indigenous and traditional knowledge along with science to enable survival under rapidly proceeding climate change.

Author Tero Mustonen is the head of the village of Selkie, the second-oldest village in North Karelia, Eastern Finland. Indigenous author Pauliina Feodoroff is a Sámi scholar from the community of Skolt Sámi, representing the last fully functioning

Indigenous governance of the *siida* (traditional Sámi governance body) historically in the region.

Our purpose is to shed light on the globally little-known dynamics of land transition from the 1600s to the present day in the context of traditional (Selkie village and more broadly Finnish wilderness/forest communities) and Indigenous (Sámi) communities in Finland and neighboring Northwest Russia. The actions on revitalization of communal lands flow from our decade-long coordination of the first full-fledged collaborative management system on the Näätämö river watershed in the Arctic part of Finland, in the Skolt Sámi homeland. Ultimately, we wish to argue that the recent developments of the Indigenous and Community-Conserved Areas (ICCAs) under the United Nations Environment Programme represent a potential vehicle for a return of communal lands through private land acquisition and subsequent handover to Indigenous and traditional governance bodies. The method for our work is an essay-style reflective dynamic. Scholars and readers wishing to access the peer-reviewed sources for the Näätämö river watershed work or ICCAs can find them on the website of Snowchange, the organization where we work.[1]

A Brief Historical View on the Finnish and Sámi Communal Lands From Prehistory to 2020

Finland is one of the youngest nations in Europe, having received independence from Russia in 1917. Sámi- and Suomi-related linguistic groups have coexisted and been in a trade-conflict-peace nexus of relations for over two thousand years in the modern space of Finland. Linguistic sciences argue that these groups are descendants from a single or shared language ethnos, while today the Sámi are the undisputed Indigenous peoples of the Finnish state by constitution.[2]

Following a 1918 civil war and a range of smaller wars with the Soviets (and Germany) in World War II, Finland had to cede territory to Russia as a compensation for the war losses. These losses especially affected the eastern region of Karelia and, in the Arctic, the Skolt Sámi homeland, which to a large extent was given to the Soviets, leading to a diaspora and a relocation of the Skolt Sámi into a new (formerly Skolt Sámi Indigenous) area of Sevettijärvi, Keväjärvi, and Nellim.

The dramatic events of the 1900s should be positioned into the rather unique history of what is today known as Finland in the extreme northeastern corner of Europe. Mostly a boreal forest ecosystem with sub-Arctic field areas in the northern part of the country, the territory of Finland historically has been the home of the Swedish-speaking populations on the Baltic Coast, inland Finnish-speaking communities, Eastern Karelian and Savo-Karelian areas toward Lake Ladoga and all the way to the Kainuu region, and then, in the northern part of the country, the three Sámi groups—the Inari, North, and Skolt Sámi.

Traditional Sámi land use, in place since prehistoric times, covered a large extent of the northern part of Fennoscandia. The map on this page represents a view of the Indigenous-controlled territory known as *Sápmi,* Sámi homeland. The territorial units of the Indigenous governance of this area have been known as siidas, Indigenous home areas of a specific nation or group controlling its resources of mostly hunting, fisheries, gathering economies, and, increasingly, reindeer herding. The siidas were historically governed by siida councils, exercising ultimate political, legal, and social power within their siida borders. These councils, consisting of family representatives of the siida, also organized the external relations of a siida to other peoples—i.e., the Swedish, Norwegians, Russians/Pomors, and so on. Already in the 1500s the rights and relations of the siidas between Skolt Sámi and the Russian Empire were documented in a range of letters known as *Gramota*. In 2015, these gramota were accepted into the UNESCO Memory of the World (with the process led by Pauliina Feodoroff), representing some of the oldest Indigenous rights and diplomatic documents.

The Finnish (Suomi) people, who call themselves *suomalaiset,* are linguistically

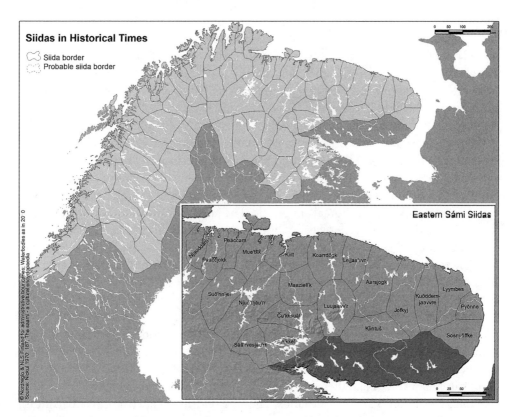

Sámi siidas in historical times. Snowchange, 2019. Created by Johanna Roto.

related to the Sámi, another Finno-Ugric language group.[3] The Finnish peoples also have included the Karelian peoples, of which today one subgroup (the Veps) is considered an Indigenous group by the Russian Federation. It is generally accepted that the Finns arrived in present-day Finland sometime in the early prehistoric Iron Age through the Kokemäenjoki river in the southwest part of the country from the Baltic home area. Subsequently, these hunter-fishers who also later practiced slash-and-burn agriculture encountered most likely inland Sámi groups in the Western Finland interior. These cultural contacts range from conflict to trade and avoidance and will not be discussed further here for the lack of space.

Of interest to the present discussion are the traditional land uses of the Finnish villages and communities. Their endemic land and water use governance has been called *erämaa*. This concept refers to the seasonal use of fishing lakes and hunting territories that could be up to 125 miles from the main winter village or home area. These erämaa lands (sometimes translated as "wilderness lands") were distinctly owned by individual families and villages. Erämaa harvest areas took a number of forms across the Finnish–Karelian space—from the inland large lake system utilization to the south coast of Karelia, where the outer-archipelago Baltic herring fishing families self-governed their islands, all the way to the sub-Arctic White Sea Karelia, the homeland of the Karelian rune singing (and the national epic *Kalevala,* which inspired Longfellow and J. R. R. Tolkien in their literary works). Central to the erämaa system were the seasonal hunting and fishing rounds combined with traplines and hunting cabins out in the boreal forest.

In 1542, the Swedish king and Crown, who had "owned" Finland since the 1200s but saw the Eastland mostly as an uninhibited northern wasteland, declared that all erämaa and siida lands of the Finns and Sámi would be annexed to the Swedish state. This transfer of community and Indigenous lands took place without any treaties or royal proclamations and represents a massive, if little-known, land acquisition by a European sovereign in the boreal and Arctic. The justification for this act was the need for more taxation and Sweden's geopolitical interest in settling what they believed to be empty wilderness in order to acquire bridgehead positions in the east and north. Sweden, the regional empire of the day, was also engaged in a number of military campaigns and wars in the region with Russia and other states for territory, and the costs of these wars was rather draining on the state coffers.

For the purpose of our view, this 1542 annexation had major consequences for all the centuries that followed, as it eroded and destroyed the communal and Indigenous-controlled lands in present-day Finland and allowed the state(s) that followed to govern them, using the 1542 decision as the basis of their rule.

In summary, since 1542, there have been only two possible forms of landownership in Finland: state lands and private lands. The land reform of 1749 (the Great Partition),

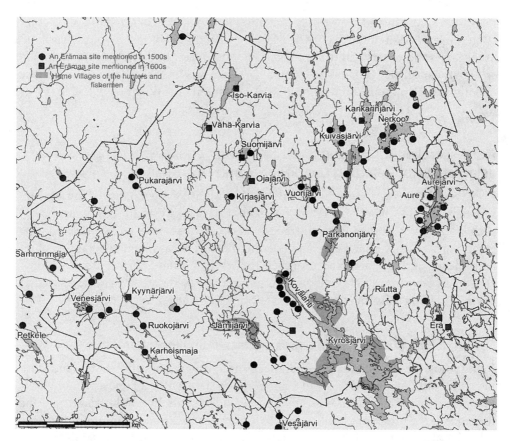

An example of erämaa territories from Western Finland. Snowchange. Created by Johanna Roto.

which reached Finland in the 1800s, was completed in the Sámi area in the mid-1900s. It reorganized farmlands and tried to rationalize private lands into profit-producing units but did not refer to the communal unceded land rights that had existed before 1542. Lastly, the 1918 Finnish civil war that pitted small-scale rental farmers against large, private landowners affected the use of communal fisheries, especially in Western Finland, but it had little impact on the Eastern Karelian or Sámi areas, where a de facto use of communal lands persisted but has not been recognized by the state since 1542. The only exception to this rule was the Skolt Sámi community of Suonjel, which remained in Russian territory until 1920 and then, between 1920 and 1944 following the peace treaty of Dorpat, was relocated to the new state of Finland. In 1944, with the Paris Peace Treaties, the Skolt Sámi home area was ceded to the Soviets, but the Skolt Sámi kept their siida council in the new homeland in Sevettijärvi and other relocation sites. Finland, as the only exception to this day, recognized this siida council in the legislation of the Skolt Act, providing some level of Indigenous governance of the lands and waters within the Skolt Sámi home area. Building on this Skolt Sámi self-governance, the Näätämö river comanagement was established in 2011 and, subsequently, the restoration and rewilding work spread into the potential ICCA sites—the topic of the next section.

North Karelian ICCAs and Skolt Sámi Indigenous Rewilding as a Vehicle of Realizing Land Rights and Governance

Even though the 1542 annexation of lands to the Swedish Crown removed the legal and formal land rights of both the Finnish erämaas and Sámi siidas, the customary uses of such lands has continued through traditional occupancies such as fisheries, hunting, gathering, and, in the Sámi case, reindeer herding. This has maintained a level of understanding of traditional land use, even though in a limited form. Also, the Nordic concept of everyman's rights has allowed some land-based practices and access to take place, providing a distinct form of access even on private lands.

Return of Finnish Communal Lands: A Case from North Karelia

In the 2010s, the Snowchange Cooperative, a nonprofit organization in Finland working with both Finnish villages and Sámi home area, installed a Landscape Rewilding Program to purchase, restore, and rebuild degraded lands after industrial ruin. All of the lands in the program are officially and legally on private land. One of the purposes of the Landscape Rewilding Program is to purchase former community lands from the open markets, restore them if needed, and then turn them over to the adjacent village, community, or Sámi organization, depending on the case. Private landownership by villages is a known issue also in Alaska, parts of Canada, Norway, and Sweden.

For the Eastern Finnish (i.e., North Karelian space), the Landscape Rewilding Program has purchased or owns the Havukkavaara old-growth forest and the Linnunsuo wetland in the Jukajoki catchment.[4] Both sites, a boreal forest and a restored and rewilded wetland, portray significant biodiversity values and are very important to the local community of Selkie. The village has installed comanagement and cogovernance of the sites for hunting and recreational value. These two sites are the first community conserved areas (CCAs) in Finland. They are important symbols of self-realized community lands through rewilding and land acquisition from the open markets back into village commons. For the first time since 1542, there are official community lands for the Finnish space. Most importantly, the return of community governance combined with high biodiversity returns—a significant issue in a century of climate change. The establishment of community lands is an important vehicle for resilience for traditional

Finnish villages who are not Indigenous by law but maintain important cultural and natural heritage values.

After many years of debates and reflection, the forest ICCA site of Havukkavaara was conceptualized as an endemic concept of CCA in Finnish: *hiisi. Hiisi,* in the older traditional village era, used to refer to sacred community groves that were thought to be the home of the spirits. They were sites of communal worship across Finno-Ugric space from Khanty to Udmurtia to Karelia to Finland before larger colonial processes.

Implementing reestablished village lands will remain a complex question in Finland, where Finns constitute the majority of the ethnic population, but it is relevant especially in the traditional villages, such as Selkie, which predate the establishment of the state (1917). Between 1945 and 2021, state natural resource governance has been built on production landscapes for timber, mining, and ditching, or the classic nature conservation of top-down protected areas, often excluding the traditional land uses (hunting, fisheries, and gathering economies) of the rural communities.

Finland has over three thousand non-Sámi Finnish villages, each dating back to prehistory in their land uses and histories. A marked east–west axis also informs how the traditional land uses and family–landscape connections have been preserved. In order to proceed with two aims—one, the equity of villages as traditional owners of their landscapes from prior to 1542 annexation, and, two, the modern necessities of nature conservation and climate security—a cogovernance dual model of CCA lands and state governance may constitute the way forward in the Finnish space, first and foremost on those (Metsähallitus, state) lands currently governed from the far-off capital city region using silo approaches.

The Difficult Question of Private Lands in Sámi Space: The Skolt Sámi Case

The Sámi have no collective land or water rights in Finland at all. Sámi Parliament has cultural and linguistic say on the issues of the Sámi, but that does not extend to land use, with the minor exception of a legal point of a need to consult if harm to the Sámi is expected. Finland has not ratified ILO 169 or other definite land use agreements or treaties with its Indigenous peoples. Officially, there are state lands and there are private lands. Of a special note are also Sámi-owned private lands and forestry collectives (the Inari and Utsjoki *yhteismetsät,* "common forests").

The only major exception to this rule is the Skolt Sámi Act, put in place in the 1940s to ensure rights and livelihoods of the displaced Skolts who needed a place to live and thrive after the land cession of the Second World War. They also preserved the siida council as an Indigenous decision-making body all the way to the present day, unlike other Sámi groups.

The Skolt Sámi Act allowed Skolt Sámi families and individuals to receive small private land allotments and, subsequently, with the Reindeer Farm Act of 1969, additional zoned lands for their reindeer economy. These sites might range from a couple acres to 250 acres being directly adjacent to state lands owned by the state of Finland. Reindeer herders could also use these large state lands for their herding economy, fisheries, and hunting, to a certain extent. Metsähallitus, Parks and Wildlife Finland (the state agency), enacted a number of water alteration and forestry projects on these state lands between 1950 and the 1990s in the Skolt Sámi home area. This included large-scale industrial clear-cuts and dredging and alteration of salmon, trout, and grayling streams for timber floating and other purposes.

A central example of these so-called improvement actions was the river Vainosjoki in the Näätämö watershed. It was significantly altered from 1968 to 1972. This included the loss of salmonid spawning areas and juvenile fish habitats, as well as alterations to the water flow. Restoration sites were chosen and prioritized using Sámi Indigenous knowledge and science, based on the level of past degradation and the loss of biodiversity.

In 2011, when the Snowchange–Skolt Sámi comanagement actions began in the Näätämö area, the most pressing driver of change was the fluctuation of climate and extreme weather events on the fish and land animals in the Sámi area as decided by the Skolts. By 2013, the Skolt Sámi teams of the comanagement identified one of the actions needed to be taken for survival—Indigenous-led ecological restoration of aquatic habitats to allow the salmonid fish more time, space, and capacity to survive under the rapidly proceeding warming. Between 2017 and 2019, the three miles of river Vainosjoki were fully restored by Snowchange and the Skolt Sámi teams using Indigenous knowledge, science, and nonmotorized means, for the most part. The restoration actions included renewed spawning areas and juvenile fish habitats, water flow stabilization, and rock replacement. Monitoring the success using Sámi knowledge and limnological science has shown grayling and trout returning to these sites and accepting them. The Vainosjoki restoration was the first ever of its kind on state lands where the Sámi governed a full ecosystem restoration of past damages using their Indigenous knowledge and customary actions.

In 2018, the view turned from aquatic ecosystems in the Skolt Sámi space to private forest lots (owned by individual Sámi and other citizens) and terrestrial sites that were currently in private hands and being used for forestry.

The central question, following the success of the Vainosjoki work, was how could the Skolt Sámi governance of these lands and restoration of terrestrial areas take place in the context of Finland, where there are only private or public (state) lands by law?

The Landscape Rewilding Program stepped in to provide an answer. Snowchange and the Skolt Sámi identified a patch of approximately 370 acres of private lands as key pilot areas for rewilding and Indigenous restoration. They were partially logged north boreal pine forests and marshmires. By being in the private market, these lots were subject to (immediate) land purchase and utilization, including further forestry, ditching and churning of soils, cabin building for non-Sámi landowners, partial loss of reindeer calving areas, and increased organic and nutrient loading into the down-stream lakes and rivers. The Landscape Rewilding Program and the Skolt Sámi nego-tiated with the private landowners and reached a land purchase agreement that was completed in 2019. Three individual lots of wilderness forest were acquired by Snow-change at the behest of the Skolts.

One of the first acts that the Skolt Sámi did was an act of reterritorialization. These new sites were given a new Skolt Sámi name: *Čuhč člåå'ddrääuhvää'r* (A Hill Where the Capercaillie Will Be Left at Peace). Capercaillie (*Tetrao urogallus*) is a forest bird central to cultural and subsistence practices. It is hunted. The renaming itself is impor-tant, marking the capacity of the Skolt Sámi to put forward new toponyms for the returning lands. Reclaiming and renaming places in the new context allows for reali-zation of Skolt Sámi governance and rights. We should not exclude the social power of such key sites, while they may be small in geographical terms at first. It restores the Indigenous epistemological and ontological specifics to these sites, which are not abstract but real, tangible evidenced locations and spatial nodes demonstrating the power of Indigenous rewilding.

Secondly, the Skolt Sámi and Snowchange have entered into a process of reviewing Sámi land use of these newly reestablished community commons, as well as restoration action needs. These may include the fencing of parts of the forest areas for regrowth of lichen stock for reindeer, controlled burns, allowing the rebuilding of capercaillie and wood ptarmigan stock on the lots, inventories of cultural and ecological places and species of significance, and so on. The parties will organize a range of community meetings of the Skolt Sámi siida in Sevettijärvi village to allow the Skolt Sámi to de-cide and provide their opinions on the uses of these newly acquired Indigenous lands from private markets. These meetings will also decide whether these lands will be offered and registered into the UNEP Indigenous and Community-Conserved Area registries in 2020 and beyond. The long-term transition of these forests will be from Snowchange to a Sámi entity capable of governance of Indigenous lands. It will also guarantee any Skolt Sámi prioritized access and use of these areas. This is planned for the mid-2020s, once the rewilding actions are complete. Until such time, they remain Sámi governed but are owned by Snowchange Cooperative.

A central question for the implementation of the concept of the Indigenous and Community-Conserved Area in the Sámi case will be scale. As no land or water rights exist, does the ICCA allocation provide benefits and support for the Sámi as a site-specific action or across landscapes? Will the former siida territories constitute the ba-sis of Sámi ICCA models? These will be defined and refined in the future by the Sámi.

Conclusion: Using Private Land Purchases to Achieve Community Land Rights in Finland

We have reviewed a historical process of loss of communal lands of both the wilderness territories of Finns (the erämaa) and the Sámi Indigenous lands (the siidas) since 1542. As these two groups share a linguistic origin and partially similar land use patterns, the cases are rather unique in the boreal and Arctic, as well as in the global, context. Today there are only either private or public lands in Finland. The only exception is the Skolt Sámi community, which has, since the 1940s, the Skolt Sámi Act defining some land use decision powers and rights, but not ownership.

After establishing the first comanagement process with the Sámi, Snowchange, together with Indigenous knowledge holders, restored a three-mile stretch of Vainosjoki river as a means of resilience under the context of climate impact and reestablishment of governance on present-day state lands. It was the first of its kind. Subsequently, the model extended to three forest lots that were purchased from open markets by 2019.

On the Finnish space, Snowchange had been purchasing, restoring, and acquiring forests and wetlands that, for the first time since 1592, reestablished village governance of these territories. Some of these sites were registered as CCAs—community-conserved areas.

Given the fact that there are no Indigenous or traditional lands by law in Finland, land purchases of private lands in key locations using the Landscape Rewilding Program have proven a viable alternative to reestablish Indigenous and traditional governance through restoration of these sites. Traditional means of nature conservation or issuing protocols for sustainable use, mainly on forestry and marshmire utilization, has not been able to prevent major negative impacts on lands that are in use. Therefore, on Finnish sites the land purchases for rewilding have enabled the land to reacquire its value in multiple streams, in addition to the financial value. Rewilding has also triggered a new sense of the history and memory of a degraded site and memory and, most importantly, a promise and realized act of a new, better, and restored future that dismisses the concept of a wasteland or a degraded site.

In the Sámi case, the purchase of key lands back into a transitional process from the private markets into a Sámi-decided and ultimately Sámi-owned site provides a powerful alternative to the concept of natural resources use of land in place since the 1940s in Finland (especially for forestry). This can also stimulate those Sámi who own private lands to reconsider the use of said lands, as allowed by the 2014 Forestry Act (a general national law, not to be associated with the Skolt Sámi Act), where a site can now be managed more freely than through clear-cuts, which used to be the norm.

The lands are held in trust by Snowchange until a village or a Sámi community wishes to transition these territories to traditional ownership. Their conservation values and traditional land use rights will be upheld. As of August 2020, the program covers over 3,200 acres of land and positively influences over 64,000 acres.

The concept of ownership and property always has some sort of value that is then reflected in psychological and social processes of how value is added. The overtaking of Sámi space has created a context for land where it has very little value unless value has been created from outside (for timber, mining, farming, tourism, and other non-Indigenous uses). The Landscape Rewilding Program has enabled the Sámi pilot sites to return new narratives of value of land and the potential of a return to community-decided forms and processes that will grow.

The Landscape Rewilding Program represents an important pilot in the very specific context of Finland (and parts of Northwest Russia) to realizing historical land rights of the traditional and Indigenous communities in an era of massive global change. The program realizes and supports other land use and rights struggles that may proceed, but as the current freeze on any land rights remains, the program provides a new step forward in a rather impossible situation.

Therefore, these rewilding sites are important as well-being ICCAs so that other nonhuman beings will also have a fighting chance under rapidly proceeding climate and ecological change.

NOTES

1. Snowchange Cooperative, www.snowchange.org.
2. See Ante Aikio, "The Study of Saami Substrate Toponyms in Finland," in *Borrowing of Place Names in the Uralian Languages,* ed. Ritva Liisa Pitkänen and Janne Saarikivi (Debrecen, Hungary: Onomastica Uralica, 2007), 159–97.
3. Aikio, "Study of Saami Substrate Toponyms in Finland."
4. "Explore Case Studies," ICCA Registry, http://www.iccaregistry.org/en/explore/finland/Havuk kavaara; and "Linnunsuo," Protected Planet, https://www.protectedplanet.net/555626081.

Settler Colonial Mexico and Indigenous Primordial Titles

KELLY S. McDONOUGH

North–south dialogues in the Americas have never come easy in Native American and Indigenous studies. Language barriers aside, one of the primary challenges to such conversations and collaborations is our propensity to think that Indigenous experiences in the U.S./Canadian and Latin American contexts are radically, if not incommensurably, distinct. Key to this misconception is that although the settler colonial dyad of land dispossession and elimination of Native bodies is widely accepted as the foundation of Anglophone colonialisms, in the Iberian context, forced Indigenous labor and resource extraction is the dominant narrative.[1] To the north the colonial process is seen as land-centric, whereas to the south it is viewed as labor-centric; one about eliminating Native bodies, the other about utilizing them. But this is a false binary, for Iberian colonialisms were just as much about Indigenous land dispossession and eliminating Native bodies as their Anglophone counterparts.[2]

To make this case, in the first section of this essay I provide a brief overview of sixteenth-century policies of *encomienda, hacienda,* and *repartimiento* (varied combinations of assigning Indigenous bodies and lands to Europeans) in New Spain, the space currently called Mexico. I follow with a more detailed discussion of the seventeenth-century policies of *congregación* (forced Indigenous removal and resettlement) and *composición* (establishment of title and rights to land). In the second section I turn to one of the many creative ways Indigenous peoples responded to such policies: the creation of Indigenous land titles—today called primordial titles. These mosaics of community histories were put to paper, in primarily alphabetic script with occasional pictographic drawings, and submitted to the Spanish courts as proof of the community's connection to its territory since time immemorial. Although the technology of alphabetic writing has long been viewed as a negative imposition forced upon Indigenous peoples of Mexico, primordial titles show that it also served as a meaningful way for them to assert rights to land and simultaneously strengthen community ties at a moment of crisis.

As Chickasaw scholar Shannon Speed argues, labor regimes in Latin America such as the encomienda, repartimiento, and hacienda "were often the very mechanisms that dispossessed Indigenous peoples of their lands, forcing them to labor in extractive undertakings on the very land that had been taken from them."[3] Encomienda, legally in effect from 1503 to 1542, was a concession by the Crown of Native peoples as tribute payers and laborers to Spaniards for the span of one to two generations as reward for their services. It was an abusive system akin to slavery. The removal of people from their homelands to the area of their forced labor became an unspoken mechanism for making additional lands available to non-Native settlers. Outright dispossession became legalized in 1529 with the hacienda system, wherein the Crown granted Indigenous lands to Spaniards. Repartimiento, a forced, but not year-round, labor system, replaced the encomienda system in the 1540s. The major difference was that Indigenous peoples reverted to belonging to the Crown, as opposed to the *encomenderos*. Working conditions remained horrific. Migration was often seen as the only way to escape part-time slavery or, for those conscripted to work in the mines, a sure death sentence.

Along with these institutionalized practices, Indigenous lands were physically emptied of Indigenous inhabitants by deaths that came with war, rampant disease, and forced labor. But it was also a tradition, since the earliest days of colonization, for Spaniards to misrecognize Indigenous lands as empty.[4] Providing a clue to this peculiar habit, Charles Gibson observes, "lands without Indian inhabitants could be categorized by Spaniards as vacant, unowned, or unappropriated (*baldías* or *realengas*), and thus available to Spanish intrusion 'without injury.'"[5] Add to this that settlers regularly mistranslated Indigenous lands as empty when they were left fallow following agricultural practices that allowed lands to rest. Without signs of human settlements or farming activity that mirrored their own, European settlers believed they were legally within their rights to claim the land for themselves.

Less well known, although no less pernicious, the systematic removal and concentrated resettlement of Indigenous peoples through the policy of congregación affected hundreds of Indigenous communities.[6] Lands emptied through congregación were regularly distributed to, or appropriated by, Spaniards. Like their counterparts in the Anglophone context, they usurped and made their homes on Indigenous lands they used for agriculture, livestock grazing, and multiple forms of resource extraction. Congregación is generally understood as having two major waves. Initially, the drastic decline of the Native population—sources estimate a 60 to 97 percent reduction in the first one hundred years of contact—had left sufficient land available for both Indigenous survivors and the Europeans.[7] Therefore, the first wave of congregación was aimed at consolidating evangelization efforts, ensuring efficient tribute collection, and providing easy access to Indigenous draft labor.[8] Natives were removed from their homelands and resettled in communities of precisely measured lots laid out on a grid, with a church and central plaza at its center. Such an arrangement facilitated the surveillance and discipline of Indigenous peoples by both religious and secular Spanish authorities.[9]

Of its many negative consequences, one of the more egregious aspects of congregación was that it disrupted the governing ethos of Nahua communities and compromised kin and other networked relationships. The Nahua *altepetl* (city-state) was a unified sociopolitical community but tended to lack contiguous borders. It consisted of several nonhierarchical subunits, each led by its own *tlatoani* (head speaker). Each subunit contributed to group obligations in a scheduled rotational pattern, and similarly, each subunit took a turn at coordinating the combined efforts of the altepetl. The center, in a word, was moveable. The Spanish vision of community that organized the congregaciones, however, was defined by a contiguous border enclosing a specific geographic space dominated by a single centralized authority. This new organization fragmented communities, since altepetl subunits were prone to resettlement in different geographic sites. Spaniards failed to understand (or perhaps astutely recognized) that spatially separated peoples could still be one people. Another challenge for congregated Indigenous peoples was that oftentimes Natives of distinct ethnolinguistic groups, many who were traditional enemies, were resettled together without concern for potential incompatibilities. Ethnolinguistic affinity did not promise harmony either, since Nahuas identified themselves first and foremost with the altepetl to which they belonged. Two groups of Nahuatl-speaking communities could very well have been just as foreign to each other as, say, speakers of Nahuatl and speakers of Otomí or Chontal.[10]

By the end of the sixteenth century, the Indigenous population had begun to stabilize, while at the same time the European and criollo (American-born European) population had steadily increased. Euro-criollo settler desires to possess Indigenous lands by legal or illegal means became increasingly pronounced. For this reason, the second major wave of congregación (1598–1607) took on a decidedly more land-oriented focus. As more Indigenous peoples and Euro-criollo settlers were competing for less and less land, the king of Spain began to take notice. In 1591, King Philip II issued a series of decrees criticizing how Spanish subjects were appropriating the best and largest portion of the lands of colonial Mexico, often under questionable circumstances. Although conceivably he was thinking in part about the lot of Indigenous peoples, this was no defense of Indigenous land rights. Instead, the point was to remind everyone that each and every parcel of land in colonial Mexico actually belonged to the Crown, unless the land had been explicitly granted by the king to the landholder in the form of a *merced* or as part of an encomienda or hacienda concession. For according to Pope Alexander VI's Bulls of Donation (*Inter caetera* [1493] and *Dudum siquidem* [1494]) and the Treaty of Tordesillas, one-half of the world belonged to Spain and the other half to Portugal.[11] That is, from the point of view of the pope and the Catholic monarchs, Indigenous peoples had no inherent right to their lands; they simply enjoyed them at the pleasure of the king. Although ideally Philip II's remonstration of Spanish land theft would ameliorate mounting tensions between Indigenous communities and Spaniards, the main objective was to reiterate and reestablish the Crown's dominion at a time when Spanish settlers were amassing more land and power in colonial Mexico with each passing day.

The king also had mounting (and related) financial concerns. Having already declared the Crown bankrupt three times during his reign, and on the verge of having to do so again, he needed a relatively quick way to fill the royal coffers. One strategy was to establish a new agrarian program called composición (composition), through which the only way to establish legal rights to land was through the acquisition of a title of landownership. The process for securing a land title included the submission of a recent physical survey of the land and any previously held titles to the courts and, of course, paying a relatively hefty fee.[12] Although the program was targeted toward settlers, Indigenous peoples astutely recognized composición as an opportunity to recover and protect their landholdings. As soon as the program became known, scores of *amparo* (protectionary) petitions were filed in Mexico City to prevent any redistribution of lands while Indigenous communities sought claim to their own legal titles.[13]

Indigenous communities did not possess previously held titles they could provide to the courts, since this was a Spanish convention, not an Indigenous one. Their ingenious response to the situation, then, was to create their own version of land titles that communicated—with alphabetic script and the occasional pictographic image—their relationship to the land since "time immemorial."[14] In the Nahuatl-language primordial title of San Matías Cuixinco, the Indigenous elder-narrator explains the rationale for having his words put to paper in alphabetic script by stating: "my children, . . . I give you the way in which you will be able to speak and respond in defense of your lands, and so that you know where the borders are and so you can defend them in a court of law."[15] Although primordial titles were ostensibly made to prove to outsiders why the lands rightfully belonged to the people, through the process of creating these manuscripts, the elders were able to remind their people that they had a history in that place and that they deserved a future there as well.[16]

At present, 122 primordial titles have been identified in Mexican archives.[17] The majority, 54, are in Nahuatl.[18]

Nahuatl	54
Maya	43
Zapotec	19
Mixtec	1
Purépecha	3
Otomí	2

Primordial titles, particularly those written in Nahuatl, are easily distinguished from other types of Indigenous-language manuscripts in the archive due to their unusual form and content. That said, they have often proved elusive, as they are usually buried within hundreds of pages of Spanish-language litigation materials for individual cases. In terms of form, unlike most Nahuatl-language sources expertly crafted by the professional Nahua scribes in their exquisitely uniform hand, primordial titles were created by nonprofessionals; their script is irregular, exceedingly difficult to parse, and loaded with hermetic regionalisms. Most primordial titles were written with black ink on *amate* (paper made from ficus bark), although red ink occasionally makes an appearance in headings or sections.[19] Simple line drawings and maps interspersed throughout the corpus pale in comparison to the extraordinary Aztec and Mixtec codices produced in other contexts, but they present valuable information, nonetheless.

In regard to content, primordial titles read as unscripted oral discourse of an elder (or elders) sharing a series of nonchronological histories in a collective setting. The collective nature of the sources is evident in the way the elder addresses an audience on multiple occasions, as in the case of the previously mentioned title of San Matías Cuixinco wherein the elder explains to his people that Spaniards are coming for their lands:

> Your grandfathers and ancestors founded our community, which they conquered with great effort. I urge you to not allow your children to take council with the Spaniards because through trickery they will try to take their lands. They will convince your children with kindness and they will feed them their foods, and [your children] will assume it all to be a great honor. And when the Spaniards begin to settle in their midst, they will remind your children of all that they had given them to eat, and all of the money they had given them. This is how they will take away their papers and before [your children] know it they will be left without any of the lands given to us by God our Lord and his Majesty in whose name they were bestowed upon us by the Marquis [Hernando Cortés].[20]

Besides such warnings from the elder narrators, an omnipresent feature of primordial titles is what I call a "narrative mapping."[21] That is, with stories they create a vision of the land, its boundaries, and their claims to both—oftentimes in the context of competing claims, whether from other Indigenous communities or colonial powers.[22] These mind's-eye maps are conveyed as if the elder and his people were actually walking the landscape as the discourse was being recorded. At regular intervals during this walk, ceremonies of possession are remembered and reenacted: grasses are pulled and braided together, arrows are launched to the four directions, and stones are stacked as markers of boundaries. At other stops along the way, musical instruments are played and the people feast.[23] Stories of past events important to the community are conveyed throughout this ambling inventory, most often on the site where it was said to have originally taken place.

Stock story lines of the genre, found in varying combinations, include feats of ancestors, migrations, inter-Indigenous war and peacemaking, and original settlement. Many mention encounters with deities, particularly as they are related to the revelation of water sources, pacts with Spaniards who acknowledge and confirm Indigenous rights to their lands, pledges of loyalty to the Spanish Crown, and the acceptance of the Catholic faith. On this final point, it is important to note that only Christian subjects of the king had access to the court system. While it is true that the vast majority of Indigenous peoples of the time did become practicing Catholics, such a declaration was requisite if the community were to have any chance at having its case considered. Woven together, the microhistories of primordial titles formed a macrohistory that portrayed the community—in a fashion ideally recognizable to the courts—as deserving of their lands.[24] They index how Nahuas strategically adopted and adapted the Roman alphabet to serve their own purposes and to engage a specific audience in a unique yet all-too-familiar scenario.

The general rationales and strategies of European colonialisms may have differed in certain ways, but the end results did not; lands were stolen and bodies were abused and eliminated. Although rarely utilized to think about Iberian colonialisms, I believe the framework of settler colonialisms can help draw attention to the often-overlooked policies of systematic Indigenous land dispossessions that went hand in hand with abusive labor regimes in Latin America. Ideally, the recognition that Latin America, too, is a settler colonial space will open new interpretive ground and signal a way to bridge the north–south divide in Native American and Indigenous studies.

To be clear, drawing attention to common settler colonial experiences here is less about lamenting shared oppression than it is about highlighting the commonality of creative tactics employed by Native peoples affected by settler colonial policies and practices. And one such tactic, the primordial titles, actually had some positive results. Of the eighteen Nahuatl primordial titles with known outcomes, eleven (60 percent) of the Indigenous communities, including San Matías Cuixinco, won their cases. Some even gained additional lands in the process. Indigenous land dispossession in Mexico is a regular occurrence to this day, with surprisingly little change in practices or justifications since colonial times. Lessons from the past, however, such as the moderately successful genre of primordial titles, may inspire renewed recourse to the documentation of memory and history as a strategy to interrupt, if not disrupt, the continued threats to Indigenous territorial and sociopolitical unity today.

NOTES

1. Aníbal Quijano, "Coloniality of Power and Eurocentrism in Latin America," *International Sociology* 15, no. 2 (2000): 215–32.
2. Shannon Speed, "Structures of Settler Capitalism in Abya Yala," *American Quarterly* 69, no. 4 (2017): 783–90.
3. Speed, "Structures of Settler Capitalism in Abya Yala," 784.
4. Daniel Nemser, *Infrastructures of Race: Concentration and Biopolitics in Colonial Mexico* (Austin: University of Texas Press, 2017), 26.
5. Charles Gibson, *The Aztecs under Spanish Rule: A History of the Indians of the Valley of Mexico, 1519–1810* (Stanford, Calif.: Stanford University Press, 1964), 282.
6. Peter Gerhard has identified 163 *congregaciones de indios* formed before 1570. Gerhard, "Congregaciones de indios en la Nueva España antes de 1570," *Historia Mexicana* 26, no. 3 (1977): 388.
7. James Lockhart, *The Nahuas after the Conquest: A Social and Cultural History of the Indians of Central Mexico, Sixteenth through Eighteenth Centuries* (Stanford, Calif.: Stanford University Press, 1992), 163–64; and Woodrow Borah and Sherburne F. Cook, "Conquest and Population: A Demographic Approach to Mexican History," *Proceedings of the American Philosophical Society* 113, no. 2 (1969): 180.
8. Brian Owensby, *Empire of Law and Indian Justice in Colonial Mexico* (Stanford, Calif.: Stanford University Press, 2008), 21.
9. Ernesto de la Torre Villar, *Las congregaciones de los pueblos de indios, fase terminal: Aprobaciones y rectificaciones* (Mexico City: UNAM, 1995).
10. Nemser, *Infrastructures of Race,* 56–58.
11. Related to the Spanish Doctrine of Discovery, see Francisco Morales Padrón, ed., *Teoría y leyes de la conquista,* Serie Historia y Geografía, no. 123 (Sevilla, Spain: Universidad de Sevilla, Secretariado de Publicaciones, 2008).
12. Gibson, *Aztecs under Spanish Rule,* 285; Ma Cristina Torales Pacheco, *Tierras de indios, tierras de españoles: confirmación y composición de tierras y aguas en la jurisdicción de Cholulu (siglos XVI–XVIII)* (Mexico City: Universidad Iberoamericana, 2006), 90, 94n1; and Robert Haskett, *Visions of Paradise* (Norman: University of Oklahoma Press, 2005), 118–19.
13. Owensby, *Empire of Law and Indian Justice in Colonial Mexico,* 20, 104.
14. Lockhart, *Nahuas after the Conquest,* 411; and Haskett, *Visions of Paradise,* 186.
15. *Tierras* 2819, exp. 9, 363r–363v, May 1702, Archivo General de la Nación, Mexico City. See López Caballero, *Los títulos primordiales del centro de México* (Mexico City: CONACULTA, 2003), 293.
16. Stephanie Wood posits that the audience of the primordial titles is the Indigenous community first and the court system second, since they contain specific warnings against showing the community's papers to Spaniards. Moreover, no primordial title specifically addresses court officials. Stephanie Wood, *Transcending Conquest: Nahua Views of Spanish Colonial Mexico* (Norman: University of Oklahoma Press, 2003), 220–23.
17. Robert Haskett and Stephanie Wood, "Primordial Titles Revisited, with a New Census and Bibliography" (unpublished manuscript, October 6, 2013); Charles Gibson, "A Survey of Middle American Prose Manuscripts in the Native Historical Tradition," in *Handbook of Middle American Indians: Guide to Ethnohistorical Sources, Part 4,* ed. Howard F. Cline (Austin: University of Texas Press, 1975), 320–21.

18. Haskett and Wood, "Primordial Titles Revisited."
19. There is no strict pattern for when the red ink appears in these manuscripts. While it is most often at the beginning of sections, wherein the elder is appealing to his people to listen to him, at times entire sections and individual terms are in red as well. It is possible that the red ink coupled with the black ink was a bridge to past forms. *In tlilli in tlapalli,* the red and the black ink, is a Nahuatl *difrasismo* that combines to stand for the pre-Hispanic intellectuals who painted the people's knowledge in codices. Equally possible is that the scribe was imitating the European convention of rubrication (the use of red text) signaling when a priest, for example, was to address his flock directly during Mass.
20. *Tierras* 2819, exp. 9, 376v, May 1702, Archivo General de la Nación, Mexico City. See also López Caballero, *Los títulos primordiales,* 293.
21. Kelly S. McDonough, "Plotting Indigenous Stories, Land, and People: Primordial Titles and Narrative Mapping Colonial Mexico," *Journal for Early Modern Cultural Studies* 17, no. 1 (2017): 1–30.
22. My understanding of narrative mapping resonates with Mishuana Goeman's work with Indigenous women's literature. Of particular importance for this study is her interrogation of how Indigenous story works to (re)define and (re)present Indigenous communities in colonial contexts, especially in relation to lands and other peoples, always with an eye on future possibilities. Goeman, *Mark My Words: Native Women Mapping Our Nations* (Minneapolis: University of Minnesota Press, 2013), 3.
23. James Lockhart, *Nahuas and Spaniards: Postconquest Central Mexican History and Philology* (Stanford, Calif.: Stanford University Press, 1991), 39–64.
24. McDonough, "Plotting Indigenous Stories, Land, and People."

"Our Divine Right to Land"

The Struggle against Privatization of Nahua Communal Lands

ARGELIA SEGOVIA LIGA

Allotment in Colonial Mexico City

From the early years of the sixteenth-century European invasion and occupation of the American territories, numerous Indigenous populations have suffered from allotment, forceful relocation, and displacement from their original lands. The consolidation of the colonial system in the territories conquered by the Spaniards and their allies resulted in the creation of new institutions that legally supported the forced relocation of Indigenous communities from their original places of origin.

In Mexico-Tenochtitlan, the state capital of the Mexica (Aztecs), later called Mexico City by the Spaniards, the forceful relocation of Indigenous peoples from their territories began during the second decade of the sixteenth century and it continued unabated throughout the entire nineteenth century. In 1821, when Mexico became an independent nation from Spain, the political transformations of the new nation encouraged both the abolition of Indigenous individuals as separate protected legal entities and the concept of collective landholdings. The Indigenous communities affected by these new measures organized themselves and used all the possible legal instances and arguments to maintain their lands under their control. The impact of these new policies resulted in a process of forced allotment of communally held Indigenous lands and properties in Mexico City.

Forced Removal in Mexico City: The *Parcialidades* from the Sixteenth to the Eighteenth Century

The city of Mexico-Tenochtitlan fell to the Spaniards on August 13, 1521. It had originally been founded in 1325, based on the incorporation and communal understanding of the Nahua peoples' complex, clan-based landholding concepts,[1] which allowed the city and its inhabitants to survive and thrive in such a unique geography.[2] The city itself became actually a composite urban conglomeration of an organized series of semiautonomous sovereign towns, called *altepetl,* or *altepemeh* in plural, which literally meant "the waters, the mountains," a concept that the Spaniards described as "Indian kingdoms." Each of these altepemeh was composed of a series of subordinate *tlaxila-calli,* or neighborhoods (barrios).[3] Once the Spaniards conquered Tenochtitlan, they modified its original concept of Indigenous landholding and simplified these original divisions so that they could better administer them. They reduced all of these semi-autonomous Indigenous towns, or altepemeh, into only two big *parcialidades:*[4] San Juan Tenochtitlan and Santiago Tlatelolco.[5] These parcialidades in the Spanish colonial legal framework existed as territorial and political units through which colonial Spanish authorities reconfigured the geopolitical organization of the former Mexica Empire and they served as a means by which the inhabitants of the city experienced the first colonial relocations and expropriations from their traditional lands. Thus, the Spanish selected the central area of the city to turn it into their principal space of colonial residence, along with the first thirteen blocks from the center of the newly founded Spanish city heading out in each direction. The Indigenous population they forcibly relocated to the peripheral lands beyond this initial thirteen-city-block radius around the central plaza.[6] For the better administration of these new territories, the colonial authorities created two major legal concepts that defined the spaces and the legal position of the Indigenous population that resided within the city: the parcialidades and the *república de indios,* or Indian republic.[7] These provided peripheral suitable lands for labor and agriculture so that Indigenous peoples could also support the growth of the city with their agricultural production surplus. This division also promoted the creation of segregated institutions to which Indigenous peoples had exclusive access, such as separate Indigenous tribunals, schools, and hospitals.

These parcialidades continued the Indigenous collective tradition of landownership, and their inhabitants had semiautonomous local government, which in turn remained under the direct control of the superior Spanish authorities. The leaders of these parcialidades had the right to elect as their representative an Indigenous member of the community,[8] who would serve before the local Indigenous cabildo and represent the Indigenous communities' interests before the Spanish town council, or ayuntamiento, of Mexico City.[9] The parcialidades also prevented land speculation and encroachment, and their representatives organized and collected tribute for the Spanish colonial authorities.

Moreover, the members of these parcialidades also contributed with their production and communal funds to endow schools of first letters (*escuelas de primeras letras*) for basic education or hospitals for the benefit of the Indigenous peoples of the city. Organized and legally protected community chests, or *cajas de comunidad,* served as a means of administering the revenues and resources collected by Indigenous officials from communal properties.[10] These also served to assist the Indigenous communities and their communal social welfare in the case of catastrophes—such as epidemics, droughts, shortages, or other mishaps—and in paying for professors at exclusively Indigenous schools.[11]

Throughout the colonial period in Mexico City, these *parcialidades* continued working to provide resources, supplies, and labor to support the economy of the city, as well as contributing to the maintenance of the social and educational fabric of the Indigenous societies.

The End of the *República de Indios*: The Political Changes of the Nineteenth Century

The Napoleonic Wars and the consequent occupation of Spain by the French resulted in the issuing of the Political Constitution of the Spanish Monarchy in 1812.[12] This so-called Constitution of Cadiz dictated the end of the colonial system of segregation in the Spanish Americas; it legally abolished the division between Spaniards and Indigenous peoples, granting to both groups Spanish citizenship, without any distinction of race or caste, and promoted a concept of equality before the law to all the inhabitants of the colonies.[13] In Mexico, this political transformation also came with the concomitant dissolution of the two separate colonial republics, the Spanish one (*república de españoles*) and the Indigenous one (república de indios). Thus, under the concept of social equality promoted by the new constitution, all segregated institutions ceased to exist. In the beginning, a few Indigenous intellectuals in Mexico City embraced the new civil order, since they considered that the constitution would also provide Indigenous peoples with both equality and equity under the law.[14] Nevertheless, what seemed like an achievement of the modern political practices of equality and self-determination actually created a new constitutional order that praised individual interests over collective groups. This led to the further detriment of Indigenous communities in Mexico and their loss of legal rights to their traditional communal landholdings.

Years later, after a series of turbulent events, Mexico officially declared its independence from Spain in 1821.[15] Influenced by both the Constitution of 1812 and the political theories of liberalism, the authorities of the new republic sought to reorganize and consolidate the governing institutions in the country to defend individual liberties and eradicate corporatism.[16] In general terms, there were two groups that fit into this liberal Mexican agenda ripe for reform: the Catholic Church and communal Indigenous properties. These two types of property holdings became intertwined with the religious sphere not only in its physical representation of the ownership of churches and temples but also because Indigenous cultural identity had remained closely attached to the religious life and activities organized around local Indigenous communal churches and ecclesiastical establishments. For instance, many Indigenous communities held lands, even outside of the city, in perpetuity as part of endowments for religious confraternities and other religious societies.

Liberal Reforms, the New Republic, and Indigenous Landholding

Amid these political transformations, several politicians and Mexican intellectuals advanced arguments about the "positive" impact that the creation of individual property could provide for the Indigenous peoples.[17] Nineteenth-century Mexican politicians considered that the continued existence of the parcialidades perpetuated paternalistic policies left over from the colonial era, and thus they represented an obstacle for the integration of the Indigenous people into the modern nation-state.[18] Based on this premise, the new independent government sought the creation of Indigenous peoples as individual landowners in order to promote the civil equality and the end of any type of special treatment to the Indigenous sectors of society.

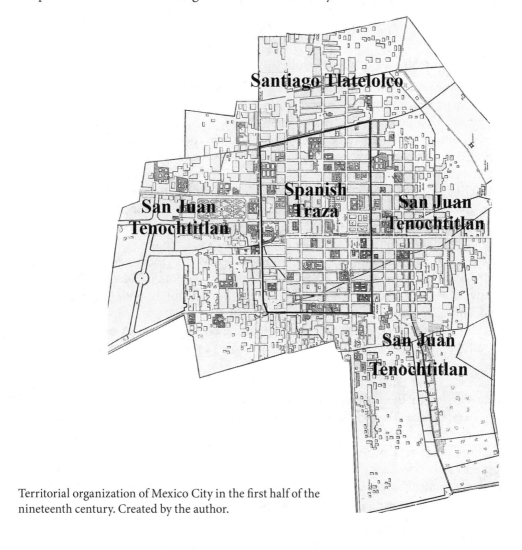

Territorial organization of Mexico City in the first half of the nineteenth century. Created by the author.

As a result, the same year Mexico City officially became the capital of the country, on November 27, 1824, Mexican Congress issued a decree formally declaring the parcialidades as extinct, proposing the distribution and allotment of these communal properties among those individuals who formed part of this corporation.[19] Originally, the decree focused on keeping the collective landholding nature of these lands in benefit of their original owners, and without providing further details, it also dictated the creation of a board of seven individuals from the former parcialidades to approve the decree and create a bylaw to regulate the way the mentioned assets would be distributed. This decree focused on eliminating the existence of corporative property; however, the termination of the parcialidades in actual practice encountered several difficulties in its execution, since this allotment process faced resistance from the Indigenous people.

The Indigenous Defense of Collective Property

At the same time, similar to the movements of white settlers in the United States, non-Indigenous land speculators attempted to benefit themselves from the new law concerning the parcialidades by interpreting the regulations about their redistribution and allotment for their own benefit. Thus, during this period, Indigenous intellectuals in Mexico City became desperately involved in the active defense of the extinguished parcialidades and other collective institutions. The regulations after 1822 positioned the Indigenous peoples in a clear disadvantage and limited their effective participation in political matters that concerned their own communities. Thus, from 1822 to 1827, several Indigenous communities in Mexico City appointed Indigenous individuals to represent their communities and defend their rights to keep their collective organizations before the new national Mexican courts of law. Most of them were trained lawyers who based the defense of communal landownership on political ideas set forth in the theory of natural law, which defended the divine and natural right of peoples to hold and administer properties for their own individual or collective benefits.

Although the decree of 1824 specified that the owners of the former parcialidades would be the Indigenous peoples, years later there were complaints about the fact that some of the lands from the parcialidades would be purchased by a handful of people who did not belong to this corporation, while the rest of these assets would be possessed by the ayuntamiento of the city. This would have left the members of the former parcialidades landless. Through their representative, the members of these communities argued that without the assets from the parcialidades, the communities would not get any benefits to continue organizing their collective celebrations, to support local schools of basic literacy, to aid the communities in times of epidemics, and to provide their communities with food during periods of shortage. Additionally, Indigenous communities in Mexico City associated land not only with the agricultural field but also with the Earth, the world, inheritance, and identity, so that the allocation of people out of the land they had traditionally occupied and worked for generations represented a deeply disruptive process for these communities.

Moreover, redistributing their Indigenous land among non-Indigenous individuals who did not belong to the community would leave Indigenous peasants without any means of subsistence, which eventually would result in the fragmentation of the cohesive element that allowed communities to keep a solid Indigenous entity.

For this reason, on November 22, 1827, the members of the extinguished parcialidades in Mexico City elected Pedro Patiño Ixtolinque to legally represent them. Patiño Ixtolinque, an Indigenous graduated artist from the Academy of Arts of San Carlos, in Mexico City, requested both chambers of the Mexican government to suspend the law of 1824 that stipulated the individual redistribution and forced allotment of the communal properties of the parcialidades.[20] Patiño Ixtolinque complained that the main goal expressed in the original law of the redistribution and allotment of land among the former owners or members of the parcialidades had been misinterpreted to allow non-Indigenous individuals to be legally able to acquire these assets.[21]

The Indigenous communities also used Patiño Ixtolinque's voice to express the importance that land had for Indigenous communities. The collective character of land, the relationship that existed in collective identity, and the sense of belonging to it, as well as the deep knowledge that people had about all sorts of practices suitable for diverse types of lands, were only a few of the core Indigenous values that had kept communities' cohesiveness throughout the colonial era. For this reason, the legal representative of these communities made sure to express their fears about the ignorance that authorities had about the nature and quality of the properties that were ready to distribute among individuals. For instance, the authorities had planned to convert most of the lands from the parcialidades into fields suitable for agriculture; however, not all the properties referred to by the law possessed the qualities to successfully develop this planned allotment. Patiño Ixtolinque explained to the authorities that some Indigenous communities based their local economy and welfare on fishing, hunting, or foraging, while others indeed relied on agriculture, but not all of them or their lands were suitable for allotment as agricultural parcels. This law, if enacted, he argued, would be deeply disruptive to the traditional and economic practices that Indigenous communities had followed for centuries. Moreover, these dramatic changes would wreak havoc on the economy of Mexico City, which would result in not having enough internal production to support the city's population. Patiño Ixtolinque alarmingly argued that, contrary to what the law pursued, its ultimate implementation could be catastrophic: instead of turning Indigenous communities into agrarian societies made up of individual allotted landowners, this law might instead turn collective farmers and fieldworkers into landless beggars.[22] Additionally, the limited flow of resources that communal properties would provide to institutions that used to benefit Indigenous communities in the city would be insufficient to provide education and other social benefits to Indigenous communities in the city, which would turn Indigenous peoples into a marginalized social group. Nevertheless, most of these appeals were ignored by the Mexican government.

As a counterresponse to these demands, the Mexico City authorities appointed Luis Velázquez de la Cadena, a non-Indigenous individual, to carry out an inventory of the properties of the extinguished parcialidades in Mexico City.[23] The relationship that existed between Velázquez de la Cadena and the members of the parcialidades remained far from optimal. Between the years 1846 and 1847, several leaders of Indigenous communities wrote and published a series of complaints about Velázquez de la Cadena's performance.[24] The leaders of these communities objected that Velázquez de la Cadena did not form part of the Indigenous community—hence, his ignorance about the Indigenous forms and means of property from the parcialidades for the benefit of the members of their own communities.[25]

Amid the increasing disputes for their communal lands, Nahua people in Mexico City also faced the Mexican–American War (1846–1848), which resulted in the occupation of Mexico City by American troops in September 1847, preventing them from fully committing to the successful defense of their properties. Nevertheless, the succeeding liberal administrations encouraged the practice of more policies that deteriorated communal property and Indigenous landownership, eventually leading to further forced allotment and the gradual loss of Indigenous landownership in the city.

Conclusion

The initial attempts to eradicate the parcialidades resulted in the ultimate reduction of Indigenous communities' political participation within their own municipal government. Indigenous people denounced the fact that the government took advantage of them by indiscriminately using their human and economic resources in the defense of the territory during the Mexican–American War, while neglecting their right to participate in political matters that deeply affected their communities and economic welfare.[26] As an immediate solution, the representatives of these Indigenous communities first requested direct participation in electing and choosing their next administrator, who they argued must be an Indigenous person. Nevertheless, the complaints and issues concerning the distribution of the assets of the parcialidades and the further allotment of their landholdings did not end during the first decades of the nineteenth century. On the contrary, this conflict extended and affected not only the parcialidades but also the lands and assets that religious organizations and the Catholic Church also held.[27]

The eradication of collective property and communal landownership in Mexico City affected both the Indigenous population and their foundational forms of social organization. The dissolution of their communal properties brought about a major dispossession of their traditional lands, which attracted the attention of non-Indigenous land speculators who purchased pieces of these properties at low prices in order to resell them for large profits. This cycle of allotment and land speculation led to the massive impoverishment of the Indigenous sector of the urban population and their subsequent conversion into landless peasants. This process allowed the creation of a wealthy class of non-Indigenous landowners that quickly accumulated a large quantity of these former Indigenous lands, turning them into large latifundios or haciendas.

The subsequent political administrations in Mexico, especially the regime of president Benito Juárez (1861–1872), focused on the total dissolution of corporate lands, both civil and religious. Contrary to the government's original intentions of making the Indigenous peoples in Mexico a group of independent landholding farmers, these measures resulted in the catastrophic decline of the welfare of Indigenous peoples. Over time, wealthy landowners required cheap labor to make the formerly Indigenous lands productive again. The wealthy non-Indigenous hacendados then hired, at extremely low wages, the Indigenous peoples to work on their very same dispossessed lands, turning these Indigenous laborers into a landless and formally debt-enslaved class of people. It can be said, then, that these forced allotments of lands initiated at the beginning of the nineteenth century led directly to the events that would spark the landless movements that clamored for access once again to communally administered lands during the Mexican Revolution of 1910.

NOTES

1. James Lockhart, *The Nahuas after the Conquest: A Social and Cultural History of the Indians of Central Mexico, Sixteenth through Eighteenth Centuries* (Stanford, Calif.: Stanford University Press, 1992), 14.
2. Frances Berdan and Patricia Rieff Anawalt, *The Essential Codex Mendoza* (Berkeley: University of California Press, 1997).
3. Lockhart, *Nahuas after the Conquest,* 28.
4. María Castañeda de la Paz, "Dos parcialidades étnicas en Azcapotzalco: Mexicapan y Tepanecapan," *Estudios de Cultura Nahuatl* 46 (July–December 2013): 230.
5. Andrés Lira, *Comunidades indígenas frente a la ciudad de México: Tenochtitlan, Tlatelolco, sus pueblos y barrios, 1812–1919* (México: El Colegio de México, 1995), 17.
6. Lucía Mier y Terán Rocha, *La primera traza de la ciudad de México 1524–1535,* vol. 1 (México: Fondo de Cultura Económica–Universidad Autónoma Metropolitana, 2005), 72–73.
7. Jay Kinsbruner, *The Colonial Spanish-American City: Urban Life in the Age of Atlantic Capitalism* (Austin: University of Texas Press, 2010), 43–44.
8. Que estas parcialidades se junten y hagan su elección de gobernador libremente, November 24, 1664, Instituciones Coloniales, Real Audiencia, Indios (58), container 14, vol. 24, file 477, Archivo General de la Nación, México (hereafter abbreviated as AGN).
9. Relación de los individuos que han sido cojidos por leva y estan reclamados, unos por sus

parcialidades de indios, y otros por sus mujeres y madres, n.d., Instituciones Coloniales/ Indiferente Virreinal, box 4205, file 13, AGN.

10. Guadalupe Nava Oteo, "Cajas de bienes de comunidades indígenas," *Anales del Museo Nacional de México* 2 (1971): 349.

11. *Ya les pesa a ciertos hombres que se ilustren los indios* (México: Imprenta del Ciudadano Alejandro Valdés, 1830), Ramo Justicia-Instrucción Pública, vol. 1, file 47, pp. 292–293, AGN.

12. Jaime E. Rodríguez O., "México, Estados Unidos y los países hispanoamericanos: Una visión comparativa de la independencia," in *México, 1808–1821: Las ideas y los hombres,* ed. Pilar Gonzalbo Aizpuru and Andrés Lira, 71–106 (México: El Colegio de México, 2014), 75.

13. Lira, *Comunidades indígenas frente a la Ciudad de México,* 22–23.

14. Juan de Dios Rodríguez Puebla, *El Indio Constitucional* (México: Oficina del Ciudadano Valdés, 1820), 1.

15. See Othón Arróniz, ed., *Los Tratados de Córdoba* (Veracruz, Mexico: Biblioteca Universidad Veracruzana, 1986).

16. Manuel Ferrer Muñoz, "El poder legislativo en México durante 1822 y la cuestión indígena," *Jurídica: Anuario del Departamento de Derecho de la Universidad Iberoamericana* 28 (1998): 287–304.

17. For instance, see José María Luis Mora, *Obras sueltas de José María Luis Mora, ciudadano mejicano* (Paris: Librería de Rosa, 1837), cvviii.

18. Donald J. Fraser, "La política de desamortización en las comunidades indígenas, 1853–1872," *Historia Mexicana* 66, no. 2 (October–December 2016): 621.

19. "Número 441. Decreto de 27 de noviembre de 1824. Sobre los bienes de las que se llamaban parcialidades de San Juan y Santiago," in *Legislación Mexicana. Colección completa de las disposiciones legislativas expedidas desde la Independencia de la República, ordenada por los licenciados Manuel Dublan y José María Lozano,* vol. 1 (México: Imprenta del Comercio, 1876), 744.

20. El gobernador del distrito acompaña la representación que hace a las cámaras Pedro Patiño como apoderado de las parcialidades para que se suspensa el reglamento formado para repartir los bienes de ellas, 1827, México Independiente, Justicia Negocios Eclesiásticos, Justicia, vol. 47, file 50, f. 373r–373v, AGN.

21. El gobernador del distrito acompaña la representación que hace a las cámaras Pedro Patiño, 366r.

22. El gobernador del distrito acompaña la representación que hace a las cámaras Pedro Patiño, 366r.

23. José María Lafragua, *Memoria de la Primera secretaria de estado y del despacho de relaciones interiores y exteriores de los Estados-Unidos Mexicanos: leída al soberano Congreso constituyente en los días 14, 15, y 16 de diciembre de 1846; Secretaría de Relaciones Exteriores* (México: Imprenta de Vicente García Torres, 1847), 228.

24. *La Presencia del indígena en la prensa capitalina del siglo XIX: catálogo de noticias,* vol. 2 (México: CIESAS, 1993), 310–11.

25. *Exposición que hacen los interesados en las parcialidades, en contra de su ilegal y mal llamado administrador D. Luis Velázquez de la Cadena* (México: Tipografía de R. Rafael, 1849).

26. *Exposición que hacen los interesados en las parcialidades,* 20.

27. *Sumisa representación de los curas párrocos de las parcialidades de San Juan y Santiago, que elevan a la augusta Cámara del Senado, para que se sirva tomar en consideración los males que se seguirán al reparto* (México: Imprenta de J. R. Navarro, 1849).

After Property

The Sakhina Struggle in Late Ottoman and British-Ruled Palestine,
1876–1948

MUNIR FAKHER ELDIN

Before the first Eastern European Jewish immigrants arrived at Palestine in the 1880s, long-term and new developments had been underway in the country. These changes are often told from the point of view of Zionism, as an invisible hand preparing the country for colonization or, as the Zionist myth goes, "land redemption."[1] The land could thus be seen as being emptied or opened up by the unfolding of market forces and so-called historical progress. The Palestinian national narrative has provided only a partial response to this narrative. While the Palestinians mark Zionist land purchases as the beginning of their national land loss and Nakba—the large-scale dispossession and ethnic cleansing suffered in 1948—the Palestinian social history of property has been largely left untouched. Rather than taking the development of Zionist colonization as the temporal frame of the story, this essay focuses on the experience of Sakhina—a small tribal village located in the Beisan valley in the northern district of Palestine—under late Ottoman and British colonial land policies.

Five or six decades before the Sakhinites lost their land to the Zionists in the 1930s, they lost their usufruct title to the Ottoman sultan Abdülhamit II (r. 1876–1909). This was a very different kind of land loss, one based on semifeudal political and economic conventions. The previous owners were secured tenancy under the banner of the sultan. Then the British colonial regime paradoxically returned the land to the possession of the local cultivators in 1921, but this progression was intended, at least in part, for unleashing market competition and increasing Zionist pressure on land resources in Palestine. To protect themselves against the adverse impact of the new rule of property, the Sakhinites trusted to return to a situation of protected tenancy under a rich Palestinian landlord. In the context of Palestine in the 1920s, with the growth of the market economy and the political boosting of the Zionist settler project, this was a huge risk that they inadvertently took. The new landlord, partnering up with a British subject residing and speculating in land in Palestine, took no real steps to develop the land and to employ the Sakhinites. A couple of years later, the partners sold to the

Jewish National Fund (JNF), which grew to lead Zionist land colonization after British occupation.

The Sakhinites fought for over a decade, between 1928 and 1939, to defend their moral entitlement to the land. They refused to evacuate, forcing the British to offer them new arrangements that partially compensated for their land loss. By telling their story, we can gain new insights on Arab–Jewish colonial relations in British-ruled Palestine. The struggle they waged is masked by the popular depiction of a holy war, an ancient feud between two faiths—Muslim and Jewish—in an old country. This was a deep struggle for political rights in a modern age. The Sakhinites, like the whole of the Palestinian people, were eventually unable to alter the imperial regime or to stop the dynamics of markets and settler colonial expansion. However, they marked a fault line of the Palestinian struggle against the settler colonial logic. This is a crooked logic of exclusion and political elimination that continues to underpin the question of Palestine today and that prescribes that the natives' loss of private titles to land (whether by sale or state expropriation) is a post-factum proof of the natives' lack of original political time and space, of political community and homeland. To tell the Sakhinites' story in this way, however, we need to resist plotting their agency on the conventional Zionist or Palestinian nationalist timelines.[2] Their story was a story of myriad struggles and middle grounds vis-à-vis various forces: Ottoman rulers, British colonial framings, and Zionist officials and settlers, as well as local agents and land brokers.

The Ottoman Background: Sultan Abdülhamit's Vision of Property and Empire

During the nineteenth century, the Ottoman Empire responded to growing European political and economic influences with a series of modern state reforms known as the Tanzimat (1839–1876), a series of centralizing state reforms drawing on both Ottoman political traditions and contemporary European models. Customary land tenure and indirect methods of tax revenue collection were central targets of reform. Ottoman reformers specifically condemned the semifeudal system of tax farming (*iltizam*) as one of the key factors weakening the state and depriving it of its wealth. In 1858 and 1859, new land tenure and usufruct registration codes were issued to centralize land revenue management and create a new land possession and tax registry.[3] However, as a sign of what one can call relative low-capital hegemony, the Ottomans kept the tithe at the core of their fiscal system. This meant, among other things, that the new system of title registration did not always eradicate existing customary uses and forms of access to land. While the reform allowed the emergence of absentee large landowners in many valleys (hitherto constituting internal tribal frontiers within the empire, including in Palestine), labor relations continued along flexible sharecropping arrangements and relied on local agents.[4] Various tenant and nontenant communities continued to live, cultivate, and access resources in lands that were registered as property of absentee landlords.[5] Early British officers noticed this fact and spoke about migrant Arab tribes that customarily moved across the frontiers of Palestine and continued to enjoy un-contested and long-standing privileges of seasonal pasturage in the plains all over the country.[6] The Beisan valley was no exception, despite the unique kind of its absentee owner—the Ottoman sultan, Abdülhamit II.

To defend his status vis-à-vis rising civil and military elites, as well as against European political and economic powers, Abdülhamit II reinvigorated and expanded a classical Ottoman institution of imperial domains, and the Beisan valley fell under it in the 1880s.[7] With these acquisitions, he indeed became a major contender for landed property and a key player in the transformation of Palestine, competing with private capital. The Beisan property allowed him to materialize a plan for a railroad connecting Haifa on the Mediterranean coast, through his estates, with the interior provincial capital, Damascus. Initially, the plan was put forward by Ottoman and British private investors, who controlled the Marj Ibn 'Amer (Jezreel) Valley adjacent to the sultan's land.[8] Abdülhamit II blocked their project and took it as his own. Moreover, his agents invested in the urban space of Beisan, building new roads and bridges, as well as storehouses and a caravansary, thus attracting new immigrants from neighboring towns. Merchants and farmers brought in small yet important investments and contributed to the development of the town and its agrarian hinterland. These private investments were instrumental in completing drainage works and land reclamations, targeting the marshlands in the valley, which bordered Sakhina's land.

Before drainage, the swamp near Sakhina was useful for raising animals, including buffaloes, and provided reeds from which the locals made baskets and rugs for domestic consumption and small commerce.[9] Proximity and control of water resources was a point of strength, a relic of the past power enjoyed by the larger Saqr tribe to which the Sakhinites belonged, before the advance of Ottoman centralization in the nineteenth century.[10] By the end of the century, the tribe's hold on power began to change, but this was a slow process. Many among the tribal communities in the valley, including the Sakhinites, began to adopt mixed forms of land uses and divisions suitable for dry cereal farming. The new demands imposed by the Ottoman sovereign-landlord were basically of a feudal nature, a claim over a share of the produce, which did not involve systematic reorganization of land tenure and land use. Despite the long-term erosion of power, communal solidarities and structures of authority persisted. Although the sultan had used a modernization and developmental discourse as part of legitimating his new land acquisitions and rule, he had also consciously cultivated older political idioms of rule.[11] This left a deep impact that outlasted his rule. When the post-Hamidian government sought to privatize the land, the inhabitants stood together and were able to resist the plan. They were supported by high-ranking Arab Ottoman officials and by the Arabic press in the various Arab provinces.[12] The greater change came later, with the British land settlement in 1921. The British recognized local entitlements to land, yet only as the basis for a new regime of private land registration. While seeming to empower the people of Beisan, the new allotment plan basically paved the way for messy land market relations and the emergence of Zionist settlements that threatened to push the natives out of their land.

Sakhina and the Beisan Land Settlement, 1918–1928

The British had committed themselves to advancing Zionist colonization in Palestine—or what is called the Jewish National Home policy, through the Balfour Declaration of 1917—before they actually defeated the Ottoman army and completed the occupation of Palestine in 1918. While this commitment prescribed key policy decisions, it was open for contestation. In preparation for the Paris Peace Conference of 1919, the Zionist leaders demanded a public right for Jewish land acquisition and development that would extend to all available state lands and include the power to fix land prices and even expropriate private (Arab) lands upon need. The British downscaled or reframed these demands. The British believed that a modern registration system (based on the colonial Australian Torrens system of titles by registration) and fiscal and legal reforms would suffice to address Zionist colonization needs. This policy was first implemented in the ex-sultan's domains in the Beisan valley in what came to be known as the Beisan land settlement. The settlement recognized existing tenancy rights as valid grounds for granting the natives property rights, disregarding the Zionist demand for a swift public land policy in their favor. However, this new allotment disregarded and broke down the local customary communal forms of access and rights to land, moving from periodical communal reallotments to permanent private allotments, irreversibly altering the human geography and landscape of the valley.

The actions of the Palestinians are key to understanding the British policy. In 1920, the Beisan valley witnessed a short and little-noticed, albeit locally significant, insurrection against the British army. Other, better-known communal clashes took place in Jerusalem and echoed anti-Zionist popular feeling all over the country. In response, the British introduced several measures to accommodate some of the demands of the Palestinians, which gave birth to the Beisan land settlement. Despite the Zionist problem, a latent core in Palestine society—that of middle-class urban liberals who envisioned national unity and social reform—could still see British rule in a positive light. Oppressed under Ottoman rule for their Arab nationalist ideology and rejection of the Turkification of the empire, this core found better conditions under the British. Like other national elites under British imperial dominion (such as in India and Egypt, among other places), they rose to new positions of popular leadership and mediation between the peasantry and their colonial rulers. British political culture related to their bourgeois sense of normative order in society and national revival based on private property. Although this compatibility between imperial rule and local bourgeoisie nationalism was always fraught with tensions, producing anticolonial politics, it was nonetheless profound and long-lasting.

In the town of Beisan, some of the new landowners, who arrived at the valley just a decade or so before the British, belonged to this elite core of Palestinian society and politics. Their alliance with the local communities proved fruitful against the Ottoman privatization plan in 1913 and, again under the British, in pushing for land settlement. Yet this alliance was also caught up in deep tensions. The nationalist elite had celebrated the settlement as a victory for all the Arabs of Palestine, a great chance for the revival and modernization of the Palestinian peasantry and an immunity against the Zionist project. Yet the terms and dynamics of the land settlement continued to be deeply contested. The settlement not only broke down communal solidarities and customary economic practices but also put heavy financial burdens on the owners, which pushed not a few to look for options to sell their land. A basic condition of the settlement stipulated that no sales were allowed to outsiders before the passage of a period of fifteen years, during which the new landowners would have paid all their dues to the government and established themselves as "good agriculturalists." However, heavy debts to the government and to moneylenders, and the high rise of prices due to Zionist land demands, undermined the basic idea of the settlement. Under those circumstances, the British decided, first tacitly in 1925 and then openly in 1928, to introduce policy changes, allowing outsiders to acquire land from the locals. Sakhina was among the first to feel the change.[13]

The early beneficiaries of this policy were not the Zionist settlers but two land developers, one Arab and the other British. Suleiman Bey Nassif, a Palestinian resident of Lebanese origins, speculated in land for oil exploration by British and American companies already before the First World War and served the British army in Egypt and Sudan before returning to Palestine after occupation. The second was a certain Captain Ross, a British national, residing in Nablus. In the early 1920s, Nassif sold land west of Sakhina to the JNF, which bought the land on behalf of the Hashomer Hatzair movement. In 1926, Nassif and Ross got a special license from the government to purchase Sakhina's land. It is likely that Nassif had tied the Sakhinites by private debts and thus they conceded to sell when he promised to keep them on the land as tenant-laborers. Like the rest of the residents of the valley, the Sakhinites were also pressed by indebtedness to the government, and the new patron-client arrangement must have appeared to them as a plausible option. Many of them agreed to sell all or part of their allotted plots to Nassif, but not all of them did. Additionally, many of the sold plots were still held in undivided shares by groups of family members, despite the desired plan intended by the Beisan land settlement. Thus, Nassif's and Ross's shares intermingled with other plots of people who refused to sell. A highly fragmented and contested space emerged. At first no change took place, and the Sakhinites continued to live on the land and use it for cultivation and as a grazing ground according to their own customs. Occasionally, some of them paid rent to Nassif in the form of a portion of the yield. And when they failed to do so, he obtained court orders to confiscate their produce. In the meantime, when the British introduced a new policy in 1928 to allow more outsiders to purchase land in the valley, Nassif and Ross divided their shares and each sold his plots separately to the JNF, which sought to facilitate the establishment of new Hashomer Hatzair settlements in the region. The Sakhinites were asked to leave the land and Nassif committed himself to the JNF to deliver the whole land free of tenants. For a whole decade they resisted eviction, waging a bitter struggle against Nassif, the JNF, the settlers, and the British police.[14]

After Property: Struggle and Perseverance, 1928–1948

In his repeating attempts to evict the Sakhinites, Nassif resorted to both negotiation and prosecution. He tried to utilize his connections within the Palestinian business and political elite to persuade the Sakhinites to leave the land for monetary compensation, while at the same time pursuing legal action. Neither of these was smooth or easy. The Sakhinites enjoyed the sympathy of influential Palestinian leaders who lobbied on their behalf with the British rulers in Jerusalem. Attempts to evacuate the tribe by police force failed due to the steadfastness of the community. The complex legal geography of undivided shares and intermingled plots of land helped the Sakhinites resist the execution of eviction orders; when execution officers showed up, they found it very difficult to demarcate the exact boundaries of the sold plots without clashes with the Sakhinites. On several occasions, the settlers sent tractors with armed guards to forcefully plow the disputed land, but they repeatedly faced physical resistance by the tribesmen and had to turn back. The police force often intervened and used violence and intimidation against the Sakhinites. But these actions helped to raise more sympathy with them.

Learning from experience, the British mandate officials generally sought to avoid the violent evacuation of Palestinian peasants; in certain cases, they were willing to freeze court decisions.[15] In the 1930s, the British came to recognize some of the adverse effects of their land policy in Palestine—mainly, the emergence of a class of landless Palestinian peasantry and a direct result of Zionist colonization. Some legal measures and a development program of resettlement of uprooted farmers were introduced. Legally speaking, the Sakhinites, having sold their own land, did not qualify for the new program. However, due to their resistance, the government decided to offer them accommodation under the resettlement program with funds to be obtained from the JNF. The Sakhinites were thus offered alternative camping and grazing ground to lease, along with a small amount of irrigated land ready for cultivation. But they did not rush to accept the offer. They continued to believe that their deal with Nassif did not end their long-standing moral right to work and live on their ancestral land; they rejected the emerging notion of exclusive property rights and demanded to pay back money to annul their sale contracts. Their call was ignored. When the Great Palestinian Revolt (1936–1939) against British rule broke out, they were emboldened and informed government officials, in an anticolonial spirit, that they would not leave Sakhina even if they were offered "a dunam for dunam."[16]

The revolt failed to overthrow British rule and in many ways strengthened the Zionist settlers. Yet, what ought to be noted is that the struggle was (and still is) not a zero-sum game. During the revolt, the Palestinians in the Beisan valley asserted possession of government and absentee owners' land with disregard to the colonial order. As part of their plan to pacify the country on the eve of World War II, the British introduced a new land regulation concerning land transfers from native Palestinian Arabs to Jewish settlers; the aim was to control Zionist immigration and land purchases and head for a form of a binational state. A zoning plan of the land market was thus put into effect. Parts of the valley fell in one zone in which land transfers from Arabs to Jews were totally prohibited; other parts fell in a zone in which transfers required government approval. The new British policy was fiercely contested by the Zionists; on the ground, the JNF continued to buy land without official registration, thus adding new problems for the British. Politically, the British failed to assert the binational option, and at the end of the war, they endorsed a new United States–backed trajectory of support for a Jewish state, which led to the UN Partition Plan of 1947, an armed conflict between the Zionist army and the neighboring Arab states, and the Palestinian Nakba in 1948.

In the meanwhile, in the decade between the end of the revolt and the Nakba, in Beisan and elsewhere, the Palestinian national movement was slowly regaining political strength. The new land regulations allowed a small, yet promising, Palestinian Arab company—the Arab Nations Fund—to invest in purchasing land to block unofficial sales to the JNF.[17] The Sakhinites benefited from this new environment. By the end of the revolt, the Hashomer Hatzair movement, with the help of the JNF and the British army, managed to install new settlement outposts in the region and to forcefully seize Sakhina's land. However, the Sakhinites did not go away. They retained the unsold plots in their possession and encroached on nearby state lands. Claiming critical land needs, the settlers encroached on the same state-owned plots and claimed tenancy rights. Considering the new zoning rules, the British rejected the settlers' claims while granting the Sakhinites legal leases to cultivate the land. Despite growing tensions in the 1940s, this state of affairs continued basically until British evacuation in 1948. It was through Zionist military conquest and the ethnic cleansing of the entire Arab population from the valley that the Sakhinites finally lost their livelihood in their homeland. Together with hundreds of thousands of their compatriots, they turned into refugees in other parts of Palestine as well as in neighboring Arab countries.

Final Remarks

Zionist historiography gave a specific name to the period in which new settlements rose in and near Sakhina: Yame Huma Umigdal, the Era of Wall and Tower. According to the Zionist narrative, a new heroic ethos of defense-by-conquest against "Arab violence" and "wilderness" was born, which Israeli historians consider to be a major factor in the establishment of the state of Israel and of settlement expansion in the 1967 Palestinian territories.[18] The Palestinians were made to disappear discursively and physically. Yet Palestinian memory and struggle were reborn after 1948 not only in militant revolutionary forms but also in a multiplicity of cultural and history-telling forms. Palestinian and pro-Palestinian commemoration books, websites, innumerable personal and communal social media pages, and cultural products all resist the colonial erasure and strive to mark the loss.[19] Critical historians, however, are presented with a more difficult task of marching against the grain of thousands of pages of historical data in order to reconnect and record many complex and long stories of loss and struggle, of Nakba and reconstruction. In this task, one is confronted with the urgency of reflexivity and distance, of distinguishing class positions and variance in experiences across and within communal lines. Sakhina's story, as I came to understand it, reminds us of the historical and varying social and political meanings of property. If we adopt a monolithic sense of property, of legal private ownership as we know it through its conventional contemporary and historical liberal/colonial lenses, we risk re-erasing the subaltern realities of the colonized and the dispossessed. In the Zionist logic, Arab loss of title to the land was constructed as a loss of a right to be in the country, to define it as their own—a zero-sum game of a logic of elimination, to borrow from Patrick Wolfe.[20] The subaltern Palestinian stories teach us that communal life (both economic and political) was possible after the loss of official titles in a stressful economic and juridical context, and it is this possibility that the settler colonial logic wishes always to deny.

NOTES

1. For a classical Zionist academic account, see Abraham Granott, *The Land System: History and Structure* (London: Eyre & Spottiswoode, 1952). A similar narrative also underlies works such as Dov Gavish, *The Survey of Palestine under the British Mandate, 1920–1948* (London: Routledge-Curzon, 2005), and Roy Fischel and Ruth Kark, "Sultan Abdülhamit II and Palestine: Private Land, Imperial Policy," *New Perspectives on Turkey* 39 (2008): 129–66.
2. Beshara Dumani, "Rediscovering Ottoman Palestine: Writing Palestinians into History," *Journal of Palestine Studies* 21, no. 2 (1992): 5–28.
3. Huri Islamoglu, "The Land Code as a Contested Domain: A Reevaluation of the Ottoman Land Code of 1858," in *New Perspectives on Property and Land in the Middle East,* ed. Roger Owen (Cambridge, Mass.: Harvard University Press and the Center for Middle Eastern Studies of Harvard University, 2000), 3–62.

4. Roger Owen, *The Middle East in the World Economy,* rev. ed. (London: I. B. Tauris Publishers, 1993), 267.

5. Raya Adler, "The Tenants of Wadi Hawarith: Another View of the Land Question in Palestine," *International Journal of Middle East Studies* 20, no. 2 (1988): 197–220.

6. Munir Fakher Eldin, "British Framing of the Frontier in Palestine, 1918–1923: Revisiting Colonial Sources on Tribal Insurrection, Land Tenure, and the Arab Intelligentsia," *Jerusalem Quarterly* 60 (2014): 42–58.

7. Fischel and Kark, "Sultan Abdülhamit II and Palestine."

8. Jacob Norris, *Land of Progress: Palestine in the Age of Colonial Development, 1905–1948* (Oxford: Oxford University Press, 2013), 47–48.

9. Sandra Sufian, *Healing the Land and the Nation: Malaria and the Zionist Project in Palestine, 1920–1947* (Chicago: University of Chicago Press, 2007).

10. Tawfiq Canaan, "The Saqr Bedouin of Bisan," *Journal of the Palestine Oriental Society* 16 (1936): 21–32.

11. Selim Deringil, *The Well-Protected Domains: Ideology and the Legitimation of Power in the Ottoman Empire, 1876–1909* (London: I. B. Tauris, 1998), 66.

12. Munir Fakher Eldin, "Communities of Owners: Land Law, Governance, and Politics in Palestine, 1858–1948" (PhD diss., New York University, 2008), chap. 1.

13. Munir Fakher Eldin, "Confronting a Colonial Rule of Property: The Al-Sakhina Case in Mandate Palestine," *Arab Studies Journal* 17, no. 1 (2019): 19.

14. Fakher Eldin, "Confronting a Colonial Rule of Property," 21–27.

15. Germey Forman and Alexandre Kedar, "Colonialism, Colonization, and Land Law in Mandate Palestine: The Zor al-Zarqa and Barrat Qisarya Land Disputes in Historical Perspective," *Theoretical Inquiries in Law* 4, no. 2 (2003): 491–539.

16. Fakher Eldin, "Confronting a Colonial Rule of Property." A dunam is an Ottoman land measure, equal to nearly a quarter of an acre.

17. Fakher Eldin, "Communities of Owners," chap. 5.

18. See Sharon Rotbard, "Wall and Tower," in *A Civilian Occupation: The Politics of Israeli Architecture,* ed. Rafi Segal and Eyal Weizman (Tel Aviv: Verso, 2003); Anita Shapira, *Land and Power: The Zionist Resort to Force, 1881–1948* (Oxford: Oxford University Press, 1992), 253–57; and Tamar Katriel and Aliza Shenhar, "Tower and Stockade: Dialogic Narration in Israeli Settlement Ethos," *Quarterly Journal of Speech* 76, no. 4 (1990): 359–81.

19. See the classical work by Walid Khalidi, *All That Remains: The Palestinian Villages Occupied and Depopulated by Israel in 1948* (Washington, D.C.: Institute for Palestine Studies, 1992). Also see the Palestine Land Society's project, led by Salman Abu Sitta, https://www.plands.org/en/home. Other popular websites include https://www.palestineremembered.com and https://zochrot .org.

20. Patrick Wolfe, "Settler Colonialism and the Elimination of the Native," *Journal of Genocide Research* 8, no. 4 (2006): 387–409.

How to Get a Home, How to Work, and How to Live

KHAL SCHNEIDER

In 1881 and 1882, the European hops crop failed. American hops prices, which had lurched between 15¢ and 40¢ per pound during the 1870s, jumped to a heady $1.10 per pound. In 1883, California growers rushed to plant more vines, and as they scrambled to find enough pickers to gather the glut of fast-spoiling flowers, they offered wages up to 50 percent higher than in previous years. And in Mendocino County, California, a group of Northern Pomo hops pickers earned enough in one season to pay off their mortgage a year early. The year before, in March 1882, Sam Hale, Billy Maze, Jack Maze, and Dutch Stevens had paid Frank Weger the first $600 for 160 acres near Ukiah. They had then borrowed $1,000 from hops grower Charles English and offered their quarter section to him as security on the mortgage. Now, after the bonanza 1883 hops harvest, they held enough money to offer English the value of the original loan plus interest—$1,117 in gold coin. But English refused to accept payment or turn over the deed.[1]

And so, the Pomos sued him. At trial, English argued that the Indians had failed to fulfill the terms of their agreement: to provide eighty people to pick English's hops, at fifty cents per one hundred pounds, in 1883 and 1884. But in the boom year of 1883, the Pomos had found other growers willing to pay as much as three times that amount, and they reasoned that English would find their immediate offer of cash a more welcome repayment method than their labor a year hence. In court, however, superior court judge Robert McGarvey, himself a hops grower, agreed with English's assertion that he had not offered home-seeking Indians a mortgage loan, but instead had contracted eighty hops pickers for two successive harvests—labor the Pomos refused to provide. The judge ruled in English's favor, and the Pomos forfeited their down payment, the land, and the "valuable" improvements they had already put in.[2]

Set against an era of rampant dispossession and an allotment policy that would severely reduce tribal holdings across western North America, it is not surprising to find this Pomo community failing to defend its land from American property owners and courts. But the success of other similar efforts would have made this failure especially frustrating for the Pomo people involved. In fact, Hale already owned two other pieces of property when he filed suit against English. In September 1878, Hale bought his first tract with a down payment earned in hops picking. The deed, finalized after the Pomos completed their payment with another year of hops picking, identified "Captain Jack, Charley, and Sam Hale, Indians," as the owners of fifty acres north of Ukiah. Three months later, Hale and seventeen other men paid one hundred dollars for another seven acres and took title as "Indians of the Redwood Valley Tribe." Other Pomo communities pooled their resources to buy parcels of land ranging in size from 10 to 120 acres, most of them clustered around Ukiah.[3] In most respects, the new parcels (known locally as rancherias) fit seamlessly into the landscape of white farms. Pomos recorded titles to them with the county, paid taxes on them, took mortgages for them, and, in some cases, produced the same crops—including hops—on them as their white neighbors. But the tracts stood out in the deed registers in one important aspect: each deed listed between two and eighteen owners of the land and identified them as Indians. Most also explicitly named an Indian tribe as the collective owner of the land.

That tribal land was a subject of interest to many people—federal officials, local white citizens, and Pomos themselves—but for different reasons. Massachusetts Senator Henry L. Dawes may not have heard about Hale's failed suit, but he did hear of the Pomo landowners, and as he was professionally interested in the effects of property ownership on Indian communities, he visited them at Ukiah just a year after the Pomos sued English and three years before passage of the act for which he would be best known. It may have seemed to Dawes, as he was informed by numerous citizens, that the purchases Pomos had worked out on their own were far superior arrangements to the reservation for getting Indians to work, save, and adopt other "civilized pursuits."[4] Local citizens and authorities encouraged Indian landownership, because unlike reservation land, the private tracts were taxable, under local jurisdiction, and purchasable only with the wages Pomos made working for white landowners—landowners like English who extended credit and sold land to Pomos to keep them close for the next harvest. To Pomos, land represented security in many forms: it held that potential as farmland to offset low wages and seasonal unemployment, equity to buy even more productive or otherwise valuable land, and even simply safety from eviction. While white citizens sought ways to reliably extract value from Pomo labor, federal officials drew moral lessons from Indian labor nationwide, and both groups sought to draw Indians into a hierarchical market order, Pomo laborers endeavored not merely to improve their position in that order but to protect themselves from it.

In the places that Americans renamed Potter Valley, Coyote Valley, and Redwood Valley, members of Northern Pomo–speaking tribelets, or sovereign village communities, charted their prospects for survival within a narrow space.[5] Bowing to pressure from California's congressional delegation, the Senate ratified no treaties with California tribes; the United States never legally quieted Indian title in California, but the private claims of thousands of American citizens extinguished it nonetheless.

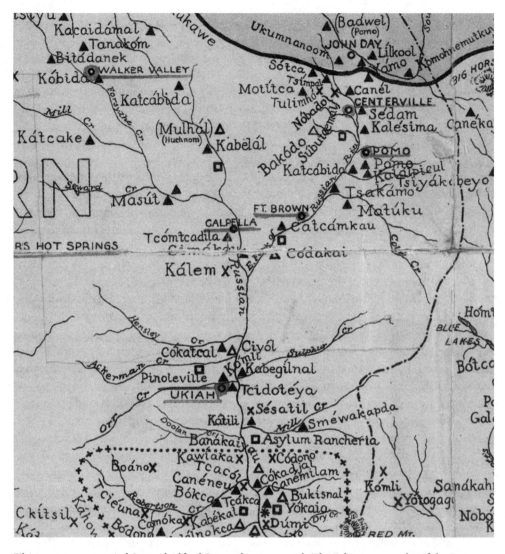

This map accompanied Samuel Alfred Barrett's monograph *The Ethno-geography of the Pomo and Neighboring Indians.* White squares represent Pomo-owned rancherias. The land Sam Hale, Billy Maze, Jack Maze, and Dutch Stevens tried to buy from Frank Weger is in the center of the map detail, south of the town of Calpella and in the approximate area of the old village site Cimákaū, just above the confluence of the East Fork and main stream of the Russian River.

S. A. Barrett, "Map of the territory of the Pomo linguistic stock and of the adjacent territories of other linguistic stocks, showing dialectic subdivisions and village sites," University Press, 1908, Map G 04361 E1 1908 M3 Case C Bancroft, courtesy of the Bancroft Library, University of California, Berkeley.

California law empowered those citizens to dispose of Indian land and people as they saw fit. In addition to the now better-known components of California's 1850 Act for the Government and Protection of Indians that permitted private citizens to indenture Indians as "apprentices" or "servants," a portion of the law also instructed *"proprietors of land on which Indians are residing"* to permit them to stay or apply to the justice of the peace to set aside a "sufficient amount of land for the necessary wants of Indians."[6] Neither component of the law offered any real protection, but both governed Indians via the relationship between white property owners and the Native people who resided on their land. The Civil War spelled doom for this system of bound Indian labor that supporters had cheered as a western analog to southern slavery, and in 1869, the state's supreme court suggested that the 1866 Civil Rights Act included Indians among those who held the "absolute rights of persons" to "the benefit of the writ of habeas corpus, to sue, to contract, hold property, etc."[7] The court meant for this to be a ceiling for Indian rights rather than an admission to fully enfranchised, voting citizenship, and white citizens still expressed their relationship to Indian workers as personal entitlement to the labor of specific groups and individual Indians. But Pomo people fell under local jurisdiction, and most Pomo laborers drew wages; in the coming years they would attempt to recover land through appeals to the laws of that local order and with the wages they earned within it.

Northern Pomo captains (hereditary and sometimes elected heads of families and allied family groups) from Potter, Redwood, and Coyote Valleys contracted with growers—the new owners of what had been the collective property of their villages—to deliver the seasonal labor of their people during harvest seasons. Those arrangements, often oral agreements with growers, could also include permission to remain on white property owners' land in the off-season. When the United States brought hundreds of Northern Pomos to Mendocino County's Round Valley Reservation in 1872, captains continued to make seasonal contracts to work off the reservation during harvest season. Agents typically permitted them to leave since they could not match the wages private citizens paid, and most reservation lands were under the control of trespassing white citizens.[8] In 1875, the district's Democratic congressman, John K. Luttrell, argued that the federal government ought to turn Round Valley over to the "worthy class of citizens" on the reservation who lived with Indians on "most amicable terms" (while they used reservation land as their own rent- and tax-free range). Luttrell pointed to the experience of off-reservation Indians to prove the soundness of the plan. The "county judge and other prominent citizens" in Ukiah, seventy miles to the south, swore to the "good conduct of the Indians" there. Those who had left Round Valley were now "industrious, frugal, and temperate," were well-clothed, made two dollars a day working for white farmers, and "had as high as $700 deposited in the savings bank." Luttrell recommended that while it dissolved the reservation, the federal government should appoint a panel of three local judges—including hop grower and judge

Robert McGarvey—to see to the Indians' education and employment and, if possible, find land for them.[9]

The government never enacted his plan, but Pomos took advantage of the space it seemed to open. The Northern Pomo head man known to white citizens as Captain Jack contracted with white growers to deliver his people's labor for four successive harvests while he was enrolled at Round Valley as a "Potter Valley Indian." In 1878, Captain Jack left the reservation for good (and this time without permission) to buy the first Pomo-owned rancheria, not in Potter Valley, where he was born, but near Ukiah, twenty miles to the south. He then hired a local lawyer who threatened the pursuing agent, Henry Sheldon, with a kidnapping charge should he try to bring the Pomos back to Round Valley. Captain Jack was joined on his deed by Charlie Bourne and Sam Hale, relatives from Potter Valley who had relatives of their own in Redwood and Coyote Valleys. Sam Hale joined with some of those relatives to buy a second piece of property, and he fended off Agent Sheldon with a receipt for the seven acres now belonging to the "Redwood Valley Indians" (whose land was not in Redwood Valley, but closer to Ukiah) and a receipt for the poll tax he had recently paid, indicating that he was no longer "not taxed" and was beyond the agent's power. Round Valley's former Peace Policy agent, the Methodist minister John L. Burchard, helped them enter their deeds with the county clerk, but they bought the land with their own wages at a site of their own choosing where, as they calculated, they stood to make the highest and most dependable wages in the future.[10]

Pomo men and women worked as domestics, washers, woodcutters, fruit pickers, and basket sellers, but hops brought them the most reliably high wages and drew them into sustained relations with some of the region's most prosperous white citizens. Although among the region's wealthiest landowners, hops growers produced a crop that was notorious for its fluctuations in price and that spoiled rapidly and required many hands in the longest harvest season of any crop in California.[11] In efforts to impose some predictability on the labor market, growers contracted Pomo laborers years in advance, extended credit to them, and arranged for them to remain close at hand for the next harvest by selling or leasing them small parcels of land. Hale and his people were able to contract debt from hops growers with the confidence that they could repay it after the next season's harvest. Although Sam Hale already owned two pieces of land by 1880, the census of that year found him living on the land of Ukiah hop grower Patrick Cunningham. In a decade's time, a group of Northern Pomo men related to Hale had bought five and a half acres of that land from Cunningham. Their deed specified that they would deliver payment to Cunningham at three stages of the hops-producing year: planting, training, and harvesting.[12] Three of those buyers, representing "three families," all "related—cousins and things," as one of their descendants recalled, later bought still another piece of land south of Ukiah for a recorded sale price of only ten dollars. The hops growers who sold it had already recouped most of the land's value in labor performed by Pomos living there.[13] In 1883, the year Hale sued English, an Indian Office inspector admitted that the Pomos around Ukiah were "accounted good hop-pickers," "earn[ed] considerable amounts of money," owned "considerable property," and had "succeed[ed] in supporting themselves tolerably well."[14] After the 1883 harvest, Hale, Billy Maze, Jack Maze, Dutch Stevens, and their families held the equivalent of a modern sum of more than $30,000 in gold coin. It was more than enough to secure enough property to make them producers on par with even the most prosperous hops growers in the county.[15]

But white citizens were not interested in seeing Pomo landowners become independent producers. Although they praised Indian workers, countenanced Indian land-ownership, and affirmed that Pomos and white citizens alike could resort to the local courts to defend their rights, white growers could be confident that the law would resolve conflicts between them and their Indian workers in their favor. In Hale's suit, Judge McGarvey reasserted the authority of local landowners over Pomo laborers in the language of common law principles. English's lawyers chided the Pomo plaintiffs with a reminder that "he who asks equity must first do equity," and the court agreed they had, by their own negligence, forfeited any claims they might make on English. Judge McGarvey was also an employer of Pomo hops pickers and a mortgage lender to a Pomo community living close to his property.[16] He sympathized with English's claim that the Indians "failed and refused to perform" their part of the bargain by failing to deliver the requisite hands in 1883, when it was "a very difficult matter to obtain hop pickers at the proper time." McGarvey agreed that English's "sole and only object" in taking possession of the land was to "secure in advance a sufficient number of hands to pick his hops." They had refused, and still refused, to labor for English, finding better pay elsewhere, and now, McGarvey continued, "they cannot be compelled to perform" that labor. The state's civil code held that "an obligation to render personal service cannot be enforced." McGarvey thus characterized Pomo labor as "personal service," a vague space in the marketplace that echoed the prior condition of Indian servitude and was seemingly immune to the laws of contract. He simultaneously (perhaps contradictorily) denied that considerations of "equity" allowed the Pomos to use cash as an equivalent for their labor. In fact, in offering cash, they had actually robbed English of the value of their labor, for which he had bargained at fifty cents per hundred pounds of hops—hops he had hoped to market at least twice that price per pound over two years. McGarvey used the opportunity to discipline laborers on whom Ukiah growers, McGarvey included, depended.[17] Although some Pomo rancherias would continue to market their own hops crops in years to come, none of the residents stopped working for white growers.

In the year after the English case, 1883's hops crop glutted the market and prices fell drastically from their 1882 high. They would stay depressed, at as little as 5 percent of 1882's price, for the rest of the decade. ("There is nothing that grows from the ground that is subject to such extreme fluctuations and uncertainties in regard to price," one market observer noted.)[18] In 1884, some Ukiah growers elected to lease their land rather than waste their time and money marketing their own hops. That year, in addition to growing hops on the rancheria to which he owned the deed along with Captain Jack and Sam Hale, Charlie Bourne rented an additional ten acres on which to grow his own hops—just as predictions came that it would be another bad year.[19] And at just that moment, a delegation from the Senate Committee on Indian Affairs, chaired by Senator Henry Dawes, called Bourne and another Northern Pomo man, Charlie Brown, to testify in Ukiah on their experience at Round Valley and their reasons for leaving the reservation.

Bourne and Brown offered the senators a detailed accounting of the value they placed on their own labor, described their prospects for the future, and eagerly used the opportunity to tell Dawes about the reservation's failures. When Dawes probed them as to "how nicely you are getting along" on their land, they directed the conversation repeatedly back to Round Valley. "He worked us too long," Charlie Brown said of his former agent. He said that the resources, animals, and tools of the reservation "belonged to the Indians, but, at the same time, we couldn't get any of it when we needed it." Brown recalled working "a whole week splitting rails, building fences, plowing, sowing grain, working in the grist-mill" and receiving only seventy-five cents in pay. "I killed 100 hogs myself and scalded them and cleaned them," Brown testified, "but the Indians didn't get any of them." Contrary to the popular nineteenth-century perception of reservation Indians living easily on government rations, Round Valley Indians worked hard on their reservation but gained nothing by it. "Every agent said" if they worked, they would have land, said Bourne, "but we didn't get anything." They "promised land and horses and everything we wanted, and they never did it," said Bourne. Bourne recalled that they wanted him to go to school, but then the agent pulled him out of school after only two months—before he "learned the ABC's"—and put him to work "like a dog." The only lessons they had learned about labor and property at the reservation were that long hours of labor would always accrue to the benefit of someone else. After commanding them to labor, the government's agents "ought to have given us something so we could live there," Bourne said. When they failed to do so, "we came away and bought our own land here the 22nd day of September, 1879." "We have our own homes here and feed ourselves well, and nobody troubles us," he told Dawes. "Nobody does any harm to me here."[20] Dawes would not have been shocked to hear that the reservation had thwarted these men's aspirations to independence; after investigating the reservation, he was sure that it was because most of the land there was in the hands of white trespassers. But even so, to hear Bourne say that white citizens did not do him "any harm" off the reservation probably confirmed for Dawes that the reinforcing virtues of hard work and self-sufficiency would win these Indians respect from white neighbors and propertied citizenship.

But he appeared perplexed by some of the lessons their exposure to the marketplace seemed to have taught these Pomos. Bourne and Brown each identified their holdings as both their own land and as their people's land. Bourne told Dawes that he and Captain Jack "run the farm" and "pay the taxes and interest," but it "belongs to all our folks and nobody can take it." When Dawes asked Charlie Brown if he would "like to work and have something of [his] own," Brown answered yes but described both of those efforts as collective. He called the people who lived on his land his "tribe" and told Dawes, "We live in a bunch." His people borrowed money to buy ten acres, worked to pay back their loan, collectively planted crops, paid taxes from a common fund, and when they worked for white hops growers, the seventy-three adults divided the combined six hundred dollars of earnings evenly between them. "Have they worked as much as you?" Dawes wondered skeptically. Brown assured him they had, and that "*we* have good living here."[21] Brown's reference to his "bunch's" "good living" invoked a view of the rancherias not as homes of autonomous households, each privately pursuing their own accumulation of wealth, but as secure and interdependent families.

Perhaps finally detecting the irony in Bourne's repeated complaint that the Indian Office never fulfilled its promise to teach the Indians how "to do no wrong to any person," and fearing that the men's private property ownership had not severed their tribal ties but seemed to have depended on and strengthened them, Dawes attempted to gauge just how far their progress toward civilization had proceeded. When Bourne told him that the agent took him out of school after only two months, Dawes interrupted clumsily, "Do all you people have more than one wife?" Bourne told Dawes, "I want to tell you about the reservation. I am not through yet," and ignored the question.[22] But as his Pomo witnesses presented evidence of the tribal means they took to counter their exploitation, Dawes repeatedly tried to determine the degree to which they conformed to the class-based, gendered, and religious imperatives of the assimilation policy. The citizenship he envisioned for Bourne and Brown and all Indian people depended on an idealized image of a white middle-class household—built by men securing their living by paid work outside of it and women secure in their proper role within it. Dawes understood what Bourne and Brown did as work, but he overlooked the wages that women made in domestic labor in other people's houses and in the sales of baskets, which they made during the winter months when farm work was impossible to find. These, too, contributed to the purchase of the land and the security of the communities. His questions—"Do you like to work and own something of your own?" "Do you drink whisky?" "Do [you] marry like white people?"—betrayed his hopes that property ownership had produced among the Pomos, especially men, the necessary acceptance of Protestant middle-class morality that would allow them to truly be included "among the citizens of this land."[23] The witnesses told Dawes—if he had ears to hear it—that those questions were immaterial to the problems they faced and the ways they were required to address them. When Dawes asked him about his people's marriages,

Brown answered yes, his people "marry like white people," but no one bothered any longer to get a marriage license. "We did that way when we were at the reservation and were Christians . . . but that didn't do us any good, so we let it go." What Dawes might have taken as a maladaptation, Brown probably considered a rational calculation: the Methodist minister who served as agent issued marriage licenses for free at Round Valley; in Ukiah, they cost at least two days' wages.[24]

Asking to retake the witness chair at the end of the day, Charlie Brown offered a summation of the lessons Pomos had drawn from their experience with federal agents and private employers, and he drew a distinction between Dawes's ideological commitment to Indian property ownership and their material realities. "Up at the reservation they told us about the Democrat and the Republican," Brown explained to the Republican senator. "They said the Republican would show us what to do," he continued, "how to get a home, how to work, and how to live, how to raise vegetables of all kinds; they said we could have our own land, 6, 7, 8, or 50 acres for ourselves." "Every agent said so, but we didn't get anything," Brown said. So, he told his people, "we better leave and go to Ukiah." Able to read and "find out things through the newspapers," Brown heeded local authorities who instructed him to "shear sheep, and make money and . . . rent hops and make money" and to "buy 15 or 20 acres and pay the interest (I understand what interest means)." "I took my people away, because I found out something about those white people," he told Dawes, and as Brown was aware that he was telling a Republican senator about the failures of "the Republican" reservation agents, his placement of the clause "I found out something about *those* white people" after "I took my people away" was likely not accidental. Brown brought his people to Ukiah, not their original homes, but the center of the political and economic order built by the people who overtook those homes, turned Pomo land into their own property, and commanded them to labor on it. "We paid $100 an acre for 10 acres," he closed, before he left the Ukiah council. "That is what I wanted to tell, and that is the last word from me."[25]

It was the last word from Brown, but Pomo landowners contributed indirectly to the discourse on Indian Affairs that would culminate in the passage of the General Allotment Act. A year after he met Bourne and Brown, when he spoke before the assembled Friends of the Indian at Lake Mohonk, Dawes bolstered his call for Indian policy reform with a reference to the "hardworking Indians in Northern California," apparently confident that his audience would be as familiar with that caricature as they were with "warlike Crows" and the "stalwart Indians of Dakota." But the speech hinted that he had not left California convinced that hard work was enough. The Indians' "friends" needed the "authority of law" to do what "necessities demand" for each tribe; that is, there needed to exist a strong federal program and continued guardianship to ensure that Indians learned the right lessons from their experience in the marketplace.[26] With his "last word," Brown affirmed that he did not need further lessons from Dawes or the Indian Office on "how to get a home, how to work, and how to live," and his testimony revealed a conflict at the center of the era of Indigenous land privatization that Dawes and other reformers barely acknowledged. Pomos were already where assimilationists hoped to place all Indians, and the lessons they learned there were not about the gentling influence of liberal citizenship but rather about the conflict over the material interests of Pomo workers and white landowners. Pomos knew how and were able to work for pay, contract debt, save, and rent and buy land, but their primary concern was insulating themselves from an economy in which their primary income was the wage they drew for picking one specific crop with wildly fluctuating prices and where their aspirations for security were subject to the demands of their employers and local legal authorities. Dawes's discomfort came when he recognized that Pomos' understanding of what "necessities demanded" inspired them to draw from whatever resources they could, including the kinship-based tribal communities that had always sustained their people, any arguments about the civilizing nature of property ownership notwithstanding.

Especially after Hale's failed suit, Pomos had few illusions about their white neighbors and employers, but they were sure that they were the authorities to which they must appeal if they had any hope of acquiring property, the only means they saw of gaining some protections against the dangers of the marketplace. A decade after their failed suit, Sam Hale and Jack Maze reunited to buy one last tract of land. They and three other men swapped the first parcel they bought in 1878 for a larger one adjacent to a large hops farm just north of town and took the deed in the names of Captain Jack, Sam Hale, Jack Maze, Fuller Williams, and Jim Reeve. Like several other rancheria deeds, it provided that the land belonged to deed holders and their "heirs and assignees" "forever," and the superior court explicitly named the five men as trustees of the land for the benefit of the "Pinoleville Indians."[27] The Pinoleville Rancheria, like others, persisted as a cocreation of Pomo laborers and white authorities, the means of collective security that Pomos entrusted uncertainly to an order founded on Indian dispossession.

NOTES

1. David Vaught, *Cultivating California: Growers, Specialty Crops, and Labor, 1875–1920* (Baltimore: Johns Hopkins University Press, 2002), 42; and Sam Hale et al. v. C. H. English, April 16, 1884, Case 2482, Mendocino County Records, Civil and Criminal Case Files, Mendocino County Superior Court, 1880–1902, California State Archives, Sacramento, Calif.
2. Hale v. English.
3. L. B. Frasier to Sam Hale et al., December 10, 1878, *Book of Deeds,* vol. 20, 373, Mendocino County Clerk-Recorder, Ukiah, Calif. (hereafter MCD); and Weger to Captain Jack et al., September 22, 1879, vol. 21, 319, MCD. See also Khal Schneider, "Making Indian Land in the Allotment Era: Northern California's Indian Rancherias," *Western Historical Quarterly* 41, no. 4 (Winter 2010): 429–50.

4. U.S. Senate, Condition of Certain Indians in California, S. Rep. No. 1522 (1885).

5. Northern Pomo is one of seven mutually unintelligible Pomo languages, speakers of which comprised as many as fifty autonomous tribelets at the time of the American invasion. The founder of professional California ethnology, Alfred Louis Kroeber, coined the term *tribelet* to describe the basic unit of California Indians' political geography—the diminutive was meant to emphasize their small geographic scale, not necessarily imply an incoherent sovereignty. Victor Golla, *California Indian Languages* (Berkeley: University of California Press, 2011); Kent Lightfoot, *Indians, Missionaries, and Merchants: The Legacy of Colonial Encounters on the California Frontiers* (Berkeley: University of California Press, 2005), 42–43; and S. A. Barrett, "The Ethno-geography of the Pomo and Neighboring Indians," *University of California Publications in American Archaeology and Ethnology* 6, no. 1 (1908): 124–27, 159–61, 182–85, 210–12, 227–28. On Native Californians and American statehood, see Brendan C. Lindsay, *Murder State: California's Native American Genocide, 1846–1873* (Lincoln: University of Nebraska Press, 2012); and Albert L. Hurtado, *Indian Survival on the California Frontier* (New Haven, Conn.: Yale University Press, 1990).

6. Stacey L. Smith, *Freedom's Frontier: California and the Struggle over Unfree Labor, Emancipation, and Reconstruction* (Chapel Hill: University of North Carolina Press, 2013), 114–19; Michael Magliari, "Free State Slavery: Bound Indian Labor and Slave Trafficking in California's Sacramento Valley, 1850–1864," *Pacific Historical Review* 81, no. 2 (April 2012): 155–92 (emphasis added).

7. The People of the State of California v. George Washington, 36 Cal. 658 (1869).

8. William J. Bauer Jr., *We Were All Like Migrant Workers Here: Work, Community, and Memory on California's Round Valley Reservation, 1850–1941* (Chapel Hill: University of North Carolina Press, 2009); and Kevin Adams and Khal Schneider, "'Washington Is a Long Way Off': The 'Round Valley War' and the Limits of Federal Power on a California Indian Reservation," *Pacific Historical Review* 80, no. 4 (October 2011): 557–96.

9. Report of Representative J. K. Luttrell, January 16, 1875, RG 75, Letters Received by the Office of Indian Affairs, 1824–1880, microfilm 234, reel 47, National Archives, Washington, D.C.

10. Schneider, "Making Indian Land," 429, 435–38, 441; and S. Hale to Trustees of M. E. Church, August 8, 1891, vol. 59, 173–74, MCD.

11. Vaught, *Cultivating California,* 60.

12. Manuscript Census of Ukiah Township, Mendocino County, Calif., Tenth Census of the United States, 1880, National Archives microfilm T9, reel 68, California State Library, Sacramento; and Schneider, "Making Indian Land," 436.

13. Sally Russell and Bruce Levine, *Voices and Dreams: A Mendocino County Native American Oral History* (Ukiah: Mendocino County Library, 1991), 15; and C. E. Diddle to Calpella Pete et al., August 24, 1892, vol. 57, 515–16, MCD.

14. Report of Inspector Champion, October 26, 1883, RG 75, Reports of Inspection of the Field Jurisdictions of the Office of Indian Affairs, 1873–1900, microfilm M1070, reel 43, National Archives, Washington, D.C.

15. In 1880, only 450 acres were in hops cultivation in the county. Pioneering hops grower L. F. Long, one of the leading producers, held only 50 cultivated acres. Manuscript Census of Ukiah Township, Mendocino County, Calif., 1880; and Manuscript Census of Agriculture, Mendocino County, Calif., 1880, Non-population Census Schedules for California, 1850–1880, microfilm reel 133, California State Library, Sacramento. See also Robert A. Burchell, "Opportunity and

the Frontier: Wealth-Holding in Twenty-Six Northern California Counties, 1848–1880," *Western Historical Quarterly* 18, no. 2 (April 1987): 177–96.

16. *Republican Press* (Ukiah, Calif.), November 28, 1902; and U.S. Senate, Condition of Certain Indians in California, 77.

17. Hale v. English.

18. Vaught, *Cultivating California,* 42.

19. U.S. Senate, Condition of Certain Indians in California, 79.

20. U.S. Senate, 75–76, 79–80.

21. U.S. Senate, 77–80 (emphasis added).

22. U.S. Senate, 80.

23. *Proceedings of the Fifth Annual Meeting of the Lake Mohonk Conference of Friends of the Indian, Held Sept. 28–30, 1887* (Philadelphia: Sherman and Co. Printers, 1887), 68.

24. U.S. Senate, Condition of Certain Indians in California, 75–77.

25. U.S. Senate, 80–81.

26. Indian Rights Association, *Proceedings of the Third Annual Meeting of the Lake Mohonk Conference of Friends of the Indian* (Philadelphia: Sherman and Co. Printers, 1886), 38.

27. I. C. Reed and Elizabeth Reed to Sam Hale et al., June 24, 1893, vol. 60, 288–90, MCD.

Petitioning Allotment

Collectivist Stories of Indigenous Solidarity

MICHAEL P. TAYLOR

On December 6, 1897, Kānaka ʻŌiwi (Native Hawaiian) leaders James Kaulia and David Kalauokalani joined Queen Liliʻuokalani in Washington, D.C., entrusted with 556 pages of signatures petitioning the unconstitutional and unwanted annexation of Hawaiʻi. Nearly thirty years later, Gertrude Bonnin (Yankton Sioux) and her newly formed National Council of American Indians submitted a petition to Congress aimed at reclaiming treaty rights and outlining the ongoing injustices against newly enfranchised American Indian citizens of the United States.[1] In 1929, at the conclusion of their annual convention, the Alaska Native Brotherhood and Sisterhood appointed five Alaska Native men to investigate "the feasibility of suing the U.S. for our lands."[2] These delegates subsequently petitioned Congress to reverse and provide recompense for the ongoing U.S. encroachment on Alaska Native lands and waters. These are but three of the many petitions that circulated among Indigenous American nations and networks throughout the allotment era, carrying with them thousands of stories that have so far been largely omitted from the Indigenous literary history of allotment because of the still-too-prevalent emphasis on single-author, continental narratives. In response to the ongoing attempts to individualize and privatize Indigenous lands, allotment-era Indigenous petitions evidence the collective rejection of such settler schemes and unequivocally assert tribal sovereignty over Indigenous lands and lifeways.

As each of these three petitions presents from within distinct geographic, cultural, and linguistic spaces of self-governance, allotment has always been much more than a covert turn-of-the-twentieth-century land grab that began with the Dawes Act (1887), ended with the New Deal (1934), and remained within the contiguous United States. Rather, allotment is a foundational settler colonial mindset, an underlying presumption that Eurowestern methods of privatized land, water, and resource ownership are fundamentally superior to collectivist Indigenous relationships with the natural world. Allotment is an ongoing ideology, a persistent "story of Indigenous deficiency,"[3] that has settled itself into the sociopolitical underpinnings of every ongoing effort of U.S. expansion and resource extraction.

Indeed, even Indigenous stories are, at times, allotted, as scholars choose to prioritize individual authors and single-author literary traditions, checkering them away from collectivist practices of community-based literature and literacy: of story making and storytelling. Thus, in addition to recovering, recontextualizing, and retelling the individual stories of allotment that are such crucial acts of "re-membering" allotted peoples to their collective cultural bodies, lands, and waters,[4] reading allotment-era petitions as stories of collective organizing and action recognizes the far-reaching impacts of allotment ideologies while simultaneously documenting hemispheric networks of Indigenous solidarity. As an alternative to the checkerboard maps of U.S. allotment that Daniel Heath Justice (Cherokee) has so effectively reimagined as "cartographic kinscapes,"[5] Indigenous petitions offer resurgent maps of interconnected Indigenous relations, resilient kinscapes that adapted the Indigenous literary and political tradition of petitioning to assert their ongoing commitment to communal relations despite ever-increasing individualist impositions.

In addition to remapping expansive networks of surviving Indigenous relations, allotment-era petitions also expand what Audra Simpson (Mohawk) theorizes as a "cartography of refusal," in their declarations of territorial integrity and their demands to "have one's *political* sovereignty acknowledged and upheld."[6] Among the many individual and collective petitions that circulated throughout the U.S. allotment era, the three petitions I have placed in conversation here emerged from distinct—often depicted as being disconnected—regions, languages, and cultures, as well as specific organizational strategies, governing principles, and imagined Indigenous futures. Each of these petitions is gendered differently, asserts a unique relational tone toward the United States, and builds upon a diverse set of legal and political precedents. Together, however, these petitions map a hemispheric story of solidarity; they coalesce into a collective refusal to relinquish the rights and responsibilities of living on and caring for Indigenous lands and waters. Together, these petitions represent a widespread participation in what Taiaiake Alfred (Kanien'kehá:ka) proposes as "rites of resurgence," of nonviolent conflict "with the hope of recreating the conditions of coexistence."[7]

These allotment-era petitions are but another chapter in the long-standing story of collective Indigenous political awareness and action. Such petitioning has been a critical avenue of voicing collective Indigenous solidarity since long before European contact. In fact, the practice of petitioning dates back at least to the Great Law of the Haudenosaunee Confederacy:

> A bunch of wampum shells on strings, three spans of the hand in
> length, the upper half of the bunch being white and the lower half
> black, . . . shall be a token that the men have combined themselves into
> one head, one body and one thought. . . . The white portion of the shell

strings represent the women and the black portion the men. . . . This
string of wampum vests the people with the right to correct their
erring Lords.[8]

Here strings become the paper and wampum shells the ink used to represent the coming together of "the people" to collectively petition the actions of their leaders.[9] In other words, rather than reading allotment-era petitions as a recognition of U.S. jurisdiction or only as the result of claiming U.S. constitutional rights, these petitions represent a return to what John Mohawk (Seneca) describes as the "traditional way," an Indigenous methodology of organizing to ensure survival,[10] of "bending and swaying but not breaking, adapting and accommodating without compromising what is core to one's being."[11] As the precolonial Haudenosaunee right to petition prescribes, allotment-era petitions present the intersecting stories of "the people" who signed in solidarity to, as Lisa Brooks (Abenaki) suggests, "pose a challenge to narratives of progressive colonial expansion."[12] While allotment ideologies still seek to structure the narratives and resulting realities of Indigenous peoples throughout and beyond the United States as always deficient, divided, or dying, allotment-era petitions posit possibilities of reconstructing such narratives into stories and sustainable systems of survivance.

Palapala Hoopii Kue Hoohuiaina of the Hui Aloha 'Āina

In 1887, ten years prior to Lili'uokalani's palapala hoopii kue hoohuiaina (petition of annexation), her brother King Kalākaua was forced to sign the now infamous Bayonet Constitution of 1887, which transferred suffrage from the common Hawaiian people to wealthy white immigrants and privatized Hawaiian Crown lands.[13] In 1893, white missionaries and planters, empowered by the Bayonet and with the backing of the U.S. Navy, overthrew the Hawaiian Kingdom and proclaimed themselves the Republic of Hawai'i. On June 16, 1897, after four years of persistent lobbying, the newly elected U.S. President William McKinley, alongside leaders of the oligarchical republic, ultimately signed the unconstitutional Treaty of Annexation.

   Rather than react in revolutionary violence, Kānaka 'Ōiwi from across the islands organized into pro–Hawaiian Kingdom activist organizations—the largest being the Hui Aloha 'Āina (Hawaiian Patriotic League)—to peacefully protest annexation, promote the restoration of the monarchy, and demand equal civil rights that were being denied within the new settler colonial Republic.[14] During a mass meeting of aloha 'āina (Hawaiian patriots) held in September, the president of the Hui Aloha 'Āina, James Kaulia (Kānaka 'Ōiwi), declared, "Let us take up the honorable field of struggle, brain against brain. . . . Do not be afraid, be steadfast in aloha for your land and be united in thought. Protest forever the annexation of Hawai'i until the very last aloha 'āina [lives]!"[15] With this call for nonviolent resistance to the unilateral privatization and subsequent theft of Hawaiian lands, leading women of the league boarded ships and canoes to neighboring islands and began to gather signatures of protest. Leaders of the men's branch soon followed. Despite having been unified by militarized force less than ninety years prior, each island welcomed the Hui Aloha ʻĀina representatives with leis and gifts of interisland solidarity. By October 1897, league delegates had gathered over twenty-one thousand signatures, making up more than half of the recorded population of Native Hawaiians at the time.[16] The sister organization of Hui Kālaiʻāina collected an additional seventeen thousand signatures.[17]

The gathering of thirty-eight thousand signatures across an archipelago spanning more than 1,500 miles at a time when Indigenous peoples of the western hemisphere were being cast by politicians and popular media as illiterate, immobile, and vanishing is a significant allotment-era story in itself. It is a textual testament of survival, relationship, solidarity, resistance, and mobilized literacies throughout Hawaiʻi. The petition that solicited so many signatures represents what Noenoe Silva (Kānaka ʻŌiwi) describes as the "hard work and hopes of the whole nation," emphasizing solidarity in the protection of collectively sustained Hawaiian lands and waters.[18] The petition's opening line is particularly telling of the League's underlying effort:

> O Makou, na poe no lakou na inoa malalalo iho, na wahine Hawaii oiwi,
> he poe makaainana a poe noho hoi no ka Apana o _____ ,
> Mokupuni o _____ .
>
> We, the undersigned, native Hawaiian women, citizens and residents of
> the District of _____ , Island of _____ .[19]

Although the league's petition speaks specifically to annexation, not directly addressing U.S. allotment legislation or the privatization of Hawaiian lands, the side-by-side publication of the petition in English and Hawaiian maintains collective land-based relations as the foundation of Hawaiian self-governance. The term ʻāina (land, earth), for example, which appears in the league's name as well as in Kaulia's plea for peaceful protest, also defines the petition's signatories. In English, the undersigned are translated as "native Hawaiian citizens and residents." In Hawaiian, they are "makaainana."

Publishing the petition bilingually emphasizes the league's multiple audiences, appealing to civil rights–supporting non-ʻŌiwi allies in Hawaiʻi and in Congress while also encouraging ʻŌiwi readers to remain committed to collectively preserving and protecting their ʻāina. Whereas the English term *citizen* signifies an "inhabitant" or "legally recognized subject,"[20] the term *makaʻāinana* can signify both "subject" and "citizen," as well as "commoner" or "people that attend to the land."[21] Understanding this underlying distinction between languages, audiences, and cultural commitments positions the 1897 petition against annexation as a representative example of collective

'Ōiwi literary action within a long-standing hemispheric tradition of petitioning, one that reasserts what Susan M. Hill (Haudenosaunee) describes as "familial relationship with the earth."[22] Still today, these petitions represent a moment of interisland mobility and ancestral solidarity in the ongoing fight to protect 'Ōiwi lands and waters against the imperialism of allotment-minded economies and industries. As Kānaka 'Ōiwi scholars Nālani Minton and Silva suggest, regarding the petition's thirty-eight thousand interconnected stories, "Our ancestors' actions to make pono [right] the wrongs of their time infuse us with the mana [spiritual power] to make pono ours. We are the continuation of a living culture: the aloha 'āina of this land."[23]

Petition of the National Council of American Indians

Distinct from the Hui Aloha 'Āina, who gathered within shared genealogies against the imperialist overthrow and unconstitutional annexation of Hawai'i, the National Council of American Indians came together as newly enfranchised citizens of the United States originally representing twenty-one distinct tribal nations at a time when federal Indian policy had shifted from direct military action to nearly thirty years of legislated land theft and systemic starvation. As then U.S. President Theodore Roosevelt extolled in his 1901 State of the Union address, the violence of the underlying allotment mindset was in full force: "The General Allotment Act is a mighty pulverizing engine to break up the tribal mass. It acts directly upon the family and the individual. Under its provisions some sixty thousand Indians have already become citizens of the United States."[24] Twenty-five years after Roosevelt celebrated the strategy of dislocating Indigenous families and their collective rights and responsibilities to Indigenous lands in exchange for U.S. citizenship, founding president of the National Council of American Indians Gertrude Bonnin offered a resurgent response: "It is imperative to join hands, unite our forces, to save our race from dying out, by actual starvation and landlessness."[25] Like the Hui Aloha 'Āina, Bonnin and her National Council accepted the responsibility to organize in order to protect Indigenous lands and livelihoods. They, too, petitioned Congress in a statement of self-governance and continental Indigenous solidarity.

The National Council's 1926 petition begins by echoing the U.S. Declaration of Independence. Rather than declaring independence under God, however, the National Council reminds readers of the Doctrine of Discovery and petitions for an increased U.S. accountability under the Great Spirit: "When in the course of human events a civilized state asserts by virtue of an alleged right of discovery the power of preemption in an aboriginal territory, it assumes before the Great Spirit . . . an obligation for those whose possession it displaces."[26] After rewriting the opening lines of the most foundational document of U.S. liberty, the National Council's petition goes on to draw precedent from a range of texts, including the Proclamation of 1783,[27] two early petitions of the Indian National Confederacy,[28] and various treaties and congressional acts dating back to as early as 1789. Together, these sources intertwine to validate Indigenous land rights and to hold Congress accountable for the ongoing breaching of constitutional treaties.

The petition then reminds Congress of the long history of preallotment, unilateral land-based legislation, including the Preemption Act of 1841, the Railway Acts of 1862 and 1864, and the Homestead Act of 1862,[29] arguing that "no adequate provision [had] been made for the protection of Indians against the lawless horde of land grabbers that was turned loose by those laws upon their lands."[30] While the petition was printed only in English, the National Council distributed at least ten thousand copies of their petition to Indigenous communities and non-Indigenous allies throughout the entire United States in an attempt to reconstruct the narrative of American Indian citizenship to one of the right to resist the ongoing onslaught against Indigenous peoples and lands.[31]

1929 Grand Camp Resolution of the Alaska Native Brotherhood and Sisterhood

Bonnin wrote her impassioned plea to join hands in solidarity against the ongoing theft of Indigenous lands and livelihoods from her D.C. office in February 1927 to Alaska Native Brotherhood (ANB) leader Rev. Sam G. Davis (Tlingit). Two years later, he attended the ANB's annual convention, where the keynote speaker, U.S. District Judge for Alaska James Wickersham, questioned, "Why haven't the Natives been paid a cent for their land?" He immediately answered, "Because nobody has asked to be paid for their land so far."[32]

Following Wickersham's speech, Davis joined other largely Tlingit and Haida convention attendees to discuss issues of landownership and citizenship. They then appointed five men to investigate the possibility and process of seeking redress from the United States for stolen lands. The investigation resulted in the following resolution:

> WHEREAS when the United States government took over Alaska from our forefathers, it was a land of plenty, with rivers teeming with all kinds of salmon, the woods with fur and game animals, and forests were free to us; and
>
> WHEREAS the United States government has locked up the forests so that what was formerly ours must now be purchased from a government that gave us nothing for it; and
>
> WHEREAS our fish streams have been taken from us by the United States Government so that we can [n]either fish nor live near our ancient fish streams, not only because in the changing civilization the same

Government has taught us to live like civilized people and not on a diet of fish like our fathers, but also because our Government without giving us a hearing has prohibited us from catching fish at our ancient fish streams for our support; and . . .

THEREFORE BE IT RESOLVED, . . . that Congress be asked to delegate a committee of fair minded men to investigate our condition, with money to get the evidence, uninfluenced by the different bureaus which are directly responsible for our condition; and

BE IT FURTHER RESOLVED, that copies of this resolution be sent to each Senator and Representative of the Congress of the United States with the hope that some day one may be touched to ask justice for us.[33]

With the approval of this resolution, the Alaska Native Brotherhood and Sisterhood transformed the conference resolution into a petition representing the protest of five thousand Alaska Native individuals working and writing collectively against the historic and ongoing theft of Alaska Native lands and waters.

Throughout their petition, the Alaska Native Brotherhood and Sisterhood speak through a communal voice, maintaining the rights and responsibilities that governed their collective land- and water-based relationships, thereby rejecting the allotment mindset of privatization. The petition refers to "*our* forefathers," forests that were "formerly *ours*," "*our* fish streams," "*our* ancient fish streams," and so on. The petition also relies on this communal voice to represent those affected by and those speaking out against the U.S. government. It describes "forests [that] were free to *us*," "a government that gave *us* nothing," waterways "taken from *us* by the United States Government so that *we* can [n]either fish nor live." The Alaska Native Brotherhood and Sisterhood then declared: "*We* petition . . . to ask justice for *us*."[34] Rather than allowing themselves and their stories to be broken up, these five thousand Alaska Native men and women, out of the approximately thirty thousand recorded Alaska Native population at the time who made up the *we, our,* and *us* of the Grand Camp Resolution, asserted their collective rights to their unceded lands and waters. They chose to interweave their individual stories into a collective story of Alaska Native solidarity.[35]

Like the Hui Aloha 'Āina and the National Council of American Indians, the Alaska Native Brotherhood and Sisterhood focused its 1929 petition on the protection of Alaska Native land and disregarded unilaterally appointed territorial government officials to directly address every individual member of Congress. The petition was also published to the public and distributed to Alaska Native Brotherhood and Sisterhood members in the organization's official newspaper, the *Alaska Fisherman*.[36] Although it has been so far impossible to trace the exact networks of distribution, readership, and individual congressional responses, this 1929 petition became the catalyst for the collective action that placed the Alaska Native Brotherhood and Sisterhood on a six-year path toward what is now known as the Tlingit and Haida Jurisdictional Act (1935), which paved the way for the subsequent Alaska Native Claims Settlement Act (1971), the most substantial land claims act up to that point in U.S. history.[37]

Interconnected Indigenous Solidarities

In 1897, ancestors of the Alaska Native Brotherhood and Sisterhood sent petitions and representatives to Washington, D.C., to protest the unlawful erasure of Alaska Native sovereignty, land, and civil rights in Alaska.[38] It was the same year that that Queen Liliʻuokalani's delegation from nearly three thousand miles across the Pacific traveled to D.C. to petition Congress against the illegal annexation of Hawaiʻi. As Danika Medak-Saltzman (Turtle Mountain Chippewa) argues, it is a colonial presumption to imagine that these two parties—as well as the many other Indigenous delegates, leaders, performers, and others, who were continually writing to and visiting D.C. and other epicenters of colonial enterprise at the turn of the twentieth century—did so in isolation from one another.[39] Such colonial pretense elides the ever-broadening recoveries and grounded reimaginings of trans-Indigenous relations and solidarity that have existed since long before European contact. Like the National Council of American Indians—which, as founding secretary Raymond Bonnin (Yankton Sioux) described, "was started by all Indian delegates from 21 different tribes who were on tribal business [in D.C.] but who saw the advantages to be had in organization"[40]—Indigenous delegations from throughout the imperial borders of the United States were conscious of and, at times, directly interacted with one another in D.C. and elsewhere. Their resulting local and intertribal petitions assure contemporary readers of existing networks of Indigenous solidarity that refuse the dominant allotment narratives of widespread Indigenous dislocation.

The 1897 petition of the Hui Aloha ʻAina, the 1926 petition of the National Council of American Indians, and the Alaska Native Brotherhood and Sisterhood's 1929 petition are but three of the many petitions that have been and continue to be written by Indigenous communities. Together, they represent the interconnected solidarities of well over forty thousand Indigenous individuals who chose to share collectivist stories against both the literal legislation and the spreading allotment ideology of American individualism. Each Indigenous collective petitioned from within specific and shared ancestral and ongoing Indigenous literary traditions that are committed to collectively preserving and sustaining Indigenous lands and lifeways. Just as the tribal delegates that came together to form the National Council of American Indians each represented nation-specific histories, knowledges, languages, priorities, protocols, and visions for Indigenous futures, each Indigenous collective petitioned from within specific and shared ancestral and ongoing literary traditions that remain committed to collectively preserving and sustaining Indigenous lands and lifeways.

As such, these petitions participate within a long-standing Indigenous literary tradition that has been, so far, deemed by the allotment-minded models of Eurowestern literary studies as not "literary" enough to be read as literature and not "traditional" enough to be read as Indigenous. As Caroline Wigginton describes, Indigenous petitions "assert their intellectual right to tell their own stories. They assert their ability to construct their own versions of history."[41] But not only history. Like today's burgeoning body of published Indigenous creativity and critical scholarship, these petitions assert Indigenous desires, abilities, and choices to imagine and direct Indigenous futures in relationship with the lands and waters of both their ancestors and their posterity. These three petitions are more of what Brooks describes as the "word[s] that could set [Indigenous peoples'] creative deliberation into motion."[42] They are the kinetic stories of solidarity written to resist allotment ideologies and actions that attempt to render Indigenous peoples as static.

NOTES

1. President Calvin Coolidge signed the Indian Citizenship Act, or Snyder Act, on June 2, 1924.
2. Alaska Native Brotherhood, "Grand Camp Alaska Native Brotherhood Convention," November 18, 1929, box 2, folder 1, MS/017, Judson Brown Papers, 1920–96, Sealaska Heritage Institute Archives, Juneau, Alaska, 6–9. The five men were Ralph Young (Tlingit), Charles Newton (Tlingit), Frank G. Johnson (Tlingit), George Haldane (Haida), and Samuel Jackson (Tlingit).
3. Daniel Heath Justice, *Why Indigenous Literatures Matter* (Waterloo, Ontario: Wilfrid Laurier University Press, 2018), 2.
4. Janice Acoose, "Iskwewak Kah' Ki Yaw Ni Wahkomakanak: Re-membering Being to Signifying Female Relations," in *Learn, Teach, Challenge: Approaching Indigenous Literatures,* ed. Deanna Reder and Linda M. Morra (Waterloo, Ontario: Wilfrid Laurier University Press, 2016), 19–36.
5. Justice, *Why Indigenous Literatures Matter,* 197.
6. Audra Simpson, *Mohawk Interruptus: Political Life across the Borders of Settler States* (Durham, N.C.: Duke University Press, 2014), 33, 11.
7. Taiaiake Alfred, *Wasáse: Indigenous Pathways of Action and Freedom* (Toronto: University of Toronto Press, 2009), 21–22.
8. Arthur C. Parker, *The Constitution of the Five Nations* (Albany: University of the State of New York, 1916), 46.
9. As a comparison, the Magna Carta (1215) reserved the right to petition solely for nobility.
10. John Mohawk, *Thinking in Indian: A John Mohawk Reader,* ed. (Golden, Colo.: Fulcrum Publishing, 2010), 212.
11. Alfred, *Wasáse,* 29.
12. Lisa Brooks, *The Common Pot: The Recovery of Native Space in the Northeast* (Minneapolis: University of Minnesota Press, 2008), 43.

13. Noenoe K. Silva, *Aloha Betrayed: Native Hawaiian Resistance to American Colonialism* (Durham, N.C.: Duke University Press, 2004), 126–27.

14. Hui Aloha 'Āina, "Ke Kumukanawai," *Ka Leo o ka Lahui,* March 22, 1893, 3.

15. Noenoe K. Silva, "The 1897 Petitions Protesting Annexation," University of Hawai'i at Manoa Libraries Special Collections, 1998, accessed September 12, 2018.

16. Silva, "1897 Petitions Protesting Annexation."

17. ku'ualoha ho'omanawanui, *Voices of Fire: Reweaving the Literary Lei of Pele and Hi'aka* (Minneapolis: University of Minnesota Press, 2014), 21.

18. Silva, "1897 Petitions Protesting Annexation."

19. Silva, "1897 Petitions Protesting Annexation." The men's petition was identical to the women's petition with the omission of "women." It reads: "We the undersigned, native Hawaiian citizens."

20. OED Online, s.v. "citizen (*n.* 1, 2)," accessed October 28, 2018, https://www.oed.com/view/Entry/33513.

21. Nā Puke Wehewehe 'Ōlelo Hawai'i (Hawaiian Dictionaries), s.v. "Maka'āinana," accessed December 4, 2015, http://wehewehe.org.

22. Susan M. Hill, *The Clay We Are Made Of: Haudenosaunee Land Tenure on the Grand River* (Winnipeg: University of Manitoba Press, 2017), 4.

23. Nālani Minton and Noenoe K. Silva, *Kū'ē: The Hui Aloha 'Āina Anti-Annexation Petitions, 1897–1898* (Honolulu: Nālani Minton and Noenoe K. Silva, 1998), viii.

24. Theodore Roosevelt, State of the Union Address, December 3, 1901, printed as "The Annual Message of the President," in *Papers Relating to the Foreign Relations of the United States* (Washington, D.C.: Government Printing Office, 1902).

25. Gertrude Bonnin to S. G. Davis, February 15, 1927, box 3, folder 14, MSS 1704, Gertrude Bonnin and Raymond Bonnin Collection, 20th–21st Century Western and Mormon Americana, L. Tom Perry Special Collections, Harold B. Lee Library, Brigham Young University.

26. Gertrude Simmons Bonnin, "Petition of the National Council of American Indians," in *Help Indians Help Themselves: The Later Writings of Gertrude Simmons Bonnin (Zitkala-Ša),* ed. P. Jane Hafen (Lubbock: Texas Tech University Press, 2020), 250–76.

27. The Proclamation of 1783 declared that the federal government must consent to any extinguishment of aboriginal title to Indigenous lands.

28. As P. Jane Hafen (Taos Pueblo) explains in *Help Indians Help Themselves,* the Indian National Confederacy was a multinational, fluctuating coalition that began as early as 1763 and moved through various stages that worked first to resist the United States during the American Revolution and then to resist U.S. claims to Indigenous lands after the retreat of Britain. Hafen, *Help Indians Help Themselves,* 352.

29. As Lisi Krall describes, the Preemption Act and Homestead Act allowed individuals to purchase or work 160 acres of unsurveyed land. Lisi Krall, *Proving Up: Domesticating Land in U.S. History* (Albany: SUNY Press, 2011), 58. The Pacific Railway Acts of 1862 and 1864 provided federal support to build the first transcontinental railroad and telegraph. John P. Davis, "The Union Pacific Railway," *Annals of the American Academy of Political and Social Science* 8, no. 2 (1896): 47–91.

30. Bonnin, "Petition of the National Council of American Indians," 255.

31. Gertrude Bonnin to Thomas F. Bayard, April 1926, box 3, folder 4, MSS 1704, Gertrude Bonnin and Raymond Bonnin Collection, 20th–21st Century Western and Mormon Americana, L. Tom Perry Special Collections, Harold B. Lee Library, Brigham Young University.

32. Alaska Native Brotherhood, "Grand Camp Alaska Native Brotherhood Convention," 5.

33. Alaska Native Brotherhood, "Grand Camp Resolution at the Haines 1929 Alaska Native Brotherhood Convention," November 25, 1929, series 1, box 2, folder 15, MS/007, Walter A. Soboleff Papers, 1920–2009, Sealaska Heritage Institute Archives, Juneau, Alaska.

34. Alaska Native Brotherhood, "Grand Camp Alaska Native Brotherhood Convention," 25–29 (emphasis added).

35. The 1930 U.S. Census Bureau entitled "Indians of Pure and Mixed Blood, by Sex, Age, and Linguistic Stock, for Alaska" accounted for 29,983 total Alaska Natives, including 15,359 men and 14,624 women.

36. The *Alaska Fisherman* was the Alaska Native Brotherhood and Sisterhood's official newspaper, published from 1923 to 1932 in Juneau.

37. The Alaska Native Claims Settlement Act also simultaneously discontinued the Alaska Native Allotment Act, which lasted nearly forty years beyond the General Allotment Act.

38. As but one example of earlier Alaska Native petitions, see Anatolii Kamenskii's *Tlingit Indians of Alaska* (Fairbanks: University of Alaska Press, 1985) for a discussion of the 1897 "Petition to the President of the United States," originally published in English and Russian in the New York–based *Russian Orthodox American Messenger.*

39. Danika Medak-Saltzman, "Transnational Indigenous Exchange: Rethinking Global Interactions of Indigenous Peoples at the 1904 St. Louis Exposition," *American Quarterly* 62, no. 3 (September 2010): 591–615. To begin further discussion of early trans-Indigenous relations in the continental United States and the Pacific, see Lisa Brooks's *Our Beloved Kin: A New History of King Philip's War* (New Haven, Conn.: Yale University Press, 2018) and Alice Te Punga Somerville's *Once Were Pacific: Māori Connections to Oceania* (Minneapolis: University of Minnesota Press, 2012).

40. Raymond Bonnin to Reverend Robert Clarkson, March 31, 1927, box 3, folder 15, MSS 1704, p. 1, Gertrude and Raymond Bonnin Collection, L. Tom Perry Special Collections, Harold B. Lee Library, Brigham Young University.

41. Caroline Wigginton, "Extending Root and Branch: Community Regeneration in the Petitions of Samson Occom," *Studies in American Indian Literatures* 20, no. 4 (2008): 21.

42. Lisa Brooks, "The Constitution of the White Earth Nation: A New Innovation in a Longstanding Indigenous Literary Tradition," *Studies in American Indian Literatures* 23, no. 4 (2011): 58.

I Do What I Do for the Language

Land and Choctaw Language and Cultural Revitalization

MEGAN BAKER

There are now empty fields in the place the Oklahoma Choctaw community called Rufe used to be. Tall grasses sway where rows of houses used to stand. The old path leading to the first Choctaw Academy Church is still visible, yet inaccessible because of the fence cordoning off the property. Just a few miles over, where a Choctaw community called Slim used to be, a Choctaw woman named Fannie Gibson and her descendants would have held their allotments. While not her father's whole 160-acre homestead allotment, she would have held title to a parcel of his allotment after it had been divided up between her and her siblings. But because Fannie was born after her father died, she was left landless. Gibson lived with her mother until she married and moved to the nearby lumber company town, Wright City. Before the establishment of the settler town, though, the U.S. Army Corps of Engineers induced families to sell their lands in Slim to make way for Pine Creek Lake, which would flood the area. Holdouts were forced to sell their lands eventually and Slim passed into memory. The community only lived on through the people who grew up there and talked about it. And for all the trouble of getting Choctaws to vacate the area, the area was never flooded as the Army Corps said it would be. Today, the land where Slim used to be has since been sold off to new landowners—non-Choctaws. All that really remains of Rufe and Slim are the old, well-worn paths, fenced off from any passing Choctaw who might want to visit the old community.

Allotment critically shaped the lives of people like Fannie Gibson, her family, and her descendants. When implemented in Choctaw Nation, allotment introduced a new economic arrangement in Choctaw territory that led many individuals to lose their assigned lands. Once allotment was finalized and everyone on the Dawes Rolls had been allocated their parcels, Choctaw land loss gradually became understood as a consequence of individual decisions rather than the effect of a policy that created the conditions that induced people to make difficult decisions regarding their allotments and contributed to a collective loss of land. In its attempt to assimilate Choctaws into a settler set of property relations, allotment dictated and reshaped the social geographies of families. Nevertheless, while faced with immense land loss that began with

Choctaw removal from their ancestral homelands and continued in Indian Territory, some Choctaws came to tie this history with a steadfast resistance to surrendering their language and culture, which uphold their political distinctiveness. For many Choctaw speakers and learners, speaking Chahta *anumpa,* or Choctaw language, is about asserting the primacy of a Choctaw way of life that is also tied to their status as members of a sovereign nation that the United States has sought to assimilate to secure land.

Drawing on ethnographic and archival research on Choctaw allotment, I share a story about the relationship between Fannie Gibson and her granddaughter Teresa "Teri" Billy to illustrate how Choctaw women, as intellectuals and theorists of post-Removal Choctaw life, have understood land dispossession and attacks on their Nation's sovereignty and how they have passed that knowledge to later generations. Equally as important, I highlight how these women have used Chahta anumpa and cultural revitalization to maintain Choctaw political distinctiveness as part of a response to ongoing land loss. In treating Gibson as a historian of Choctaw land dispossession and by taking Gibson's stories and warnings to her granddaughter as enactment of felt theory,[1] I highlight how her life experiences are an archive of historical knowledge. That knowledge then informed her refusal to allow Choctaw political distinctiveness to disappear in what is now Oklahoma.[2] Not only do Gibson's stories of land dispossession provide a robust account of Choctaw land relations in understudied rural southeastern Oklahoma, she also shows a particular significance of Chahta anumpa to individuals without land. Lastly, her stories about Choctaw land loss and white encroachment reveal her intimate knowledge of its impact on everyday life.

Perhaps since the possibility of owning her own land had been foreclosed early in her life, Fannie Gibson understood the impact of not holding title to land and its implications for Choctaws' life possibilities. Growing up in the 1910s, Gibson lived through a turbulent period in which Congress squabbled over federal laws regulating Choctaw land titles and restrictions. This created uncertainty for Choctaws who received little information regarding the shenanigans of Washington, D.C.[3] In rural Slim, she witnessed friends and families lose their land to white settlers who squatted on their lands or because they sold land to put food on the table on account of the limited economic opportunities in the region. When she raised her granddaughter, Gibson instilled not only an awareness about land dispossession and its ramifications for Choctaw lives but also a critique of the white settlers who facilitated that loss. When reflecting on her grandmother's life, Billy credited her as a keen observer of the world. She recalled:

> She would always say, "Choctaws owned all this land and the white people
> knew what they were doing." They were probably doing encroachment—
> which is right and fair if you stay there long enough and develop the
> land. That's what it's all about: developing the land. She said Choctaws

owned saddles, all the tools that it would take to have a farm, cultivate everything, and the large acreage. Then the white people would come and settle in the corner and say, "If you'd let us grow crops here or let us grow corn or whatever, we'll share with you." [My grandmother] said she saw as a child that lot of Choctaws worked the land. But then slowly became people who—because of this encroachment—didn't have to work so hard no more.[4]

For Gibson of the Slim community, Choctaw people's biggest problem was the white settlers who came to Choctaw territory, encroached on their lands, and dispossessed them of that land using a Lockean logic of productivity.[5] Land squatting, as she described here, was one method of taking Choctaw land and homes, and this informed her lifelong distrust of white settlers. In pointing out how white settlers lived and farmed on a portion of a Choctaw allotment that enabled them to claim squatter's rights, Gibson drew attention to the Lockean logic in which labor legitimated a man's claiming of land as his property. And although Choctaws held title to their allotments, they still faced the danger of losing that land if they did not labor over the land, which would then be sanctioned by Oklahoma law.[6] The same system of U.S. law that removed Choctaws to this new land now also authorized and sanctioned settler claims to Choctaw land. Gibson looked out for others by warning them that white people could not be trusted because they would take advantage of Choctaw generosity. Such distrust of white people continues to circulate in informal advice today, since squatting laws have not changed.

Adverse possession laws are a critical site of Oklahoma Choctaw land loss where responsibility to prevent squatting rests on individual landowners. Indians holding land title have to be proactive about defending their land. When I spoke about my own family's restricted land with an Oklahoma lawyer who frequently handles Indian allotment probate cases, he recommended fencing off the land and periodically checking in on it to watch for squatters. He also recommended maintaining the land in visible ways like mowing the lawn along the property lines.[7] In dispensing this bit of advice, this called to mind the well-maintained lawns in the middle of the forests I could always recall seeing throughout my life. Perhaps such stringent land mowing was part of Choctaws internalizing the need to demonstrate ownership through land improvement—even though their 1830 removal treaty had already secured these lands.

Between the 1898 Curtis Act that authorized Choctaw allotment and Oklahoma statehood in 1907, the status of Choctaw landownership was in flux and uncertain.[8] Throughout this period, white settlers married Choctaw women to secure access to their lands, badgered the Bureau of Indian Affairs for allotments, and squatted on land to secure Choctaw land for themselves, claiming territory that was supposed to be Choctaws' homeland. Responding to these changes, Choctaw national attorneys filed numerous lawsuits in the U.S. Court of Claims for compensation for treaty violations and land losses. Gibson was born in 1908, and she would see massive changes over her lifetime: the increased influx of white settlers and their growing influence, the growth of nearby railroad towns like Idabel and Broken Bow, and steady Choctaw land dispossession by individuals and lumber companies that legally and illegally purchased allotments for the valuable timber. Struggle over land was a defining feature of Choctaw life in Oklahoma despite the 1830 Treaty of Dancing Rabbit Creek that promised Indian territory as a land where Choctaws would "exist as a nation." Despite massive land dispossession and the steady influx of white settlers overwhelming Choctaw community life in the region, Gibson asserted Choctaw distinctiveness by only speaking Chahta anumpa, embodying a commitment to Choctaw social and political life in Oklahoma.

Deep in and around the Kiamichi Mountains in southeastern Oklahoma are the old Choctaw communities from which Gibson and Billy hail. This region, now geographically contained within the county borders of McCurtain County, is well known among Oklahoma Choctaws as having a large concentration of full-blooded Choctaws, as well as the majority of living Choctaw first-language speakers (individuals whose first language was Chahta) relative to other counties.[9] While there are Chahta anumpa speakers and teachers who live throughout the Nation's boundaries and across the United States, the history of the Chahta anumpa in McCurtain County is unique and critical to the history of the language's rigorous documentation and relative vitality.

After the U.S. government forced Choctaws to relocate to Indian Territory, Choctaw settlement patterns in the new homelands had a lasting impact on the course of history for Chahta anumpa and its speakers. Many full-blood families stayed in this southeastern corner of Choctaw treaty territory, while white-Choctaw mixed-blood families settled westward, where they lived with or alongside white settler communities. Full-bloods of this region composed the bulk of what is now McCurtain County, where the majority only spoke Chahta. It is here that the land itself provided the conditions in which Chahta anumpa would flourish. The dense forests and rocky mountain roads kept Choctaws in relative geographical isolation from the white settlers who came in and settled in the southern portion of the county. Up until the mid-1900s, these Choctaw communities largely kept to themselves with families venturing into town only when needed and where elders recalled white store owners speaking Chahta to conduct business.

Furthermore, this physical isolation enabled Choctaws to transform the colonial institution of the church into centers where Chahta anumpa and cultural practices thrived. The Choctaws who settled in what is now McCurtain County were accompanied by Cyrus Byington, a Presbyterian missionary who lived with them in the homelands. Byington, in his effort to convert Choctaws, learned Choctaw with the help of numerous parishioners. In the new Choctaw homelands, he developed a church circuit where he delivered sermons and provided medical aid. Byington's periodic visits facilitated churches becoming a central hub for community gathering—especially after allotment decades later. Although allotments separated out extended families into individual family plots, they would come together again at their family church. Gathering at church allowed families to mitigate the distance that allotment had instituted. In his efforts to convert Choctaws, Byington assembled dictionaries and translated the Bible into Chahta anumpa to deliver sermons and proselytize.[10] Using Byington, Choctaws developed the language's written form, which they later taught in their local, Choctaw Nation–run schools. This emphasis on literacy was also passed on to later generations, including Gibson, who used to make her granddaughter practice Choctaw by reading and writing scripture.

While Chahta anumpa was key to maintaining community coherence, it also made Choctaws vulnerable to white settlers seeking allotted lands. One major case of fraud was discovered in 1907 when the BIA Commissioner of the Five Tribes investigated a case involving white settlers Eli, Elmer, and Charles Williams. They developed a scheme that targeted Choctaw-only speakers to transfer title of their lands to them. Using an interpreter who organized Choctaws to sign legal documents that he himself did not understand, the Williamses secured power of attorney, which allowed them to sell, convey, and transfer Choctaws' land in fee simple to their discretion. Many of the affected were full-bloods from Rufe, Valliant, Lukfata, Garvin, and Alikchi—the communities surrounding Gibson's home in Slim.[11] Timber companies, particularly the Dierks Lumber and Coal Company, secured Choctaw allotments in a similar way to gain access to the valuable timber.[12] Gibson heard these warnings about signing documents and land loss circulated among community members and this informed her and others' distrust of white people.

The history of this region and how Chahta anumpa thrived in it is key to understanding how Chahta anumpa came to stand for Choctaws' understanding of what it means to be Choctaw. Being Choctaw was not just about speaking Choctaw and eating *banaha* (a type of shuck bread); it also meant living with a constant threat of losing their land and homes. This was intertwined in the lessons that Fannie Gibson taught her granddaughter. In turn, speaking Chahta anumpa was about a Choctaw way of life, which was also shaped by a history of continual land dispossession. By speaking only Chahta anumpa, Gibson enacted a refusal to let the language and the way of life tied to it to fade away or disappear. This was a lasting lesson that would in turn shape the life trajectory of her granddaughter's career and the Chahta language revitalization that she would later usher in with her husband, Curtis "Tody" Billy.

Today, Teri Billy is the assistant director of Chahta Anumpa Aiikhvna, or Choctaw School of Language, and works to ensure that there are new generations of Choctaw speakers. She attended Southeastern Oklahoma State University to join the then-new

Choctaw bilingual program. After over twenty-eight years of teaching elementary school, which included accolades like Broken Bow's Teacher of the Year and a nomination for Oklahoma State Teacher of the Year, Billy took her teaching experiences to the then-small Choctaw Nation language program. In 2003, the director of education called Billy and offered her a job to oversee the early childhood component of the Choctaw language department. At the time, they were developing a curriculum and felt that Billy's first-language speaker status and extensive experience creating her own lesson plans would make her invaluable to the project. Billy took the opportunity. In her time working for Choctaw Nation, she helped the language program transition into a school. As assistant director, she is now responsible for the language program in the Nation's Head Starts, community language classes, college-credit language classes, and the high school language program, where nineteen instructors teach Chahta anumpa in Oklahoma public schools. Students learn not only language and culture but also Choctaw perspectives on Oklahoma history, which often glorifies and monumentalizes Indigenous land dispossession through celebrations and reenactments of land runs.

Teri Billy's work is a testament not only to her deep commitment to Choctaw language and its people but also to her relationship with her grandmother. Because Billy's mother worked away from home to support her family, Gibson raised Billy alongside her children. Billy and her aunt Eleanor Caldwell, now a famed Choctaw painter, describe Gibson as a fiercely intelligent woman. Growing up, Billy only spoke Choctaw because that was all that her grandmother spoke. Before going to elementary school, the only exposure to English she had was when her aunts and uncle would speak it because they were in school. When she started school, Billy saw her friends start to turn away from speaking Choctaw. In an interview she stated: "I couldn't get away from it because it didn't matter where I went: the post office, the grocery store. Wherever, [Gibson] would say 'Teri, go get this, go get that' so I couldn't pretend that I didn't know Choctaw. I couldn't get away with it publicly."[13] Billy saw herself as a contrast to her peers because she never felt that she could act like she did not speak Choctaw, since that was the only way that her grandmother communicated with her. As she watched her peers around her giving up Choctaw for English, Billy made a conscious decision to do otherwise. She continued: "And another part of that was I didn't want to dishonor her. That was the language that she was comfortable in, our home, and it was everything to her and I never would have turned my back and no, there's no way." Language, not only a mode of communication, also stood in for the deep and storied history of Choctaw struggle in Indian Territory.

When Gibson's daughter got a job in Lawton in 1965, Gibson and Billy followed her there. Western Oklahoma, they found, was vastly different from their home in McCurtain County. Gibson was quickly homesick. She missed singing Choctaw hymns in church and speaking Chahta anumpa with everyone. After three years, the two moved back to Wright City. Returning in this way, Gibson demonstrated her commitment to living her life as a Choctaw woman in their home territory, participating in Choctaw church life where Chahta hymn-singing and conversation were part of the fabric of daily life. Language speaking and going to Choctaw churches are often understood as part of Choctaw culture or being Choctaw. In a place where white settlers attempted to eliminate Choctaw modes of being by targeting the language and communities themselves via the missions and allotment, it is important to see how language and culture are political acts and about political commitments.[14] Within the settler colonial society that is the United States, Choctaw ways of life—which Choctaws themselves often understood as living in accordance with their particular culture—should be understood as a political orientation, since their life in Oklahoma was created because of their membership as part of Indigenous polities that had to engage an American settler state set on their political elimination.

While Gibson understood limited English—she often verified with her children whether her translations of white people speaking to her were correct (and they typically were)—she actively did not speak it. This suggests that for her, being Choctaw was the only way of life that she cared for, and in that she refused the settler techniques of impinging upon the well-being of that world. She keenly understood and had a critique of the settlers who took from Choctaws. Gibson refused to accept the legitimacy of a settler narrative of history and articulated that through her linguistic choice. Only speaking Chahta foregrounded the importance of being Choctaw, which was grounded in the particularity of Choctaw experiences and the conditions that produced it. Gibson's knowledge of the world, acquired through her experiences growing up and living in southeastern Oklahoma, hinged upon land dispossession that shaped the trajectory of Choctaws' lives in the region. Her life experiences taught her that there was something about being Choctaw that made them targets, and as the lessons she passed onto her granddaughter would show, this was contingent on land itself. In spite of the economic costs, to Gibson there was something more meaningful about being Choctaw. She insisted on speaking Choctaw every day to ensure that traditional ways continued on to the next generation. Learning from her grandmother's refusal through language, Billy carries on that legacy of asserting Choctaw lifeways and sovereignty through her life's work with the language.

As the arc of Teri Billy's career and everyday labors demonstrates, she has dedicated herself to work in service of Choctaw people. Growing up, Billy witnessed increasing economic disparity between Choctaws and non-Choctaws in McCurtain County. To mitigate this inequality, she worked to ensure that Choctaw children had the same opportunities as white children. Simultaneously, she did not want improving one's economic lot in life to come at the expense of being Choctaw and she found a way to ensure Choctaw life passed on to the next generation. After Teri and her husband, Tody, graduated college, they returned home and worked for Broken Bow public schools, helping Choctaw-speaking children learn English and integrating Chahta culture into classrooms. They continued this work with their second careers as teachers and administrators for Chahta Anumpa Aiikhvna. Not only do they ensure the language's survival, but they teach it to Choctaw and non-Choctaw students alike in Oklahoma public schools. Teaching within the Nation's territorial boundaries via satellite teaching, they remind Oklahomans of Choctaws' claim to their treaty territory and how their nation has not diminished—even if many individuals no longer own the land itself. Furthermore, the existence of the schools underscores the strength and vitality of contemporary Choctaw political life, particularly since such an extensive statewide program would not be possible without Choctaw Nation's growing economic and political power in state politics.[15] Through this work, Teri and Tody importantly remind settlers across southeastern Oklahoma that they live in Choctaw territory.

Land dispossession produced the injustices that both Billy and Gibson lived with throughout their lives. These lived experiences led them to theorize the relationship between whiteness and Choctaw land dispossession to their status as members of a Choctaw polity. In this essay, I argued that their actions to assert the importance of Choctaw language are a mode of counteracting attacks on Choctaw nationhood through the theft of land. In Gibson's warnings about white settlers and theft through the telling of stories marking the Choctaw landscape, she reveals her recognition of the structured way that land loss continues to shape Choctaw life. In her active decision to only speak Choctaw, Gibson enacted a form of refusal through language that asserted the preeminence of Choctaw nationhood—a political alternative to the society that settlers had erected around them. She came to embody this history and taught it to those around her, particularly her granddaughter Teri Billy, who has been instrumental in Chahta anumpa's revitalization and resurgence through her careers as a teacher, language curriculum specialist, and now assistant director of Chahta Anumpa Aiikhvna.

In their new homelands, Oklahoma Choctaws persist as a polity and have found avenues for maintaining Choctaw distinctiveness. While the landscape of McCurtain County has had critical bearing on the institutions where Chahta anumpa and culture was maintained, Teri and Tody's work as Choctaw educators has brought the language and culture to new heights and audiences, expanding people's knowledge. As demonstrated by the new generations of students of the language and cultural programs that the Billys organized, as well as those returning to the language after years of silence, Choctaw politics will continue to live on through the language, education, and culture—further strengthening Choctaw sovereignty.

NOTES

1. Dian Million, "Felt Theory: An Indigenous Feminist Approach to Affect and History," *Wicazo Sa Review* 24, no. 2 (2009): 53–76.

2. Audra Simpson, "On Ethnographic Refusal: Indigeneity, 'Voice,' and Colonial Citizenship," *Junctures* 9 (2007): 67–80.

3. "Indian Lands, Taxation of, 1913–30," folder 3, box 7, Hampton Tucker Collections, Western History Collections, University of Oklahoma, Norman, Okla.

4. Teresa Billy, interview with author, September 12, 2016.

5. Indigenous land dispossession was largely premised upon the idea that Native people did not own land because they failed to make land productive. Under the Lockean logic, land mixed with work becomes transformed into property. For more, see K-Sue Park, "Money, Mortgages, and the Conquest of America," *Law & Social Inquiry* 41, no. 4 (2016): 1006–35.

6. Robert Nichols, "Theft Is Property! The Recursive Logic of Dispossession," *Political Theory* 46, no. 11 (2018): 3–28.

7. Peary Robinson, personal communication with author, July 21, 2016.

8. Given the stipulations of their removal treaty, Choctaws were exempt from the Dawes Act. Choctaw allotment had to be negotiated separately.

9. Billy, interview, 2016. Anthropologist Sandra Faiman-Silva also notes: "Long home to traditionally oriented Choctaws, [the McCurtain and Pushmataha County timber region] still is the largest number of full blood Choctaws of any Choctaw Nation county." See Sandra Faiman-Silva, *Choctaws at the Crossroads: The Political Economy of Class and Culture in the Oklahoma Timber Region* (Lincoln: University of Nebraska Press, 1997), 103; and Shelia Kirven, "Chahta Anumpa Ikhvnanchi Yvt Im Okla Isht Atokoli Okchalinchi," *Biskinik,* May 2020, https://www.choctawnation.com/sites/default/files/May%20Biskinik.pdf. Additionally, the high concentration of Choctaw first-language speakers and full-bloods in this region led linguists to focus their studies of Choctaw language in this region. See Robert S. Williams, "Language Obsolescence and Structural Change: The Case of Oklahoma Choctaws" (PhD diss., UCLA, 1995).

10. Louis Coleman, *Cyrus Byington: Missionary and Choctaw Linguist* (Kearney, Nebr.: Morris Publishing, 1996).

11. Department of the Interior Commissioner to the Five Civilized Tribes, Decimal 054 (Councils—Acts of Tribal Council), Bureau of Indian Affairs Central Classified Files, 1907–1939, RG 75, National Archives, Washington D.C.

12. Faiman-Silva, *Choctaws at the Crossroads.*

13. Billy, interview, 2016.

14. See Glen S. Coulthard, *Red Skin, White Masks: Rejecting the Colonial Politics of Recognition* (Minneapolis: University of Minnesota Press, 2014); Elizabeth A. Povinelli, *The Cunning of Recognition: Indigenous Alterities and the Making of Australian Multiculturalism* (Durham, N.C.: Duke University Press, 2008); and Audra Simpson, *Mohawk Interruptus: Political Life across the Borders of Settler States* (Durham, N.C.: Duke University Press, 2014).

15. Megan Baker, "(Re)Developing Sovereignty: Choctaw Reconfigurations of Culture and Politics through Economic Development in Oklahoma" (master's thesis, UCLA, 2017).

Tse Wahzhazhe

RUBY HANSEN MURRAY

In the fall of 2017, I was organizing a visit to John Joseph Matthew's stone cabin on the Tallgrass Prairie when chief Geoffrey Standing Bear invited me to see the first bison delivered to the Bluestem Ranch, a 43,000-acre tract the Osage Nation had recently purchased from billionaire Ted Turner. Jane Fonda, Turner's ex-wife, may have been interested in social justice, but Turner sold the Osage our own ancestral land for $74 million, a property he'd bought fifteen years earlier from the Drummond family for $15 million.

The bison would form a herd on the Osage Nation's ranch and recreate the days when we hunted buffalo that migrated north and south across what is now called Oklahoma. I live along the lower Columbia River, about forty-one river miles from the Pacific Ocean. Unless I'm at home in the Osage driving on the Tallgrass Prairie Preserve, the closest I come to bison is on YouTube: a bison turning quickly to chase a tourist around a tree or a young man visiting Yellowstone, sitting in the passenger seat filming a bison walking deliberately along the narrow edge of a road beside a line of RVs. From the car ahead, a man's hand appears and slaps the bison's narrow rear. Lightning fast, the animal kicks the car and the guy filming turns to his friend open-mouthed.

Once I drove with a cousin after dusk on the Tallgrass Prairie when luminous eyes bounced like ping-pong balls as bison ran across a wash in front of us. I've felt the stink eye of a big bull, viscerally aware that I was too close, that he was bigger than my car.

I've never lived full-time in the Osage. My Dad was born on the reservation and lived there as a child. My grandmother moved her family to Denver in the late 1920s. Like many Osages, my father enlisted in World War II. We were a military family, living in France and Japan. When we were in the States, we visited my aunt and uncle on their allotments toward Bartlesville. I regret that I don't know the patchwork of ranches in the Osage the way I've come to know the valleys off the lower Columbia.

The 1906 act ultimately forced allotment of our 1.57-million-acre reservation to the 2,229 Osages alive in 1906. The State of Oklahoma proceeded to create Osage County on top of the reservation boundary. Not surprisingly, white settlers, some of whom had been put off the reservation multiple times before it was allotted, took this as affirmation that Osage sovereignty was over.[1]

Negotiations for a new reservation in what is now northeastern Oklahoma began after the Civil War when the Osages in Kansas were overrun by settlers trespassing on tribal land. The Osage had observed the disastrous results of the allotment of the Omaha, our Dhegiha Siouan relatives, in 1854. Under the influence of Osage band chief Joseph Paw-ne-no-pashe, language in the treaty of removal from Kansas stipulated that the new reservation would be protected from trespassers, owned communally, and not allotted to individuals. Because we held title to the reservation, the Osage were exempt from the General Allotment Act of 1887, sponsored by Henry Dawes. Allotment usually opened tribal land in excess of homestead-sized parcels deeded to tribal members to settlers, but the Osage leaders ensured that the entire surface of the Osage Reservation would be divided among the 2,229 tribal members in parcels of 657 acres, with exceptions for townships, Indian villages, schools, and a cemetery. More importantly, mineral rights were reserved to the Osage tribe and held in common.

That fall day, I drove west on Highway 60 toward Ponca City, following the cloud of dust from the chief's truck and bumping over cattle guards toward the Ferguson pens. Cars and trucks were parked around loading chutes. People visited in small groups. Assistant Chief Raymond Red Corn, Congresswomen Maria Whitehorn and Angela Pratt, and artists Addie and Anya Roanhorse and Yatika Fields were there. Reporters and editors from the *Fairfax Chief, Big Heart Times, Pawhuska Journal-Capital, Bartlesville Examiner-Enterprise,* and *Osage News* stood around with cameras slung over their shoulders. Wearing a crisp white shirt, Minerals Council Chairman Everett Waller sat in a circle of folks in the shade of a pickup.

While we waited for the twenty yearlings on their way from the Wichita Mountains Wildlife Refuge near Lawton, Oklahoma, an Osage wildland firefighter, who had been at the fires in Montana, noticed my canvas bag from the Zon-Zo-Lin district.

"I'm Pawhuska," he said. I told him I wouldn't hold it against him, and we laughed.

When the stock trailer arrived, women put on their Osage blankets. The animals ran out of the trailer into a narrow pen in a blur of rusty brown. We waited again, while the driver climbed onto the truck, calling and slapping the sides, trying to induce the stragglers out. Finally, three young animals bolted.

Everett Waller draped a red broadcloth blanket over his shoulders. Raising an eagle wing fan above his head, the claw splayed in the air, Waller prayed in Wahzhazhe ie welcoming those animals home. I can't do justice to his prayer, but what I heard him say spoke to the fulfillment of generations of Osages, of the promise and desire for the Wahzhazhe to be whole again as our Creator wanted, our people on our land with our ways.

At last, the gates opened and the bison started running down a long chute toward where I stood with the editor of the *Osage News* behind what I hoped was a solid gate of red steel pipe. Killdeer peeped and flashed white as sun hit their wings. The animals ran, slopping through puddles, while I shot with a telephoto lens until I had to lower it to see exactly how close they were going to come. Our ancestors hunted these rushing bison, the women working the hides and meat of the large animals. The bison stopped and, when they'd looked us over, ran to an adjacent corral. That day Shannon Shaw Duty, the editor of the Nation's newspaper, asked me to write a monthly column about Osage culture.

Pawhuska has changed in the decades I've been coming home. The Nation has invested in economic development, built casinos, and founded an immersion school. Ree Drummond, a celebrity chef who married into a family descended from a man who parlayed a trading license with the Osage into a fortune, is filling Pawhuska with restaurants that draw upward of six thousand tourists most days, almost twice the town's population. The Drummond family is one of the largest landowners in the United States, and, as the old people say, no friend of the Osage.

For years, the five-storied Triangle Building, a symbol of graft, home to entrepreneurs and opportunists drawn to the Osage Mineral Reserve, deteriorated. Windows fell out and were boarded up. Proposed renovations faltered. In 2018, the building that housed lawyers who had preyed on Osages reopened as the Frontier Hotel. The old office building feels like the setting for a 1940s detective novel, with frosted glass doors and oddly shaped rooms on concrete floors. The head of a bison is mounted in the lobby beside narrow, winding stairs.

Allotment changed the trajectory of the Osage Nation, as did the discovery and development of oil resources. Together they culminated in the murder of at least 60 Osages out of an enrolled population of 2,229. As the mineral resource was developed, the proceeds were distributed among the Osages on the tribal roll in 1906 in shares called headrights. Huge oil fields generated substantial income for individual Osages, whose wealth made them both a national curiosity and objects of derision. White entrepreneurs and professional scammers appeared; some married Osages and murdered them to gain control of their headrights. Lawyers and guardians stole millions. The majority of the murders were neither resolved nor prosecuted, despite the presence and efforts of the FBI.[2]

A century later, Osage annuitants—as well as the State of Oklahoma—depend on the price of oil for income, suffering the environmental disturbance of oil and gas production in a state unwilling to pay teachers a living wage. The Osage Nation is recovering land that has been fractionated and is working to rehabilitate land scarred by oil and gas production. It is nurturing Wahzhazhe people with language, culture, and economic development.

In the parking area near the corral that October day, ranchers in cowboy hats stood near their trucks. I spoke to friends while people went home to family and dinner. I had a good feeling when I drove the county road through veils of dust dissolving in evening light. As the sky turned gold, I thought of ten-year-old Anya getting down from the tail-gate where she was sitting to hug me and introduce me as her grandmother's friend. As the house prices in Osage County soar and rental houses turn into high-end lodging, I wondered if I'll have enough money to buy a home here and whether Anya will have work that sustains her.

NOTES

1. The U.S. Congress set out the provisions of the allotment process in the Osage Allotment Act of 1906. Terry Wilson provides a succinct description of the process in *The Osage* (New York: Chelsea House, 1988) and a comprehensive discussion of the politics of land, oil, and sovereignty in *The Underground Reservation: Osage Oil* (Norman: University of Oklahoma Press, 1985).
2. See *The Deaths of Sybil Bolton* by Dennis McAuliffe (New York: Times Books, 1994) and *A Pipe for February* by Charles Red Corn (Norman: University of Oklahoma Press, 2002) for books by Osage authors.

Afterword

Indigenous Foresight under Duress and the
Modern Applicability of Allotment Agreements

STACY L. LEEDS

The allotment process, from inception to hindsight, gives rise to countless stories similar to those included in this collection. For the United States, a successful and complete allotment process required the erasure of Indigenous stories and lifeways, but most importantly, it demanded an end to Indigenous laws, governance, and autonomy. Pre-existing tribal property law systems that had flourished for centuries were necessarily ignored and replaced by the colonizer's laws.[1]

When allotment was implemented by the federal government, there was a clear exit strategy. Tribal government control of land would be eliminated in the short term. Federal involvement in Indian land transactions would eventually be phased out in the long term.[2]

Allotment proceeded with or without tribal consent and sometimes over strong objections and resistance, including tribally filed cases in federal courts to halt the process as an unconstitutional taking of property rights. At the time, federal courts either dismissed the cases as political questions, to which the judicial branch could not intervene to provide a remedy, or acquiesced to unfettered power in the United States to effectuate allotment.

First, the United States compelled the redistribution of the tribal land base from tribal government (communal) ownership to individual Indian ownership. Federal agents, as self-appointed temporary trustees over the newly allotted Indian lands, would then ensure the requisite legal documents were executed to complete the initial real estate transaction. At the conclusion of an adjustment period for the "new" individual Indigenous landowner, the federal trusteeship would terminate and the individual Indigenous landowner would be in the same position and subject to the same laws as any other private landowner within the United States.

The United States presumed that once the allotment process reached finality, tribal governments would cease to exist, Indians would become fully assimilated U.S. citizens, and federal Indian law and policy would be nothing more than a chapter in American history books. Although some Indigenous families have successfully retained allotment lands to the present generation, the original intent of the allotment process was to make all Indian lands freely alienable for future conveyances. When allotment was complete, the American melting pot theory would be fully realized, as to Indians.

In the intervening century from allotment to present, many legal and practical changes have occurred that reshape Indigenous rights, both within the United States and internationally. Allotment was repudiated as a failed policy experiment. For tribes, the legacy of a failed allotment policy goes far beyond catastrophic land loss and suppression of tribal laws and lifeways. Left intact is a strained tribal–federal relationship rooted in contradiction. Following allotment, the federal government continues as the self-imposed federal trustee over many Indigenous lands and natural resources, while simultaneously subscribing to tribal self-determination over other retained tribal governmental powers.

If time travel were possible, the policy architects of Indian allotment would be shocked to see what the year 2021 reveals. They would see that despite the loss of millions of acres of Indigenous-owned land as a direct result of allotment, Indigenous nations persist and many tribes retain the territorial boundaries originally set forth in treaties that predate allotment. Within Indigenous national boundaries, tribal government entities often include institutions of higher education, judiciaries, law enforcement, comprehensive health-care systems, environmental regulatory agencies, diverse economies (including international trade), and Indigenous language protectors.

If the allotment policy architects could read this collection of stories penned by Indigenous scholars, most of whom are citizens of modern-day Indigenous nations, they might learn that allotment almost did many of us in. Across the globe, Indigenous families and communities remain wounded by allotment and other colonial weapons, but we are definitely on the mend.

Among the many different perspectives conveyed in this collection, one truth cannot be denied: we have collectively survived our predicted end. We are the thriving great-grandchildren of those who would never be divided and carved out as a single parcel: not as individuals, not as acreage.

The Legal Mechanics of Allotment

The United States experimented with allotment on a smaller scale earlier in the nineteenth century, as evinced in a few treaty provisions providing for individual allotments.[3] The passage of the General Allotment Act of 1887 (GAA) ushered in a federal comprehensive plan, but the GAA was not a magic wand. Just like the Indian Removal Act before it, the GAA was a federal policy statement that was not self-executing.

Perpetual tribal land rights (and ownership) in post-removal tribal territories were previously guaranteed in many treaties. This legal reality complicated the federal desire for a quick and painless Indian allotment process. Acting on the belief that there was no unquestionable legal mechanism to allot tribal lands without tribal consent, United States agents set out to negotiate allotment agreements with individual tribes. United States agents had previously effectuated the Indian Removal policy by negotiating land cessions from tribes in the removal-era treaties that situated tribes in the new territories for which allotment was now sought.

These allotment agreements were later codified in federal legislation detailing how the allotment would be uniquely implemented specific to each Indian reservation, with the GAA as the conceptual framework. These tribal-specific allotment agreements are central to many modern-day legal challenges that may define where tribal jurisdiction begins and state jurisdiction ends. The unique allotment aftermath experienced by each tribal community is an outgrowth of these series of events brought to life in legal documents.

Similar to treaties, most allotment agreements were negotiated under extreme duress with an unbalanced federal–tribal power dynamic. When consent could not be obtained from the tribe, the federal government moved forward with allotment over tribal objection. When tribes tried to challenge unilateral federally forced allotment as an unconstitutional taking in federal courts, the United States Supreme Court refused to intervene, noting that the allotment transaction only amounted to a change in the way Indian lands were held. Converting lands from tribal government (communal) ownership to individual Indian ownership still left land in Indian hands.

In some cases, after tribal land bases were divided and individual parcels of land were conveyed to individual tribal citizens, acreage was left over and the federal government concluded that the tribe no longer needed the land. These surplus lands were subsequently returned to the federal domain for redistribution to non-Indian settlers.[4]

Mechanically, the allotment process was effectuated in different ways within each Indigenous nation, based on the size of land base, the number of tribal citizens, and, most notably, the unique political and legal circumstances of the Indigenous nations relative to the colonizing power. Globally, Indigenous peoples experienced remarkably similar regimes intended to undermine autonomy with similar paths in resistance.

A Post-Allotment Five Tribes Story: *McGirt v. Oklahoma*

The Muscogee (Creek) Nation, Cherokee Nation, Chickasaw Nation, Choctaw Nation, and Seminole Nation share a common history of removal from their homelands in the southeastern United States to Indian Territory, now in present-day eastern Oklahoma.[5] At the time of removal, each of the Five Tribes negotiated ownership of a new territory with treaty-guaranteed perpetual self-governance and dominion over a fixed political and territory boundary, or reservation. To ensure that the lands did not remain under control of the United States, or otherwise vulnerable to non-Indian pressure, each of the Five Tribes negotiated outright ownership of the new territory. To memorialize those agreements, the United States issued fee patents to each of the Five Tribes as required in each removal treaty.

Due to the nature of the Five Tribes' ownership in their respective territories, the United States knew the allotment would be more difficult to compel. Although the GAA applies to many tribes, the Five Tribes were expressly exempted from the GAA's reach, and instead, other federal laws were passed to pressure the Five Tribes to consent to allotment. Such legislation purported to lease the mineral estates of the Five Tribes without tribal consent and set expiration dates whereby Congress would abolish the powerful tribal judiciaries in each of the Five Tribes by a specific date, unless the tribe adopted an allotment agreement. Throughout the United States, the GAA was enacted under implicit threats to compel tribal consent. With the Five Tribes, federal threats were more overt and intended to combat tribal resistance with punitive measures, including termination of tribal government institutions and loss of federal recognition of rights and territories should the tribes fail to agree.

Eventually, each of the Five Tribes agreed to allotment, as a means to preserve what could be preserved of a tribal existence. These agreements were negotiated over several years and are among many hidden stories of tribal resistance and international diplomacy that are just now being understood and highlighted.

Tribal citizens and their leaders explored all paths of resistance, including civil disobedience leading to incarceration, community violence, lawsuits, and eventual agreements to end tribal existence on a given date, in favor of banding together to seek statehood within the United States as the State of Sequoyah. A failed endeavor that would have never been on the table had the United States honored prior legal and moral obligations.

The Five Tribes eventually adopted allotment agreements after finding themselves in a stark yet familiar situation: after unsuccessful appeals to federal courts, the tribes could either do nothing and watch the federal government unilaterally take tribal lands in contravention of express treaty guarantees, or the tribes could negotiate and secure to themselves the best possible legal scenario for the future.

Fast forward to July 2020 when *McGirt v. Oklahoma* was decided by the United States Supreme Court.[6] The court ruled that Oklahoma had overstepped its governmental authority for over a century by exercising state criminal jurisdiction over Indians inside the boundaries of the Muscogee (Creek) Nation. The court noted that "once a reservation is established, it retains the status 'until Congress explicitly indicates otherwise.'"[7] Squarely at issue in the case was the legal impact of the allotment process and subsequent Oklahoma statehood on the Muscogee (Creek) Nation.

With respect to the allotment process, the court noted: "Starting in the 1880s, Congress sought to pressure many tribes to abandon their communal lifestyles and parcel their lands into smaller lots owned by individual tribe members."[8] Once "all the lands had been allotted and the trust period expired, [then] the reservation could be abolished."[9] In finding that the Muscogee (Creek) Nation retains territorial integrity despite the loss of ownership of all lands inside those boundaries, the court noted that a reservation is never disestablished simply because Congress had a plan to eventually do so. Even if it almost did. The Muscogee (Creek) Nation resisted at the time of allotment and has now recommitted to doing what it has done several times before: survive, rebuild, reinvent.

The United States Supreme Court decision in *McGirt v. Oklahoma* begins with a remarkable opening: "On the far end of the Trail of Tears was a promise." The contributors to this collection are beneficiaries of that promise and similar intergenerational guarantees, with contexts as rich as their complexities. Allotment was a series of events that will undoubtedly loom large in the collective Indigenous experience, influencing the stories of future generations. Allotment will never be situated as the final chapter.

NOTES

1. Kenneth H. Bobroff, "Retelling Allotment: Indian Property Rights and the Myth of Common Ownership," *Vanderbilt Law Review* 54, no. 4 (2001): 1559–1623 (dispelling myths and common misconceptions in federal rationales for allotment).
2. For the most comprehensive legal review of the implementation and aftermath of allotment policy, see Judith V. Royster, "The Legacy of Allotment," *Arizona State Law Journal* 27 (1995): 1–78.
3. See Treaty with the Shawnee of May 10, 1854, 10 Stat. 1053, which provided for allotment of certain lands in Kansas.
4. See Stacy L. Leeds, "By Eminent Domain or Some Other Name: A Tribal Perspective on Taking Land," *Tulsa Law Review* 41 (2005): 66–67 (describing the federal surplus lands policy as forced wealth transfer).
5. The land was conveyed from the United States, which "gives and grants" the lands to the Cherokee Nation "to have and to hold the same, together with all the rights, privileges, and appurtenances thereto belonging to the said Cherokee Nation forever." Cherokee Nation v. Hitchcock, 187 U.S. 294 (1902). The language contains no reservation of rights in the United States.
6. McGirt v. Oklahoma, 140 S. Ct. 2452 (2020).
7. McGirt v. Oklahoma at 2468–69.
8. McGirt v. Oklahoma at 2463.
9. McGirt v. Oklahoma at 2464–65.

Acknowledgments

Our contributors answered the original call for papers with such enthusiasm, brought such richly textured work to the volume, and have been so consistently generous, thoughtful, and conscientious along the way. We are so proud to be part of this project with you. Wado and Miigwech.

The University of Minnesota Press has been the ideal home for this project. Jason Weidemann saw our vision from the very beginning and has been a constant source of support and encouragement. Zenyse Miller, Rachel Moeller, Mike Stoffel, cover designer Catherine Casalino, and the entire Press team have gone above and beyond in realizing not only a meaningful book but a beautiful one. And we are so appreciative to Robert Warrior, a steadfast advocate for the very best work in Indigenous studies, for including *Allotment Stories* in the Indigenous Americas series. Wado and Miigwech.

Our external readers, Mishuana Goeman and Alyosha Goldstein, provided some of the most helpful and comprehensive reader responses we have ever seen in our respective careers, and the volume is even better as a result of their generous recommendations. All scholars should be so fortunate as to have readers of this care and caliber!

Special thanks to Joshua Althoff for his careful and incisive work in compiling the volume's substantial index, and to Douglas C. Harris, Nathan T. Nemetz Chair in Legal History at the Peter A. Allard School of Law at the University of British Columbia, for giving the legal terms in the glossary such careful attention, and on short notice, too. Wado and Miigwech.

Daniel: I'm enormously grateful to the Digadatseli'i ᏗᎦᏓᏤᎵ Cherokee citizen scholars group for their commitments to Cherokee legal, political, and intellectual sovereignty, and for the conversations that have helped inform so much of the thinking behind this project. I also want to thank fellow Cherokee Nation citizens Twila Barnes, Joseph Pierce, and Rebecca Nagle for their friendship, courage, and determination in speaking truth to power. My husband, Kent Dunn, is not only my best friend and reader but my stalwart source of love and support. Last, but certainly not least, my deepest thanks to Jeani O'Brien—I truly couldn't have asked for a better editorial partner for this project. I will treasure this experience as one of the high points of my career, in large part because of her laughter, her brilliance, and her tenacity. Wado ginali.

Jeani: The American Indian and Indigenous Studies Workshop at the University of Minnesota, now well over twenty years in the making, contributed their usual wisdom and exuberance for this project since its initial formation in 2017 and through multiple iterations. I'm enormously grateful to our brilliant graduate student and faculty participants who brought their insights to this project. My very first conversation with the wonderful Daniel Heath Justice in Vancouver about our mutual scholarly interests initiated a completely unexpected synergy that has continued to mark work on this project. It's such a great honor to have been able to bask in Daniel's brilliance and cocreate this book. Heartfelt thanks to our amazing authors for contributing their important work to this volume. And thanks as always to Tim Kehoe for love, support, and endless fun. Miigwech!

Glossary

Aboriginal title: Aboriginal title is a legal doctrine affirming that an Indigenous group's land rights and tenure are unique ("of their own kind," or sui generis), existed before European colonization, and persist in spite of settler assertions of sovereignty; such title is based on and derives from Indigenous peoples' historic use and occupation of land. Compensation and recognition of land rights varies by authority and jurisdiction and requires proof for the recognition of Aboriginal title, the content of title, and the methods of extinguishing title.

adverse possession: The formal legal doctrine for the more nebulous concept of squatter's rights, in which a trespasser can claim interest in and apply to quiet title (and therefore gain ownership) of real property (land) provided they meet particular legal conditions, such as possession over a certain period of time. Many jurisdictions have limited or abolished the scope of adverse possession claims, but in others it remains in full force; it continues to be used by settlers to target remaining Native-held allotment lands in Oklahoma. In the United States, tribal trust lands are typically exempt from adverse possession claims, but allotments, as private property, are not.

Alaska Native Claims Settlement Act (ANCSA): The Alaska Native Claims Settlement Act (Pub. L. 92–203) was an untried case in the extinguishment of aboriginal title. President Richard Nixon signed ANCSA into law on December 18, 1971. Alaska Natives received fee simple absolute title of up to forty-five million acres of land and a total sum of $962.5 million as compensation for the extinguishment of land claims. ANCSA mandated the establishment of thirteen for-profit Alaska Native regional corporations and over two hundred Alaska Native village corporations tasked to manage the land and payments. ANCSA rejected traditional trusteeship—the land is owned by enrolled Alaska Native shareholders through privately held stock in regional and village corporations.

allotment: A parcel of individually owned land designated for a particular named recipient, inheritable by descendants, typically carved out of a larger, collective land base, with remaining surplus lands made available to other groups for ownership and possession. The average size of allotments and the distribution mechanisms vary according to the historical era of allotment, the geographical features of the land being divided, the number of eligible allottees, and the social expectations of authorities determining the process of how the land can and should be used. Under

U.S. allotment policy, the division of collectively held tribal lands into individual allotments was part of the larger so-called civilization policy to assimilate Indigenous people into U.S. citizens. Restricted allotments could be inherited but not sold or otherwise lost; unrestricted allotments could be inherited, sold, exchanged, or lost to tax seizure or other mechanisms.

altepetl (s.), altepemeh (pl.): Nahuatl word that literally means "the waters, the mountains"; also translated as "the waters, the hills." Spaniards understood this Indigenous concept of land as "Indian kingdoms." More accurately described as a Nahua community, a pueblo, or polities.

American Indian Movement (AIM): Founded in 1968 in Minneapolis, this activist organization emerged in response to endemic poverty and systemic police brutality against the urban Indian community. It formed Indian Patrols, modeled after Black Patrols, that responded to police harassment against Indians and advocated for Indian citizens, resulting in a marked decline in arrest rates. AIM made bold demands around the recognition of Indian treaties and sovereignty and rights. It grew increasingly militant in the early 1970s and is best known for such high-profile events such as the Trail of Broken Treaties, which culminated in the takeover of the Bureau of Indian Affairs in 1972 and the Occupation of Wounded Knee in 1973. AIM chapters proliferated across the United States and it continues to work in defense of Indian sovereignty and against issues such as Indian mascots.

Arab Nations Fund: Sunduq al-Ummah (Arabic) is a company established by financially capable Palestinian national leaders in the 1930s and 1940s with the aim of blocking Zionist land acquisitions by offering to buy lands from indebted peasants. This was a significant development in the Palestinian elite's strategy, which had previously trusted private investments in land as a measure to block colonization. In the 1940s, the ANF strategy posed a serious challenge to Zionist colonization, until the military expulsion of most of the Palestinians from their homes and villages in 1948.

Beisan Land Settlement: A British project launched in 1921 to allot the ex-sultan's land in Beisan to the local cultivators as private property. This was part of a larger land settlement and survey policy that aimed to establish a new land registry based on the colonial Australian Torrens land registration system. These projects stepped up the dynamics of land alienation, which fed into increasing Palestinian popular resistance and a major anticolonial revolt—the Great Revolt, 1936–1939.

bona fide settlers: A common phrase in the nineteenth-century United States that distinguished farmers who were ideologically entitled to access to the public domain from speculators who reaped unearned profits by manipulating the market for those lands. It also distinguished Americans from the Indigenous people whose land the public domain once was. Indigenous people by definition could not be settlers because, as so-called savages, they were ostensibly nomadic.

Bulls of Donation: Papal bulls issued by Pope Alexander VI at the end of the fifteenth century granting the "right to spread the faith" (i.e., conquer and convert) to the Spanish and Portuguese Crowns. The pope divided the world in two, with Spain receiving rights for half and Portugal the other half.

Bureau of Indian Affairs (BIA): Located in the Department of the Interior since 1849 (and previously in the Department of War after its creation in 1824), the BIA is the federal agency that oversees Indian affairs in the United States. It is responsible for upholding the trust responsibilities of the federal government toward the 574 federally recognized Indian nations and is embedded in the government-to-government relationship as it has unfolded over time.

Cherokee Male and Female Seminaries: Preparatory educational institutions conceived of, administered by, and funded by the Cherokee Nation and its citizenry, in operation with short interruptions from 1851 to just after Oklahoma statehood. Unlike U.S.- and missionary-led boarding and residential schools that largely focused on industrial training and working-class service, the seminaries prepared elite Cherokee and other Five Tribes citizens for leadership along the lines of eastern white preparatory schools. Lessons included Latin, Greek, French, German, English grammar, classical literature, physical geography, physiology, rhetoric, natural philosophy, surveying, calculus, trigonometry, analytical geometry, astronomy, zoology, and other subjects. The seminaries were transferred from Cherokee control after Oklahoma statehood; the Male Seminary burned in 1910, but parts of the Female Seminary form the architecture of Northeastern State University's Seminary Hall.

Choctaw and Chickasaw Citizenship Court (CCCC): Established through an arrangement between the Dawes Commission and the Choctaw and Chickasaw Nations, the CCCC was a special tribunal charged with addressing the legitimacy to claims of citizenship and thus legal entitlement to allotment land in the Choctaw and Chickasaw Nations from 1902 to 1904. Its primary focus was on the largely fraudulent claims of so-called court citizens who were placed on initial tribal rolls by federal judges in Indian Territory.

citizenship categories: There were three primary categories for citizen status in the Five Tribes for land allotment purposes, which largely reflected a mix of tribal and federal laws and treaties defining citizenship and citizen rights: by blood, intermarried white, and Freedmen. The Cherokee Nation had the added complexity of Delaware and Loyal Shawnee citizens by treaty who were noted in Dawes records as both Cherokee by blood and as adopted Delaware or Shawnee, respectively. The

Choctaw Nation had an additional identification category for Mississippi Choctaws who had not moved to Indian Territory (but who would be required to do so to receive their allotment).

Clapp Act of 1906: This act, technically a rider to an appropriation act, followed up on the Burke Act of 1906 that authorized the secretary of the interior to shorten the twenty-five-year trust period built into the Dawes General Allotment Act to protect Indian allottees from being defrauded of their land if an Indian was deemed "competent and capable" to manage their own affairs. This provision led to major abuses and widespread land loss among six of the seven Ojibwe nations in Minnesota (Red Lake was exempt from allotment). The Clapp Act enabled Indians who were judged to be mixed blood as categorically competent and capable, institutionalizing racist notions of physical anthropology in the process and opening the door to sweeping Indian dispossession.

Cobell (Education) Scholarship: Authorized under the Cobell settlement, and partially funded through the Land Buy-Back Program, this scholarship provides postsecondary funding for American Indian and Alaska Native students.

Cobell settlement: The 2009 settlement of *Cobell v. Salazar,* which was a class action lawsuit brought forward in 1996 against two U.S. government departments for mismanagement of Indian trust funds. In the settlement, $1.4 billion was to be paid to the plaintiffs and $2 billion to the Land Buy-Back Program to return fractionated lands to tribal ownership. In addition, the Cobell Education Scholarship was established.

composición: A 1591 agrarian reform program in which legalized titles of land ownership (often to Indigenous lands) were issued by the Spanish Crown in exchange for paying a fee and submitting a physical survey of the land in New Spain (colonial Mexico).

congregación: Late sixteenth- to early eighteenth-century forced Indigenous removal and resettlement in New Spain (colonial Mexico).

Crown land (Canada): In Canada, *Crown land* refers to land that is owned by the provincial or federal governments whose control resides with the Crown. These lands account for approximately 89 percent of all lands in Canada, leaving less than 11 percent in private ownership. The territories of Nunavut, Northwest Territories, and Yukon account for most federal Crown lands, which are administered by Indigenous and Northern Affairs Canada. Four percent of Crown land in the provinces is federal, consisting of Indian reserves, national parks, and military bases.

cultural revival: *Cultural revival* is a term used to describe an ongoing effort by a group of people to restore the cultural fabric that once defined that group's common traditions, customs, practices, institutions, and overall way of life. Cultural revival often occurs in response to a loss of culture from colonization, ethnic cleansing, assimilation, relocation, removal, or oppression.

Curtis Act (1898): Although the allotment provisions of the 1887 Dawes Act would initially exempt the Five Tribes of Indian Territory, the passage of the Curtis Act a decade later was specifically focused on those nations and their lands, extending the Dawes Act's provisions over the territory and imposing federal jurisdiction over legal and criminal matters previously addressed by tribal legislation and authority. The law was named for Senator Charles Curtis (Kaw).

customary Ottoman land tenure: Ottoman land tenure was a revenue-based system that allowed a host of local land and labor arrangements. Village communities could practice periodic reallotments of their lands without state interference. Long-standing sharecropping and customary land access privileges were widely practiced on absentee landlords' estates. While British land settlement targeted communal landholdings, Zionist colonization abolished the sharecropping agrarian culture to make room for exclusive Jewish land control.

customary rights: Rights that are acquired by custom—established, traditional patterns of norms that can be observed within a specific social or cultural setting.

Dawes Act of 1887: The Dawes Act of 1887, named after its sponsor, Senator Henry Dawes of Massachusetts, and also known as the General Allotment Act or the Dawes Severalty Act, authorized the president to divide the collective lands of Indian reservations into individually owned parcels of land—in other words, it sought to privatize previously communally owned Indian lands as a means to speed up Indian assimilation. Under this system, land privatization was imposed on tribes on a piecemeal basis between 1887 and 1934, when the process was halted as part of a new Indian Self-Determination Policy. (Allotment came to Indian Territory through a separate but related process. *See* allotment and the Curtis Act [1898].) Allotment was imposed on 118 reservations in all, resulting in the loss of around 100 million acres of Indian land, or roughly two-thirds of the lands remaining in Indian hands prior to allotment, reducing tribal control over their homelands and introducing infinite complexity in the status of Indian lands.

Dayunisi: In the Cherokee creation story, Dayunisi, Water Beetle, Beaver's Grandmother (or Grandchild), is the animal relative who dives into the primordial ocean and retrieves a small bit of mud from the depths after larger, stronger birds and animals are unable to do so. Upon touching the air, this mud expands, becoming the Earth and providing land for the other animals and eventually humans to live on.

Delgamuukw case (*Delgamuukw v. British Columbia*): A landmark 1997 ruling from the Supreme Court of Canada (SCC) that addressed the scope, nature, and limits of Aboriginal title, affirmed the government's duty to consult with Indigenous peoples regarding their lands (especially when the Crown or its agents seek to impose their authority and access for resource extraction), and recognized oral tradition as having equal evidentiary value in court proceedings. A significant decision in defining Aboriginal title as a property interest, and one that dismissed nineteenth-century decisions defining Aboriginal title as a political and moral issue rather than a legal one. While recognizing cultural and ancestral rights and the significance of Aboriginal title, *Delgamuukw* affirmed the Crown's underlying title and positioned Aboriginal title as a burden on the Crown's underlying title. The SCC defined the nature or scope of Aboriginal title and set out the test for proof but did not address how it was that the Crown's title was the underlying form. For all its significance, *Delgamuukw* nevertheless leaves much latitude for governments to infringe upon Indigenous rights, provided the infringement meets "legitimate government objectives," especially those of resource extraction and industry.

encomienda: Legally in effect from 1503 to 1542, encomienda was a concession by the Spanish Crown of Native peoples as tribute payers and laborers to Spaniards for the span of one to two generations as reward for their services. An abusive and dispossessive system akin to slavery, with particular emphasis on removing people from their homelands.

enfranchisement: Under Canada's Indian Act, enfranchisement was a compulsory legal process that involved terminating Indian status (and removing its associated rights) and imposing Canadian citizenship, thus substantively an enforced exchange of Indigenous belonging with that of nation-state obligation. Enfranchisement could be triggered by receiving a university education, taking a medical or law degree or becoming clergy, serving in the Canadian Armed Forces, or, for women, marrying a non-Status man. Enfranchisement meant being removed from band lists and often meant losing access to housing on reserve as well. The most punitive enfranchisement rules were in effect from 1876 to 1951, but for women they continued until 1985 (with revisions in 2017) and continue to have impacts on their descendants today. Enfranchisement in the United States refers to citizenship/voting rights.

fee simple: In common law, the most complete form of private landownership (also known as freehold), in which the estate can be bought, sold, inherited, mortgaged, or otherwise used to the benefit of the owner. Fee simple status is commonly transferable, a feature recognized by early settler advocates of allotment who understood that resource-rich and collectively held Indigenous lands would be easier to move into white hands under fee simple status. (*See* Dawes Act of 1887, allotment.)

Five (Civilized) Tribes: From the early nineteenth century onward, white social reformers identified the Cherokee, Chickasaw, Choctaw, Muscogee (Creek), and

Seminole Nations from the U.S. Southeast as the Five Civilized Tribes for the willingness of their leadership and many of their citizens to adopt particular white American economic, social, and political structures as their own (including chattel slavery), while still retaining their political and cultural distinctiveness. The Five Tribes would face similar social and demographic upheaval under Removal and the U.S. Civil War and would share similar pressures in the years leading up to allotment.

fractionation: After the death of an allottee under the General Allotment Act of 1887 (Dawes Act), ownership of an allotment passes to their heirs in equal portions. As generations pass, heirs receive smaller and smaller fractions of the original allotment.

Freedmen: Many Five Tribes citizens practiced chattel Black slavery from the late eighteenth and early nineteenth centuries onward, and many brought enslaved people with them to Indian Territory during Removal. The Five Tribes rebuilt in these new lands in part with enslaved labor and, after siding with the South during the U.S. Civil War, agreed to emancipation as part of a set of treaty negotiations with the victorious U.S. government. The further federal stipulation that Freedmen be granted citizenship in their respective Indian nations proved to be more controversial, even though many Freedmen were also Native by heritage, culture, language, and kinship. Each of the Five Tribes responded differently to this demand: some reluctantly enfranchised Freedmen while others outright refused. The status of Five Tribes Freedmen became even more complicated when the matter of allotment and land distribution arose, with varying degrees of obstruction to Freedmen citizenship and land rights. Freedmen descendants continue to struggle for recognition of rights in the Five Tribes today.

golgadit, buođđut: Two forms of traditional net fishing in Deatnu. Golgadit is practiced with a drift net and buođđut with a weir.

Gradual Enfranchisement Act (1869): A precursor to Canada's paternalistic Indian Act, the Gradual Enfranchisement Act set strict guidelines on the property rights of Indigenous people, defined limited band council and chief duties and extensive restrictions on local authority, imposed gendered and moralizing restrictions on leadership and property, linked enfranchisement with loss of Indian status, and otherwise imposed wide-ranging authority by the superintendent general of Indian Affairs over nearly every aspect of Indigenous life and relations.

Grand Allotment: A land reform in Sweden that began in the mid-eighteenth century and continued up until the 1960s in northernmost Finland. The purpose of the Grand Allotment (*isojako* in Finnish, *storskiftet* in Swedish) was to eliminate the problems caused by the traditional division of the farmland for the purposes of increasing agricultural production and its efficiency. In the process, the previous narrow, scattered strips of farmland were consolidated into fewer and bigger blocks. In addition to the consolidation of fields, the common forest and pasture lands of the village were privatized by dividing them up among the farms. It was further stipulated that the "leftover commons" after the farms had been allotted were declared as Crown (state) land. This was the start of state forest ownership, which is significant especially in northern Finland, where the state still owns 90 percent of all land.

grounded relationalities: Proposed by Jodi A. Byrd, Alyosha Goldstein, Jodi Melamed, and Chandan Reddy ("Predatory Value: Economies of Dispossession and Disturbed Relationalities," *Social Text* 36, no. 2 [June 2018]: 1–18) as an alternative to the logics of settler colonialism and racial capitalism. They note that *grounded* is meant in a literal sense, as relating to the shared earth/land itself, while not precluding migrations, movement, or the flows of air or water. The relational, in this sense, is meant to open up the concept of agency for other-than-human subjectivities, exceeding liberal conceptions of the human and centering on Indigenous epistemologies and forms of interconnectivity.

hacienda: Legalized (in 1529) dispossession wherein the Crown granted Indigenous lands to Spaniards.

half-breed tracts: Parcels of land set aside by U.S. authorities specifically for mixed-race Native individuals and families in the American Midwest. Small in size, often coveted by surrounding settler populations, and frequently not even recognized by authorities, most half-breed tracts were lost within a generation through a combination of outright theft and manipulation.

Hashomer Hatzair movement: A socialist-Zionist movement founded in Galicia, Austria-Hungary, in 1913. In Palestine, the movement established a network of *kibbutzim* (socialist agrarian settlements) based on a strict ideology of excluding Arab labor.

Haudenosaunee Confederacy: The Haudenosaunee Confederacy consists of the Mohawks, Oneidas, Onondagas, Cayugas, Senecas, and Tuscaroras (who joined in 1720). Known as the Iroquois Confederacy by the French and the League of Five (later Six) Nations by the English, the Haudenosaunee continue to participate in a long-standing political and cultural alliance that formed centuries prior to European contact.

headright: For Osages, a headright is the right to receive a portion of the Osage Mineral Estate, which consists of the oil, gas, and other minerals beneath the Osage Reservation. The Osage Allotment Act of 1906 allotted the surface of the reservation to tribal members in 657-acre parcels, while the United States held the mineral rights in trust for the Osage Nation.

Homestead Acts: The 1862 act expanded the earlier Preemption Act by allowing men and single women who lived on the land for at least five years and made minimal structural and agricultural improvements to file claims on 160 acres of federal land. They could acquire title by living on the land for five years, building a permanent dwelling, and preparing some acreage for cultivation. The 1872 act allowed some Anishinaabe people in northern Michigan to file homestead claims under the 1862 act within areas reserved for them under the 1855 Treaty of Detroit. The 1875 Indian Homestead Act allowed Indigenous people to file under the 1862 act if they gave up their tribal affiliation. The General Allotment or Dawes Act of 1887 used the provisions of the 1862 act to carve up tribal reservations into allotments. The remaining land in the reservations after allotment was then opened to white settlement.

Indian Child Welfare Act (ICWA): The Indian Child Welfare Act, passed in 1978, is a federal law aimed at redressing the disproportionate number of Indigenous children that were removed from their kin and placed in foster care. In the 1960s and 1970s, in some communities up to 35 percent of Indigenous children were forcibly removed and placed in non-Indigenous adoptive homes. This removal was carried out by social workers, religious organizations, and state and federal officials, who saw Indigenous families as inherently defective and Indigenous mothers as unfit. Though the ICWA was meant to protect the best interests of Indian children, tribes, and families, compliance remains inconsistent and there are ongoing legal proceedings at the state and federal levels regarding child custody and foster placement.

Indian New Deal: Also known as the Indian Reorganization Act or Wheeler-Howard Act, the Indian New Deal of 1934 entreated tribes to reorganize tribal governments according to a U.S. constitutional model in exchange for federal recognition and subsidies.

Indian Territory: Both a place   with ever shifting boundaries—and an idea, Indian Territory was marked on maps following the Royal Proclamation of 1763 as that area to the west of the Appalachian Mountains, a boundary intended to prevent the expansion of European settlement without a prior agreement between the Crown and Indigenous peoples (and thus serving as a precipitating factor in the American Revolution). It was later proposed by U.S. officials as that region beyond the Mississippi River and immediate American control where Indigenous nations would, for a limited period, maintain autonomy and authority until such time as they disappeared or were absorbed into the U.S. body politic. First formally described by the Indian Trade and Intercourse Act of 1834, it became the relocation site for those nations dispossessed by the 1830 Indian Removal Act. It would gradually shrink in size and scope as westward expansion, transcontinental railroads, and unending settler land hunger impinged further on Indigenous sovereignty, until what remained was reduced to the eastern half of what would become the state of Oklahoma. In 1905, the leadership of the Five Tribes attempted to reconstitute Indian Territory as a Native-governed state called Sequoyah, but President Theodore Roosevelt's opposition meant that the Indian and Oklahoma Territories were merged into the single state of Oklahoma. Indian Territory is still a common reference to the comprehensive jurisdictional and reservation boundaries of the Five Tribes.

Jewish National Fund (JNF): Keren Kayemet LeYisrael (Hebrew) was established in London in 1901 after the first Zionist Congress (1897) to acquire land for Jewish colonization in Palestine. Benefiting from British rule, the JNF became a major landlord in Palestine by 1948, developing and allocating land exclusively for Jewish settlers and expelling Palestinian Arab tenants from the land. After 1948, it was endowed a large part of the Palestinian refugees' properties by the state of Israel and continues today to push for Jewish-Israeli settlement expansion in the 1967-occupied Palestinian and Syrian territories.

Kanaka ʻŌiwi: A Kanaka ʻŌiwi, Kanaka Maoli, is a Native Hawaiian person who has a direct ancestral or genealogical relationship with the lands and waters of Hawaiʻi.

kuleana: In the Hawaiian language, a concept and set of reciprocal values that, depending on context, variously refers to privilege, concern, right, responsibility, title, property, jurisdiction, and authority.

Land Buy-Back Program: A part of the Cobell settlement, this program purchases fractionated land interests that were allotted under the Dawes Act and returns these lands to tribal trust ownership.

language revitalization: The revival of languages that are in decline in usage. For Indigenous communities worldwide, such revitalization is crucially tied to reviving culture and ancestral knowledge.

McGirt decision/*McGirt v. Oklahoma*: A 2020 U.S. Supreme Court decision that affirmed that, in spite of the land losses accompanying allotment, the reservation and jurisdictional boundaries of the Five Tribes had never been disestablished by Congress and were therefore intact.

Métis: Along with First Nations and Inuit, one of the recognized Aboriginal peoples in Section 35 of Canada's Constitution Act, 1982. A distinct Indigenous people and nation whose ethnogenesis dates to eighteenth-century prairie First Nations and European fur trade kinship and cultural exchange, especially in the Red River region of what is now Manitoba. As many settler Canadians conflate distinct Métis peoplehood with any degree of mixed Indigenous heritage, settler self-Indigenization and claims to Métis identity are on the rise, especially in eastern Canada.

parcialidad (s.), parcialidades (pl.): Spanish colonial concept to organize land. This concept was used to organize the territory of Mexico Tenochtitlan after it fell to

Spanish conquistadors. These units served the colonial rule to administer the local production, labor, and Indigenous population of the city.

Pick-Sloan Missouri River Basin Program: Known as the Pick-Sloan Plan, this megainfrastructure project was carried out by the Army Corps of Engineers in violation of numerous treaties with Indigenous nations and was completed in 1962. By creating five earthen, rolled dams along the Missouri River, the Pick-Sloan Plan flooded vast areas belonging to the Yankton, Lower Brule, Crow Creek, Cheyenne River, Standing Rock, Rosebud, Santee, and Fort Berthold reservations. In so doing, the plan illegally condemned hundreds of thousands of acres of Indigenous land, forced entire communities to relocate, and destroyed the habitats of countless plant and animal species.

Pomo: A collective name for seven related but distinct languages spoken by people in the Coastal Ranges of Northern California north of San Francisco and for the people themselves. The word derives from a Northern Pomo word, *Po'mo* (also *Po'ma*), signifying a village or group of people living together. It was also contained in the name of a specific Northern Pomo village, called Po'mo Po'ma, in what became known as Potter Valley in Mendocino County.

Preemption Act of 1841: This act allowed adult male squatters who were living on federally claimed lands to purchase up to 160 acres at $1.25 per acre.

Proclamation of 1783: The Proclamation of 1783 declared that Congress, not individual U.S. states, had the sole authority to deal directly with Indigenous nations.

quiet title action: A legal proceeding to determine ownership of real property. This usually takes form in a lawsuit to settle property disputes when multiple parties have claims to a single piece of land, when one of the owners sues the remaining parties to "quiet" title (other challenges or claims to the land).

Railway Acts of 1862 and 1864: These acts offered federal land and financial subsidies to expedite the construction of the U.S. transcontinental railroad.

rancheria: A Spanish word that referred to both an independent Indian village and the residential quarters of the Indian laborers on a rancho. English-speaking Americans in California adopted the word, and through the nineteenth century it continued to denote a settlement of Indian laborers and an Indian community that derived its specific occupancy rights to land through the work its members performed for non-Indian landowners. By the early twentieth century it signified a small reservation.

Red Power Movement: The Red Power Movement emerged in the 1960s and 1970s as Indigenous youth in the United States organized to demand self-determination, the honoring of treaty rights, and the defense of Indigenous cultures through organizations such as the American Indian Movement, the National Indian Youth Council, Indians of All Nations, and Women of All Red Nations. These and other groups protested against the antisovereignty termination policy of the 1950s and 1960s, and they emerged largely in urban areas where the companion Relocation policy expanded the number of Indian people in cities where they organized and engaged in daily acts of resistance, cultural revitalization, and highly visible protests such as the Occupation of Alcatraz Island in 1967.

Reindeer Acts in Finland: There are multiple laws impacting Sámi herding in Finland, and they have a long and conflicted history. As part of its powers as a subject state of the Russian Empire from 1809 to 1917, the Finnish Senate determined the distribution of reindeer husbandry territories (*paliskunta*) in 1898; they were further refined in 1916. The PorotilaL 590/1969 (Reindeer Farm Act) was presented as a mechanism to provide financial support for the reindeer herders and their families to receive financial support to construct houses and reindeer farms with financial support of up to 70 percent of the costs. Critics, however, saw this legal act as a mechanism to force the Sámi to settle down and direct the reindeer herding toward reindeer husbandry, a more Finnish, farmer-style reindeer economy. The current Reindeer Husbandry Act (1990) governs reindeer husbandry in the territory of the husbandry zone in Finland and includes both Sámi and Finnish herders. There is no specific Sámi herding act in Finland; rather, there are legal frameworks inside the Finnish state. Sweden and Norway also have reindeer legislation.

relocation program: Also known as the Indian Relocation Act of 1956 or the Adult Vocational Training Program. This was a program operated by the Bureau of Indian Affairs that intended to assist American Indians in leaving their reservations, relocating to urban areas, and assimilating into the general population.

repartimiento: A forced, seasonal Indigenous labor system in New Spain (colonial Mexico).

restricted/unrestricted land: In the United States, restrictions on allotment and other tribal lands prevent their title from being sold, mortgaged, taxed, or otherwise transferred, although leasing is permitted with permission from the secretary of the interior. Unrestricted status means that such lands can be transferred or lost through means fair and foul.

Sakhina Village (the Sakhinites): A locality in the Beisan valley, in the northern section of the Jordan valley. Sakhina was inhabited by a branch of the Arab Saqr tribe, which had once been a major force in the lower Galilee in Ottoman Palestine during the eighteenth and nineteenth centuries. In the late 1930s, the inhabitants (the Sakhinites) were evicted from most of their lands and struggled to preserve access to new resources in the vicinity. In 1948, they were expelled by the Zionist army to become refugees in other parts of Palestine and in the nearby Arab states.

Sámi Parliament (Finland): One of three Sámi parliaments, the Sámi Parliament in Finland is, according to its website, "the supreme political body of the Sámi in Finland representing the Sámi in national and international connections. It is an independent legal entity of public law which, due to its self-governmental nature, is not a state authority or part of the public administration." There are also Sámi parliaments in Norway and Sweden, and the extent to which their mandate is the exercise of self-governance versus advisory/consultation is an ongoing matter of discussion and debate among Sámi.

scrip: A substitute or alternative for legal tender entitling the bearer to exchange it for things such as money or an allotment of land. Scrip was a primary mechanism used by unscrupulous grafters and agents of the Canadian state to dispossess Métis of land, leading to extensive poverty, itinerant wage labor, homelessness, and marginalized settlements on Crown land for the first half of the twentieth century. The Métis nickname "the road-allowance people" dates to this period.

seasonal round: The form taken by the traditional family economies of many North American Indigenous peoples. In the case of the Anishinaabeg, the round combined agriculture, gathering, maple sugaring, fishing, and hunting and was carried out by specific groups of people in specific places at specific times of the year. Although work roles were flexible, the activities of the round were gendered, associating women with agriculture, gathering, and maple sugaring and men with hunting and fishing.

Skolt Sámi Act (Finland): Originally enacted in the post–World War II years in Finland, the current Skolt Sámi Act is from 1995. As the Skolt Sámi were forcefully removed from their ancestral home areas in Pechenga, which is today in Russia, the act was created to support the Skolt Sámi to maintain their traditional livelihoods, well-being, and culture. The state of Finland provides loans and financial support for Skolt Sámi residential home construction, fisheries, reindeer herding, and services. The act also contains decrees regarding the Skolt Sámi Village Council and traditional siida governance and land uses.

Steenerson Act of 1904: This act responded to the demands of the logging industry, which sought to enrich itself by gaining access to Indian allotments through the Dawes Act. Industry lobbyists persuaded legislators to enable the secretary of the interior to allot additional plots of land to Indians in order to make them available for exploitation by timber companies.

Sultan Abdülhamit's private-imperial estates (çiftlik-i hümayun): In the 1880s and 1890s the famous late-Ottoman sultan Abdülhamit II (r. 1976–1909) expanded his private-imperial estates to secure his autocratic rule. The policy especially targeted tribal regions, turning their inhabitants into direct tenants of the sultan. In 1909, the land reverted back to the state, but Abdülhamit II's status quo was largely preserved.

termination: Ushered in by House concurrent resolution 108 in 1953, termination policy called for the immediate end to federal recognition of tribal sovereignty to be implemented on a case-by-case basis through federal legislation. Termination aimed to sever the trust relationship of the government toward tribes; terminate federal support for health, education, and services; break up tribal communal resources; and close the rolls to future tribal citizens as a way to "get out of the Indian business." This devastating policy affected more than one hundred tribes and bands (more than twelve thousand individuals), and around 2.5 million acres of tribal lands lost trust status (and much was sold into non-Indian hands). The trust relationship was subsequently restored to more than sixty tribes following the successful activism of the Menominee Nation in regaining recognition. Although not officially rescinded as official policy until 1988, termination withered in the early 1960s.

tlaxilacalli: A Nahua term to define neighborhoods subordinated to the *altepemeh*. Spaniards identified these units as barrios.

Tlingit-Haida Jurisdictional Act: Passed in 1935, the Tlingit-Haida Jurisdictional Act legally defined Tlingit and Haida personhood and authorized each tribe to sue the United States.

Treaty of Tordesillas: A June 7, 1494, agreement between Spanish and Portuguese Crowns as to jurisdiction over lands supposedly discovered by Christopher Columbus.

White Earth Land Settlement Act of 1986: This controversial settlement sought to address the illegal transfer of Indian land allotments under the Dawes Act through a cash settlement in order to clear the title of the more than one hundred thousand acres of White Earth Indian land that had been fraudulently obtained by non-Indians. This act created a mechanism for researching the history of land title at White Earth and retroactively settled these illegal land transfers with a cash payment to heirs of the allotments, as well as providing additional considerations for the White Earth Nation, such as funding for tribal economic development.

Contributors

Jennifer Adese (Otipemisiwak/Métis) is the Canada Research Chair in Métis Women, Politics, and Community and associate professor in the Department of Sociology at University of Toronto Mississauga (UTM). She is coeditor of *A People and a Nation: New Directions in Contemporary Métis Studies* (with Chris Andersen) and *Indigenous Celebrity: Entanglements with Fame* (with Robert Alexander Innes).

Megan Baker (Choctaw Nation of Oklahoma) is a PhD candidate in anthropology at the University of California, Los Angeles, and a research associate in the Choctaw Nation Historic Preservation Department.

William Bauer (Wailacki and Concow of the Round Valley Indian Tribes) is professor of history and program director for American Indian and Indigenous Studies at the University of Nevada, Las Vegas. He is the author of *California through Native Eyes: Reclaiming History.*

Christine Taitano DeLisle (CHamoru) is associate professor in American Indian Studies at the University of Minnesota, Twin Cities. She is the author of *Placental Politics: CHamoru Women, White Womanhood, and Indigeneity under U.S. Colonialism in Guam.*

Vicente M. Diaz (Pohnpeian and Filipino) is on the faculty in the Department of American Indian Studies at the University of Minnesota, Twin Cities, where he heads the Native Canoe Program. He is the author of *Repositioning the Missionary: Rewriting the Histories of Colonialism, Native Catholicism, and Indigeneity in Guam.*

Sarah Biscarra Dilley (yak tit ͬu tit ͬu yak tiɬhini) is an artist, educator, and PhD candidate in Native American Studies at the University of California, Davis, nitspu titit ͬu tsʔitɨnɨ patwin, in the unceded homeland of the Patwin-speaking people (unratified Treaty "J" region).

Poet, writer, and professor **Marilyn Dumont** (Cree/Métis) teaches for the Faculty of Native Studies and Department of English and Film Studies at the University of Alberta. Her most recent book of poetry is *The Pemmican Eaters.*

Munir Fakher Eldin is a member of the Syrian native community in the Israeli-occupied Golan Heights, assistant professor of philosophy and cultural studies, and dean of the Faculty of Arts at Birzeit University, Palestine. He is the chief editor of the fourth edition of the critical Arabic-language volume *The General Survey of Israel 2020*.

Nick Estes (Kul Wicasa, Lower Brule Sioux Tribe) is a historian and the author of *Our History Is the Future: Standing Rock versus the Dakota Access Pipeline, and the Long Tradition of Indigenous Resistance*. He is coeditor, with Jaskiran Dhillon, of *Standing with Standing Rock: Voices from the #NoDAPL Movement* (Minnesota, 2019).

A filmmaker, playwright, and traditional Sámi livelihood practitioner, **Pauliina Feodoroff** (Skolt Sámi) leads the Näätämö River Catchment Co-management Project in Finland and coordinates the large-scale land use and ecological assessment process with the Muddusjärvi Reindeer Co-op in Inari.

Susan E. Gray is associate professor of history emerita in the School of Historical, Philosophical, and Religious Studies at Arizona State University. She is the coeditor of *Contingent Maps: Rethinking Western Women's History and the North American West* (with Gayle Gullett).

Daniel Heath Justice (Cherokee Nation) is professor of Critical Indigenous Studies and English at the University of British Columbia on unceded Musqueam territory. His recent books include *Why Indigenous Literatures Matter* and *Raccoon*.

J. Kēhaulani Kauanui (Kanaka Maoli) is professor of American studies and affiliate faculty in anthropology at Wesleyan University. She is the author of *Paradoxes of Hawaiian Sovereignty: Land, Sex, and the Colonial Politics of State Nationalism* and *Hawaiian Blood: Colonialism and the Politics of Sovereignty and Indigeneity* and editor of *Speaking of Indigenous Politics: Conversations with Activists, Scholars, and Tribal Leaders* (Minnesota, 2018).

Rauna Kuokkanen (Sámi) is research professor of Arctic Indigenous Studies at the University of Lapland and adjunct professor of Indigenous Studies at the University of Toronto. She is the author of *Restructuring Relations: Indigenous Self-Determination, Governance, and Gender*.

Stacy L. Leeds (Cherokee Nation) is the Foundation Professor of Law and Leadership at Sandra Day O'Connor College of Law, Arizona State University. The first woman to serve on the Cherokee Nation Supreme Court, she is a district judge for the Muscogee (Creek) Nation and an appellate court judge for the Prairie Band Potawatomi Nation. She is the coauthor of *Mastering American Indian Law,* second edition (with Angelique EagleWoman).

Sheryl Lightfoot (Anishinaabe, Lake Superior Band) is Canada Research Chair in Global Indigenous Rights and Politics at the University of British Columbia (Vancouver), with academic appointments in political science, First Nations and Indigenous Studies, and the School of Public Policy and Global Affairs. She is the author of *Global Indigenous Politics: A Subtle Revolution.*

Kelly S. McDonough (Anishinaabe [White Earth] and Irish descent) is associate professor of Latin American literary and cultural studies and Indigenous studies in the Department of Spanish and Portuguese at the University of Texas at Austin. She is the author of *The Learned Ones: Nahua Intellectuals in Postconquest Mexico.*

Ruby Hansen Murray (Osage Nation) is an award-winning columnist for the *Osage News,* writer, and educator. Her work has been published in the *Massachusetts Review, Moss, High Desert Journal, Shapes of Native Nonfiction, Native Voices: Indigenous American Poetry, Craft, and Conversations, World Literature Today, CutBank,* and *The Rumpus.*

Tero Mustonen, a Finn, is adjunct professor at the Department of Geographical and Historical Studies, University of Eastern Finland. He is the lead author for the Sixth IPCC Assessment Report, a winter seiner, and the head of the Kesälahti fish base.

Jean M. O'Brien (White Earth Ojibwe) is Distinguished McKnight University Professor and Northrop Professor at the University of Minnesota. She is the coauthor of *Monumental Mobility: The Memory Work of Massasoit* (with Lisa Blee) and the author of *Firsting and Lasting: Writing Indians Out of Existence in New England* (Minnesota, 2010).

Darren O'Toole (Métis) is associate professor in the Faculty of Law and the Faculty of Social Sciences at the University of Ottawa. He has published on the historical, legal, and political aspects of Métis land claims.

Shiri Pasternak (Ashkenazi Jew) is assistant professor of criminology and cofounder of the Yellowhead Institute, a First Nations–focused think tank at Ryerson University. She is the author of *Grounded Authority: The Algonquins of Barriere Lake against the State* (Minnesota, 2017).

Dione Payne (Waikato, Ngāti Tūwharetoa) is assistant vice chancellor (Māori and Pasifika) at Te Whare Wānaka o Aoraki/Lincoln University and oversees the Mātauraka Māori Research Theme. She convenes the Mahika Kai Conference and is the journal manager for the *Mahika Kai Journal*.

Joseph M. Pierce (Cherokee Nation) is associate professor in the Department of Hispanic Languages and Literature at Stony Brook University. He is the author of *Argentine Intimacies: Queer Kinship in an Age of Splendor, 1890–1910* and, with S.J Norman (Koori, Wiradjuri descent), cocurator of the Indigenous-led performance series *Knowledge of Wounds.*

Khal Schneider (Federated Indians of Graton Rancheria) is associate professor of history at California State University, Sacramento. He is completing a book on the history of Pomo communities, their work, their land, and the founding of California's Indian rancherias.

Argelia Segovia Liga works as professor-researcher at the Colegio de Michoacán at the Centro de Estudios de las Tradiciones in Mexico. Her research considers nineteenth-century Indigenous intellectualism in Mesoamerica, Nahua culture in Mexico City during the nineteenth century, trans-Indigenous relations in Mexico and the United States, and Indigenous land allotment in Mexico and the Southwest of the modern United States.

Leanne Betasamosake Simpson (Michi Saagiig Nishnaabe) is a writer, academic, and musician. She is the author of *As We Have Always Done: Indigenous Freedom through Radical Resistance* (Minnesota, 2017) and the novel *Noopiming: The Cure for White Ladies* (Minnesota, 2021).

Jameson R. Sweet (Lakota/Dakota) is associate professor in American studies at Rutgers University. His current book project, "The 'Mixed-Blood' Moment: Race, Law, and Mixed-Ancestry Dakota Indians in the Nineteenth-Century Midwest," expands on this family history and legal and racial issues surrounding Indians of mixed ancestry.

Michael P. Taylor is assistant professor of English and associate director of American Indian Studies at Brigham Young University. He is coauthor of *Returning Home: Diné Creative Works from the Intermountain Indian School.* His current book project, "Co-national Networks: Writing Indigenous Solidarity into the Twentieth Century," analyzes Indigenous constitutions, petitions, and newspapers to remember Indigenous modernism as an era of maintaining longstanding networks of Indigenous solidarity.

Named a Cherokee National Treasure for skill and artistry in oblique and warpface fingerweaving, ᏔᏯ ᎠᎦ / **iya dihi** / **Candessa Tehee** (Cherokee Nation) is assistant professor in the Department of Cherokee and Indigenous Studies and the coordinator of the Cherokee language education and Cherokee cultural studies programs at Northeastern State University in Tahlequah, Oklahoma. She was raised in northeastern Oklahoma and continues to be guided by Cherokee ᏨᎾᏫ᎐ᏍᏗᏛᏓᏯ / *iyunadvnelidasdi* / *the way we used to live, the way we live now, and the way we should live.*

Benjamin Hugh Velaise (Koyukon Athabascan) is a JD/MBA candidate at the University of Chicago. He is a shareholder in Doyon Limited, an Alaska Native corporation, and formerly worked as a lead for the Google American Indian Network, which addresses the digital divide for tribal communities and encourages the use of technology to benefit Native peoples and cultures. He graduated from Wesleyan University in 2018, where his senior thesis, "From Life and Death to Gain and Loss: The Alaska Native Claims Settlement Act," earned the M. G. White Prize for the best Honors Thesis in American Studies.

Index